PROVERBS & ECCLESIASTES

Brazos Theological Commentary on the Bible

Series Editors

R. R. Reno, General Editor
First Things
New York, New York

Robert W. Jenson (1930–2017)
Center of Theological Inquiry
Princeton, New Jersey

Robert Louis Wilken
University of Virginia
Charlottesville, Virginia

Ephraim Radner
Wycliffe College
Toronto, Ontario

Michael Root
Catholic University of America
Washington, DC

George Sumner
Episcopal Diocese of Dallas
Dallas, Texas

PROVERBS & ECCLESIASTES

DANIEL J. TREIER

BrazosPress
a division of Baker Publishing Group
Grand Rapids, Michigan

© 2011 by Daniel J. Treier

Published by Brazos Press
a division of Baker Publishing Group
P.O. Box 6287, Grand Rapids, MI 49516-6287
www.brazospress.com

Paperback edition published 2015
ISBN 978-1-58743-388-7

Printed and bound by CPI Group (UK) Ltd, Croydon, CR0 4YY

All rights reserved. No part of this publication may be reproduced, stored in a retrieval system, or transmitted in any form or by any means—for example, electronic, photocopy, recording—without the prior written permission of the publisher. The only exception is brief quotations in printed reviews.

The Library of Congress has cataloged the hardcover edition as follows:
Treier, Daniel J., 1972–
Proverbs & Ecclesiastes / Daniel J. Treier.
p. cm. — (Brazos theological commentary on the Bible)
Includes bibliographical references and indexes.
ISBN 978-1-58743-148-7 (cloth)
1. Bible. O.T. Proverbs—Commentaries. 2. Bible. O.T. Ecclesiastes—Commentaries. I. Title.
II. Title: Proverbs and Eclesiastes.
BS1465.53.T75 2011
223'.707—dc22 2010051565

Unless otherwise indicated, scripture quotations are from the New Revised Standard Version of the Bible (NRSV), copyright ©1989, by the Division of Christian Education of the National Council of the Churches of Christ in the United States of America. Used by permission. All rights reserved.

Scripture quotations marked ESV are from The Holy Bible, English Standard Version® (ESV®), copyright © 2001 by Crossway, a publishing ministry of Good News Publishers. Used by permission. All rights reserved. ESV Text Edition: 2007

Scripture quotations marked KJV are from the King James Version of the Bible.

Scripture quotations marked NASB are from the New American Standard Bible®, copyright © 1960, 1962, 1963, 1968, 1971, 1972, 1973, 1975, 1977, 1995 by The Lockman Foundation. Used by permission.

Scripture quotations marked NIV are from the Holy Bible, New International Version®. NIV®. Copyright © 1973, 1978, 1984, 2011 by Biblica, Inc.™ Used by permission of Zondervan. All rights reserved worldwide. www.zondervan.com

Scripture quotations marked RSV are from the Revised Standard Version of the Bible, copyright 1952 [2nd edition, 1971] by the Division of Christian Education of the National Council of the Churches of Christ in the United States of America. Used by permission. All rights reserved.

Scripture quotations marked TNIV are from the Holy Bible, Today's New International Version®. TNIV®. Copyright © 2001, 2005 by Biblica, Inc.™ Used by permission of Zondervan. All rights reserved worldwide. www.zondervan.com

Baker Publishing Group publications use paper produced from sustainable forestry practices and post-consumer waste whenever possible.

To Amy

Walking through life with you,
I encounter the truth of Proverbs 31:10–31 and
Ecclesiastes 4:9–12 with profound joy

CONTENTS

SERIES PREFACE

Near the beginning of his treatise against Gnostic interpretations of the Bible, *Against the Heresies*, Irenaeus observes that scripture is like a great mosaic depicting a handsome king. It is as if we were owners of a villa in Gaul who had ordered a mosaic from Rome. It arrives, and the beautifully colored tiles need to be taken out of their packaging and put into proper order according to the plan of the artist. The difficulty, of course, is that scripture provides us with the individual pieces, but the order and sequence of various elements are not obvious. The Bible does not come with instructions that would allow interpreters to simply place verses, episodes, images, and parables in order as a worker might follow a schematic drawing in assembling the pieces to depict the handsome king. The mosaic must be puzzled out. This is precisely the work of scriptural interpretation.

Origen has his own image to express the difficulty of working out the proper approach to reading the Bible. When preparing to offer a commentary on the Psalms he tells of a tradition handed down to him by his Hebrew teacher:

> The Hebrew said that the whole divinely inspired scripture may be likened, because of its obscurity, to many locked rooms in our house. By each room is placed a key, but not the one that corresponds to it, so that the keys are scattered about beside the rooms, none of them matching the room by which it is placed. It is a difficult task to find the keys and match them to the rooms that they can open. We therefore know the scriptures that are obscure only by taking the points of departure for understanding them from another place because they have their interpretive principle scattered among them.[1]

1. Fragment from the preface to *Commentary on Psalms 1–25*, preserved in the *Philokalia* (trans. Joseph W. Trigg; London: Routledge, 1998), 70–71.

As is the case for Irenaeus, scriptural interpretation is not purely local. The key in Genesis may best fit the door of Isaiah, which in turn opens up the meaning of Matthew. The mosaic must be put together with an eye toward the overall plan.

Irenaeus, Origen, and the great cloud of premodern biblical interpreters assumed that puzzling out the mosaic of scripture must be a communal project. The Bible is vast, heterogeneous, full of confusing passages and obscure words, and difficult to understand. Only a fool would imagine that he or she could work out solutions alone. The way forward must rely upon a tradition of reading that Irenaeus reports has been passed on as the rule or canon of truth that functions as a confession of faith. "Anyone," he says, "who keeps unchangeable in himself the rule of truth received through baptism will recognize the names and sayings and parables of the scriptures."[2] Modern scholars debate the content of the rule on which Irenaeus relies and commends, not the least because the terms and formulations Irenaeus himself uses shift and slide. Nonetheless, Irenaeus assumes that there is a body of apostolic doctrine sustained by a tradition of teaching in the church. This doctrine provides the clarifying principles that guide exegetical judgment toward a coherent overall reading of scripture as a unified witness. Doctrine, then, is the schematic drawing that will allow the reader to organize the vast heterogeneity of the words, images, and stories of the Bible into a readable, coherent whole. It is the rule that guides us toward the proper matching of keys to doors.

If self-consciousness about the role of history in shaping human consciousness makes modern historical-critical study critical, then what makes modern study of the Bible modern is the consensus that classical Christian doctrine distorts interpretive understanding. Benjamin Jowett, the influential nineteenth-century English classical scholar, is representative. In his programmatic essay "On the Interpretation of scripture," he exhorts the biblical reader to disengage from doctrine and break its hold over the interpretive imagination. "The simple words of that book," writes Jowett of the modern reader, "he tries to preserve absolutely pure from the refinements or distinctions of later times." The modern interpreter wishes to "clear away the remains of dogmas, systems, controversies, which are encrusted upon" the words of scripture. The disciplines of close philological analysis "would enable us to separate the elements of doctrine and tradition with which the meaning of scripture is encumbered in our own day."[3] The lens of understanding must be wiped clear of the hazy and distorting film of doctrine.

Postmodernity, in turn, has encouraged us to criticize the critics. Jowett imagined that when he wiped away doctrine he would encounter the biblical text in its purity and uncover what he called "the original spirit and intention of the authors."[4] We are not now so sanguine, and the postmodern mind thinks

2. *Against the Heretics* 9.4.

3. Benjamin Jowett, "On the Interpretation of Scripture," in *Essays and Reviews* (London: Parker, 1860), 338–39.

4. Ibid., 340.

interpretive frameworks inevitable. Nonetheless, we tend to remain modern in at least one sense. We read Athanasius and think him stage-managing the diversity of scripture to support his positions against the Arians. We read Bernard of Clairvaux and assume that his monastic ideals structure his reading of the Song of Songs. In the wake of the Reformation, we can see how the doctrinal divisions of the time shaped biblical interpretation. Luther famously described the Epistle of James as a "strawy letter," for, as he said, "it has nothing of the nature of the Gospel about it."[5] In these and many other instances, often written in the heat of ecclesiastical controversy or out of the passion of ascetic commitment, we tend to think Jowett correct: doctrine is a distorting film on the lens of understanding.

However, is what we commonly think actually the case? Are readers naturally perceptive? Do we have an unblemished, reliable aptitude for the divine? Have we no need for disciplines of vision? Do our attention and judgment need to be trained, especially as we seek to read scripture as the living word of God? According to Augustine, we all struggle to journey toward God, who is our rest and peace. Yet our vision is darkened and the fetters of worldly habit corrupt our judgment. We need training and instruction in order to cleanse our minds so that we might find our way toward God.[6] To this end, "the whole temporal dispensation was made by divine Providence for our salvation."[7] The covenant with Israel, the coming of Christ, the gathering of the nations into the church—all these things are gathered up into the rule of faith, and they guide the vision and form of the soul toward the end of fellowship with God. In Augustine's view, the reading of scripture both contributes to and benefits from this divine pedagogy. With countless variations in both exegetical conclusions and theological frameworks, the same pedagogy of a doctrinally ruled reading of scripture characterizes the broad sweep of the Christian tradition from Gregory the Great through Bernard and Bonaventure, continuing across Reformation differences in both John Calvin and Cornelius Lapide, Patrick Henry and Bishop Bossuet, and on to more recent figures such as Karl Barth and Hans Urs von Balthasar.

Is doctrine, then, not a moldering scrim of antique prejudice obscuring the Bible, but instead a clarifying agent, an enduring tradition of theological judgments that amplifies the living voice of scripture? And what of the scholarly dispassion advocated by Jowett? Is a noncommitted reading, an interpretation unprejudiced, the way toward objectivity, or does it simply invite the languid intellectual apathy that stands aside to make room for the false truism and easy answers of the age?

This series of biblical commentaries was born out of the conviction that dogma clarifies rather than obscures. The Brazos Theological Commentary on the Bible advances upon the assumption that the Nicene tradition, in all its diversity and controversy, provides the proper basis for the interpretation of the Bible as Christian

5. *Luther's Works*, vol. 35 (ed. E. Theodore Bachmann; Philadelphia: Fortress, 1959), 362.
6. *On Christian Doctrine* 1.10.
7. *On Christian Doctrine* 1.35.

scripture. God the Father Almighty, who sends his only begotten Son to die for us and for our salvation and who raises the crucified Son in the power of the Holy Spirit so that the baptized may be joined in one body—faith in *this* God with *this* vocation of love for the world is the lens through which to view the heterogeneity and particularity of the biblical texts. Doctrine, then, is not a moldering scrim of antique prejudice obscuring the meaning of the Bible. It is a crucial aspect of the divine pedagogy, a clarifying agent for our minds fogged by self-deceptions, a challenge to our languid intellectual apathy that will too often rest in false truisms and the easy spiritual nostrums of the present age rather than search more deeply and widely for the dispersed keys to the many doors of scripture.

For this reason, the commentators in this series have not been chosen because of their historical or philological expertise. In the main, they are not biblical scholars in the conventional, modern sense of the term. Instead, the commentators were chosen because of their knowledge of and expertise in using the Christian doctrinal tradition. They are qualified by virtue of the doctrinal formation of their mental habits, for it is the conceit of this series of biblical commentaries that theological training in the Nicene tradition prepares one for biblical interpretation, and thus it is to theologians and not biblical scholars that we have turned. "War is too important," it has been said, "to leave to the generals."

We do hope, however, that readers do not draw the wrong impression. The Nicene tradition does not provide a set formula for the solution of exegetical problems. The great tradition of Christian doctrine was not transcribed, bound in folio, and issued in an official, critical edition. We have the Niceno-Constantinopolitan Creed, used for centuries in many traditions of Christian worship. We have ancient baptismal affirmations of faith. The Chalcedonian definition and the creeds and canons of other church councils have their places in official church documents. Yet the rule of faith cannot be limited to a specific set of words, sentences, and creeds. It is instead a pervasive habit of thought, the animating culture of the church in its intellectual aspect. As Augustine observed, commenting on Jer. 31:33, "The creed is learned by listening; it is written, not on stone tablets nor on any material, but on the heart."[8] This is why Irenaeus is able to appeal to the rule of faith more than a century before the first ecumenical council, and this is why we need not itemize the contents of the Nicene tradition in order to appeal to its potency and role in the work of interpretation.

Because doctrine is intrinsically fluid on the margins and most powerful as a habit of mind rather than a list of propositions, this commentary series cannot settle difficult questions of method and content at the outset. The editors of the series impose no particular method of doctrinal interpretation. We cannot say in advance how doctrine helps the Christian reader assemble the mosaic of scripture. We have no clear answer to the question of whether exegesis guided by doctrine is antithetical to or compatible with the now-old modern methods of

8. *Sermon* 212.2.

historical-critical inquiry. Truth—historical, mathematical, or doctrinal—knows no contradiction. But method is a discipline of vision and judgment, and we cannot know in advance what aspects of historical-critical inquiry are functions of modernism that shape the soul to be at odds with Christian discipline. Still further, the editors do not hold the commentators to any particular hermeneutical theory that specifies how to define the plain sense of scripture—or the role this plain sense should play in interpretation. Here the commentary series is tentative and exploratory.

Can we proceed in any other way? European and North American intellectual culture has been de-Christianized. The effect has not been a cessation of Christian activity. Theological work continues. Sermons are preached. Biblical scholars turn out monographs. Church leaders have meetings. But each dimension of a formerly unified Christian practice now tends to function independently. It is as if a weakened army had been fragmented, and various corps had retreated to isolated fortresses in order to survive. Theology has lost its competence in exegesis. Scripture scholars function with minimal theological training. Each decade finds new theories of preaching to cover the nakedness of seminary training that provides theology without exegesis and exegesis without theology.

Not the least of the causes of the fragmentation of Christian intellectual practice has been the divisions of the church. Since the Reformation, the role of the rule of faith in interpretation has been obscured by polemics and counterpolemics about *sola scriptura* and the necessity of a magisterial teaching authority. The Brazos Theological Commentary on the Bible series is deliberately ecumenical in scope, because the editors are convinced that early church fathers were correct: church doctrine does not compete with scripture in a limited economy of epistemic authority. We wish to encourage unashamedly dogmatic interpretation of scripture, confident that the concrete consequences of such a reading will cast far more light on the great divisive questions of the Reformation than either reengaging in old theological polemics or chasing the fantasy of a pure exegesis that will somehow adjudicate between competing theological positions. You shall know the truth of doctrine by its interpretive fruits, and therefore in hopes of contributing to the unity of the church, we have deliberately chosen a wide range of theologians whose commitment to doctrine will allow readers to see real interpretive consequences rather than the shadow boxing of theological concepts.

Brazos Theological Commentary on the Bible has no dog in the current translation fights, and we endorse a textual ecumenism that parallels our diversity of ecclesial backgrounds. We do not impose the thankfully modest inclusive-language agenda of the New Revised Standard Version, nor do we insist upon the glories of the Authorized Version, nor do we require our commentators to create a new translation. In our communal worship, in our private devotions, in our theological scholarship, we use a range of scriptural translations. Precisely as scripture—a living, functioning text in the present life of faith—the Bible is not semantically fixed. Only a modernist, literalist hermeneutic could imagine that this modest fluidity is a liability. Philological precision and stability is a consequence of, not a basis for, exegesis. Judgments about the meaning of a text fix its literal sense, not the other way around. As a result, readers should expect an eclectic use of biblical translations, both across the different volumes of the series and within individual commentaries.

We cannot speak for contemporary biblical scholars, but as theologians we know that we have long been trained to defend our fortresses of theological concepts and formulations. And we have forgotten the skills of interpretation. Like stroke victims, we must rehabilitate our exegetical imaginations, and there are likely to be different strategies of recovery. Readers should expect this reconstructive—not reactionary—series to provide them with experiments in postcritical doctrinal interpretation, not commentaries written according to the settled principles of a well-functioning tradition. Some commentators will follow classical typological and allegorical readings from the premodern tradition; others will draw on contemporary historical study. Some will comment verse by verse; others will highlight passages, even single words that trigger theological analysis of scripture. No reading strategies are proscribed, no interpretive methods foresworn. The central premise in this commentary series is that doctrine provides structure and cogency to scriptural interpretation. We trust in this premise with the hope that the Nicene tradition can guide us, however imperfectly, diversely, and haltingly, toward a reading of scripture in which the right keys open the right doors.

R. R. Reno

AUTHOR'S PREFACE

Since Proverbs and Ecclesiastes call us into concrete communal relationships, it is especially important to acknowledge others who contributed to this project. Rusty Reno, Rodney Clapp, and the editorial board of the Brazos Theological Commentary on the Bible took great risk in having me write for this series and then graciously pushed me to take worthwhile risks beyond my native inclinations. Whatever complaints I would like to nurse, "faithful are the wounds of a friend": Rusty's editorial crucible made this a far better book, and I will never be the same as a writer. David Aiken was very helpful in the editorial process, and John Muether generated the indexes. For several years, student assistants—Barry Jones, Carrie Littauer, Lissy Verseput, and especially Uche Anizor, Emily Bergen, and Steve Pardue—handled numerous research details, including heroic attempts to uncover resources on liturgical usage and Jewish exegesis.

Colleagues in Old Testament studies, particularly Michael Graves, Richard Schultz, and Andrew Hill, gave not only encouragement during this endeavor but also concrete help. Michael commented on the entire manuscript and stoked my courage. Richard offered comments on key portions and deserves undying gratitude for welcoming me to "Advanced Hebrew Exegesis: Ecclesiastes" without humiliation for my impoverished language skills. His helpful perspectives also appear from draft forms of forthcoming commentaries. Craig Bartholomew and Amy Plantinga Pauw likewise graciously gave previews of their commentary efforts, with Craig providing his valuable manuscript ahead of publication. All the folks thanked here should of course be exonerated for occasions on which this book reflects my stubborn and/or theologically adventuresome spirit.

Wheaton College granted a course release through the G. W. Aldeen Memorial Fund and then a sabbatical during which the project finally neared completion. I am very grateful to administrators Jeff Greenman, Jill Peláez Baumgaertner, and Stan Jones for their generous support. Others connected to the college who either read portions of the manuscript, enhanced my cultural resources, and/

or sustained me in this weariness of the flesh include Alan Jacobs, Jon Laansma, Tim Larsen, Kevin Vanhoozer, doctoral students at the systematic theology colloquium, and others from the Café Padre gang. Michael Allen commented on the entire manuscript—at multiple draft stages, no less—offering inestimable resources and encouragement. Without these folks, particularly Michael, I could never have finished.

It remains to thank the family members who are so integral to pursuing the path of wisdom, for which especially my parents and grandparents never stop praying. Thanks to the birth of daughter Anna, I have encountered anew the human delights and limitations of which Proverbs and Ecclesiastes speak. Through my wife, Amy, to whom this book is dedicated, God further confronts my misguided scholarly ambitions while making the joys of Prov. 18:22 concrete: "He who finds a wife finds a good thing, / and obtains favor from the LORD." This proverb is true in myriad ways, far beyond Amy teaching me to embrace finitude joyfully. But I am all the more grateful that she and Anna love me through the stresses of learning about human toil.

ABBREVIATIONS

Bibliographic

→	indicates a cross-reference to commentary on a passage in Proverbs or Ecclesiastes
ANF	The Ante-Nicene Fathers. 10 vols. Reprinted Grand Rapids: Eerdmans, 1957.
FC	Fathers of the Church: A New Translation. Washington DC: Catholic University of America Press, 1947–.
NPNF[1]	A Select Library of the Nicene and Post-Nicene Fathers of the Christian Church, first series. 14 vols. Reprinted Grand Rapids: Eerdmans, 1956.
NPNF[2]	A Select Library of the Nicene and Post-Nicene Fathers of the Christian Church, second series. 14 vols. Reprinted Grand Rapids: Eerdmans, 1956.
PTA	Papyrologische Texte und Abhandlungen. Edited by D. Hagedorn et al. Bonn: Habelt, 1968–.
WSA	Works of St. Augustine: A Translation for the Twenty-First Century. Edited by J. E. Rotelle. Hyde Park, NY: New City, 1995.

Bible Versions

ESV	English Standard Version
KJV	King James Version
NASB	New American Standard Bible
NIV	New International Version
NRSV	New Revised Standard Version
RSV	Revised Standard Version
TNIV	Today's New International Version

Biblical Books

Acts	Acts
Amos	Amos
1 Chr.	1 Chronicles
2 Chr.	2 Chronicles
Col.	Colossians
1 Cor.	1 Corinthians
2 Cor.	2 Corinthians
Dan.	Daniel
Deut.	Deuteronomy
Eccl.	Ecclesiastes
Eph.	Ephesians
Esth.	Esther
Exod.	Exodus
Ezek.	Ezekiel
Ezra	Ezra
Gal.	Galatians
Gen.	Genesis
Hab.	Habakkuk
Hag.	Haggai
Heb.	Hebrews
Hos.	Hosea
Isa.	Isaiah
Jas.	James
Jer.	Jeremiah
Job	Job
Joel	Joel
John	John
1 John	1 John
2 John	2 John
3 John	3 John
Jonah	Jonah
Josh.	Joshua
Jude	Jude
Judg.	Judges
1 Kgs.	1 Kings
2 Kgs.	2 Kings
Lam.	Lamentations
Lev.	Leviticus
Luke	Luke
Mal.	Malachi
Mark	Mark
Matt.	Matthew
Mic.	Micah
Nah.	Nahum
Neh.	Nehemiah
Num.	Numbers
Obad.	Obadiah
1 Pet.	1 Peter
2 Pet.	2 Peter
Phil.	Philippians
Phlm.	Philemon
Prov.	Proverbs
Ps.	Psalms
Rev.	Revelation
Rom.	Romans
Ruth	Ruth
1 Sam.	1 Samuel
2 Sam.	2 Samuel
Song	Song of Songs
1 Thess.	1 Thessalonians
2 Thess.	2 Thessalonians
1 Tim.	1 Timothy
2 Tim.	2 Timothy
Titus	Titus
Zech.	Zechariah
Zeph.	Zephaniah

INTRODUCTION

Sage Theological Commentary

The temptation is overwhelming for commentaries on Ecclesiastes to begin brazenly, by citing Eccl. 12:12b: "Of making many books there is no end, and much study is a weariness of the flesh." The commentators acknowledge the obvious irony of writing still another book on Ecclesiastes, yet, after appearing to be appropriately sheepish, they proceed anyway. Lately there is no end to the making of methodological prefaces either. Accordingly, it was this author's original intention to avoid such weariness. Hermeneutics, which theologians engage both too much and too little, must not substitute for exegesis.

However, two rather different commentaries appear within this volume, which calls for explanation. Moreover, Eccl. 12:9–14 presents a paradigm for the act of commentary itself. In this passage we have third-person commentary on the character and work of Qoheleth, the book's main voice, describing the Sage's approach to preceding wisdom tradition(s): "Besides being wise, the Teacher also taught the people knowledge, weighing and studying and arranging many proverbs. The Teacher sought to find pleasing words, and he wrote words of truth plainly" (12:9–10). The ensuing reflections in the epilogue to Ecclesiastes interpret the rest of the book positively as wisdom. Via emphasis on fearing God and keeping the commandments, Ecclesiastes relates not only to Proverbs but also to the Torah—divine instruction for living—in the rest of scripture. Therefore the epilogue's portrayal of Qoheleth as a wise collector and purveyor of divine truth can guide contemporary commentary on Proverbs and Ecclesiastes.

Character

The portrayal begins by ascribing wisdom to Qoheleth. For this reason the term "Sage" is preferable to "Teacher" or "Preacher," since these usual translations have modern professional connotations that could mislead English readers. Ecclesiastes certainly evinces skepticism regarding elements of wisdom, as that tradition is typically depicted in critical Old Testament scholarship. Nevertheless, Eccl. 12:9 is not ironic in predicating wisdom to the Sage, since the argument of this passage needs to bolster the book's canonical propriety. The text is counteracting potential skepticism, not winking at it. Therefore we have before us ideals toward which a theological commentator should aspire. The textual ethos—its tone, subtexts, judgment, and so forth—should manifest and encourage the fear of God.

Wisdom denotes not just the subject matter of Proverbs and Ecclesiastes, but also the proper pursuit of interpretation. Sage commentary therefore attends not only to the biblical text and its author(s), but also to its readers' contexts and responses. Hence, in a particular sense the adjective "devotional" would be a compliment for the present work. Sage commentary ought to reflect reverence for scripture, not as an end in itself but as the means by which we hear God speaking in order to live.

Wisdom literature seeks to align the character of its readers with the divine design in creation. The Torah, as embodied in the Pentateuch, orders the life of the people of Israel around their covenant with God. Therefore its literary forms are primarily laws and narratives. The narratives provide the history of salvation. The laws provide the civic framework and cultus for the community, along with the moral boundaries for life in covenant with God. But if laws are to be more than guardrails, they require prudence for particular people to implement, especially across time and place. Hypotheses about the development of wisdom via schools, possibly associated with royal courts—and how this might relate to the development of Torah—are only speculative. In terms of canonical significance, though, wisdom literature addresses the need for prudence to help the divine teaching of Torah result in communities of character. Though rooted in God's created world, wisdom material does not depart from the covenant. Beyond setting up the cultic practices and specific identity of Israel, wisdom literature relates God's people to all of creation and to the learning of outsiders; beyond setting out Israel's civic order, wisdom fosters communal life; beyond setting forth basic moral order, it builds personal character and judgment. The affinities between Deuteronomy and Proverbs, for instance, suggest complementary harmony, rather than competition, between wisdom and Torah. Rightly read, wisdom presumes the salvation-historical narratives as the framework within which Torah can be simultaneously personalized and situated within community and cosmos. In this way wisdom literature orders the particular narratives of ordinary lives around salvation history, guiding members of the covenant community toward the fear of the Lord.

Clarity and Conciseness

Not unrelated to the textual ethos is the clarity of its logos. According to Eccl. 12:9 once again, the Sage focused on teaching "the people." This is a reminder that the theological commentator should not address academic colleagues as an exclusive—or, in the present case, even primary—audience. The Sage "arrang[ed] . . . proverbs" (12:9) and "sought . . . pleasing words" (12:10). Thus it is appropriate to strive for delightful rather than boring writing. The goal is to convey "truth plainly" (12:10) in a way that people can remember for the sake of prodding and guidance (12:11). Moreover, we should expect interpretative judgments to coincide with the promotion of virtue. Moral exhortation is appropriate in a commentary that engages the text as scripture, although such exhortation should not be so blunt as to detract from proper esthetic sensibilities (12:10–11). The sharpness ought to lie in memorable divine address, not authorial moralizing.

Moving from 12:11 to 12:12, we encounter a somewhat abrupt change in tone. The editor warns against moving beyond the sayings of the wise, kept in mind for the sake of living well. Study eventually degenerates into tedium. And not just tedium—proliferation of various voices and complex ideas can put us in moral danger. Concrete implications follow for the present commentary, both in its writing and in the reading of others.

The discussion of Proverbs is not expository in detail like the treatment of Ecclesiastes. This decision stems partly from assigned word counts, but also from the nature of the material. Ecclesiastes begs for close engagement, as themes subtly build on their various appearances and on each other. Though not a linear argument, neither is the text a slapdash hodgepodge in which one occurrence of "vanity" is the same as another. Literary context matters greatly for how we understand the oft-bold declarations. Ecclesiastes elicits careful reflection and different points of identification with the Sage's quest. Hence occasionally meandering commentary matches substance with style: Ecclesiastes itself meanders, and effort should be made to convey this. In a haunting essay, R. R. Reno cautions against "drawing out" theology from the text, since focusing on doctrinal inference can produce conceptual abstraction from scriptural language.[1] By extension, the present commentary tries to avoid abstraction from the dialectical style of Ecclesiastes as well, thus rejecting an overly simplistic rhetorical line that leaves no conundrums intact.[2]

Meanwhile, Proverbs has significant stretches in which the literary connections are either tenuous or nonexistent. Scholarly inventions to the contrary are usually

1. R. R. Reno, "Biblical Theology and Theological Exegesis," in *Out of Egypt: Biblical Theology and Theological Interpretation*, ed. Craig Bartholomew et al., Scripture and Hermeneutics 5 (Grand Rapids: Zondervan, 2004), 385–408.

2. Many readers, of course, use a commentary sporadically for preaching and teaching, not reading the volume straight through. Cross-references to other relevant passages in Proverbs and Ecclesiastes are thus indicated with an arrow (→) to reduce repetition.

too clever by half. As a collection of various wisdom materials, Proverbs itself invites multiple thematic intersections between them. As proverbs are encountered, they resonate with other lessons one has already learned. While Ecclesiastes contains numerous proverbs as well, these are usually ordered in small sections contributing to a larger movement of thought. By contrast, Proverbs overall creates much less demand for linear engagement or exposition.

The commentary on Prov. 1–9 treats these chapters sequentially, although more briefly and less thoroughly than Ecclesiastes. The overarching theme of "two ways" becomes the theological framework within which the exposition fits. A lengthy subsection addresses the passage fraught with significance for later christological debates (8:22–36). In Prov. 10–29, where we largely encounter strings of proverbs, moral frameworks from the Christian tradition structure the presentation of material, before Prov. 30–31 closes the book. On the one hand, we seek to become people of virtue—four cardinal virtues and three theological virtues. On the other hand, we must learn to avoid seven "deadly sins" or capital vices. This mode of organization allows for illustrative and thematic, instead of comprehensive, engagement with the panoply of individual proverbs. The book of Proverbs by nature invites the use of external paradigms to appropriate its teaching. As the exposition will show, the classic virtues and vices do justice to that teaching. Not only do their contents cover the array of proverbial ethics; the classification of virtues as cardinal or theological enables the reader to engage how Proverbs relates to nature and grace. And the various classifications of interrelationships between capital vices hold true to the moral complexity of Proverbs.

Criticism

Conciseness also entails that no commentary can do everything, so here discussions of historical-critical scholarship are limited to forms of philology that serve theological proclamation. Readers seeking thorough exegetical treatment of each proverb or passage in Proverbs have other fine commentaries from which to choose. This has not always been the case. Now, however, we have not only an increasing number of commentaries treating Proverbs carefully, but also commentators exuding a measure of theological interest. Thus I gratefully see no need to reinvent such wheels.

Still, theological interest in a critical commentary is not the same as a theological commentary. Quite often, learned biblical scholars carefully engage textual particulars in pursuit of theological answers. Yet, when it comes to allowing theology to shape the questions or to suggest possible answers while precluding certain alternatives, there is wariness or downright refusal. The movement proceeds in one linear direction, from biblical text to theology. A modest contribution of the present commentary as theological, then, is to sift through the exegetical cornucopia for essential bounty without methodologically holding off theology until dessert or even an after-dinner snack. Furthermore, the reflective movement proceeds back and forth within *scripture*—not just an isolated biblical text—and thus between scripture and theology. The canon is not merely a source of possible historical parallels, but primarily a treasure chest of complementary teaching to proclaim.

Ecclesiastes has frequently garnered more theological attention than Proverbs. Its existential and cultural resonances elicit more open-ended forms of engagement, and so numerous books have been my teachers, whether or not they come to prominent citation. Just as I do not reinvent the wheels of exegetical detail regarding Proverbs, so also I try not to regurgitate the theological history of others' engagement with Ecclesiastes, in particular Ellul's 1990 unique achievement.[3] Ellul states early on that he studied Ecclesiastes for decades, yet resolved not to read secondary literature in the years immediately before he actually wrote his commentary. While youth and time constraints prevented following this model entirely, I sought to do so in my own way. Many faithful, gifted authors will therefore look in vain for direct engagement with their work.

Nevertheless, for both Proverbs and Ecclesiastes I refer frequently to a limited number of so-called historical-critical commentaries—for Proverbs, Longman 2006 and Waltke 2004–2005; for Ecclesiastes, Bartholomew 2009, Krüger 2004, and Longman 1998—providing in-text citations only when reasonably sure that a distinctively creative insight was in play. Otherwise I depended on them to mediate the most important elements from additional scholars. The Ancient Christian Commentary on Scripture (Wright 2005) played an analogous role with respect to much of the patristic material cited, proving to be an invaluable pointer to primary texts. These reading choices were intentionally representative of different regions and approaches—such as finding more or less structure in the Proverbs collections and having more or less positive approaches to Ecclesiastes. Doubtless many alternatives were possible, but I sought to serve busy pastors and laypeople by imitating them in accepting limitations: one can read only so much. According to the Sage, one *should* read only so much. The Sage's pursuit of wisdom served, ultimately, his presentation of wisdom. The theological commentator today undertakes a task that must eventually result in proclamation of what he or she hears as the word of God. We cannot go on listening forever to secondary voices before venturing our own, however tentative, speech.[4]

3. In addition, for a masterful survey of the history of effects of Ecclesiastes, see Christianson 2007; for its hermeneutical treatment, see Craig G. Bartholomew, *Reading Ecclesiastes: Old Testament Exegesis and Hermeneutical Theory*, Analecta Biblica 139 (Rome: Pontifical Biblical Institute Press, 1998); for resonances with film, see Robert K. Johnston, *Useless Beauty: Ecclesiastes through the Lens of Contemporary Film* (Grand Rapids: Baker, 2004); and for its postmodern relevance, see Peter J. Leithart, *Solomon among the Postmoderns* (Grand Rapids: Brazos, 2008).

4. David H. Kelsey's *Eccentric Existence: A Theological Anthropology*, 2 vols. (Louisville: Westminster John Knox, 2009) reflects important interaction with wisdom literature but came into my hands after submission of this manuscript to the publisher—thus, unfortunately, too late to engage in detail.

Commentary stands in an odd position between what we might call first and second iterations of a text. Bound up with ascertaining what the text even is and how to render it in translation—whether literally in a language or metaphorically in mind—commentary is a practice of direct encounter with the material. However, commentators are inevitably aware of mediation—prior translations and commentaries on the one hand, a reading audience on the other. The commentary's audience encounters the text even more indirectly, reading for someone else's understanding that mediates the text itself to them. In this way we can discern an analogy with practices of the church: there is scripture reading on the one hand, preaching on the other. Even scripture reading involves translation, but certainly preaching involves a stronger dimension of mediation. The preacher stands at this awkward bridge—encountering scripture and mediating its message to others, all the while encountering a tradition of interpretation (more and less consciously). So it is, likewise, with the theological commentator, who pursues this task as an act of participation in tradition(s) that mediate the text.

I belabor this point to emphasize the commentator's goal that the text should remain primary, with his or her creativity modestly in the background. Tradition is inescapable and fruitful because the text is in one sense inexhaustible, so the commentator's goal must be that the prominence of the latter might become greater, and the former less (Eccl. 12:12). That is, faithful tradition ministers the message of the text more than drawing attention to itself. A commentary points toward the founding text and away from itself all the more, since no commentator's work claims normative influence within a tradition until it has stood a test of time. My goal is therefore to imitate the Sage in sifting through the wealth of words connected to Ecclesiastes for what is particularly pleasing and theologically edifying. It is no shame if the present work reflects little of me, much of Proverbs and Ecclesiastes, and many good words said about them.

Why, then, does this theologically ordered commentary engage the historical-critical tradition at all? A first response concerns the difficulty of definitions: both "historical criticism" and "theological interpretation of scripture" are notoriously tricky to pinpoint. So-called precritical exegetes appropriated the scholarly resources of their day and surprisingly often challenged what many would expect to be churchly assumptions. The point is not to speculate that patristic commentators would be historical critics if they were alive now, but rather to recognize that historical and literary methods are not intrinsically antagonistic to theological reading. The root question concerns what is servant and what is master—which conception reigns regarding the nature of the Bible and the aims of its reading.

A second response stems specifically from Ecclesiastes once again. It is difficult to ignore "the way the words go," given the positive portrayal of the Sage's attention to words. From early on, the history of interpretation has involved both focusing on the Sage's persona(s) even more than his words and confronting some basic hermeneutical dilemmas over and over (Christianson 2007: 18). Thus it would be arbitrary either to ignore classic interpreters *or* to stop this ongoing conversation prior to the modern critical tradition. Though the rest of the scriptural canon provides a fertile field of meaning for Ecclesiastes, its unique words, uses of words, grammatical features, and so forth call for philological expertise. Some experts provide resources friendlier to theological interpretation than others; it is arguable that such believing criticism even stands within a tributary of the contemporary stream called theological exegesis. Selective engagement with critical, philological scholarship can supplement large deficits in my own expertise without being co-opted by the speculative elements of many historical hypotheses. Avoiding conjectures about date, setting, and the like is especially important regarding Ecclesiastes, for which these hypotheses have consistently tenuous connections with the text itself.

Canon and Christ

To sum up, this commentary counts as theological by hearing Proverbs and Ecclesiastes as words from God and about God, within the one word of God. The assumed audience therefore embraces any readers—scholarly, pastoral, lay—who wish to explore what it means to apply theological commitments operationally, not just notionally or methodologically, to the reading of Proverbs and Ecclesiastes. The goal is not just to derive theological commitments from these texts at the end of the reading process, as important as that is. More boldly, with prayerful vigilance, appealing to Christian doctrine can foster, rather than hinder, the scriptures having their say. Though I write as an evangelical Protestant—which influences questions asked, illustrations used, even books regarded as canonical, in ways beyond my full awareness—Catholic and Orthodox readers likewise share the commitments of Nicene Christianity prominent here. Others outside such Christian orthodoxy are also welcome to join this exploratory journey of theological reading. All are welcome to criticize, not just celebrate: "Iron sharpens iron, / and one person sharpens the wits of another" (Prov. 27:17).

As scriptural, these texts present words *from* God, but not in an easy manner—so this commentary notes particularly at the beginning of Ecclesiastes. As scriptural, these books also present words *about* God, although again not always directly. For, as wisdom texts, they concern themselves primarily with the lives of particular human beings set within the contexts of the created cosmos and the covenant community. The explicit subject matter is frequently anthropological. Yet, if knowledge of God and true knowledge of self coinhere, then Proverbs and Ecclesiastes are no less theological than other scriptural texts, even if this is less explicit.

No theory of spiritual interpretation fully determines how this theological knowledge arises, in advance of engaging the textual details. Commitment to character formation, mentioned above, elicits the extension of the literal sense to apply to faith, hope, and charity—what ancient interpreters pursued as allegorical, anagogical, and tropological senses. The chief complication involves properly finding belief about Christ in these Old Testament books and then allowing such belief to shape their interpretation further. Proverbs 8 and other wisdom texts, along with the persona of "Solomon" in Ecclesiastes, clearly raise questions of possible convergence with New Testament Christology. Beyond these particulars, two rules of thumb seem prudent.

First, any Old Testament pointers must remain partial and indirect, in order to fit the structure of biblical salvation history. Therefore, we should look not only for persons, institutions, and events that positively correspond to ultimate fulfillment in Christ and his church—what often goes today under the rubric of typology—but also for ways in which human realities are inversely related to Christ. What, in other words, are the human callings and hopes that have not yet become reality? In Proverbs and Ecclesiastes we learn about Christ not only from what Solomon was but also from what he was supposed to be; Christology accords with wisdom yet addresses folly.

Second, because we have wisdom material that *is* christologically relevant, prudence demands restraint in the rest of the texts. There is no need to force christological connections into particular words or items—via the sort of external, symbolic logic that moderns often label allegory—since the message of the literal sense can be drawn coherently into the larger canonical narrative. Complex and controversial terms like "typology" and "allegory" aside, the point is that figural reading usually recognizes the figure of Jesus by implication from extending the text's literal sense into the future, only rarely by reading Christ into isolated details. When the latter occurs (e.g., Eccl. 4:9–12), there should be an element of mystery in the Old Testament text that seems unaddressed without the unfolding of further revelation it anticipates.

Ultimately, Proverbs and Ecclesiastes are read in fullness only as part of the *one* word of God we must hear. This means reading them as scripture, comprising together—with the rest of the biblical canon—one book. Its complex unity requires acknowledging tensions, so that in the present case neither Proverbs nor Ecclesiastes, taken to extremes, may stand on its own. Together, however, these books provide checks and balances whereby the truth may be properly heard as their distinctive voices operate both antiphonally and polyphonically (→Eccl. 12:9). More broadly, this affirmation of the oneness of the word of God means reading scripture as witnessing to God's final speech-act in Jesus Christ. Here again Proverbs and Ecclesiastes confront us with unique challenges, since only some of their subject matter directly refers to Israel's hope for the blessing of the nations. Yet these wisdom books' discernment of and struggle over the nature of God's creation can, by grace, depict both the shape of what Jesus Christ came to redeem and a sketch of why that redemption is so necessary.

PROVERBS

TWO WAYS

PROVERBS 1–9

Roland Murphy suggests that the history of interpretation of Proverbs involves "benign neglect," with the book serving "as little more than an 'enforcer' for moral guidance."[1] After all, there is a relative dearth of surviving classical commentaries—with the intriguing exception of Philip Melanchthon producing various volumes on the book in the sixteenth century—and modern, critical scholars prioritize the Torah over Proverbs for Israelite ethics. Even modern commentaries on Proverbs were relatively few until the last couple of decades. Yet the present commentary begins with another side of the story: Proverbs influenced the Christian pattern of thought right from the church's beginning.

The Basic Framework

As evidence for this claim, consider the *Didache*, the so-called Teaching of the Twelve Apostles, which provides Christian instruction from as early as the second century, possibly even the first. The manual begins as follows: "There are two ways, one of life and one of death, and there is a great difference between these two ways" (*Didache* 1.1).[2] The twofold commandment to love God and neighbor starts the explication of the way of life, leading into elements of the

1. Roland E. Murphy, "Proverbs and Theological Exegesis," in *The Hermeneutical Quest: Essays in Honor of James Luther Mays on His Sixty-Fifth Birthday*, ed. Donald G. Miller (Allison Park, PA: Pickwick, 1986), 87–88.

2. Michael W. Holmes, ed., *The Apostolic Fathers: Greek Texts and English Translations*, 2nd ed. (Grand Rapids: Baker, 1999), 251.

Sermon on the Mount about loving one's enemies and giving to others. The next chapter appeals to several of the Ten Commandments. It might be tempting to dismiss the *Didache* as a law-oriented rather than wisdom-oriented source, given some of these legal elements. Yet, although the text soon unfolds God's law in many respects, the commands are not simply "do not" prohibitions but instead character-driven exhortations: "Be not [such-and-such a person]." Ensuing themes such as judging righteously and teaching youths the fear of God clearly resonate with Proverbs. Rather than treating the *Didache* as merely Torah-like, it would be better to acknowledge the degree to which its harmony of legal and sapiential elements parallels the scriptures.

Aaron Milavec proposes that the *Didache* be called "The Training of the Twelve Apostles," since it apparently presumes a one-on-one, apprentice-to-master relationship of discipleship, probably for Gentile converts in particular.[3] This training privileged orality,[4] as do proverbs. The decision to structure the material around the two ways reflects Jewish traditions that persisted into early Christianity. Famously, Ps. 1 contrasts "the way of the righteous" with "the way of the wicked." Jeremiah 21:8 juxtaposes "the way of life and the way of death." The blessings-and-curses structure in Deuteronomy (e.g., 11:26–28) is similarly binary. Jesus contrasts the broad path to destruction with the narrow path to life (Matt. 7:13–14), so that his followers dubbed their movement "the Way," according to a number of passages in the book of Acts.[5]

The *Didache* appropriates the two-ways framework to prepare catechumens for Christian baptism. This is the means by which children and adult converts publicly enter into covenant with the triune God of Israel, being joined with the Son of God in his death and resurrection while the Holy Spirit thereby connects them to the church. Christian faith kills the old self walking the way of death and makes alive the new self, created in Christ Jesus to pursue the true way of life. As the two-ways tradition developed after Proverbs, focus increased on the in-breaking of divine judgment and salvation. With the end of the ages dawning in Christ, who poured out the Spirit for making us wise unto salvation, Gal. 5:17–25 provides an instructive New Testament bridge to the *Didache*: a duality of Spirit versus flesh (in the sense of weak, earth-bound, sinful existence, not simply the body); a catalog of virtues and vices; and an eschatological incentive, within which God's in-breaking future of judgment and salvation shapes moral and spiritual life.[6]

After the *Didache* begins by setting forth the way of life, warnings appear against the way of death and false teachers who promote it. It would be easy to

3. Aaron Milavec, *The Didache: Text, Translation, Analysis, Commentary* (Collegeville, MN: Liturgical Press, 2003), 47.

4. Ibid., 41.

5. Ibid., 45.

6. Especially Gal. 5:21b but also 5:24; so M. Jack Suggs, "The Christian Two Ways Tradition: Its Antiquity, Form, and Function," in *Studies in New Testament and Early Christian Literature: Essays in Honor of Allen P. Wikgren*, ed. David E. Aune (Leiden: Brill, 1972), 69.

think that succeeding chapters change the subject, since they address a variety of churchly and pastoral practices with very concrete instructions and prohibitions. However, some of this material offers wisdom regarding how to discern true teachers from false ones, for which money is a chief concern. Hence we never stray so far from Proverbs-type material as one might think. Without entering into historical debates over the two-ways tradition, the larger point is that the mindset of Proverbs does not lie far off the beaten path of early Christian teaching. Possibly we should say this the other way: early Christian teaching continues in the canonical trajectory that Proverbs helps to set. Its demand for us to become wise as an outgrowth of fearing the Lord finds parallels throughout the New Testament. Early Christian texts do not separate law from wisdom, or individual from community formation, in the ways that modern form critics might prefer.

Beyond the explicit framing of the *Didache* around the two ways, there is the added consideration that much patristic exegesis never resulted in a commentary as such. Instead, early Christian interpretation of scripture poured forth in sermons, catechesis, and the like. In this way much patristic material remains connected to Proverbs, appealing regularly to its wisdom in ways that are appropriate to its genre. Despite the absence of formal commentary, Proverbs is not as foreign to Christian theology as are modern scholarly assumptions about what constitutes theology and whether the book meets that standard. Not only may theology transcend the systematic genre so familiar in the modern West; it may also broaden beyond theology proper (regarding the divine attributes) to include the economy of divine action (and thus the privileges and responsibilities of creatures). Insofar as Proverbs treats ethics in the context of the fear of the Lord, the book is theological whether or not it labors to develop a systematic doctrine of God, for Proverbs instead presupposes a body of teaching about God's character and will.

A few centuries after the *Didache*, Anicius Manlius Severinus Boethius wrote *The Consolation of Philosophy*. Born around AD 480, Boethius rose to prominence in the Roman Empire, though he eventually fell into disfavor and was falsely accused of conspiracy. While in prison he authored his paean to wisdom before death in 524. The *Consolation* unfolds in five books. Early in book 1, Philosophy appears as a woman to the despairing Boethius. Since Philosophy etymologically points to love of wisdom, we recognize a striking parallel to Proverbs, wherein Lady Wisdom appears to woo us away from Dame Folly. Boethius's *Consolation* therefore extends the sapiential two-ways trajectory of the *Didache*, offering an additional form of early Christian literary parallels to Proverbs.

Initially Philosophy calls Boethius out of self-pity, noting the consistent persecution that seekers of wisdom have undergone over the centuries. Boethius responds with a harbinger of issues to come: his complaint is not about the persecution, which should be expected; instead he is frustrated over the evil of its success

(*Consolation* 1.4 [153]).[7] Ironically, common opinion assumed Boethius's guilt precisely because of an ingrained retribution principle: if he suffers, there must be a reason (1.4 [157]). At this point the book signals that it will address not merely the subject matter of Proverbs, but also the tensions with wisdom that are evoked by Ecclesiastes: Why do bad things happen to good people?

Philosophy announces its goal: "I seek not so much a library with its walls ornamented with ivory and glass, as the storeroom of your mind, in which I have laid up not books, but what makes them of any value, the opinions set down in my books in times past" (1.5 [163]). The goal is reorientation of Boethius's inward compass, to be tugged into line with the truth handed down by faithful tradition. Proverbs likewise pursues fidelity of heart—"the fear of the LORD is the beginning of knowledge" (1:7)—to the best of tradition (its primary address is to "the young"; 1:4). "Men's minds are obviously such that when they lose true opinions they have to take up false ones, and then a fog arises from these false ideas, which obscures that true vision" (Boethius 1.7 [171]). There is no neutrality: there are only two ways of thinking and living. Ecclesiastes comes circuitously to the same conclusion: "Remember your creator in the days of your youth. . . . Of anything beyond these, my child, beware. . . . Fear God, and keep his commandments; for that is the whole duty of everyone" (Eccl. 12:1, 12, 13).

Book 2 takes up Boethius's concern over his loss of good fortune: "You have given yourself over to fortune's rule: you must accommodate yourself to your mistress's ways. Will you really try to stop the whirl of her turning wheel? Why, you are the biggest fool alive—if it once stop, it ceases to be the wheel of fortune" (2.1 [179]). Sounding like Ecclesiastes in confronting human insatiability, Philosophy provides a counterweight to many readings of Proverbs on retribution. According to such extreme scholarly portrayals, Proverbs simplistically suggests that good people or actions result almost automatically in good consequences, and so too bad people or actions get just what they deserve. Later on, Proverbs itself will counteract this portrayal at a number of points. But for now, one piece of the puzzle is strikingly clear in the *Consolation* (2.2 [185]) right along with Proverbs and Ecclesiastes—namely, money cannot buy happiness:

> Should Plenty pour from cornucopia full
> As much in riches as the sand
> Stirred up by wind-whipped seas, or as the countless stars
> That shine in a clear night sky,
> And never stay her hand,
> Still would mankind not cease
> Complaining of their wretchedness.
> Even were God with much gold prodigal,

7. Square brackets contain page numbers from Boethius, *The Theological Tractates; The Consolation of Philosophy*, trans. H. F. Stewart, E. K. Rand, and S. J. Tester; Loeb Classical Library 74 (Cambridge: Harvard University Press, 1978).

Answering men's prayers,
And heaped bright honours on those wanting them,
Their gains would seem to them
Nothing: ever their cruel gain-devouring greed
Opens new maws. What curbs
Could check within firm bounds this headlong lust,
When even in those whose wealth is overflowing
The thirst for gain still burns?
He is never rich
Who trembles and sighs, thinking himself in need.

The wise person does not conclude that riches constitute good fortune. Not only does the sand provide an inadequate foundation, but so also does the mountaintop, by subjecting a house to high winds. The wise person builds a house on the low rock (Boethius 2.4 [199]), as Jesus teaches (Matt. 7:24–27).

So Boethius needs to learn contentment, seeking the measure of goods appropriate to his identity. As a human being, he reduces himself below God's esteem for him if he clings to earthly goods (2.5 [205]). Similar considerations pertain, beyond riches, to power and prominent offices. After concluding book 2 with a song suggesting that love is what makes the world go round (2.8 [227]), the *Consolation* therefore treats true happiness in book 3: "The most sacred kind of good is that of friendship, a good reckoned not a matter of fortune but of virtue" (3.2 [235]). Rival possibilities by which we seek happiness, such as fame, fortune, and bodily satisfactions, undergo deconstruction. They fail to last and deny true freedom by making us wrongly depend on factors outside God and ourselves. Happiness comes from the supreme good; our recognition that these other goods are deficient requires that a perfect good exists by which to measure the rest (3.10 [275]). All other goods—to the extent that they are good—must not be separate rivals but instead aspects of participation in the one good, God, whose simplicity brings unity to all the rest (3.10 [281, 289]).

More controversially, Boethius's Philosophy concludes that everything must be seeking this good, at least by nature and in principle, even when defectively seeking this or that worldly good. "There is therefore nothing . . . which while remaining true to its nature would try to go against God" (3.12 [303]). Standing behind this conclusion is a concept of order such as we have in Proverbs. It is not that the world lacks fools, but such folly is out of step with our God-given nature—inconsistent with what we see happening when the world around us works according to divine design.

Yet evil people and fools often seem to get on quite well; we can hear echoes of the Sage musing in Ecclesiastes. Why does God not make the way of the world more straightforwardly conducive to virtue alone? This is the preoccupation of books 4–5 in the *Consolation*. Lengthy exposition of Philosophy's answer to Boethius lies beyond our present purpose, which is simply to affirm that the moral life, for which Proverbs exhorts and equips us, readily raises theological questions.

One cannot avoid deciding whether people have true happiness just because they persist in health and wealth, or that they might be longing for union with God their supreme good even though they do not know it. These issues require an account of divine judgment, both in this life and regarding life hereafter. The *Consolation* actually argues that the wicked should recognize themselves to be better off punished, because in this way God maintains the moral integrity of the universe with which (in principle) they aspire to be in harmony (4.4 [343]).

It is not always appropriate—pastorally or biblically—merely to exhort pitying rather than hating the wicked, as Boethius's Philosophy does here (4.4 [351]). The *Consolation* may overstate the goodness of evil due to divinely superintended results (4.6 [371]), and its ultimate answer to questions of God, freedom, and evil may be unsatisfying if its commitment to divine simplicity is unsatisfying—which is, to say the least, controversial these days. But Boethius's work reflects the classic Christian commitment to uphold the integrity of God's creation and, on that basis, to pursue truth about living well, wherever it might be found. Boethius's *Consolation* also manifests the limits of, and the tensions provoked by, such encounters with philosophy. When allusions to scripture and Jesus Christ are rare, do we have the Christian message about wise living in harmony with the rest of creation? Or is this liable to end (even unintentionally) in distortion as a natural theology? Boethius raises this question for us as acutely as Proverbs itself.

In any case, one cannot say that the early church resisted the excellence of wisdom. The *Didache* and Boethius's *Consolation* reflect a two-ways trajectory from Proverbs into classic Christian teaching. It is fair to suggest that Proverbs eventually declined in theological influence as the church's doctrinal heritage became more christologically focused and then ever more subject to abstract speculation. Aside from debates over 8:22–36, the church's primary uses of the book inevitably regarded moral instruction. Yet, even so, it is dubious to suggest that such instruction is inherently nontheological or moralistic. The example of Boethius attests to the theological relevance of Proverbs, and Murphy himself does too when he starts to unfold the underlying theology of creation and human experience in Proverbs. Various perennial debates over nature and grace, from the medieval period onward, further demonstrate the book's dogmatic relevance.

At minimum, resistance against natural theology must not result in neglecting a theology of nature. At maximum, Proverbs embodies the canonical legitimacy of addressing the Creator and creation without explicitly accounting for redemption at every point. The Protestant Reformation and subsequent centuries play an ironic part in this proverbial drama, resisting medieval moralism with respect to justifying grace on the one hand while heightening the divine affirmation of ordinary life on the other. Thus the stakes involved in reading Proverbs simultaneously fell and rose, and today's pastoral climate for reading Proverbs intensifies these extremes.

On the one hand, sectors of Protestantism turn justification by faith alone into an offer of cheap grace. Many Christians claim to be evangelical despite disconnecting redemption from creation, thereby living foolishly, as if they do not fear the Lord. Some, who seek to recover creation within the Christian worldview, nevertheless enjoy and exploit its goods without a moral framework disciplined by the gospel of Jesus Christ. Meanwhile, sectors of Roman Catholicism and Eastern Orthodoxy also fail to exert nurturing influence over the daily moral lives of their members—whether or not they have a version of Paul trumping other, James-like, canonical literature in the way that Protestants sometimes do.

On the other hand, contemporary readers face the temptation to encounter Proverbs, if not moralistically, then at least pragmatically. The book becomes a source of parenting tips, offering advice on the level of a self-help manual—with divine guarantees. In uses of this sort, the theological framework of Proverbs becomes either so prominent that its shape is distorted or else so obscure that it can exert little influence. Either God blesses automatically the people who do the right things or else the God of "moralistic therapeutic deism"[8] offers people the platitudes they need to help themselves. In neither case do we have the comprehensive, creation-oriented ethics of Proverbs, which gets supplanted instead by piecemeal moralism reinforcing our current economic practices and ethical prejudices.

Concerned to avoid such errors, therefore, we now turn to the text itself. The structural benchmarks of the proverbial collections are fairly clear. Proverbs 1–9 consists of extended speeches from parents and Wisdom personified, while the rest of the book contains a series of collections offering proverbs in the shorter, usually two-line sense to which most people are accustomed. Within Prov. 1–9, the structure of the speeches is again relatively clear. Interludes have Wisdom speaking in 1:20–33 and Prov. 8. In between, parental lectures address "my child" or "children" (2:1; 3:1, 11, 21; 4:1, 10, 20; 5:1, 7; 6:1, 3, 20; 7:1, 24; 8:32). Not all of these vocatives are necessarily equal in force, indicating key structural divisions; 6:3 reinforces direct address at the beginning of a lecture, while 7:24 and in a different sense 8:32 do so at the end of another. The divisions in the middle of Prov. 3 are minor, without interrupting the major flow of thought. Though more wisdom vocabulary occurs after 3:12 than before, the positive and negative admonitions along with the context of providential protection do not fundamentally differ from the first half of the chapter. Similarly, the parental admonitions and proffered life remain consistent throughout possible subsections in Prov. 4. Proverbs 5 begins with a description of the wayward woman (5:1–6), providing context for warnings against her (5:7–23). After another lecture begins in 6:1, the vocatives in 6:20; 7:1; and 7:24 relate to further warnings against the wayward woman. While various structural possibilities are arguable, the view taken here sees a connection between the warning of 6:20 and the preceding material in 6:1–19. The youth must avoid being ensnared by a foolish pledge (6:1–3), excessive sleep (6:4–11), crooked speech (6:12–15), or the abominations cataloged in 6:16–19.

8. Christian Smith and Melinda Lundquist Denton, *Soul Searching: The Religious and Spiritual Lives of American Teenagers* (New York: Oxford University Press, 2005).

Likewise the adulteress would entangle the youth with a vengeful husband and likely disgrace (6:20–35). By contrast, in Prov. 7 the adulteress plays an extended speaking part in the public square, an obvious contrast with Lady Wisdom in Prov. 8. This suggests that, in addition to the literal level, at a metaphorical level the adulteress by now embodies Dame Folly.

As a result, we can read Prov. 2–9 thematically using the standard chapter divisions. Proverbs 2, 3, 4, and 6 are parental speeches lauding Wisdom, with progression in their focus—from accepting her offer (Prov. 2) to holding on to her (Prov. 3) to maintaining commitment to this parental path (Prov. 4) to avoiding entanglements that could divert one from the path (Prov. 6). Proverbs 5 and Prov. 7 intersperse parental warnings against Folly. The signal danger from which a person needs to guard the heart (4:20–27) is adultery (Prov. 5). Married or not, youths face grave spiritual dangers from listening to seductive voices (Prov. 7) instead of Lady Wisdom, who speaks in Prov. 8. Proverbs 9 offers summary versions of the opposing invitations from Lady Wisdom (9:1–6) and Dame Folly (9:13–18), framing axioms about the single-mindedness necessary for wisdom (9:7–12).

Of course, this dramatic movement transpires at the broad level of an overarching framework, within which are many highways and byways. Put differently, within this drama lie the twists and turns of numerous subplots, yet these are usually variations on the basic theme of two ways—one leading to life and the other to death. The overlapping vocabulary and motifs across Prov. 1–9 stem from this basic duality, while it remains possible to glimpse elements of progression in its portrayal. Ancient theological and moral frameworks, such as the two ways, by doing justice to the Bible's subject matter, help us to recognize and remove the blinders of current religious fashion.

Prologue (1:1–7)

Proverbs 1:1 indeed confronts us with another world, attributing to King Solomon the proverbs that follow. Surely not the author of each one, he nevertheless is the hub of their creation and collection. As "son of David" and "king of Israel," Solomon connects these proverbs to Israel's salvation history, however obliquely. That connection becomes more overt within a few verses, as the fear of YHWH—not just any god or Most Perfect Being—stands as the narrow gate for entering into pursuit of wisdom (1:7). Solomon's name associates him with peace (Hippolytus, *Fragments from Commentary on Proverbs*, in ANF 5.172), not just in the negative sense of avoiding war but rather in the holistic sense of flourishing—enjoying harmony with God, God's people, and the rest of creation. The wisdom for such *shalom* is mediated through Israel's officials—in this case, the Davidic king—from which line Jesus the Messiah ultimately came.

The purpose of the proverbs appears in 1:2–6. These verses heap repeated words for wisdom on top of each other. Excessive precision with fine lexical distinctions is not the aim. Yet, within this dense network of signifiers pointing to wisdom, a number of theological lessons emerge.

First, wisdom is not merely personal but also social in its orientation. The insight gained from proverbial instruction enables wise dealing and promotes justice (1:3). The proverbs enable not only learning or gaining instruction, but also teaching (1:4)—these constructions are parallel, so the latter pertains for the recipient of Proverbs just as much as the former. The truly wise person does not hoard the instruction he or she receives, but passes it on to the simple and the young. Proverbs 1:4 further pushes wisdom beyond the moral and spiritual priorities of 1:3 into the hurly-burly of interpreting everyday life, since the connotations of its "shrewdness" vocabulary are not uniformly positive throughout the Old Testament—recalling the serpent in Gen. 3. We need to become "wise as serpents," not just "innocent as doves" (Matt. 10:16). Thus Proverbs describes the way of the world without always prescribing appropriate responses. This hint of the need not only to pass on wisdom but also to grapple with the world's moral complexity appears before the hermeneutical function of wisdom in 1:5–6. Wisdom builds on itself: learning and teaching wisdom are foundational for growing in ability to hear and discern its meaning. Wisdom's riches are accordingly inexhaustible: the wise are to increase in skill for understanding these words—boundless not in potential meanings on any given occasion (since, requiring skill, they must be somewhat determinate), but rather in fullness of meaning over time, especially as they encounter new and complex situations.

Second, biblical wisdom addresses everyone, at a level appropriate to where they are. This is evident initially in the lack of an explicit addressee in 1:1. Next it is evident in the way wisdom accumulates, even for the wise, as just noted; one never gets wise enough to stop needing more. Moreover, we can teach wisdom to the simple and the young. Thus Proverbs does not trouble itself over virtue's paradox, the idea that only the virtuous can grow in virtue, which seems to preclude anyone ever starting to become virtuous in the first place. Wisdom for the next step—even the first step on the path to life—is always available, unless a person has walked so far down the road from simplicity to prideful folly that he or she utterly refuses to turn around.

Third, 1:7 directs us toward resolving this virtuous paradox theologically: beginning with "the fear of the LORD," wisdom is therefore a gift from God, evoking a posture of reception. God's name is YHWH, by which the Creator reveals himself in covenant with Israel. Wisdom begins with a proper response to this God. The givenness of YHWH's revelation is taken for granted; 1:7 depicts the either-or of the two ways: people respond either appropriately with fear or else inappropriately with folly. But God has given the gift.

Fools despise the instruction offered to them because, by implication, they do not take God seriously. At that point, of course, wisdom no longer addresses everyone in quite the same way. Folly harms ability to gain understanding in a manner roughly parallel to the way wisdom accumulates. Thus in Matt. 7:6 Jesus our wisdom instructs: "Do not give what is holy to dogs; and do not throw your pearls before swine, or they will trample them under foot and turn and maul you." People become so hardened in folly that wisdom makes an offer they no longer can accept. At the same time, we must be cautious in discerning when others "despise wisdom," for great danger lies in presuming our own: first we ought to remove the log in our own eye before attempting to help with the speck in our brother's or sister's (7:1–5). Far from encouraging us to be wise in our own eyes, Jesus's exhortation in 7:6 merely acknowledges that obvious cases exist in which people will be unreceptive; giving them what they despise will only worsen the situation.

Fools are prideful—a root, if not the root, of the so-called deadly sins. Meanwhile, an early indicator of the need for grace is the aura of mystery involved in the very idea of a "proverb"—*māšāl*, a term that can also designate a "parable." The twofold reality of Jesus's parabolic teaching is likewise pertinent to Proverbs. On the one hand, the concrete earthiness of the sayings enables some understanding for even the simplest audience, inserting the teaching into the ordinary practices of life. On the other hand, "to those who have, more will be given, and they will have an abundance; but from those who have nothing, even what they have will be taken away" (Matt. 13:12). For, "seeing they do not perceive, and hearing they do not listen, nor do they understand" (13:13–15, quoting Isa. 6:9–10). Proverbs and parables seem deceptively simple, with layers of meaning reserved for those wise enough to fear God.

The fear of the Lord is not terror that creates further distance. Instead, this Old Testament synonym (roughly speaking) for faith emphasizes initial recognition that God is the Creator to whom we account for ourselves. God confronts our lives with a claim to which we must respond—one way or the other. Our response can never exhaust this claim. Bede distinguishes "servile fear" from subsequent "holy fear": upon initial torment over our sin, God's perfect love casts out servile fear of punishment (1 John 4:18), so that charity can instill in us the holy fear of disappointing our beloved Father (*Commentary on Proverbs*, in Corpus Christianorum: Series Latina 119B.25 and Wright 2005: 7).

Therefore Jas. 1:5–8 offers the necessary gloss on how this fear enables acquisition of wisdom: "If any of you is lacking in wisdom, ask God, who gives to all generously and ungrudgingly, and it will be given you. But ask in faith, never doubting, for the one who doubts is like a wave of the sea, driven and tossed by the wind; for the doubter, being double-minded and unstable in every way, must not expect to receive anything from the Lord." Wisdom begins in acknowledging our need and desire for the Creator to reveal how we might join creation's harmony. Because the grace involved in the gift of wisdom concerns all of creation, in principle fools—as we all are, apart from grace—do not lie beyond divine reach. God still addresses them as their Creator; they do not need developed knowledge of redemption to change course and begin acquiring wisdom. For starters they merely need to acknowledge their lack and quit despising God's provision. The basic duality of the two ways does not run simplistically between the wise and the foolish, the righteous and the unrighteous, or Christians and non-Christians. It also snakes more complexly through the hearts of the wise. James 1 makes clear that the righteous too can become double-minded and unstable, asking God for wisdom though having little or no intention to follow through on God's gift. However bizarre it seems, people sometimes counter all our expectations by receiving a gift without opening it. If this is true at times for the people of God, how much more can others become seemingly foolish beyond redemption, due not to lack of divine power or provision but rather to their hardened refusal even to receive a gift?

Since wisdom begins in acknowledging need for divine grace, we must intend to obey what we learn. Otherwise our need names a deficit in our lives, but not a true desire to have it filled. Fear of God is the beginning of wisdom not just in sequence, as if it were a hurdle over which to leap, after which to move on. Such fear is the beginning of wisdom in series; since wisdom is a path on which to walk, its beginning always points to the next step. If a person gives up fearing God, then the problem is not just stalled progress but rather the double-mindedness of looking in too many directions at once. Not to progress in wisdom by fearing the Lord is already to take a detour, if not start backward. The fear of the Lord endures forever (Ps. 19:9).

As a biblical exemplar, Reno offers Job—at the end of his story—to show that fear of God accompanies the demanding reality of recognizing who God really is:

> The created nature of the human person remains forever distinct from the divine nature of the Holy Trinity. This chasm is bridged by grace, but never eliminated. God becomes incarnate, not created, and salvation is a deification of our humanity, not our absorption into the divine nature. . . . An analogy might help. When we walk across bridges we may enjoy every confidence that the engineers have done a good job and the span will not collapse—and yet, who does not feel hints of terror when looking over the edge and into the depths of the ocean below.[9]

The ongoing need for holy fear follows still further from the recursive nature of wisdom, in which the wise keep receiving greater facility to grow. Again, the two ways concern not just starting points but also one's direction.

This duality involved in the teaching of two ways is not the dualism with which the Christian tradition is so readily charged these days. Exactly to the contrary, the two ways stem from there being only one true God. All of life, for everyone, is subject to the lordship of YHWH, the Creator. This holds in principle for body and soul, now and not yet, church and world. The faulty dualism into which Christians sometimes fall—perhaps on occasion due to Greek influence, however much that is overblown—splits these realities into utterly separate categories, in which one or the other has priority with respect to God. By contrast, Jerome

9. R. R. Reno, "Fear of the Lord," in *Christian Reflection: A Series in Faith and Ethics* (Waco: Baylor University Press, 2009), 15–16.

finds in the exhortations of Prov. 1 a call to engage secular philosophy (Letter 70, in NPNF[2] 6.149). Everything in the world must be subject to the fear of God.

Rejecting dualism does not obliterate legitimate distinctions, within which all spheres of life remain subject to the God of Israel revealed in Jesus Christ. Some distinctions must remain if we are to account for the one God's rule awaiting fullness on earth, to match its fullness in heaven (Matt. 6:9–13). The most basic distinction lies in the human heart, not in its perfection but its direction—walking according to God's way or away from that wisdom. Eschatological dualism follows from this: we do not yet see all things subjected to the Lord Jesus Christ (Heb. 2:8), though someday we will (Phil. 2:9–11), when every knee bows and every tongue confesses the sovereignty that God exercises in his Son. It is appropriate and even necessary to care for bodies and to engage human culture, yet we must do so without the world supplanting the Lord whom the church must fear. In other words, speaking biblically of the world requires double entendre—duality, not dualism. Though "God so loved the world that he gave his only Son" (John 3:16), he did so "that the world might be saved through him" (3:17), not simply left as it is, hiding in the darkness (3:19–21). Though "everything created by God is good" (1 Tim. 4:4a), to be "received with thanksgiving . . . sanctified by God's word and by prayer" (4:4b–5), the direction of the human heart is no longer good, turning these gifts into idols. Thanks to the flesh and the devil, apart from the divine light of Jesus Christ we forget that "the world and its desire are passing away, but those who do the will of God live forever" (1 John 2:17).

Fourth and finally, then, the corollary of wisdom's social, democratic, and theological dimensions has surfaced numerous times above: wisdom is progressive. Its teacher, while always vitally active, moves progressively from giving basic direction to stimulating complex discernment, as youths overcome their simplicity and grow in wisdom. The goal is not slavish repetition of traditional formulas but the freedom of sonship, in which the learner becomes ever more able to recognize truth and live accordingly, without constant direction. The growth necessary to realize that goal, though, requires initial instruction and ongoing guidance.

Hearing No Evil (1:8–19)

Thus, among the sinews binding these early verses together is "instruction" (*mûsār*). The sequence in 1:2—"knowledge/learning" (*daʿat*), "wisdom" (*ḥokmâ*), "instruction" (*mûsār*)—reappears in 1:7. Now appearing again in 1:8 (in addition to 1:3), *mûsār* leads into the main exhortation.

The text presents two speakers, offering two different paths leading toward two different ends. The speakers are parents (1:8–9) and "sinners" (1:10–19). The sinners are enticing (1:10, 14, 17–18) and violent (1:11–12, 16) for the sake of greed (1:13–14, 19). Yet their end is death, portrayed starkly in terms of self-destruction (1:18–19, as well as double entendre involving evil in 1:16). The implication, by contrast, is that the end of parental instruction is life. The imagery of 1:9 is not merely ornate, but a fitting indication of ultimate rest in victory. The irony of violent folly becomes transparent in 1:17–19, as those who set a trap for others entrap themselves; they lack the bird's-eye view being offered to the proverbial youth. The parallelism extends to the ambushes, "for blood" (1:11) versus "for their own lives" (1:18). The tragedy of the gang extends to their desires and even their definitive destinies.

Among the underlying concepts, first, is striking integration of truth, goodness, and beauty, the three classic transcendentals of human participation in the created order and thereby the divine life. Truth is at stake as always in Proverbs, for that is what the parental instruction enables us to know. Goodness too is at stake, which is particularly obvious in the present section, as the two paths of godly obedience and gang violence lie in sharp contrast. Their different ends point toward not only God's goodness but also beauty. God displays goodness by providing instruction for living in harmony with creation so that—in general, all things being equal—we may flourish. The portrayal of this flourishing comes in esthetic terms (1:9), with the parental instruction itself serving as adornment. Truth, goodness, and beauty are not separate realities to be played off against each other in tension, but integral dimensions of one reality—a form of divine simplicity. Responding to divine instruction conveyed via delegated authority brings the social and natural harmony whereby creaturely life reflects the character of our Maker.

"Transcendental" is a misnomer for truth, goodness, or beauty if it conveys abstraction to some realm far beyond human experience. Proverbs portrays this integrated reality as quite immanent, concretely touching choices we make in daily life. Transcendence lies not in abstraction, but in the connection between a person's ordinary life and the Creator who relates to all other people as well. There is a regrettable absence of obedience to divine instruction in most human lives. To use obvious examples near to hand, humans are constantly caving in to peer pressure (1:10), ambushing the innocent without cause (1:11), filling houses with the spoils of conquest (1:13), agreeing to share only in dubious enterprises (1:14), hurrying to hurt others (1:16), and so forth. Supposedly enlightened Western societies have scarcely conquered so much as tried to manage violence—purloining newer and more subtle forms, even offering it as entertainment. Yet here in Proverbs truth, goodness, and beauty lie beyond us not in principle so much as in practice.

Second, the preponderance of 1:8–19 communicates the character and pervasiveness of sinners. One of the two ways often seems more enticing than the other—the way of death. Humans are sufficiently vulnerable to its wiles that biblical warnings must be extensive. Its pervasiveness aside, the way of death inextricably links rejection of God and violence, idolatry, and injustice. To despise the Lord's way of instruction enmeshes a person in greed leading to bloodshed. It is tempting to view the references to murder (1:11, 16) as extreme, so that the robbers are outliers from the community, the exception rather than the rule.

Indeed, these warnings uphold a social order in which there are more robbed than robbers, more warned than warned against. However, "houses" (1:13) indicate some social status. Moreover, 1:19 broadens the field of vision: "Such is the end of all who are greedy for gain"—the robbers enact an extreme form of the corrupted desire that infiltrates everyone. The upshot is that contemporary social reforms predicated on dealing with strife and radical violence via managed self-interest—tolerance—cannot offer definitive solutions. The aberrance that leads to school shootings and the like—as well as the more pervasively ordinary road rage, wrongful competitiveness, ethnic suspicions, and hatred—is impossible to address fully without reconciling people to their Creator. Conversely, those who believe they love God without loving their neighbor deceive themselves.

Third, sinners offer enticing forms of alternative community (1:14). They even promise forms of sharing to which the godly might aspire. Not all theological strategies for arriving at this conclusion are appropriate, but the observation itself is sound: humans are peculiarly relational animals. The robbers appeal for the youth to join in a common purse. The pathology in the robbers' appeal is subtle, since Proverbs itself appeals to genuinely enlightened self-interest when leading us toward wisdom. Proverbs, however, does not appeal to self-interest at the expense of others' well-being in the community or the stability of the community as a whole. Nor does the book treat self-interest as a matter of sharing in unlimited goods: "Sinners love wealth and use people; saints love people and use wealth to help others" (Waltke 2004: 193). The blessing generally conveyed by obedience does not reward those "greedy for gain" (1:19).

Fourth, the positive side of community in this passage concerns familial tradition. To "honor your father and mother" means more than grudgingly obeying direct commands until reaching a certain age of independence. Beyond obeying parents one must prize the spiritual heritage they pass on, respecting their God-given vocation and treasuring their faithful teaching. Spiritual interpretations of God as father and church as mother are problematic in this text if they obscure the primary focus on human families: the flourishing of the covenant community depends on familial harmony in the perpetuation of wisdom. The most direct ecclesiastical implication in 1:8–19 is that the church needs to catechize in a way that equips parents to instruct their children. Beyond this, the church needs to foster a climate in which older and wiser members guide younger ones, and the younger ones heed—even seek—such guidance.

Fifth and finally, there is a strong connection between hearing and doing. It is wrong to take this as guaranteed, one-way linear movement from knowledge to obedience. People can know the good they ought to do without doing it (Jas. 4:17). However, those to whom one listens influence how one lives. Put negatively, "Bad company corrupts good character" (1 Cor. 15:33 TNIV). Put positively, divine instruction received with heartfelt commitment keeps a person on the straight and narrow. Aside from our need for biblical teaching, this reaffirms the centrality of hearing in how we profitably receive such a tradition of instruction. Biblical teaching has a personal and oral character that we must not neglect in our rush to address an image-dominated society. The acquisition of information is not primary; neither is the vividness of the images. The parent uses a strategy of narrative depiction to convey warnings; hence in their own way some of the verbal images are quite striking, such as lying "in wait for blood" and "ambush[ing] the innocent" (Prov. 1:11), "swallow[ing] . . . alive" yet "go[ing] down to the Pit" (1:12), "fill[ing] . . . houses with booty" (1:13), "feet run[ning] to evil" and bloodshed (1:16), or ensnaring a bird (1:17). However, certain visually vivid images could actually mislead youth, being used to make elements of gang life seem attractive. So, while oral instruction is important for its personal directness—having the words of warning delivered in a context of authority, integrity, and caring relationship—its visually indirect element may likewise be significant. The parent matches the imagery of the wicked appeal with depictions of destruction, but does so with verbal warnings rather than an alternative tableau of visualized promises. We certainly cannot and should not reject visual arts. But the appeal of wickedness is often sensory, so that replacing the hearing of parental teaching with other modes of conveying these warnings might ironically play on the opposition's home turf. To put the matter bluntly, it is not clear that an R-rated movie portraying the destruction of the wicked would catch the spirit of this text in the same way as a personal warning, and its cleverness might even backfire, providing the violence with romantic allure. Prudential disagreements about parental means of conveying warnings are appropriate, of course, but we should not embrace substitutes for our words. Parental wisdom tries to reach the youthful will by appealing to authority and relationship, in order to elicit rational deliberation about the ultimate consequences of various courses of action.

This section introduces themes not only for the familial household but also for the spiritual life of the household of God. In fact, while not exactly one and the same, these overlap: it is no accident that the New Testament frequently uses the household metaphor regarding the church (e.g., 1 Tim. 3). Proverbs teaches how to "be subject to one another out of reverence for Christ" (Eph. 5:21), focusing early and often on the initial, most intimate churchly context in which we do so—our families. Proverbs portrays the joyous harmony that results when husbands and wives love each other, when parents train children wisely, and especially when children obey their parents in the Lord—fulfilling thereby the fifth commandment with a promise, "so that it may be well with you and you may live long on the earth" (Eph. 6:1–3). As a Father who only knows best (Matt. 7:9–11), God nurtures us through the daily dramas of family living as an analogy of life in his covenant. The teaching and learning, even commanding and obeying, about which we read in Proverbs, are instructive regarding the fear of the Lord precisely because they are so integral to it. Literary devices such as Lady Wisdom and Dame Folly are apropos precisely because they can be more than metaphors: the literal sense has spiritual significance, and the spiritual meaning truly is grounded in the letter. In this case the analogy does not compare two realities extrinsic to each other. Rather, our daily participation in a proximate dimension nurtures our connection to the ultimate reality. God is the Father who defines what parental instruction really means, but God chooses to instruct by way of our having—and becoming—fathers and mothers ourselves (Prov. 1:8).

Hearing Wisdom's Offer (1:20–33)

This personal character of biblical teaching manifests a new dimension beginning in 1:20, as Wisdom—personified—cries out in the public square. She begins to issue her invitation here and then expands it starting in 8:1. Otherwise the speeches in Prov. 1–9 come from the parents, particularly the father, in the home; they seek to maintain the youth within the familial traditions of the covenant community. Wisdom's offers similarly pertain to all youth but then travel a step further, pursuing those who have already fallen victim to Folly and seeking their return to the fold. The speeches are mutually reinforcing. Wisdom reproves as parents do (1:23) and requires the fear of YHWH (1:29), remaining vulnerable to being despised just as parental teaching is (1:7–8). The parental lectures repeatedly seek to inculcate Wisdom by first stirring up openness to hear her (2:2) and desire to pursue her when outside the home (2:3–4).

In fact, the first parental lecture (1:8–19) introduces Wisdom's initial interlude (1:20–33), at which we now arrive. Three elements are immediately significant: Wisdom is publicly available, personally active, and already scorned.

First, Wisdom is very publicly available. The text emphasizes how loud and centrally located she is as she cries out (1:20–21). She does not risk excessive subtlety, addressing the simple and the scoffers directly (1:22) with an imperative invitation (1:23). How strong is the contrast, at first glance, with Job 28: "But where shall wisdom be found? / And where is the place of understanding? / Mortals do not know the way to it, / and it is not found in the land of the living. / . . . Where then does wisdom come from? / And where is the place of understanding? / It is hidden from the eyes of all living, / and concealed from the birds of the air" (28:12–13, 20–21). Yet, while it might appear as if Job renders wisdom unattainable, on closer inspection Job 28 and Prov. 1 are complementary. Job emphasizes that wisdom is not a creaturely given, evident in the cosmos for the taking. It is hidden from the eyes, whereas "God understands the way to it, / and he knows its place. / For he looks to the ends of the earth, / and sees everything under the heavens. . . . / He saw it and declared it; / he established it, and searched it out. / And he said to humankind, / 'Truly, the fear of the Lord, that is wisdom; / and to depart from evil is understanding'" (28:23–24, 27–28). As Rom. 1:18–32 makes clear, looking at creation without departing from evil merely reinforces idolatry.

Proverbs arrives at the same place as Job—the fear of the Lord is wisdom—by a different route. Emphasis lies on God's making wisdom available to humans, not at first sight but upon hearing the divine voice. Wisdom's depths may be unfathomable yet their entrance is not, for the possibility of fearing the Lord is not far off; God personally pursues us. According to Job 28, some might find the path to fearing the Lord only after wandering around in an exasperated search for wisdom. According to Prov. 1, such folks need to listen. This raises the question of how to identify Wisdom more closely: how might one listen to the right voice? Given the surrounding context, Wisdom is divine teaching, parentally given in the covenant community. But regarding the broader world or even parental sources, the text does not belabor any of the additional nuances about Wisdom's relation to divine attributes, the order of creation, types of personification, and so forth.

Second, Wisdom is personally active, a crucial distinction from Job 28. In Prov. 1 Wisdom is crying out, promising to pour out thoughts and words (1:23), calling and experiencing refusal (1:24–25), therefore laughing and mocking (1:26), choosing not to respond or to give herself (1:28). Job rules out the possibility of finding Wisdom latent in the cosmos. Proverbs agrees, for Wisdom is not only mediated by creaturely realities but also comes between us and the rest of creation. The situations portrayed by Job work the other way around, as mortals try (and fail) to go straight through the created world to get Wisdom. By contrast, the nearest explanation of Wisdom's character at this point in Proverbs is parental instruction (1:8–19) as a vehicle of personal divine address (1:20–33), which guides us toward the treasure we seek in the cosmos (Prov. 2). Parents warn against evil companions and so preserve—even prepare—us for paying attention to God. While the nuances are not yet explicit, Wisdom already begins to have a divine aura.

For, third, Wisdom is already scorned. Its refusal is treated as fact in 1:24–25, 29–30. The structure of this language is reminiscent of the personal rejection that evokes divine jealousy, even the covenant curses forecast for Israel in Deuteronomy. So these young fools are not outside the community; they are the next generation of God's covenant people, who always begin their journey tempted by waywardness. At the end of such a self-destructive path, some cry out once they realize the consequences, begging to enter life. The New Testament heightens this drama with its description of those who cry out, "Lord, Lord" yet whom God never knew (Matt. 7:21–23).[10] Even doing good works in the divine name provides no guarantee of genuinely fearing the Lord in a life-giving way.

"Hell hath no fury like a woman scorned"—whatever the general truth of this saying, it summarizes a very poignant reality in Prov. 1. As a consequence of her rejection, Wisdom promises to respond in ways that only God can do. Only God can laugh at the tragic fate of the nations (1:26–27). Psalm 2 is apposite: "Why do the nations conspire, / and the peoples plot in vain? / . . . He who sits in the heavens laughs; / the Lord has them in derision" (2:1, 4). Only God can

10. Also Matt. 25:11, mentioned by Gregory the Great, *Forty Gospel Homilies* 10 (12), trans. David Hurst, Cistercian Studies 123 (Kalamazoo, MI: Cistercian Publications, 1990), 73: there the ten foolish virgins, whose lamps ran out of oil, beg to enter the wedding feast; surely they were part of the community in some sense if they received an invitation, but the bridegroom refuses to acknowledge them.

determine when people are past the possibility of genuine repentance. This is of course the flip side of the truth that only God gives the necessary self-revelation in the first place:

> At that time Jesus said, "I thank you, Father, Lord of heaven and earth, because you have hidden these things from the wise and the intelligent and have revealed them to infants; yes, Father, for such was your gracious will. All things have been handed over to me by my Father; and no one knows the Son except the Father, and no one knows the Father except the Son and anyone to whom the Son chooses to reveal him." (Matt. 11:25–27)

> But, as it is written,
>
> "What no eye has seen, nor ear heard,
> nor the human heart conceived,
> what God has prepared for those who love him"—
>
> these things God has revealed to us through the Spirit; for the Spirit searches everything, even the depths of God. For what human being knows what is truly human except the human spirit that is within? So also no one comprehends what is truly God's except the Spirit of God. (1 Cor. 2:9–11)

The parallel from 1 Cor. 2 is instructive in light of Prov. 1:23, where Wisdom offers to "pour out [her] thoughts to you." "Thoughts" is a translation of *rûaḥ* ("spirit"), dealing at the most basic level with what Wisdom breathes out her mouth in speaking. At another level we realize that she is offering to pour out the divine Spirit, the one who knows and makes known to us the mind of God.

The two ways are as clear as ever. One can respond to Wisdom's divine invitation and live securely at rest (1:33) or else reject her advances and suffer divine judgment. The judgment may come via apparently dramatic divine intervention, now or later. Or instead via more immanent processes one may reap what one sows in the created order—the usual focus of wisdom literature. Here the judgment clearly has a temporal dimension, dealing with calamity (1:26–27) and the destruction that attends foolish complacency (1:32). There is some kind of eternal dimension too, since one can reach a point of no return or repentance (1:28), the consequence of which is self-consumption (1:31, evoking memories of 1:18). While any notion of an afterlife remains unstated and at most implicit, nevertheless we sense the seriousness of the consequences at stake. The language of lament is present in 1:22: "How long?" Insofar as parents are preparing all the community's children to listen to Wisdom, this addresses everyone. We all start out as "simple," awaiting formation in virtue or vice that occurs only over time, as experiences and responses engender habits. Though Proverbs does not articulate this situation in terms of original sin and total depravity, nevertheless the state of simplicity is clearly perilous—if for no other reason than its temporary character. How long, then, can we delight in folly—or vacillation, which comes to the same end—before our refusal of Wisdom becomes decisive (1:24–32)?

The depiction of Wisdom mocking the mockers does not portray God as a morally suspect sadist. Nor does it simply depict the two ways' version of "an eye for an eye," although the punishment does fit the crime (e.g., Wisdom calls and is rejected [1:24]; those who subsequently call on her when facing judgment receive no response [1:28]). Here Wisdom is consistent with—that is, God upholds—moral order. Those who take such a God to be morally dubious demonstrate how far contemporary culture has strayed from biblical perspectives, especially regarding the kind of deity found palatable. Proverbs 1:20–33 portrays God as personal, not merely a robotic retribution principle. Wisdom/God mocks because mere humans mock the divine initiative to embrace them in covenant. Divine mocking appropriately puts Folly in a bad light because God personally sought the flourishing of those who scorn Wisdom's offer.

Whereas Job 28 precludes those versions of natural theology in which people easily read the created cosmos like a revelatory book, Prov. 1 supports a theology of nature—tied to culture—according to which parents in the covenant community are able to instruct their children about the likely consequences of unwise actions. Here the possibilities of God's personal appeal as Wisdom for developing a redemptive natural theology pose unanswered questions, on which Prov. 8 will later come to bear. God's Wisdom is "secret and hidden" (1 Cor. 2:7), newly and more clearly sought after its redemptive-historical disclosure in Jesus Christ—"in whom are hidden all the treasures of wisdom and knowledge" (Col. 2:3). This treasure, like a fine pearl, is worth everything to possess, yet finding it does not depend on human skill despite the requisite single-mindedness (Matt. 13:44–45). When it comes to the implications of Wisdom's invitation for those outside the covenant community, again we are left with unanswered questions at this point. Perhaps, given Wisdom's elusive nature located in personal divine invitation, this is as it should be.

Accepting Wisdom's Offer (2)

We are never neutral. From the perspective of Prov. 1, people not only have two potential destinies; at any given moment their path heads either toward Wisdom and life or away from God and toward death. Even the youth of God's people, ostensibly on the path of life, begin precariously, tempted by alternative voices. God passionately calls out, wooing them toward Wisdom before they begin to harden themselves against instruction and move from gullibility to Folly. In Prov. 2 the speaking part switches back from personified Wisdom to the parent, but the message remains basically the same: seek understanding. The passage assumes that while the youth can hear and respond to such an offer, they remain vulnerable. They are, we might say, depraved yet no longer totally depraved. There is no easy theological transfer into contemporary ecclesiastical or dogmatic categories: should we view these solely as children of the covenant since they have parents teaching them God's way, or might they in another sense represent all children since God's Wisdom is on offer throughout the cosmos for their hearing? Perhaps there are implications in both spheres.

Though the passage resists fitting into some doctrinal categories and easily answering certain contemporary questions, still we may sketch its place within the unfolding drama of Proverbs. It addresses whatever scenes in which we find ourselves, regarding the urgency of what we pursue from here on out. The emphasis changes: whereas in Prov. 1 wisdom began with fearing the Lord and maintained its focus on listening—reception of revelation—here in Prov. 2 wisdom calls for active pursuit. In Prov. 1 active pursuit was problematic, because it involved either throwing one's lot in with sinners (1:8–19) or else trying to attain Wisdom once judgment for her rejection became imminent (1:20–33). In Prov. 2, however, a string of imperatives pictures active pursuit of wisdom *now* (2:1–4). The verbs begin with acceptance of revelation and progress toward wholehearted seeking. It is "the LORD [who] gives wisdom" (2:6), which requires that we approach scripture not just zealously but prayerfully.[11] Wisdom cries out, yet we also cry out for more in response. In Prov. 2, therefore, the primacy of revelation remains, but a complementary accent on human seeking is added.

In other words, Prov. 2 describes "faith seeking understanding," the classic Christian posture regarding knowledge that runs so contrary to modern instincts. "I believe in order to understand," said Augustine and others: without faith it is impossible to find oneself on the holy treadmill whereby wisdom accumulates in the wise. Yet those who take faith in terms of fideism, who rest content or even overconfident in the understanding they presently have, receive no comfort in this passage. We must "treasure up [God's] commandments within" (2:1) *and* listen, reflect, and passionately pursue greater understanding (2:2–4). Only with such a disposition, refusing to become intellectually complacent, will we truly "understand the fear of the LORD"—the faith we claim in the first place (2:5). Indeed, the passage is replete with forms of *tĕbûnâ* ("understanding") (2:2, 3, 5, 6, 9, 11).

This understanding is not primarily *theōria*, whether in the worst abstract or best contemplative, worshipful sense. The concept of understanding in Proverbs is usually closer to *phronēsis*, the practical reason for living well in concrete, worldly situations. However, though emphasis lies on the resulting obedience, nevertheless a contemplative element remains, as for example in the rumination and attentiveness implied in 2:1–2, the desperate pursuit of 2:4, the storing up of 2:7, the internalization of 2:10, and so forth. Modern epistemology tends to favor neither contemplative *theōria* nor more active *phronēsis*, instead fostering a dichotomy between abstract *theōria* and wholly active *technē*, the productive

11. Augustine, *On Christian Doctrine* 3.37.59, trans. D. W. Robertson Jr. (Indianapolis: Bobbs-Merrill, 1958), 117.

"practical" skill to which pure knowledge must lead if it is worth anything. In all this the goal becomes human mastery, so that these definitions of knowledge come to determine how we pursue it. If the goal is *technē* by which to control the cosmos, then knowledge itself must be gained by human mastery over unyielding objects of study. To modern people the risks involved in entrusting oneself to another—and ultimately to God in reverent fear—seem unacceptable. Wisdom's promise to guard us—and the justice of our communities—must be refused; we will protect ourselves by way of our critical methods and otherwise tolerant indifference, thank you.

The parental paean to wisdom in Proverbs addresses both opportunities and threats, to use language from the business world. Yet Proverbs speaks quite differently than modern epistemologies of self-salvation. In terms of opportunity, "treasure" is the privileged metaphor (2:1, 4, 7), besides "understanding," from which it stems. Wisdom provides what we should not seek directly by casting our lot in with the gang (1:13–14). "Strive first for the kingdom of God and his righteousness, and all these things will be given to you as well" (Matt. 6:33). Augustine (Sermon 399.11, in WSA 3/10.465) recognizes a troubling possibility in comparing wisdom and money: since there is no fitting comparison of their value, this could insult wisdom. But the actual point of comparison here concerns two possible loves—pursuit of wisdom or money. Given the shrewdness, self-restraint, future orientation, and even reckless abandon with which people pursue money, it is fitting to insist that wisdom is even more valuable.

In terms of threats, the Lord's wisdom is a protective shield (Prov. 2:7), a guardrail for one's path (2:8), a bodyguard of sorts (2:11, the last reference to "understanding" in the chapter). The second half of Prov. 2 promises wisdom's deliverance from the many who with perverse joy pursue the way of death (2:12–15) and particularly from the adulteress (2:16–19). We save ourselves by refusing their offers as well as by refusing to save ourselves, since wisdom is necessary to save us from these branches of the path of death. The parental lectures in Prov. 1–9 follow a pattern: an exordium or opening appeal to listen, complete with motivation for doing so; the substance of the lesson; and then a conclusion, usually outlining consequences for whether or not one chooses the good character enjoined in the lesson. In Prov. 2 the exordium is lengthy (arguably 2:1–11), and the chief lesson enjoins accepting wisdom's deliverance from destructive people (saved "from the way of evil" in 2:12; saved "from the adulteress" in 2:16).

The chapter's structure subtly emphasizes something further. The twenty-two verses equal the number of letters in the Hebrew alphabet, and 2:11–12 bisects the chapter according to the dominance of two letters. Stanzas in 2:1–4 (after the direct address), 5–8, 9–11 begin with *ʾālep*, the alphabet's first letter; stanzas in 2:12–15, 16–19, 20–22 begin with *lāmed*, the alphabet's middle (twelfth) letter. The subsections are remarkably parallel in length: the text emphasizes the completeness of divinely provided order. Nothing escapes God's notice or good providence for covenant people who walk in the way of life. The additional theme of walking straight or upright as opposed to crooked (e.g., 2:15), while alternatively avoiding seductive smoothness (2:16), gives esthetic support to this emphasis on order. Humans tend to associate certain concepts or metaphors with related manifestations across various domains and with favorable or unfavorable scenarios. So, for instance, the Bible regularly associates light with righteousness and darkness with wickedness, or height with strength and depths with danger. Such metaphorical transposition can go too far, but has value if responsibly used. Cosmic and moral harmony is esthetically consistent with the value of order in Proverbs. Conversely, the book associates the moral disorder of beguiling speech with esthetic concern about the delight of pure smoothness or that which is too easy. For Proverbs, style conveys substance—both positively and negatively.

Moving on from structural implications at the macro level, the text is saturated in covenant language: commandments and righteousness early on, *ḥesed* ("loyal lovingkindness") in 2:8, a description of what theologians call "regeneration" in 2:10, and vocabulary often used for apostasy ("forsake," *ʿāzab*) in 2:13. The covenant thrust really breaks out in earnest near the conclusion. The adulteress breaks the marriage covenant she made before God (2:17), is outside the covenant community given her end (2:18), and leads astray her victim(s) to a hopeless point of no repentance (2:19). To walk in the way of life is a shared enterprise involving righteousness (2:20), and the practical ramifications of one's choice include Deuteronomy's language of dwelling in the promised land (2:21) or else being uprooted and cut off from it (2:22). This hints at a motif that will gain momentum later. Choice of companions—especially maritally or sexually—is a trope for covenant fidelity to God. People still speak today of communal ethics with such relational and sexual language, when for instance we reference politicians "prostituting" themselves to special interests or advertisers "seducing" the public. At stake is not merely symbolic truth; rather, there is an integral relation between the realms of human friendship and/or sexuality and the spiritual direction of a life. One cannot dwell with God and God's people in *shalom* while rejecting the divine path for human relationships, particularly familial ones. Nor can people participate in faithful, life-giving human relationships without experiencing a dimension of God's goodness, which ought to entice them to seek the wise Creator behind such harmony. For this reason it is all the more appropriate that the proverbial parent should call on us to accept Wisdom's offer, to pursue her.

> It is clearly we, I say, who make rough the straight and smooth paths of the Lord with the wicked and hard rocks of our desires, who very foolishly abandon the royal road paved with apostolic and prophetic stones and made level by the footsteps of all the holy ones and of the Lord himself, and who pursue byways and brambly roads. Blinded by the seductions of present pleasures, we crawl along the dark and obstructed trails, our feet lacerated by the thorns of vice and our wedding garment in tatters, and we are not only pierced by the sharp needles of thorny bushes but also brought low by the stings of the poisonous serpents and the scorpions that lie in wait there. (John Cassian, *Conference* 24.24.5, in Ancient Christian Writers 57.845)

Such wedding of marital—and even seductive—imagery with the ubiquity of two-ways metaphorical language (count the occurrences!) in Prov. 2 is a harbinger of what is to come.

Holding on to Wisdom (3)

Much in Prov. 3 and succeeding chapters substantially repeats vocabulary and motifs encountered by now. Yet slight shifts in emphasis signal dramatic progression. In Prov. 3 this progression involves holding on to Wisdom one has already decided to embrace. So, "do not forget my teaching" (3:1); "do not let loyalty and faithfulness forsake you" (3:3); "happy are those who [in an ongoing sense] find wisdom, / and those who get understanding" (3:13); "she is a tree of life to those who lay hold of her; / those who hold her fast are called happy" (3:18); "my child, do not let these escape from your sight: / keep sound wisdom and prudence" (3:21). Undoubtedly exhortations also address those who are not yet initiated into wisdom, but emphasis increases upon persevering in a relationship one has already begun to pursue.

The exordium in 3:1–12 contains six sets of exhortations, generally matched pairs negative and positive, followed by reasons or motivations. So, do not forget parental teaching but keep the commandments (3:1), for the sake of long, successful life (3:2). Do not let go of covenant fidelity but make this integral to how you adorn yourself before others (3:3), for the sake of favor with God and other humans (3:4). Do not trust your native wisdom but rather God (3:5), for the sake of providential security (3:6). Once again, do not think of yourself as smarter than God, savvy enough to sin and get away with it (3:7), for the sake of your health (3:8). Give back to God the first and best of your wealth (3:9), for the sake of further blessing (3:10). Do not reject the hard times with which God disciplines you (3:11), for the sake of rest in God's fatherly love (3:12). The progression is fairly evident: from general exhortations to maintain what one has been given for the sake of living well, to more particular warnings against self-sufficient waywardness detracting from a blessed life, to very specific admonitions regarding how to handle apparent blessing or struggle.

The last command, regarding divine discipline, tacitly acknowledges that simplistic forms of retribution theology, according to which God makes good things happen to good people and bad things happen to bad people, are wrong. Good people do not always enjoy good circumstances, or else this exhortation would not be necessary for such people to interpret their lives and respond rightly. Proverbs 24:16 provides even more obvious nuance about righteous suffering: "The righteous falls seven times and rises again, / but the wicked stumble in times of calamity" (ESV). So-called retribution, not always manifest in circumstantial moments, ultimately pertains to final ends. Proverbs 3:11–12 echoes in Heb.

12:1–13, especially 12:5–6. To undergo chastening, though difficult, should encourage us regarding our genuine status as God's children: the Father disciplines those he loves.

The promise of Prov. 3:4, regarding favor in both divine and human sight, "assumes that the son is not shameless" (Waltke 2004: 242). If that assumption ever could be self-evident, then it certainly cannot be now, in an era of reality TV shows. What does it say about contemporary Western societies that many have no shame? Probably our culture is incapable of valuing and appropriating biblical wisdom. We show little ability to factor long-term safety rather than short-term success into our decision-making. Standing behind this situation, if the context of Prov. 3 is any indication, is a tragic lack of good parenting.

An interlude in 3:13–20 follows the exordium with praise of Wisdom. It is an interlude in the sense that direct exhortation subsides, but it is not a sidetrack; 3:13–18 lauds Wisdom's value for humanity, 3:19–20 for God. Thus her value is greater than the alternatives that might lead away from covenant fidelity, about which exhortations resume in 3:21. She is the source of the long life, wealth, and status that people seek by other means (3:16). People mistakenly think that peace—*shalom* as positive flourishing, not just lack of conflict—comes from these goods in themselves rather than from relationship with God, which is integral to the genuine enjoyment that Wisdom provides (3:17). In the image of 3:16, God does not take back with the right hand what the left gives, but offers everything—if we keep hold of Wisdom. All the same, the right hand does entail valuing long life even more highly than riches and honor. The relativized value of earthly goods in 3:14–17 further demonstrates that Proverbs does not teach naïve or indulgent forms of retribution theology.

The personification of Wisdom intensifies in this section. In 3:17 she is a trustworthy guide, taking on the Lord's role (3:6). Taking hold of her brings stability and success (3:17–18), like parental teaching (e.g., 3:2), unlike the destructive results of an adulteress taking hold of a person (7:13). We ought to pursue Wisdom as a marriage partner, yet in doing so we hug a tree of life, so to speak (3:18)! These verses were among possible selections in synagogue services, following the reading of the scroll as it was raised up for rebinding.[12] They are important because they prepare for the development of Wisdom's relation to creation in 3:19–20, offering a glimpse of the fuller treatment in Prov. 8. In 3:19–20 comes a preliminary claim about Wisdom as the means by which the Lord created the cosmos to be stable and secure. Divine Wisdom provides order, restraining potential chaos, as well as refreshment. In other words, Wisdom need designate no more than a divine attribute in these two verses, while indicating in the surrounding context that God personally offers fellowship. In this way humans can participate in divine wisdom at a creaturely level. The imagery does not teach a scientific cosmology, but instead reflects treatment of creation as the divine temple along with deconstruction of

12. A. Z. Idelsohn, *Jewish Liturgy and Its Development* (repr., New York: Schocken, 1960), 115.

ancient battle myths regarding deep waters. God's wisdom means that creation was no struggle at all and that the cosmos is full of the divine presence. Meanwhile, readers needing plenty of rainfall can recognize what a gift dew would be in an arid climate such as Canaan.

How then does the tree of life emphasize divine giving even further? References elsewhere in Proverbs (11:30; 13:12; 15:4), the rest of the Old Testament (Ps. 1; Ezek. 31; 47), and Revelation (2:7; 22:2, 14, 19) indicate that the tree is a symbol. In most if not all cases in the Old Testament, the quality of earthly life is primarily in view, although ultimate ends are pertinent, since relationship with God is so crucial to eating from the tree. In Genesis, the two trees present stark alternatives: Adam and Eve could pursue moral autonomy offered by the tree of "knowledge of good and evil" (a set phrase in the Old Testament), thereby suffering the penalty of death, or else continue to receive life as a gift from God's guiding hand. This clarifies that wisdom is ambiguous: pursued on one's own, it can be a vehicle for precisely the declaration of human independence that proved deadly in the first place. If, however, wisdom is received as a divine gift, then it can be the means by which God fosters our flourishing. Dame Folly and Lady Wisdom are emblematic: pursued autonomously, Wisdom is a disastrous alternative; pursued within covenant bonds and in response to God's initiative, Wisdom is a blessing.

The resumption of direct address in Prov. 3:21, with "my child," introduces the next subsection, containing the heart of the lesson. First, 3:21–26 promotes holding on to wisdom as our source of security; the second-person pronouns, the parts of the body, and the vocabulary of "guarding" (*nṣr* in 3:21, *šāmar* in 3:26) unify the subunit. The initial metaphors echo from earlier: wisdom adorns the neck (3:22) and protects one's way (3:23). The theme of protection receives additional emphasis (3:24–25), to the extent that YHWH stands in for Wisdom to provide the promised security (3:26). Second, in light of these motivating factors, a series of exhortations follow (3:27–31). We ought to meet others' needs without delay (3:27–28). We must not plan violence (3:29) or execute verbal violence (3:30) against others, who have no reason to expect it. We must not envy those who commit such violence (3:31), for "their day is coming" in light of how God views them (3:32–35). The couplets alternate between action and speech as their focus. In the move from omission to commission there is both an ascending pattern, from an interacting neighbor to a trusting neighbor to humans in general, and a descending pattern, from withholding help to plotting harm to addressing actual violence. Proverbs 3:27 conveys an obligation to help others in need, further implying that those others have a corresponding right to this aid. Notwithstanding all the dangers of "rights" language in contemporary Western culture, nevertheless it appears that Nicholas Wolterstorff is correct to preserve and carefully interpret the concept of rights in developing a Christian account of justice.[13] It may be, however, that such rights are best claimed on behalf of

13. Nicholas Wolterstorff, *Justice: Rights and Wrongs* (Princeton: Princeton University Press, 2008).

others rather than oneself, since what usually becomes explicit in Proverbs is the corresponding obligation.

Additionally worth pondering is the distinctive nature of the biblical prudence enjoined here. Genuine wisdom does not lie in isolated calculation of self-interest. Rather, such wisdom essentially equals love of God and, accordingly, of neighbor. This stands in some contrast with those Greek models in which humility and even charity or magnanimity would not constitute virtues. More directly, Prov. 3 indicates that wisdom focuses on our money and our mouths. Do we honor the Lord by giving back what we have received? Do we give to others in need? Or do we attack those whom God loves, especially with our speech? Those are the diagnostic questions by which to recognize whether we are wise.

Resonances with the book of James are therefore obvious. The vocabulary of blessing appears in both (e.g., Jas. 1:12; Prov. 3:13, 33), as do the theme of trusting God wholeheartedly instead of leaning on one's own understanding (Jas. 1:1–8; Prov. 3:5–8); the requirement of wisdom to triumph over desire (Jas. 1:13–21; Prov. 3:14–15); wise people being known by good deeds, especially regarding uses of words and wealth (Jas. 1:22–27; 2:1–3:18; 4:11–5:11; Prov. 3:9–10, 27–31); exhortations that people must be generous when able to help their neighbors, instead of dismissing them with well-wishing platitudes (Jas. 2:14–26; Prov. 3:27–28); and prohibitions of self-interested quarreling (Jas. 3–4; Prov. 3:29–30) along with envy (Jas. 2:1–7; Prov. 3:31) of those on whom the Lord's curse rests (Jas. 5:1–6; Prov. 3:32–35). James even quotes the Septuagint (Greek translation) of Prov. 3:34: "God opposes the proud, / but gives grace to the humble" (Jas. 4:6). Augustine rightly suggests that "there is hardly a page in the holy books" in which this truth about humility does not appear.[14] The conclusion of this chapter (Prov. 3:32–35) provides a fitting summary of why Wisdom consists in the fear of the Lord, and why finding the way to true life consists in the pursuit of Wisdom.

The unity of theological depiction and social-ethical exhortation in Proverbs, like two sides of a coin, is evident and important. Words such as "grace" are not only present (e.g., 3:34) but also do ethical work. In this way Prov. 3 ought to allay fears that the metaphor of divine fatherhood lapses into merely human projection of ancient, patriarchal, cultural patterns onto the deity. To be sure, the language of discipline appears in the tight correlation between parental teaching and Wisdom's divine self-giving. But we need not interpret such discipline through the lens of fears about paternal abuses then or now. The Lord *graciously* disciplines covenant children—literally and metaphorically via parents. And discipline forms God's children so that they in turn will manifest God's gracious character, treating others as neighbors rather than pawns or obstacles.

Moreover, "favor" may better convey the concept of "grace" in these contexts, since favor points to divine approval, whether or not this is undeserved in every sense. To borrow Augustine's refrain from his *Confessions*: "Grant what

14. Augustine, *On Christian Doctrine* 3.23.33 (trans. Robertson), 99.

you command; command what you will."[15] It is not that we earn favor with God by starting our righteousness from scratch. But God's grace fosters treatment of others according to recognition of our own need. When people respond favorably to grace, the biblical text conveys divine delight in the righteousness thus bestowed. Conversely, to claim God's fatherly love without welcoming others into the family—when, apart from God's welcome, one could not claim sonship either—is terribly prideful.

The God portrayed in Prov. 3 is gracious, not lording tyrannically over human beings but wanting them to flourish. Proverbs 3:3 uses the language of "steadfast love and faithfulness," made definitive for God's character via the divine self-revelation when Moses hid in the cleft of the rock (Exod. 34:6). Because God is just and gracious, wanting everyone to flourish, all undergo discipline sometimes, and some must undergo definitive judgment. Far from pitting justice and grace against each other, then, a biblical understanding of divine fatherhood actually liberates us from cultural dead-ends. That which God's character joins together, let no humans put asunder—in either theological understanding or social practice.

Prizing and Protecting the Parental Path (4)

The next lecture, Prov. 4, is remarkably straightforward. Direct address distinguishes three units. The first, 4:1–9, involves the father bearing witness to the family's wisdom tradition, quoting his father's instruction from childhood. The society reflected in Proverbs is undoubtedly patriarchal, but 4:3 contains a distinctive reference to the mother, so the biblical text gives her honor as well. The unusual plural "children" (4:1) is probably diachronic rather than solely synchronic: that is, the father hands down instruction to succeeding generations, not simply multiple children of his own (Waltke 2004: 276). Making no explicit distinction between the teaching of the father and that of the grandfather emphasizes the family's unbroken heritage of honoring parental wisdom.[16] The basic admonition is to "get wisdom," highlighting the accumulation motif noted earlier (1:1–7): "From everyone to whom much has been given, much will be required; and from the one to whom much has been entrusted, even more will be demanded" (Luke 12:48); "from those who have nothing, even what they have will be taken away" (Matt. 13:12). Language of love and honor in Prov. 4:6, 8 indicates that the metaphor is not merely economic ("get" = "buy," its basic sense) but again marital; Wisdom is a wife to which one clings.

The second unit, 4:10–19, emphasizes the present father's faithfulness in teaching, to which the son must now adhere. The vocabulary of teaching and leading

15. Augustine, *Confessions* 10.40, trans. Henry Chadwick (Oxford: Oxford University Press, 1991), 202.

16. Tewoldemedhin Habtu, "Proverbs," in *Africa Bible Commentary*, ed. Tokunboh Adeyemo (Grand Rapids: Zondervan, 2006), 753.

in 4:11 is not open-ended guidance toward self-discovery; the father has strongly shaped the son's path. Now the time has come, though, at which the son must decide to maintain the same direction. The first half of the unit (4:10–13) states this positively, while the second half (4:14–17) provides the negative corollary—avoiding the path of the wicked—before the overarching contrast is provisionally summarized in 4:18–19. The classic association of righteousness with light and wickedness with darkness recurs, just after the wicked are depicted in terms of bread and wine. The red color shared with blood may lie behind the association of wine with violence. For some people, wickedness becomes the staple of their diet and violence is that on which they joyfully feast.

The third and final subunit, 4:20–27, is full of body parts and senses, along with verbs of physical position and movement. At its heart is the heart (4:23), from which action flows. The Lord "will bring to light the things now hidden in darkness and will disclose the purposes of the heart" (1 Cor. 4:5). We guard the heart especially by way of the eyes, mouth, and ears, namely what we see, say, and hear. Church fathers frequently address spiritual warfare at this stage, concerned to ward off demonic influence. In fact, "our struggle is not against enemies of blood and flesh, but against . . . the spiritual forces of evil" (Eph. 6:12). We must ask God to "turn [our] eyes from looking at vanities; / give [us] life in your ways" (Ps. 119:37) (Caesarius of Arles, Sermon 41.5, in FC 31.207–8). Those who can read ought to be looking at the scriptures (Prov. 4:21). Moreover, wise teaching ought to have our ear (4:20). Since out of the heart the mouth speaks (Matt. 12:33–37, esp. 12:34), if garbage comes out of us (Prov. 4:24), chances are that garbage is going in. Many contemporary Christians, fearful of any return to legalism from bygone fundamentalist days, celebrate as "freedom in Christ" the opportunity to watch or hear whatever they want. To be sure, prudish lists of do's and don'ts are unhelpful regarding entertainment choices, since they often ignore the subtler forms of error by which people get sidetracked from the way of wisdom. However, besides Proverbs neither Phil. 4:8 nor Eph. 5:4 has been removed from the Bible on account of conservative excess: "Finally, beloved, whatever is true, whatever is honorable, whatever is just, whatever is pure, whatever is pleasing, whatever is commendable, if there is any excellence [*aretē*, "virtue"] and if there is anything worthy of praise, think about these things"; and, "entirely out of place is obscene, silly, and vulgar talk; but instead, let there be thanksgiving." Whether specific correlations can always be empirically demonstrated, the scriptures accept a general version of the "garbage in, garbage out" principle. This is not a matter of silly, linear rationalism according to which ideas inexorably and only produce certain behaviors. It is, instead, acknowledgment of the ways in which all our sensory operations both manifest and reshape the heart. This is not a matter of conservative obsessions with sex, either; although plenty of material on that subject lies ahead in Prov. 5 and Prov. 7, violence (and the greed that leads to it) is likewise at stake (4:17).

Having explored Prov. 4's recapitulation of the two ways, we must now reflect on whether or how the New Testament alters its redemptive-historical context.

Such reshaping of this chapter's emphasis on maintaining the parental path is possible in two ways.

A first challenge: does the principle "keep my commandments, and live," identifying the parental teaching with God's Torah, still hold after the coming of Christ? Paul cites a similar formulation, "The person who does these things will live by them" (Rom. 10:5, quoting Lev. 18:5), in contrast to "the righteousness that comes by faith" (Rom. 10:6), the principle operative in the current era of redemptive history. Does Paul dispense with wisdom alongside Torah? Without claiming to resolve today's massive debates over "Paul and the law," we have hints that the teaching of Proverbs pertains, as always, in the new era of Christ.

For one reason, Cyril of Alexandria directs attention to Phil. 3:13–14, an exemplary Pauline text with a journey-oriented metaphor that incorporates human choosing and striving (Letter 31.3, in FC 76.123): "Beloved, I do not consider that I have made it my own; but this one thing I do: forgetting what lies behind and straining forward to what lies ahead, I press on toward the goal for the prize of the heavenly call of God in Christ Jesus." Whatever one does with Paul's constriction of Torah usage—set forth just previously in the very same chapter (Phil. 3:2–11)—it does not preclude strenuous effort to please God by taking on righteousness found in Christ. Another reason favoring the Christian relevance of wisdom and Torah is the fear of the Lord, which functions in Proverbs parallel to faith in the New Testament. Such a starting point becomes definitive for the whole of life; one never moves on from faith to something else such as good works, inevitable though they be. Likewise, in Proverbs the fear of God initiates a journey toward wisdom while remaining ingredient within that wisdom every step of the way (Prov. 1:1–7). A third consideration is the vocabulary of *tôrâ* ("teaching") in 4:2. In 4:3 the son is "tender, and my mother's favorite," which Aquila, Symmachus, and Theodotion came to describe using the Greek *monogenēs*: as God's "one and only" (e.g., John 3:16); Jesus Christ distinctly fulfills the role of faithful son, listening to his father and ultimately the Father, keeping the commandments, gaining wisdom, and being crowned. He does not fulfill this vocation so that people may chase after wickedness, but so that we might—at an appropriate level—share in divine sonship. The continuity, not just difference, of this sonship metaphor between Jesus and other humans—tied to wise Torah observance—maintains the paradigmatic significance of Prov. 4 for Christian life.

Second among possible New Testament challenges: while Prov. 4 heavily prioritizes parental instruction, is this emphasis excessive with respect to the church being our "first family"? Rodney Clapp rightly critiques the excesses, even idolization, of the nuclear family within the rhetoric of "family values" so dominant on the religious right.[17] It would be particularly naïve to defend a family structure unknown when the relevant biblical texts were written! Moreover, it would be

17. Rodney Clapp, *Families at the Crossroads: Beyond Traditional and Modern Options* (Downers Grove IL: InterVarsity, 1993).

doubly ironic to defend this structure against the church's encroachment on its time, only to have much or even most "family time" being spent around the television—thus undoubtedly violating the strictures of 4:23 about guarding our hearts! At this juncture the problem of church versus nuclear family becomes largely a red herring. The real concern ought to be whether we pass on a heritage of wisdom to our children or simply cave in to what we see and hear in the surrounding culture. It is likely that churches need to integrate age groups and family members more in their educational efforts, rather than segregating them so thoroughly according to interest-group politics or niche marketing. Parents, meanwhile, need to integrate their instructional efforts more with churchly aims and catechetical resources. If churches would devote themselves as ardently to teaching parents the faith as they do to teaching parenting, then families might more closely approximate the ideal set forth in Prov. 4.

Yes, the home is the original small group of the church, and parents have primary responsibility for passing on Christian wisdom to children. "The church" is an abstraction that cannot entirely inculcate wisdom in the required detail; only parents (usually today, anyway) live with their children so as to reward and punish behavior that reflects and reinforces wise dispositions. Yet Prov. 4 addresses any potential crisis of fatigue, in which youths struggle to maintain a listening ear toward their parents and a heart protected from the wicked. If ever such a chapter were timely in Western culture, it is now! The struggles of contemporary young people threaten to overwhelm even the most dedicated parents. Thus, in light of Prov. 4, we need to reinforce the privilege and responsibility of parenting as a front line of churchly spiritual formation.

Avoiding the Adulteress (5)

A crucial dimension of parental teaching concerns sexual fidelity, the explicit subject of Prov. 5 that implicitly speaks to covenant relations more generally. The chapter begins with a call for listening to such teaching, equated with wisdom (5:1–2); a rationale starts to unfold in terms of waywardness being deadly (5:3–6); emphatic direct address (5:7) leads into the crucial exhortation about avoiding the adulteress (5:8) in order to avoid disastrous consequences (5:9–14); a second exhortation then unfolds the positive counterpart of sexual delight within marriage (5:15–20); and finally a theological conclusion regards the dangerous consequences at stake (5:21–23).

Cyril of Jerusalem confronts straightforwardly the temptation to divorce dogmatic theology from sexual ethics: "What does it profit a man to be an expert theologian if he is a shameless fornicator; or to be nobly temperate but an impious blasphemer?" (*Catechetical Lectures* 4.2, in FC 61.120). The strong identification of wisdom with parental teaching on sexual fidelity in 5:1 opposes contemporary appeals to wisdom or virtue by which some seek to undermine biblical standards.

Wisdom is not a cipher for doing as people like or think best, and then finding a rationale to match, along the lines of finding it "easier to ask forgiveness than permission." Matthew 7:13–14 is cautionary regarding the two paths presented in Proverbs: the path to life is indeed narrow, making difficult and unpopular demands. Wisdom is not an excuse to reconstruct the biblical road broadly.

The lips of the adulteress in Prov. 5:3 possibly introduce the main subject of sex by way of double entendre. Yet the theme of speech continues throughout the chapter. The proverbial son should not only listen but also protect wisdom in his own speech (5:2). Again in 5:7 listening is crucial. By contrast, 5:11 brings the physical suffering of the wayward to the point of groaning, and 5:12–14 presents the wistful speech of the son who would not follow paternal instruction. The drinking of 5:15–20 addresses the mouth, with which 20:17 likewise reinforces the theme of short-term versus long-term satisfaction: "Bread gained by deceit is sweet, / but afterward the mouth will be full of gravel" (Athanasius, Letter 7.5, in NPNF[2] 4.525). The Septuagint catches a related idea by rendering the adulteress in 5:3 as one "who for a season pleases your palate." Biblical exemplars abound regarding the frequent need to reject instant gratification. Moses, preeminent as a faithful son in God's house until the revelation of the Messiah (Heb. 3:1–6), chose "rather to share ill-treatment with the people of God than to enjoy the fleeting pleasures of sin" (11:25). Joseph too stands in the Old Testament background with his self-sacrificing refusal of Potiphar's wife (Gen. 39). By contrast, in today's societies, the endurance required for sexual fidelity is in short supply.

Like the rest of the book, Prov. 5 is chock full of bodily metaphors. Not only the lips and ears but also the feet are prominent, beginning in 5:5 with explicit resumption of the two-ways theme. There is a jarring claim that the adulteress pursues her missteps ignorantly (5:6). It would be hard to believe that she is ignorant of her dubious morality, so in context her ignorance concerns the deadly consequences. Before we are tempted to shake our heads, it is worth taking a serious look at the human condition. Numerous politicians, with everything to gain by keeping their pants zipped, fall into disgrace. Hubris correlates strongly with what people have to lose. Witness further the myriad athletes who thought they could get away forever with taking steroids, or the governor of my own state, recently impeached and thrown out of office, or the senator appointed by him without disclosing the dubious circumstances. We should marvel not, "How can people be so sinful?" but "How can people be so stupid, thinking they could get away with it?" All the while, however, it is very easy to fall into the same pattern or excuse our own small sins, which we think we can pursue without falling into self-defeating folly.

The line is not so easily drawn. For this reason 5:8 warns people not to flirt with disaster—not even to go near the adulteress's house. If this command (and it is a command, not mere advice) strikes contemporary readers as legalism, building an arbitrary fence around the law so that people do not cross the actual boundary, then we ought to realize that some fences do make good neighbors! This is not substitution of a whimsical human decree for the law of God, but rather a tried-and-true parental parameter integrally tied to divine command. Too many, wise in their own eyes, have ignored warnings about what they see and hear, where and with whom they go, to their peril. Proverbs 5 implicitly acknowledges the power of sexual desire as well as speech; we must not tempt fate by acting as if private forms of personal proximity are irrelevant.

Proverbs 5:9–11 offers the alternative to blessing in retribution theology (→Prov. 3). The blessings offered by wisdom—long life and significant status (5:9), wealth (5:10), and physical health (5:11)—are systematically denied to the victim of the adulteress. Quite likely this victim, once found out, would not only face public humiliation but also be in thrall to the cuckolded husband and his family. The contemporary consequences may be different but are no less severe. Wisdom, again, is not merely the craftiness or skill for quickly getting what we want; it is the fear of the Lord that grants endurance, which is necessary for pursuing blessing in the proper order and thereby avoiding disastrous consequences: "Now since our life in this world is known to be, as it were, a road, it is necessary for us to reach rest as the result of our labor rather than labor as the result of rest" (Caesarius of Arles, Sermon 231.6, in FC 66.188–89).

The victim realizes too late the cost of ignoring parental and other teachers (5:12–14). Several repeated sounds in 5:13 convey the impression of monotony, which may have been on the mind of the son who did not mind paternal instruction. From the parental side, talking about sex often seems to be an awkward chore worth delegating, as much as possible, to the youth minister or someone else. But Proverbs presents such instruction as a crucial dimension of the parental task, essential for ensuring the life and joy of children. It is not necessarily the exclusive provenance of parents, since the plural "teachers" and "instructors" of 5:13 might include other voices from the covenant community. However, all of these people must ultimately speak with one voice.

Frank depiction of sexual pleasure within marriage (5:15–20) orbits around the theme of drinking. A cistern might not hold much water in reserve within an arid climate, but still enough water flows in what God has provided to that particular person. Divinely ordained forms of sexual pleasure are provision enough, even though sexual desire is very basic to human life. The wicked person who disregards this, as John Chrysostom states, "perished through folly, not through desire: he had his own wife for the satisfaction of his desire. Let no one blame nature, but rather his own incontinence; no fault lies with nature" (*Commentary on the Proverbs of Solomon* 5.23).[18]

Two theological questions naturally arise concerning this teaching about sexuality.

First, what should we make of the obviously male-oriented framework within which Prov. 5 presents the material? At one level this literary frame makes sense

18. John Chrysostom, *Commentaries on the Sages*, vol. 2: *Commentary on Proverbs, Commentary on Ecclesiastes*, trans. Robert Charles Hill (Brookline, MA: Holy Cross Orthodox Press, 2006), 84.

in light of Wisdom's female persona, in addition to the patriarchal father teaching his sons. At a canonical level such a literary situation and strategy need not be scandalous, whatever initial reactions might be. Nothing in Proverbs denies the relevance of its teaching for young women; to the contrary, its covenant framework, rooted in the fear of the Lord, suggests that the son is a literary placeholder for both male and female youth, in terms of theologically defined recipients. More particularly, nothing in Prov. 5 denies the relevance of sexual fidelity or pleasure for young women; again, to the contrary, the larger scriptural context teaches that men and women have mutual claims upon each other's bodies in marriage (1 Cor. 7). Furthermore, whatever the beliefs of ancient cultures may have been, nothing in Prov. 5 itself teaches that women are more sexually promiscuous or dangerous than men; to the contrary, paeans to Lady Wisdom and the virtuous wife in Proverbs hold women in noble esteem, even as literary representatives of God. At issue, therefore, is the patriarchal nature of the context in which Proverbs originated—and of most societies since, arguably even our own cultures despite their supposedly heightened sensitivities. The concern of Prov. 5 regarding the self-destruction of the adulteress, not just her potential victim, seems at least as noble as the contemporary West's supposed rejection of patriarchy, within which women continue to be treated as merely sexual objects and offered forms of liberation that simply democratize the predatory behavior of men. As 5:21–23 demonstrates, true freedom lies not in thinking we can do whatever we want (5:22)—only to follow the self-destructive patterns of everybody else—but in accepting the discipline of the Lord's watchful eye (5:21, 23).

Second, then, what is the contribution of Prov. 5 to a biblical understanding of sexual ethics? Proverbs 5 does not relate children inherently to the nature of the sexual act or enjoin the avoidance of adultery "for the sake of the kids." Instead some of its imagery calls to mind the erotic poetry in Song of Songs, as for instance in the parallel between Prov. 5:19 and Song 4:5. The metaphor of intoxication—so disastrous if it occurs at the hands of the adulteress (Prov. 5:20)—portrays positively giving oneself over to a spouse without inhibition (5:19). Whatever one concludes about other biblical teaching, here sexual pleasure is integral to the moral calculus by which fidelity is enjoined upon the youth. And 1 Cor. 7:9 faithfully echoes the theme with its aphorism that "it is better to marry than to burn" (KJV), whether in passion or self-destruction.

We have already encountered the intensely personal character of sexual life in Prov. 5, notably with 5:15–17. The chapter is replete with the pronoun "your." At the same time, sexual choices are anything but private. They not only involve another person—"it takes two to tango"—but also, in biblical perspective, have ripple effects throughout families and communities. Sex is therefore a primary subject of parental instruction and communal interest. Christians dare not succumb to ridicule for rejecting the naïve idea that a politician's sex life can have nothing to do with how s/he governs or for recognizing that churchly debates over sexual ethics may concern primary rather than secondary matters. In Jude

4 the way in which false teachers denied the lordship of Jesus Christ involved their perversion of divine grace into "licentiousness": to disagree about sexual ethics means, to some degree, disagreeing about "the faith"—a sobering reality for many of our churches.

On this basis Proverbs accumulates momentum for a spiritual layer of meaning, in which marital fidelity both partially constitutes and depicts fidelity in covenant with God. It is no accident that the metaphor of marriage is essential to a biblical understanding of God's interaction with Israel and the church and that covenant language applies across these spheres. The appropriate spiritual reading of Prov. 5 builds on the literal level without obscuring it. Some particulars cannot be pressed too far at a spiritual level; for instance, to apply "drink from your own cistern" bluntly as a rejection of secular education or life outside the covenant community would be inappropriate, since it is impossible to leave the world entirely (1 Cor. 5:10). However, it remains fitting to consider analogies between the need or the strategies for maintaining sexual fidelity and those for maintaining spiritual fidelity. What, in other words, might be the safeguards for our lips, ears, eyes, feet, and hands—for both particular persons and congregations—through which to pursue faithfulness and perpetuate the bonds of our covenant identity?

As Prov. 5:21–23 makes clear, this teaching is not safely cordoned off as ethical—it is theological too. Wisdom and righteousness, wickedness and folly, strongly correlate and overlap. In God's providence the usual form of punishment for infidelity can transpire by natural means during this earthly life: "Be sure your sin will find you out." Yet these means are not solely natural: the Creator of the universe ordained that people should flourish by being faithful in covenant with other humans. This God, who initiated a redemptive covenant with humankind through Israel, superintends the historical course of the cosmos so as to promote the integrity of covenant relationships, whereby we manifest the faithful character of our Creator.

Avoiding Various Entanglements (6)

Proverbs 6 demonstrates another mode of spiritual interpretation, in the movement from 6:1–5 to 6:6–11. The first five verses warn the proverbial son not to serve as a guarantor for a neighbor's debts, concluding in 6:3b–5 with a string of exhortations to hurry when extricating oneself from such a pledge. The particular instance of sluggishness worrying the father in 6:4–5 leads into a more general exhortation against laziness in 6:6–11. Seeing this kind of movement offers a first step toward applying such a principle to more distinctly pious matters: the ant offers a trope for the Christian learner, who stores up divine wisdom for the inevitable spiritual winter. Jerome even sees in ant society a trope for the monastic community, with its seemingly endless consistency in a quiet yet common life (*Life of Malchus* 7, in FC 15.294). These images are fecund in their possibilities for applying more broadly and/or more specifically. In the present case, the apparent insignificance of the ant recalls Jesus's appeal to the tiny mustard seed: even a small amount of faith can move a mountain by drawing God's interest in advancing Christ's rule (Matt. 17:20; also 13:31–32).

In Proverbs the one who fears God learns from the ant's investment over the long haul, in an appeal to the cosmos as a source of moral knowledge. This occurs not only with the example of the ant, but likewise with gazelles and birds being hunted and trapped (6:5), in attention paid to physical manifestations of villainy (especially regarding the eyes in 6:13, 25), in analogies of playing with fire (6:27–28), and of course elsewhere in the book. Attention to the ant is careful; appeal is made to the relative lack of hierarchical organization, a claim still frequently referenced in contemporary discussions of emergent communities and properties. God's wondrous design prepares the ants to follow through on meeting their own needs; similarly, the proverbial son should not need parental nagging forever.

The son may not yet be a sluggard, but parental warning is a necessary preventative measure. Neither is the sluggard yet a villain (as in 6:12–19) or an adulteress or her victim (as in 6:20–35), but he or she has started down that road. Failure to prepare for personal security results more broadly in failure to provide for the needs of others in the family or community. Attacks upon familial and communal bonds ultimately ensue. Naturally 2 Thess. 3:10 garnered frequent citations in the early church: "Anyone unwilling to work should not eat." The context of Paul's command makes clear that "idle hands are the devil's playground" in a community.

The overarching theme of Prov. 6, therefore, echoes in the language of Heb. 12:1: "Let us also lay aside every weight and the sin that clings so closely, and let us run with perseverance the race that is set before us." As 12:2 notes, we may be very thankful that Jesus is not a son who rested on his laurels! The various people against which Prov. 6 warns all have potential to take our eyes off the path of life. Once they incite us to wander, we become entangled in the ways of death.

At first glance the problem of surety for one's "neighbor" in 6:1–5 hardly fits into the same category as other items in the progression noted above—certainly not adultery. After all, the Bible is not categorically opposed to all forms of lending (though Proverbs generally seems to be). Should we not "bear one another's burdens" (Gal. 6:2), "whenever we have an opportunity," working "for the good of all, and especially for those of the family of faith" (6:10)? One might argue that, as a wisdom text, Prov. 6:1–5 does not simplistically say what to do but intentionally evokes questions in our minds, eliciting a process of reflection whereby we grow in the wisdom required for various situations. Obviously, then, the principle against surety holds in general, but cases might arise in which one could legitimately help a trustworthy neighbor without putting an entire livelihood at stake.

There is insight in this approach to wisdom literature, but reasons remain for taking the prohibition more categorically. The seven admonitions in 6:1–5 tie in nicely with the sixes and sevens in the rest of the chapter. Just because people are not inclined to take such pledging as seriously as committing adultery does not automatically entail that the book of Proverbs agrees! There is clearly progression from least bad to worst in Prov. 6, as noted above, yet the chapter may bluntly depict evils throughout, thus confronting us with a prohibition we find difficult but necessary to stomach. The scope of the prohibition is ambiguous due to difficulties with rendering "neighbor" (*rēaʿ*). Does it have a broad sense designating any other person, or a narrow sense of someone close and trusted? The parallel with "another" (*zār*) could favor the broad sense. Waltke's suggestion (2004: 332) is intriguing: "neighbor" could designate the son's careless claim about the person, while "another" (in the sense of "outsider" or "foreigner") provides the father's considered assessment. Beyond factors in the immediate literary context, Gal. 6:5 balances out the New Testament teaching referenced earlier: "All must carry their own loads." In fact, another option besides surety exists for taking care of neighbors. One could leave them to their own devices regarding debts for which they are genuinely responsible (since the Bible distinguishes poverty due to laziness, folly, and the like from poverty imposed by injustice or uncontrollable circumstances), while providing the direct charity they need in order to eat. In this way one is generous without being foolishly entangled. Surety always makes a person vulnerable, since the neighbor's guarantee may lack good will or just the means to pay back the debt.

Modern economies built around the sophisticated incursion of debt and interest raise genuine dilemmas of application.[19] Before making easy allowances for cultural difference to blunt the force of 6:1–5, however, it is worth pondering the financial mess in which the world found itself after 2008. If ever we should exercise caution about loan guarantees and complex debt arrangements, even concerning the basic investment of home ownership, that time is now. Many people find themselves standing surety for others they do not even know, whose decisions have had catastrophic consequences. Our passage does not directly bear on whether to recover the ancient church's prohibition of usury, the lending of money at interest—high interest, at any rate. Biblical opposition to usury usually traces back to Exod. 22:25; Lev. 25:35–38; Deut. 23:19–20; Ps. 15:5; and Luke 6:34–35. There is need, alternatively, to address the parable of the talents involving interest (Matt. 25:27 || Luke 19:23). Nevertheless, Prov. 6 reflects the seriousness of debt, confronting us about what kind of community we ought to pursue:

> The usury prohibition is not a single rule to be applied indiscriminately across times and places. . . . This is a function of practical reason that needs a communal context in order to work it out; it requires a community on a quest for holiness that is capable of and knows how to confess its sins. The proper social location for the usury prohibition is not the state, civil society, or any kind of blueprint for a universal economic system. It is first and foremost the confessional. If there is no global Christian community

19. It is perhaps no accident that the *Africa Bible Commentary* (ed. Tokunboh Adeyem, 779) places an inset box addressing debt within its Proverbs section. Written by Stephen Adei, it contains a helpful summary of basic biblical teaching.

seeking holiness by recognizing the vice of pleonexia as well as the virtues of charity and justice, then the Christian usury prohibition will make no sense.[20]

The further admonitions of 6:1–11 regarding sleep do not promote workaholism. The Bible values the sweet sleep of the laborer (Eccl. 5:12). Workaholism is a far cry from avoiding a life dominated by the snooze button. In fact, workaholism is frequently a symptom of the self-promotion condemned by Proverbs, which leads to the aggressive villainy of 6:12–19. Six descriptions, again heavily concentrated on bodily actions, frame the portrait of such scoundrels in 6:12–14 before the seventh depicts their undoing in 6:15. The term rendered "scoundrel" or "Belial" (*bĕlîyaʿal*) in 6:12 can even refer to the devil, our fundamental adversary (2 Cor. 6:15). The six/seven pattern continues more explicitly in Prov. 6:16–19, from which to discern the most distinctive trait of such a villain. Lists of this kind (x, x + 1) typically highlight the final item (+ 1), so for Proverbs what is most villainous concerns the breakdown of familial unity. This conclusion has profound implications not just for the nuclear or biological family but ultimately for covenant bonds within the household of God, the church. Once again, human households are a prime literal concern because of their dramatic spiritual implications; they are the parables through which we learn life with God.

Human divisions sometimes occur due to legitimate ambiguities or disagreements (e.g., Paul and Barnabas over whether to have John Mark accompany them in Acts 15:36–41). On other occasions discord occurs due to a failure of charity and mutual restraint (e.g., Euodia and Syntyche in Phil. 4:2–3, or the situation in Rom. 14–15). Yet not all discord falls under these categories, as the New Testament handling of false teachers implies and 1 Cor. 11:19 expresses: "Indeed, there have to be factions among you, for only so will it become clear who among you are genuine." Whether the family or the church is in view, it is overly simplistic to say that disunity is always a failure of love, as if disagreements are of no account and the more tolerant position must win the day. The Bible quite clearly puts responsibility for many instances of discord at the feet of those who introduce error into a community.

Proverbs 6:16–19 reads like the anti-Beatitudes, with "haughty eyes" at the beginning in contrast to poverty of spirit; "hands that shed innocent blood" in contrast to meekness and mercy; "a heart that devises wicked plans" in contrast to purity of heart; "a lying witness who testifies falsely" in contrast to suffering from those who revile; and of course "one who sows discord in a family" in contrast to peacemaking. The prominence of sibilant sounds gives the effect of hissing throughout the list in Proverbs. It is no accident that pride comes first in the catalog of sins, while the list moves down from head to feet (Waltke 2004: 346–47). The heart, inevitably, is at the center.

20. D. Stephen Long, "Usury: Avarice as a Capital Vice," in *Calculated Futures: Theology, Ethics, and Economics*, ed. D. Stephen Long and Nancy Ruth Fox (Waco: Baylor University Press, 2007), 157.

Parental direct address reappears in 6:20, this time (unlike 6:1) with standard framing exhortations to maintain obedience. These lead into promises that parental teaching will protect children—in all of life: walking, lying down, and waking up (6:22)—from the adulteress in particular. This theme has already been prominent in Prov. 2 and Prov. 5, with the present occurrence leading into still another discussion in Prov. 7. The consistency of the theme (and of the woman's identity as an adulteress) is evident in another reference to smoothness (6:24) along with emphases on speech and eyes. New strategies of avoidance appear: having the commandment enables seeing the path (6:23), not letting one's heart succumb to contemplation of desire, regarding beauty or flirtation (6:25), and counting the cost (6:26–35).

The point of 6:26 is not that hiring a prostitute is permissible. The argument from lesser to greater underscores the exponentially higher cost of entanglement with the adulteress. Doubtless this holds true temporally, emotionally, financially—ultimately. The cuckolded husband will pursue vengeance to the full extent of the law and possibly even beyond (6:34–35). Another lesser-to-greater argument occurs with thievery (6:30–31). People might sympathize with a poor person stealing in order to eat, but Robin Hoods are still punished severely if caught; the completeness of the penalty appears in the sevenfold payment of 6:31 that, if it were more than metaphorical, would press beyond all the punishment and restitution demanded in the Torah. How much more will the cuckolded husband demand his pound of flesh! The son would get off easily if he only faced public disgrace (6:33), but in fact he puts his very life at stake (6:26), as the playing-with-fire motif dramatically portrays (6:27–28).

According to 6:29, "no one who touches her will go unpunished," echoing the covenant formulation in Exod. 20:7; 34:7; Num. 14:18; Deut. 5:11; and Nah. 1:3. Sexual infidelity is a covenant breach with God, on par with misusing the divine name. Caesarius of Arles (Sermon 41.3, in FC 31.206) summarizes poignantly: "Truly lamentable and miserable is the condition whereby what brings delight passes away at once, while what causes torture endures without end."

Avoiding Dame Folly (7)

At the literal level Prov. 7 follows with another lecture warning against the adulteress. An extended introduction (7:1–5) contains the standard exhortations to listen along with an attendant promise of guidance and protection. A seduction scenario is narrated in stark terms (7:6–23), concluded with summary exhortations and warnings (7:24–27). The language of these warnings echoes 2:16–19, Prov. 5 regarding the social self-preservation at stake for avoiding adultery, and 6:20–35 on the heightened dangers involving the cuckolded husband. Now Prov. 7 serves as the climactic lecture, with the literal sense pointing additionally to a spiritual level of reading, for several reasons.

First, the surrounding context involves not just the climactic position of this lecture but also its juxtaposition with Prov. 8 regarding Lady Wisdom. Personification there and in Prov. 9 regarding both Lady Wisdom (9:1–6) and Dame Folly (9:13–18) suggests that the adulteress of Prov. 7 is more than initially meets the eye. Dame Folly in Prov. 9 similarly sweet-talks passersby, with Prov. 7 already anticipating this.

Second, the extended introduction in Prov. 7 puts added emphasis on fidelity to traditional teaching—in part by linking to Lady Wisdom in Prov. 8, since "you are my sister" in 7:4 conveys the intimacy of marriage rather than simple sisterhood. For a sample parallel, consider Song 4:9: "You have ravished my heart, my sister, my bride."

Third, without claiming to know much about life in this text's original setting, elements of the seduction scenario hint that more is going on than meets the eye. How likely is it that the wise parent could watch the scenario unfolding (Prov. 7:6–7)? Given the apparent wealth of the woman as the wife of a merchant, how likely is it that the youth just happens to walk in her neighborhood? Would such a woman dress like a prostitute only to seduce him or avoid identification—especially since she remains easily identifiable to the neighborhood watchers? Is the predatory violence of the narrative hyperbolic solely to depict the danger of seduction, or does it have further overtones? Granted that the adulteress is brazen, the descriptions in 7:11–13, 26 remain striking in contrast to what we expect from a woman of leisure.

Fourth, religion enters into the scenario. In 7:14 the *zebaḥ* probably refers to a "fellowship sacrifice," from Canaanite practices, involving a meal (Waltke 2004: 377). No doubt people throughout history have blended sex and spirituality, but even so this seems like a bizarre pickup line. The specific personal attention (7:15), the sensual appeal using wealth (7:16–17), the language of love (7:18), the promise of safety from the husband (7:19–20)—these are closer to what we expect, although they can represent elements of religious seduction as well.

Fifth, some language suggests double entendre. The "chambers" of death in 7:27, *ḥeder*, "elsewhere in Proverbs . . . refers to 'innermost parts of the body or being' (18:8 = 26:22; 20:27, 30)." In 7:26 "the imagery is closely related to the Babylonian Ishtar and the Sumerian Inanna, both of whom have the double function of being goddesses of love and war" (Waltke 2004: 385–86). Earlier, in 7:11, "feet" may refer to genitalia and hence to the woman's public sexuality (Longman 2006: 189).

How, then, should we proceed? There is no need to deny that a warning persists against succumbing physically to the adulteress. But it is unlikely that Proverbs needs to repeat itself (yet again!) merely to reinforce that point. The deadly financial, social, and even physical consequences have already been set forth. Hence this scenario instructs us not only regarding the seductive tactics of the adulteress—in exaggerated register that instruction is truly present—but also regarding the seductive potential of foreign religions and alternative wisdom.

Spiritual reading begins by recognizing the counterpoint to Folly in obedience to parental instruction, regarding how to embody divine law. People need to internalize God's teaching (7:1–3) even as such Wisdom expresses itself in external forms (7:4–5). Wisdom cannot be acquired all at once; it requires ongoing growth. We never attain Wisdom exhaustively, but we can grow into adulthood. At that point of relative maturity, the fundamental course of life is not as vulnerable as in youth. The young lack sense (7:7) and need the watchful eye of those older and wiser. In particular, the immature tend to place themselves unwittingly in jeopardy, being at the wrong time and place (7:8–9, 25). It can be a profound mistake to be so naïve, but this need not be fatal. If the seduction were a fait accompli solely due to the young man going near the adulteress's house, then the rest of the chapter—with its careful attention to Folly's aggressive tactics and speech—would be superfluous.

Folly's aggression (7:13) is most likely to be successful when people think no one is watching. It is both literally and spiritually true that night is the time most strongly associated with deeds of darkness (Rom. 13:12–13). Folly does much to draw attention toward itself—and simultaneously to hide its true reality (Prov. 7:10). Folly seems to be everywhere (7:11–12). And it feels no compunction about appealing to religious practices that fit a generic spirituality (7:14). Everyone wants to think they are involved with something that reveals their basic inner goodness, while making no stringent demands but in fact letting them live as they like. Folly's invitations are personally tailored (7:15). They cloak themselves in sensual joys with a touch of the exotic (7:16), while in and of themselves resting on created goods (7:17). The problem lies not in the created structures but in the mistaken direction of their use.[21] In Augustine's terms, these goods are not used for the enjoyment of God, either regarding their end or their proportion or their context. Yet so often we convince ourselves that, since something is obviously good, divine strictures on its use do not matter. Another part of Folly's lie, of course, concerns a lack of harmful consequences (7:19). The husband's absence with a full purse (7:20) could merely be part of the scenario whereby the lovers are safe, but the money could moreover suggest that the youth is not really hurting him anyway. Folly convinces people that sin hurts no one else.

Folly presents itself as alternative wisdom, with seductive speech. We live in a supposedly postmodern age full of appeals to wisdom. This can recover important elements of the Christian tradition, yet also provides a cloak for opposition to divine law, careful precision, and other elements deemed modern—as if they automatically entail preoccupation with knowledge or control for its own sake. Seductive speech has hardly gone away in our era, and parodies of wisdom are a likely form for that danger to take. Who then should lead us by the hand? Not the "other" we scarcely know, but traditional teaching from trusted members of

21. Albert M. Wolters, *Creation Regained: Biblical Basics for a Reformational Worldview* (Grand Rapids: Eerdmans, 1985).

our covenant community—against which, we are sometimes able to recognize, the tempter tries to set us in opposition. Reference to Egypt in 7:16 hints at the lure of non-Yahwistic religion, and today the possibility is very real that seductive talk of wisdom could actually lead to folly, breaching covenant with the one true God. It is no accident that certain liberal forms of Christian faith that deemphasize the particularity of Jesus Christ—and especially Old Testament precedents for his vocation—in favor of generalized spirituality that can be found inside and outside multiple religions tend toward laxity regarding traditional sexual ethics. Such a correlation makes perfect sense of the religion-sexuality dynamic found in Prov. 7: treating the marriage covenant lightly figures literally and metaphorically into treating fidelity toward YHWH lightly—and vice versa.

So, again, the dynamics of spiritual reading integrally relate to the literal meaning. In the present case sexuality and spirituality intermingle. Not only is that true theologically for the concept of "covenant"; more mundanely, Proverbs spends several segments of its first nine chapters warning against the adulteress because true wisdom addresses our covenant with God in terms of embodied practices and family relationships. Sex goes to the core of both these realities. In terms of the body, consider 1 Cor. 6:18–20: "Shun fornication! Every sin that a person commits is outside the body; but the fornicator sins against the body itself. Or do you not know that your body is a temple of the Holy Spirit within you, which you have from God, and that you are not your own? For you were bought with a price; therefore glorify God in your body." In terms of family relationships, Proverbs makes clear that the stability of family ties is basic to the community's faithful perpetuation of divine tradition. There is no neutrality; Folly appeals to self-interest and may come in the form of alternative religion. Both are rivals of the true God, whom alone we should fear.

Accordingly, departures from traditional Jewish and Christian teaching about sexual fidelity are not idle controversies. Disagreements on these matters go to the core of communal identity and the practice of fearing God. This is in part because humans need, but prefer to refuse, divine discipline. Sex is a prime instance of how tempted we are to rationalize what looks good at a particular moment, rather than undergoing the demanding transformation required to keep our promises or meet divine standards. Spirituality, like sex, meets primal human needs and longings, both personal and communal. By engaging our bodies in acts of self-transcendence, both sex and spirituality present powerful temptations for treating ourselves and others—even God—as tools for idolatrous use. The literal and spiritual adulteress tells us what we want to hear but know at some level to be false. Folly is everywhere, she is loud, she is aggressive, and she is seductive—deadly so. Present-day churches should therefore not be surprised that such disagreements arise and run so deep, for the issues at stake concern the heart of covenant life with God as embodied, familial, and social creatures—and whether we will submit to long-term divine demands that do not always seem wise in our own eyes.

Hearing Lady Wisdom's Offer Again (8)

In Prov. 8 Lady Wisdom, like Dame Folly, cries out very publicly. She seeks to be winsome but her appeal has its limits, trying to gain a suitor's long-term attraction rather than practicing Dame Folly's short-term aggression. Lady Wisdom cries out but does not kiss the young man impudently. She desires to persuade with the truthful content of her speech. Proverbs 8:1–3 presents her return to the stage, and 8:4–11 offers her initial appeal in a new act of the unfolding drama. This addresses everyone (8:4), with particular reference to the simple who need to start paying attention (8:5). The basis for this initial aspect of the appeal concerns the truth of her words: they not merely convey mental knowledge, but more profoundly are righteous, straightforward rather than devious and deceptive (8:6–9). Hence they have greater value than the choicest metals and jewels (8:10–11). This claim is not modest; the extent of the comparison is such that Wisdom should be chosen rather than—not simply in addition to or before—the alternatives.

The next ten verses, 8:12–21, unfold Wisdom's value even further. The section ends with a series of claims about Lady Wisdom's bestowal of riches and honor, again comparing her favorably to gold and silver (8:18–21). Proverbs 8:12–13 begins the section similarly to the previous one, connecting Wisdom with prudence and distancing her from perverted speech. In the middle, 8:14–17 relates Wisdom to kingship, as the principle by which rulers govern rightly. In this way the rule of God is reflected: "With God are wisdom and strength; / he has counsel and understanding" (Job 12:13). It is important for "the spirit of wisdom and understanding" to rest upon the shoot of Jesse that will someday rule Israel and the nations for God (Isa. 11:2). Joshua presaged this, "full of the spirit of wisdom" (Deut. 34:9), as did Solomon in his initial request to the Lord (1 Kgs. 3). Likewise, after the exile and in anticipation of the Messiah, Ezra employed wisdom in efforts to organize and instruct the people (Ezra 7:25). God's design is for leaders to mediate divine rule by way of Wisdom. The translation of *ṣedeq* in Prov. 8:18 is usefully ambiguous, regarding whether it designates righteousness or "prosperity," as in the NRSV. Either way, these go together, not in the seeking of prosperity itself but rather in its attainment by seeking first God's Wisdom. "But seek first His kingdom, and His righteousness; and all these things shall be added to you" (Matt. 6:33 NASB).

The end of Prov. 8 contains the expected conclusion (8:32–36); Lady Wisdom offers blessing to those who listen—carefully and constantly—in order to keep her ways. This blessing consists in life and, more profoundly than purely physical existence, favor from the Lord. Alternatively, those who spurn Wisdom love death—which, by implication, is not solely physical. Notice the parallel with the end of Prov. 7: both chapters end with the starkness of death as the result of spurning Lady Wisdom. The rabbis took references to gates and doors in 8:34—vis-à-vis the synagogue, in their case—as enjoining prayer along with the study involved in pursuing Wisdom.[22] In light of the temple allusions soon to follow and the vocabulary of "watching," this seems appropriate. We should not simply listen to Wisdom by studying, but more holistically pursue her via personal relationship; study must therefore be prayerful, pursuing covenant fellowship with God. The metaphorical—and literal—importance of marriage registers in a parallel between 8:35 and 18:22. In the former, finding Wisdom obtains "favor from the LORD"; in the latter, finding a good wife does so. The relational context of pursuing Wisdom is frequent and consistent.

In this way Prov. 8 serves as the apex of a background argument supporting Lady Wisdom's climactic invitation in Prov. 9. The name "Lady Wisdom" pertains, like the contrastive "Dame Folly," because the preface "Woman" would be too generic and vague. Dame Folly is indeed dubious in character, a connotation that "Dame" begins to convey. And Lady Wisdom, while not aristocratic in an obnoxious sense, is regal in bearing, as references to jewels and kings in Prov. 8, along with her house and sumptuous feast in Prov. 9, connote. Choosing Lady Wisdom over Dame Folly opts for long-term, dare we say sophisticated, flourishing over short-term pleasures.

The apex of Prov. 8 strengthens Lady Wisdom's case by tying her comprehensively to God's rule of the cosmos (8:22–31), not just in the present but also in the remotest past—its creation—and (by implication) future. The passage is famously disputed at several points regarding Christology—or whether it even has christological implications in the first place. Wisdom's claim that "the LORD created me at the beginning of his work, / the first of his acts of long ago. / Ages ago I was set up, / at the first, before the beginning of the earth" (8:22–23) juxtaposes intriguingly but awkwardly with "in the beginning was the Word, and the Word was with God, and the Word was God. He was in the beginning with God. All things came into being through him" (John 1:1–3a). The matched "beginnings" tempt Christian readers to equate Wisdom with Jesus Christ, God's Son, through whom God created; yet heretical Arian Christology could treat this Logos as the mediator of creation while playing up the language of Prov. 8 to suggest that the Son remained a creature—not the one, self-existent Creator. For both historical-critical and doctrinal reasons, then, many scholars downplay or outright deny the christological overtones of our text.

Yet one should not get the idea that Prov. 8 would be simple if we kept Jesus out of it; problems of translation and interpretation abound in any case. Among these are (1) the meaning of the verbs in 8:22–26; (2) the meaning of *ʾāmôn*, translated "master worker" by the NRSV, in 8:30; (3) the timing of various acts; and (4) the literary function and identity of Wisdom. Building upon these considerations we can finally return to addressing (5) the christological relevance of the passage.

22. See *Proverbs Rabbah* on this verse in Burton L. Visotzky, trans., *The Midrash on Proverbs*, Yale Judaica 27 (New Haven: Yale University Press, 1992), 47.

The meaning of the verbs in 8:22–26. The first debated verb is *qnh* in 8:22. Its normal usage in the Old Testament involves acquiring or possessing, and this is frequently the case elsewhere in Proverbs. Aquila, Symmachus, and Theodotion, followed by the Vulgate, took this line. However, in some passages "create" seems better; the Septuagint, Targum, and Peshitta take this route in 8:22. A third option involves procreation, as in Gen. 4:1, which best fits parallels in Prov. 8:23–25. A contemporary parallel to the range of this term is the pair "get" and "beget" (Longman 2006: 204). Here the mode of acquisition appears to be specific, in terms of "bringing forth." This begetting of Wisdom transpired at the beginning of the Lord's way, onto which the audience is invited. Following that way would align the wise person with God's design from the outset. There are clearly temporal markers in 8:22, such as "beginning," but it will be important to note their points of comparison ("first" of what?) as we proceed, instead of quickly assuming that they depict Wisdom as a creature.

The root of the second verb, *nissaktî* in 8:23, is unclear. The concept is either "formed" or "shaped" if the root is *skk*, or else "installed" or "set up" if the root is *nsk*. Psalm 2:6 offers a possible parallel, in which the same consonants are used: "I have set my king on Zion, my holy hill," thus leading scholars to see Wisdom receiving royal investiture in Prov. 8:23. However, others see "weave" as a possible translation for either root, with the metaphor involving gestation: this would follow nicely from 8:22 and lead into the repetition of origination metaphors in 8:24–25. Though the latter view seems more likely given the nearest context, either way is again a temporal marker for the activity. So far, then, 8:22–23 has Lady Wisdom claiming, "The LORD acquired/possessed me by bringing me forth at the beginning of his way (which you can follow), before his other earliest works. From everlasting I was woven together, from the very beginning, from the earliest times of the earth."

As if that were not enough emphasis, 8:24 chimes in, attaching a series of states (currently in place) and events (subsequent) to the bringing forth (*ḥwll*) of Wisdom. This passive verb highlights divine agency, unquestionably introducing a birth metaphor, repeated at the end of 8:25. The pattern of 8:24–26 on the whole moves from down to up and from waters and mountains toward what is for human habitation (Waltke 2004: 411). The text places the waters, a source of potential chaos, firmly in hand under God's Wisdom so that they can be a source of life and blessing instead. This anticipates the movement of 8:29–31, which mirrors water elsewhere in Proverbs profiling the dangers and delights of sexuality: within divinely set, wise limits, there is profound joy, but outside those limits lies destruction.

The meaning of ʾāmôn in 8:30. The pattern of 8:27–29 moves in the opposite direction of 8:24–26, from up to down. The reason is similar though: God wisely makes the cosmos fit for human habitation. The chaos associated with water, so feared by the ancients, cannot escape the boundaries marked out by the same Lord whose commands in the Torah also set boundaries for human life. Rabbinic exegesis, almost ubiquitously, equates Wisdom with Torah (e.g., *Leviticus Rabbah* 35.4). Once this entered the tradition it could be assumed, rather than proven, in particular places. But the vocabulary of divine command does appear in 8:29. Parallels for not violating the word from God's mouth, such as Balaam (Num. 22:18; 24:13),[23] reinforce the personal, active dimension of divine law for both the sea and the sage. The limits for the sea are not merely the chance result of evolutionary processes (however much these may have been involved); they stem ultimately from the divine decree.

Temporal clauses lead up to Wisdom's claim that "I was beside" the Lord who created, "like a master worker; / and I was daily his delight" in 8:30. Translating this proves to be very difficult. Among the possibilities for *ʾāmôn* are "artisan," as in "master worker" (NRSV), but this rests on such a meaning in Jer. 52:15, itself disputable. Proverbs 3:19 might offer support by suggesting that Wisdom was God's agent in creation; however, it could also entail no more than Wisdom serving as God's instrument. Plus, other contextual reasons make this first possible meaning unlikely. The dominant alternative to "artisan" until recently was "nursling" or "child," usually based on emending the (Hebrew) Masoretic Text, following Aquila. Some opt for this second possibility because they view the "artisan" interpretation to be theologically troubling—introducing a second Creator, so to speak. However, lack of an expected feminine form (to cohere with the *Lady* Wisdom motif) is problematic at a more basic level—as are other grammatical routes for getting to this interpretation. Moreover, contextually this is not a snug fit. Despite the apparent progression from preoccupation with birth earlier in the section, the playful delight of a little child is not the best case Proverbs could make for Wisdom having gravitas due to involvement with creation.

A more promising possibility has recently surfaced. Waltke 2004: 391, 420 translates the first phrase of 8:30 as "and I was beside him constantly," taking the root of *ʾmn* as "to be firm, faithful." Stuart Weeks similarly highlights this lexical background, translating the term "faithfully," according to which "Wisdom is either existing '(as) a faithful one' or '(in) faithfulness.'"[24] The fidelity involved may transcend merely temporal presence to connote religious piety as well.[25] In that case the possible allusion to 8:30 in Rev. 3:14 makes more sense: "The words of the Amen, the faithful and true witness, the origin of God's creation." There is no need to make *archē* ("origin") in Rev. 3:14, which is complex enough in its own right, correspond directly to *ʾāmôn* in Prov. 8:30. Rather, there is an allusion that stays both closer to the "Amen" and within the overall unfolding of the entire phrase. Therefore it seems that interpreting 8:30 in relation to constancy or faithfulness was not unknown in early Christianity.[26]

23. So Raymond C. Van Leeuwen, "Liminality and Worldview in Proverbs 1–9," *Semeia* 50 (1990): 124.

24. Stuart Weeks, "The Context and Meaning of Proverbs 8:30a," *Journal of Biblical Literature* 125 (2006): 440.

25. Ibid., 441.

26. Ibid., 439n24.

The timing of various acts. If we opt for this interpretation of 8:30, then the verse raises new questions about the timing of the states and events described. According to the usual understanding, 8:30 places Wisdom beside God during creation, with the delight of 8:31 presumably being subsequent to this act or process of creation itself. However, against such an interpretation, (1) the "when" clauses introduced by *beth* in 8:27–29 could already go with "I was there" in 8:27 rather than "I was beside him" in 8:30, and (2) the catchwords linking 8:30–31 render a temporal shift therein less likely.[27] The day-by-day dimension of delight in 8:30b more naturally fits with 8:31, subsequent to creation. It is preferable, therefore, to view 8:27–29 as depicting Wisdom's presence during creation, with 8:30–31 depicting her delight in the divine presence ever since. The passage "is not merely a statement that Wisdom was with God early on, but a declaration that she has been with God throughout the history of the world, and still is."[28] This qualifies her all the more to be the principle by which kings rule and humans find *shalom*.

It remains to work backward, addressing the manner in which Wisdom precedes the cosmos (8:22–26). There is repeated verbal emphasis on her being begotten (8:22, 23, 24, 25). Each of the latter three verses makes clear that prior to Wisdom some feature of the cosmos did not exist or had not yet transpired. This is perfectly compatible with the claims of John's Gospel, and Nicene Christology, about the Logos through whom all things were made. The most challenging question appears in 8:22. Wisdom is not necessarily a creature according to the first clause. The verb, as we saw above, probably means either less ("acquired") or, most likely, more ("begot") than "created." Furthermore, as Athanasius points out, "the Lord created me" would not be automatically equivalent to "I am a creature" in the sense of passing from nonexistence into existence (*Four Discourses against the Arians* 2.19.44, in NPNF^2 4.372). Metaphorical uses are frequent for the concept of creation in scripture, and after all this text is poetry. Nevertheless, begetting is probably the issue, and what we must address theologically concerns its nature and timing. A nonliteral understanding of begetting is entirely consistent with the poetic nature of the passage and the symbolic force of household imagery throughout Proverbs. Classic Christian theology rightly highlights the text's metaphorical establishment of Wisdom's divine pedigree.

In some respects, then, the more challenging clause in 8:22 is the second one. Does "the first of his acts of long ago" place Wisdom's begetting at the beginning of a series of cosmic, temporal works? Not necessarily. The term rendered "first," *qedem*, conveys remoteness in time, yet can further point to the divine sphere, as in Hab. 1:12: "Are you not from of old [*qedem*], / O Lord my God, my Holy One? / You shall not die." The addition of *mēʾāz* ("of long ago") at the end of Prov. 8:22 is significant. Not only does this emphasize Wisdom's ancient character; it also calls to mind Ps. 93:2: "Your [the Lord's] throne is established from of old;

27. Ibid., 437.
28. Ibid., 438.

you are from everlasting." The phrasing gives every appearance of trying to convey Wisdom's distinctiveness, not her fit within creaturely patterns. To be sure, the vocabulary is not precise enough to rule by itself on technical theological questions that arose later in a Christian context. When we now pose such questions to the text, though, our options are limited and canonically guided, as shall become clear.

The literary function and identity of Wisdom. To begin with the obvious, when seeking to identify Lady Wisdom with some theological referent: her personification is a literary motif in the middle of a passage that takes poetic license. Of course no claim is directly made regarding a hypostasis named Wisdom, divine or otherwise. The parallel with Dame Folly makes this clear.

Yet Wisdom cannot refer simply to a divine attribute. It would make no sense, even metaphorically, to claim that God gave birth to God's own character or could act in such a way before (and therefore without) Wisdom. Proverbs 8 is not suggesting that there was a time when divine wisdom was not. By definition a divine attribute is not subsequently created. Nor can we settle for Wisdom personifying the book of Proverbs itself, treated as a solely creaturely reality. Whatever may be the case regarding Prov. 8–9 as preparation for Prov. 10–31, such teaching provides revelation via strikingly personal divine condescension. It cannot be merely human wisdom writ large, for that would be inconsistent with the extent of Wisdom's divine association in this passage.

The text associates its personal invitation to receive divine self-revelation with mysterious origins connected to God's life—from the very beginning, as it were. It is not appropriate for Christian theologians to tell Jewish readers how they ought to read Old Testament texts as *their* scriptures, but it is understandable how readings by the early (Jewish) Christians would naturally involve the messianic hopes, connected to future divine self-revelation, that were now thought to reach fulfillment. "Then they will know that I am the LORD," Isaiah and Ezekiel declare over and over again. Such a work of God would have to fulfill expectations about fuller knowledge of YHWH accompanying Israel's redemption, without altering commitment to practical monotheism.[29] The hope would be that the mysterious relationality of the divine life, at which Old Testament texts occasionally hint, might come to fuller light with God's new activity in redemptive history. The resulting quandaries of interpretation for Christians naturally concern the Creator-creature dynamic, since Wisdom clearly is beyond just another created reality (on the one hand) while not solely identifiable with God either (on the other hand). Hence the eventual debate between Athanasius and the Arians is perfectly appropriate to the subject matter of Prov. 8 even though Jesus Christ is not present

29. On the special implications of Isaiah in this connection see, e.g., Richard Bauckham, *God Crucified: Monotheism and Christology in the New Testament* (Grand Rapids: Eerdmans, 1999); and David S. Yeago, "The New Testament and the Nicene Dogma: A Contribution to the Recovery of Theological Exegesis," in *The Theological Interpretation of Scripture: Classic and Contemporary Readings*, ed. Stephen E. Fowl (Oxford: Blackwell, 1997), 87–100. This point holds regardless of the checkered nature and history of monotheism as a technical concept.

directly on the text's surface. Although on some technical matters today we may reach different conclusions than earlier Christian interpreters, almost certainly incorporating other forms of reasoning, still the classic theologians teach us to address the revelatory and redemptive logic of the text.[30]

If Wisdom here cannot be solely a feature of creation or a divine attribute, then its mysterious origination from within the divine life begs for exploration. Wisdom has a mediating role between God and the world, particularly God and humanity: YHWH is the first word in this text, and Adam (or son of *ʾādām*, "man") is the last. In the original context of Prov. 8, part of the emphasis lies in "Wisdom, not simply the monarchy or the temple, serv[ing] as the link between heaven and earth,"[31] for Wisdom is God present, teaching and ruling through not only kings and priests but also parents and nonhuman creatures. The resulting challenge lies in discerning the nature of this mediation—whether Wisdom is quasidivine but ultimately a creature of some kind, as the Arians held, or indeed fully divine in some form of condescension, as the orthodox came to hold. Such an interpretative challenge takes particular shape in light of Jesus Christ claiming to be the Son of God, yet stems from a mystery already latent in the text itself. If Wisdom has some kind of creaturely connection but is chronologically and otherwise distinct from everything else in the cosmos, what are we to make of its identity? The begetting metaphor, far from subordinating the Son to the Father as creature to Creator, actually indicates continuity of divine life and character.

Philippians 2:5 states the goal of wisdom, "Let the same mind be in you that was in Christ Jesus," even using the terminology of *phronēsis* (the impossible to translate "let the same mind"; →Prov. 2): Wisdom is the way God has made for humans to walk. Philippians 2:6–11 points to the divine source of Wisdom by narrating its vocational shape in Jesus Christ: first descent, then ascent; humiliation before exaltation. Humans softly echo the crescendo of divine condescension, but Paul's appeal in Philippians works precisely because in Jesus we see *divine* condescension. The exaltation of Phil. 2:9–11 returns Christ to the enjoyment of equality with God that he let go in 2:6–8; the exaltation involves not a new status (divinity he never had) but a new identity with which to enjoy that status (the Lord is now the God-*man*). Only on this basis do humans have the possibility of imitating

30. It is disappointing to find a brilliant contemporary commentary repeat the older cheap shot of R. P. C. Hanson, in which he dubbed the patristic conflict "two blindfolded men trying to hit each other" (cited in Waltke 2004: 128). Of course, modern commentators treat particular grammatical and historical details with sophisticated new resources, but the reduction of exegesis to those details—as implied by Hanson-like comments—results in theologically impoverished analysis. Neglecting classic Christian theological exegesis helps to produce and circulate problematic views such as Wisdom being merely a divine attribute. Moreover, given the numerous speculative and conflicting hypotheses in modern, critical literature on Prov. 8, contemporary scholars appear to be just as vulnerable as Hanson's targets to swinging wildly without landing many punches. Theological exegetes should read both classic and contemporary critical scholarship with grateful yet cautious attention, open to the respective contributions of each.

31. Leo G. Perdue, *Proverbs*, Interpretation (Louisville: Westminster John Knox, 2000), 140.

the mindset of Christ Jesus: our exaltation is securely rooted as participation in exaltation already begun and sure to be completed; and our sinful self-exaltation is decisively interrupted by divine, redemptive condescension. Philippians 2 narrates the incarnation; Prov. 8 does not. Yet Phil. 2 has parallel logic, insofar as wisdom requires *both* divine condescension *and* human form for us to attain. And Prov. 8 poetically establishes Wisdom's divine pedigree presumed in Phil. 2, while presuming throughout that her invitation takes a form people can accept. This satisfies the conceptual challenge of human finitude, but there remains the historical challenge of human fallenness. According to Phil. 2, in fulfilling Israel's redemptive hope for final revelation of YHWH, Jesus Christ provides the theological resolution of both.

Christological relevance. Jesus Christ therefore does not finally complicate the interpretation of Prov. 8 but presents instead the resolution of a mystery latent in the text, though not always clearly recognized. The Arian solution lay in treating the Son of God as a creature, albeit an eminently unique one. In this way, some thought, the monotheistic commitment of biblical faith could be protected. The LORD alone is Creator, whose greatness is preserved by keeping an arm's length from creation. The mediator of the process, whose timeless begetting began it all, is Jesus Christ, God's Son. Even so, for the Arians "there was a time when he was not"; his is not the eternity of the uncreated God and Father of all, but rather the derivative being of a mediating creature through whom all others receive existence.

Athanasius correctly recognized the problematic character of such a mediator. If creation required mediation because direct contact with the divine was unendurable, then what would that entail for the Word as a creature through whom this mediation transpired?

> It follows either that, if he could endure it [direct contact], all could endure it, or, it being endurable by none, it was not endurable by the Word, for you say that he is one of originate things. And again, if because originate nature could not endure to be God's own handy work, there arose need of a mediator, it must follow, that, the Word being originate and a creature, there is need of medium [*sic*] in his framing also, since he too is of that originate nature which endures not to be made of God, but needs a medium. (*Four Discourses against the Arians* 2.17.26, in NPNF^2 4.362)

In other words, without a mediator who originates from the divine life, we are stuck with infinite regress—always dealing with creatures that need a mediator through which to endure divine contact. Sooner or later there must be a form of mediation that is itself divine.

What if "Arians" attempt to respond by making wisdom "a constituent or complement of his [God's] Essence, unoriginate as well as himself, which moreover they pretend to be the framer of the world, that so they may deprive the Son of the framing of it" (*Four Discourses against the Arians* 2.18.38, in NPNF^2

4.368–69)? Then God's simplicity would be threatened.[32] In that case it would appear as if God were a compound being, composed of parts or aspects, including wisdom. In the end this would threaten the practical monotheism to which Prov. 8 doubtless remains true. Wisdom cannot be merely an attribute that God creates (poetically or not) or through which God creates. God's perfections are neither divine components nor instruments doing the divine bidding while keeping creation at arm's length from the divine being. Rather, God's perfections denote human ways of speaking analogically about the mystery of the sole Creator acting to reveal himself and to redeem us.

As a mediator the Son is guarded from being imprisoned in temporality by the titles of Word and Wisdom, which are associated with the divine means behind the speech-act of creation. Unless these titles imply eternity of the Son, they recoil upon the work of the Father, as if God had to "devise for himself" the offspring by which to create (*Four Discourses against the Arians* 1.7.25, in NPNF[2] 4.321). As already noted, this creates the absurdity of God (unwisely?) creating Wisdom in order to act wisely—in the future, as it were. And it presumes what Prov. 8 counteracts, namely the idea that God cannot be directly engaged with the cosmos but must create through an intermediary to avoid getting his own hands dirty. But Prov. 8 has Wisdom rejoicing *with* God in creation as *God's* work, not serving as a quasidivine pinch hitter. Nor, according to Athanasius, could there be a separation of Word and Son, so as to associate the divine act of creation with the former but not the latter. The Word is from God, *the speaker*, so he must be the Son, a chip off the old speaking block as it were; the Son is from everlasting, so he must be the Word, spoken right from the beginning (*Four Discourses against the Arians* 4.15–24, in NPNF[2] 4.438–43). Accordingly the Father is the Father of the Son, in a distinctive sense, as compared to being the Father of the many children whom the Son brings to glory (Heb. 2:10).

God is the Father of the eternally begotten Son by nature, yet the Father of humanity by grace (*Four Discourses against the Arians* 2.21.59, in NPNF[2] 4.380–81). Athanasius correctly teaches that titles stemming from Prov. 8 in the New Testament, "only begotten" and "firstborn of all creation," conflict unless they respectively concern these different relations. The Son is only begotten with respect to the Father, by nature, as just noted. The Son is firstborn, implying the Father's begetting others, by grace, with respect to both creation and redemption. The former deals with the Son's existence, while the latter pertains to the Son's economic activity (*Four Discourses against the Arians* 2.20.51–2.21.62, in NPNF[2] 4.375–82).

At this juncture, however, some of Athanasius's exegetical conclusions are doubtful. He parallels Marcellus of Ancyra by referring the begetting of 8:22 to the incarnation, to the humanity of the Son in Jesus Christ (e.g., *Statement*

32. For a demonstration that this appeal to divine simplicity was pervasive throughout pro-Nicene early Christian theology and did not owe distinctively to Neoplatonic influence, see Lewis Ayres, "'Remember That You Are Catholic' (*serm.* 52.2): Augustine on the Unity of the Triune God," *Journal of Early Christian Studies* 8 (2000): 39–82, esp. 69–80.

of Faith 3–4, in NPNF² 4.85). Yet the begetting of 8:25 is the eternal begetting of the Son by the Father.[33] Thus Prov. 8 would reverse the sequence of existence and economy, introducing the earthly economy of the Son first in 8:22 before moving backward to the Son's (pre)existence in 8:25. But it seems quite unlikely that these verses would have different events in view or that God would have Prov. 8 foresee the incarnation with this much specificity. A narrative beginning with the incarnation—with the begetting of the Son's humanity in Jesus Christ—then flashing back to his preexistent divine sonship, is not impossible, but should contain textual signals to that effect. Instead the clues point the other way, as shown earlier: the verbs of 8:22–25 are repetitive and linked together, as are the (pre)temporal markers. All the material prior to 8:26 concerns Wisdom's precedence before any of the cosmos; 8:27–29 proceeds to Wisdom's presence at the creation of the cosmos; 8:30–31 finally affirms Wisdom's present rejoicing in the cosmos God has made, so as to call for our embrace of this mediator in 8:32–36. Athanasius's interpretation at this point is an unnecessary expedient if we dismiss "created" from our translation of 8:22a or even simply accept that such poetic license would not entail an Arian ontology in any case. Here is an instance in which the Septuagint, rendering 8:22 with *ektise* ("created"), creates an avoidable problem.[34] It is no wonder that Arians pounced on this as perhaps their primary proof-text. But Athanasius's solution, however much a theological improvement over the alternatives, was not radical enough.

Nevertheless, Athanasius points toward the fundamental issue that determines how to read this text: is Wisdom the divine presence, outgoing in creation; or is Wisdom some kind of supercreature or supracreature? Generally, structural analysis highlights Wisdom's uniqueness while relegating claims about the created cosmos to subordinate temporal clauses.[35] More specifically, as early as 8:10–11 Wisdom's value is not just quantitatively but qualitatively unique in comparison with creation. "Again it is written: *And* all things desirable *are not to be compared unto* Her, [which means] that even things that are of Heaven's desire are not comparable to Her?" (Babylonian Talmud, tractate *Mo'ed Qaṭan* 9b). Reflecting on these verses, Athanasius asks: "Is there any similarity between things eternal and spiritual, and things temporal and mortal?" (*Four Discourses against the Arians* 1.13.55, in NPNF² 4.338–39). The exhortation to choose Wisdom instead of, not just as better than, such creaturely treasures, hints at a qualitative distinction according to which Wisdom is divinely valuable, associated first with the Creator rather than just the creature. The claim in 8:15–16 that Wisdom enables kings to rule suggests her divine identity, since elsewhere in

33. Athanasius, *Four Discourses against the Arians* 2.21.59; and Origen, *Homilies on Jeremiah* 9.5, in FC 97.93.

34. Aloys Grillmeier, *Christ in Christian Tradition*, vol. 1: *From the Apostolic Age to Chalcedon (451)*, trans. John Bowden, 2nd ed. (Atlanta: John Knox, 1975), 246, suggests that the essential, defining characteristic of Arianism is treating the Son in relation to the term *ktisma* ("creature").

35. Jean-Noel Aletti, "Proverbes 8,22–31: Etude de structure," *Biblica* 57 (1976): 35.

Proverbs and the Old Testament as a whole this is the provenance of YHWH. Likewise, claims such as 8:17 ("I love those who love me") make the most sense by relating Wisdom to the identity of the LORD who makes similar claims elsewhere: "When you search for me, you will find me; if you seek me with all your heart" (Jer. 29:13); "If any of you is lacking in wisdom, ask God" (Jas. 1:5; also Matt. 7:7–8).[36] Even Sirach 24, which speaks of Wisdom's creation (24:9), lauds her in this extraordinary language of divine identity: "Those who eat of me will hunger for more, / and those who drink of me will thirst for more. / Whoever obeys me will not be put to shame, / and those who work with me will not sin" (24:21–22). Christian readers soon realize that this language ultimately points to one who creates more hunger and thirst by satisfying all other hunger and thirst (John 4:13–15, 31–34; 7:37–39). And that is because this Word who gives us God's Spirit "came forth from the mouth of the Most High" (Sir. 24:3). Precise speech about eternal begetting rather than creation may have taken considerable time and debate for the tradition to discern, but the necessity of the mediator's divine origin is latent in the foundational texts.

Later, in Prov. 8:30–31, the mention of rejoicing further contributes to a cumulative case for Wisdom's eternity, since God has never not rejoiced (*Four Discourses against the Arians* 2.22.82, in NPNF^2 4.392–93). The catalog of creaturely realities preceding these verses is deliberately comprehensive, a merism communicating that Wisdom is uncreated because it is "before" everything God made. If by contrast the Son excels other creatures on only a relative basis, as one star differs from another, then Wisdom cannot be a cause or power to frame others but is itself caused (*Four Discourses against the Arians* 2.16.21, in NPNF^2 4.359)—with all the attendant problems noted earlier of treating Wisdom as either fundamentally a creature or else merely a divine attribute. The Bible knows of only two categories, Creator and creature, not three—there are no quasidivine mediating creatures. Even if neither Jewish nor Christian traditions are entirely uniform in discerning this fundamental implication of biblical teaching, still it bolsters the basic Athanasian logic by which to make sense of the mysteries of Prov. 8.

At the same time, Athanasius does not provide the only manner of identifying Wisdom according to patristic orthodoxy. In fact, Theophilus of Antioch and Irenaeus actually identified this Wisdom with not the second, but the third, person of the Trinity—the Holy Spirit.[37] Although the images of sonship are dominant enough to preclude this identification and favor a christological one, this example prompts us to recognize significant parallels between 8:22–31 and Gen. 1: the distinction of works of creation from one another; the heavens being created first, with the setting apart of the waters; and *rēʾšît* at the beginning of

36. Habtu, "Proverbs," 758.

37. Henri Cazelles, "La sagesse de Proverbes 8:22 peut-elle être considérée comme une hypostase," in *Trinité et liturgie*, ed. Achille M. Triacca and Alessandro Pistoia (Rome: Edizioni Liturgiche, 1984), 51.

both texts.[38] In a broader context Wisdom points to a theology of Word and Spirit: while order, distinction, and cohesion are appropriated to the Logos who prevents cosmic chaos, the vitality and delights of communion involve the divine presence of the Spirit as well.[39]

Among those who treat Wisdom christologically yet differently from Athanasius, Basil of Caesarea correctly acknowledges that Prov. 8:22 refers to the preexistent Son. Yet he recognizes that this does not entail the Son being only a creature, since (1) this position would have to overcome the weight of scriptural evidence on the other side, (2) proverbs as a genre are complex and demand interpretation that goes beyond a simplistic literal sense, and (3) one could translate "acquired" instead of "created."[40] Whatever one makes of this rationale, Basil illustrates the breadth of options and debates within the classic tradition. Nor is that tradition frozen in time. The proposal adopted in the present commentary fits its revelatory and soteriological substructure while updating some of the lexical and grammatical reference points.

Christian orthodoxy freely appealed to New Testament texts for understanding 8:22–31. John 1 offers an aforementioned parallel, since the Logos has overtones of Old Testament Wisdom in the background. This Word was "with God" yet also "was God," through whom "all things came into being" (1:1, 3). The passage goes on to call this Son *monogenēs* (1:18), designating the favorite or privileged son, the unique heir. Regardless of one's text-critical decision, the surrounding context of 1:18 makes a strong claim for the divinity of this Son. Incidentally, Wisdom makes several "I am" claims in Prov. 8 and is God's "way" (8:13, 32), the "truth" (8:7), and the "life" (8:35), thereby fitting the pattern elsewhere in John's Gospel, notably in 14:6.

The terminology of divine "fullness" (John 1:16) also appears in Col. 1:19 as dwelling in the Son. Colossians 1:15 famously speaks of the Son as "the firstborn [*prōtotokos*] of all creation." When interpreting this statement, again we find distinction between the Son and the invisible one now understood as God the Father ("he is the image of the invisible God"; 1:15), along with strong statements of divine identity for the Son ("he himself is before all things, and in him all things hold together"; 1:17). It is difficult to put the Son solely or primarily on the side of creatures when the emphasis of 1:16 is on all creation—even of the great powers that transcend this earthly cosmos—occurring in and through and for him. Proverbs 8:22b, placing Wisdom at the beginning of God's way, makes this begotten one the model point of reference for the work of creation. Orthodox creedal formulas set forth the grammar by which to make sense of these various statements.

38. Michaela Bauks and Gerluch Baumann, "Im Anfang war . . . ? Gen 1,1ff und Prov 8,22–31 im Vergleich," *Biblische Notizen* 71 (1994): 24–52.

39. Henri Blocher, *La doctrine du péché et de la rédemption* (Vaux-sur-Seine, France: Edifac, 2001), 221.

40. Mark DelCogliano, "Basil of Caesarea on Proverbs 8:22 and the Sources of Pro-Nicene Theology," *Journal of Theological Studies*, n.s. 59 (2008): 183–90, esp. 184–87.

Matthew 11:25–30 and like passages unfold the logic of revelation through which to understand Wisdom's divine self-giving in Prov. 8. The Father initiates the divine condescension—and remarkable condescension it is, bypassing any qualifications of human wisdom and addressing relative infants. Even so, the Son by whom we receive this revelation is fit to share all things with the Father. Thus the Son's knowledge of the Father is self-knowledge. Athanasius puts the claim in terms of the Son being able to call him both "Father" and "Lord" (*Four Discourses against the Arians* 2.19.50, in NPNF^2 4.375): this is the form of mediation that sets the pieces of 8:22–31 into place.

After citing Matt. 11:27, Augustine explicates the necessary distinctions for situating Jesus Christ as Wisdom within a theology of the Holy Trinity.[41] Some terms, such as "Word," are relational and pertain to particular persons. Other terms, such as "Wisdom," are substantial, pertaining to the divine nature of all three persons. That said, it is appropriate for some substantial terms, such as "Wisdom," to be associated especially with one of the three divine persons on account of salvation history; theologians often call this "appropriation." The Nicene Creed exemplifies appropriation in the realm of action, associating creation especially with the Father, redemption with the Son, and the perfection of all things with the Spirit. Thus, pertaining to divine attributes, "it is not surprising that scripture should be speaking about the Son when it speaks about wisdom, on account of the model which the image who is equal to the Father provides us with that we may be refashioned to the image of God; for we follow the Son by living wisely."[42] This is not to deny that the Father is wise or that the Spirit is strongly connected with our attainment of wisdom in the Son. Even so, the Bible particularly associates wisdom with Christ, the crucified one who *is* Wisdom for us.

"Wisdom Christology" has currently become popular, treating wisdom as a crucial category for understanding the identity of Jesus Christ. For some this is a historical claim about the influence of Old Testament or intertestamental Jewish texts upon New Testament or early Christian understandings. For others, such historical influences are more Greco-Roman, whether in terms of Jesus's self-presentation as a wandering sage or in regard to philosophical motifs. For still others, "Sophia" presents feminist possibilities for reinterpreting traditional theological categories or the male Jesus in woman-friendlier ways. Some of these claims are not mutually exclusive, but other scholars caution against inflated Wisdom Christologies, sensing that various agendas spawn the myriad historical hypotheses. Though certain historical cautions are warranted, and in this case some feminist theological claims are overblown, we should not overreact. It will not do to minimize Pauline and other New Testament Wisdom vocabulary entirely, as if it were only and always minimal and polemical. To take one example, polemical or

41. Augustine, *The Trinity* 7.1–6, trans. Edmund Hill (New York: New City, 1991), 217–24.
42. Augustine, *The Trinity* 7.5, in ibid., 223.

not, the hymn in Col. 1 reflects a positive, even glorious pattern of appropriating the christological implications of Prov. 8.

Interpreting Prov. 8 as having christological relevance helps to hold together creation and redemption rather than prioritizing either in lopsided fashion. Even if we assume with Athanasius and most traditional theologians that the incarnation occurred only due to God's redemptive plan for counteracting the effects of our fall into sin, still the Redeemer is the Logos by whom the world came into being. On the other hand, lest Wisdom devolve into mere common sense immanent to creation—a matter of opinion polling among sinful humans taking their own looks at a created order that is actually under a curse—in Christ God confronts us with true Wisdom that is personal and redemptive, entailing response to divine initiative. Covenant life means the renewal of creation, while creaturely life is ultimately designed for covenant fellowship with God. Athanasius once again strikes the proper balance: "Creation was there all the time, but it did not prevent men from wallowing in error," yet "*the renewal of creation has been wrought by the Self-same Word Who made it in the beginning*" (*On the Incarnation* 1.14, 1.1).[43]

Thus 8:31 comes alive in light of Jesus Christ. The verse identifies humanity as integral to God's delight. As already noted, YHWH is the first word in 8:22, and *ʾādām* ("humanity") the last in 8:31; at the end of the first eleven stichs and before the second eleven stichs, Wisdom—the Mediator—says, "I was there" (8:27).[44]

> The LORD, your God, is in your midst,
>   a warrior who gives victory;
> he will rejoice over you with gladness,
>   he will renew you in his love;
> he will exult over you with loud singing
>   as on a day of festival. (Zeph. 3:17)

Jesus Christ endured the cross for the joy set before him (Heb. 12:1–2), because of God's commitment to creation and particularly to humans who bear the divine image. This Son shares the Father's character, so that by grace we might do so in turn.

Final Offers from Wisdom and Folly (9)

Proverbs 9 follows the winsome invitation of Lady Wisdom in Prov. 8 with final offers from both her and Dame Folly. These offers reach the climax of what has been carefully orchestrated in preceding chapters. Wisdom made an early appearance to offer life (1:20–33), after which parental addresses repeatedly urge

43. Quotation from Athanasius, *On the Incarnation* (Crestwood, NY: St. Vladimir's Seminary Press, 2002), 42, 26 (emphasis original).

44. Aletti, "Proverbes 8,22–31," 28.

accepting this invitation, clinging to her as a beloved spouse, and protecting the heart from going an alternative route toward the wayward woman or any other entanglement. Juxtaposed with Dame Folly by the time we reach Prov. 7, Lady Wisdom returns to center stage in Prov. 8, supplementing her call with claims about her role in creation itself.

Climactically now in 9:1–6 Wisdom offers a place at table in her house—a metaphor no doubt connected, in the first instance, to the ongoing theme of family stability. The seven pillars suggest that the house is fully constructed—pleasing to look at, as well as secure. The number seven indicates that elements of the passage operate in a symbolic register. Subsequent readers are tempted to refer the pillars to the sevenfold Spirit of God (Isa. 11:2; Rev. 1:4) and/or the seven churches of Rev. 2–3. Such possibilities depend on how we interpret the house. The theme of family stability suffuses Proverbs; thus Prov. 9 shapes how we read the succeeding collections, which form at least the foundation of the house. It is not inappropriate, though, additionally to see a broader principle at work, namely Wisdom's project in creation. This project in creation involves the Lord Jesus Christ taking on human flesh, as some church fathers note (e.g., Hippolytus, *Fragments from Commentary on Proverbs*, in ANF 5.175): "And the Word became flesh and lived among us, and we have seen his glory" (John 1:14). Ultimately that house—the body of Christ—grows into the church. Wisdom's construction project is a covenant community that will become the dwelling of God in the world, so that no longer will she merely cry out from the temple on high (as she does in Prov. 9:3). Indeed, Lady Wisdom in Proverbs manages to bring holiness home, beyond the temple into the city and even the household.[45] People and place become one in the city of God—as dramatized in the book of Revelation—so Wisdom's house pervasively makes visible the life she offers. At that point the Holy Spirit's work in the church becomes relevant to a fully canonical understanding of Wisdom's endeavor.

Her invitation echoes in Jesus's invitations to wedding banquets, notably Luke 14:15–24. As in that parable, first she sends her servants—the prophets. (Folly, by contrast, has no such servants in Prov. 9:13–18.) Then Wisdom goes and speaks herself. The incarnation of God in Jesus Christ is the fitting embodiment—finally—of the extent of divine condescension. Lady Wisdom is noble yet addresses the simple—those who are not so far gone toward Folly that they mock the offer instead of accepting it. These largely are not other noble people; the invitation addresses folks all around in a wide variety of places (1 Cor. 1–2). Table fellowship bespeaks the intimacy into which God remarkably invites everyone.

By contrast mockers, the preoccupation of Prov. 9:7–12, simply abuse the wise person who addresses them. We cannot always know in advance who will respond appropriately or inappropriately to our rebuke, but in some cases the result is obvious and so we should not cast our pearls before swine (→1:1–7). Meanwhile the

45. William P. Brown, *The Ethos of the Cosmos: The Genesis of Moral Imagination in the Bible* (Grand Rapids: Eerdmans, 1999), 313–16.

wise are on the way to accumulating more wisdom since they fear the Lord. The expected results—long life or else suffering—follow for these two types of people on two different paths.[46] Hebrews 10:24–25 supplements our understanding of the context for the wise receiving instruction. We need the church, not just the biological family: "Let us consider how to provoke one another to love and good deeds, not neglecting to meet together, as is the habit of some, but encouraging one another, and all the more as you see the Day approaching." Anticipating that people will attend only one banquet or the other, Prov. 9 bears similar eschatological freight. It is true that people bear the consequences for their own choices (9:12), but we very much need others' help to remain on Wisdom's path.

Folly makes her counteroffer in 9:13–18. She too has a house and mimics Wisdom's invitation from "high places" all her own—which, as we know from the rest of the Old Testament, are frequently associated with the idolatrous seduction of God's people. The Moabite seduction of Israel in Num. 25—and "seduction" is the right word, with all its overtones—provides another example of the dangers in view (Longman 2006: 222). This is a struggle to the death, a clash of titans. Folly goes after not only the simple, but everyone—even those who are "making their paths straight" (Prov. 9:15 ESV). Proverbs 9 as a whole makes clear that "God has no grandchildren," since the proverbial son always hears the call of Folly in the air and begins in a state of gullibility out of which he must grow into maturity. Even the wise are not perfect, as 9:9–10 makes evident: the difference is that the wise fear the Lord and therefore can grow by receiving correction. Tertullian warns us to recognize heretics with reference to whether they promote this fear of the Lord; heretics render the church void of God's presence by voiding it of truth, which is connected to godly discipline (*Prescriptions against Heretics* 43, in Library of Christian Classics 5.63).

Folly is deceptive, hiding her dead guests inside the house while highlighting the sensual delights of living on the edge. She tries to make of simplicity a virtue rather than a vice: if all one has is water, it can taste sweet if stolen; if the food is nondescript, it can be delicious if the adrenaline is flowing due to a feeling of dangerously getting away with something (9:16–17). Folly's sensual appeals are not always blunt instruments; there is nuance regarding the human spirit and what really activates our sense of delight. Yet these appeals to forbidden fruit are Folly's attempts to cover for laziness, since she has not prepared a proper meal and actually just sits around (9:14). Matthew 7:24–27 echoes elements of Proverbs: a fool builds a house on the sand, in which case storms eventually prove deadly; whereas those who listen to Jesus and act on his words build their house on a stable, safe foundation. Use of the house image is slightly different, but the point is the same: there are only two ways to go, one of which is deadly. Whereas Wisdom promises a reward on her own (Prov. 9:11), Folly's destructive end is narrated for her (9:18) by the sage.

46. In addition to 9:11, note the theme of turning aside in 9:6, so important for this motif of two ways.

The overall context of Prov. 9 is a meal. The Jewish reader could not help but see here the framework of salvation history. A meal gone horribly wrong in God's garden temple led to the expulsion of Adam and Eve, and everyone else since then. The ill-gotten food came at the instigation of the "crafty" serpent—alternative wisdom terminology, designating wisdom used merely as a skillful means to a desirable end. But now God's redemptive promise offers moments of table fellowship anticipating an eschatological banquet: "On this mountain the LORD of hosts will make for all peoples / a feast of rich food, a feast of well-aged wines, / of rich food filled with marrow, of well-aged wines strained clear" (Isa. 25:6). God's invitation is not narrow, for it goes to everyone. But the way to the feast *is* narrow, for we must trust the one true God for salvation, to the detriment of our pride (25:7–12).

The Christian reader cannot help but see particular anticipations of this future meal in the Eucharist rather than elements of the old covenant sacrificial system. We reaffirm our commitment to divine Wisdom and rejoice in God's commitment to us by celebrating the Passover meal fulfilled in Jesus Christ—who is the sacrificial victim from which the meal comes (Prov. 9:2). Proverbs 9 bears on this celebration by reminding us that the Lord's Supper is not solely a memorial of Christ's past work or an expression of future hope. It is a small-scale version, in the present, of a big celebration to come. That celebration does not leave behind the good gifts of creation but instead sanctifies them for use in divine-human fellowship. Some eucharistic celebrations hardly merit the appellation "celebration"—they are far too somber and solo. We need forms of celebration that integrate members of the community with each other and with the created goods of which they partake.

Indeed, that is the message of Prov. 1–9: only by fearing one's Maker can a person truly flourish, wisely knowing how to live in harmony with the cosmos and the covenant community. Such fear does not repel but attracts (→1:1–7). The household metaphor in Prov. 9 is profoundly appropriate: ultimately God invites us to a joyful family celebration. Although, depending on the context, the host is a powerful patriarch or a regal lady, this greatness does not terrify us but instead elicits our delight at the profound privilege involved in the invitation. And the household is more than a metaphor, for the family and the celebration are realities in which we already participate analogously. The table is set, and we will reach that ultimate feast by partaking now of divine Wisdom, staying on the parental path near her house.

THE VIRTUES OF PROVERBS

PROVERBS 10–29

Beginning with Prov. 10, proverbs appear regularly in their most familiar form. Such pithy, usually two-line, statements dominate the rest of the book, running through Prov. 29. The sayings in Prov. 30–31 conclude with some unique features, including sources named from outside Israel, so they receive distinct treatment at the end.

Overview

Proverbs 10 announces that the next section contains "the proverbs of Solomon," which continue at a titular level until 25:1. There the proverbs, while also stemming from Solomon, underwent acknowledged editorial work during Hezekiah's time. Readers need not linger long over the precise role of Solomon, since the text does nothing more definitive than associating these proverbs with Israel's royal, God-given paragon of wisdom.

Within 10:1–24:34, additional divisions are proposed. It is clear that 10:1–15:33 is distinct in emphasis from 16:1–22:16: the former is dominated by the antithesis between righteousness and wickedness, whereas the latter is more wide-ranging in its ethical form and subject matter. Then 22:17–24:34 takes another new form and is often compared with an Egyptian collection, *Instruction of Amenemope*. There are minititles regarding "sayings/words of the wise" in 22:17

and 24:23.[1] Since scholars continue to debate the nature and extent of such extrabiblical parallels, there is no need to make interpretation dependent upon them. Neither do conjectures—and that is what they are—assist interpretation when it comes to compositional settings for particular proverbs. Though the titles bear witness to courtly editing, there is no reason to believe that all the proverbs were composed within a given setting—such as a royal school—or within the settings they depict—such as an agricultural context. Nor would knowing which proverbs stemmed from outside Israel necessarily influence our interpretations in detail. At minimum, the titles in Prov. 30–31 indicate that international material appears in the book, as we would expect, given Solomon's status portrayed elsewhere in scripture (esp. 1 Kgs. 4:29–34). These broader dealings with non-Israelite wisdom are theologically significant, as we shall eventually see. Yet the most important features for interpreting particular proverbs concern their recontextualization within or relation to the fear of YHWH, Israel's God. As Maker of the entire universe, this God embraces all of the cosmos within the wisdom presented by Proverbs, so most salient to the various sayings are their depictions of personal integrity in covenant community rather than disparate settings or origins.

Genre

Proverbs do not offer ironclad guarantees, because they chew on the reality of creation in bite-sized comments. These aphorisms make no pretense of examining every side of a situation. A famous example is 22:6: "Train up a child in the way he should go, / Even when he is old he will not depart from it" (NASB). Its function is not to serve as an absolute promise, thereby leading parents of wayward children toward automatic guilt. However one interprets the statement's details—descriptively or prescriptively, applying to a particular age or setting—it refutes debilitating literalism. Proverbs provide punchy confirmation of general truths that people already observe, without denying the existence of contrary cases. Moreover, by design proverbs evoke questions in their audiences rather than always serving up straightforward answers. Thus, the very question of whether 22:6 describes what generally happens—for parenting both good and bad—or instead prescribes a commitment to good parenting that usually goes rewarded evokes reflection on the importance of teaching children.

In line with their interesting mix of generality and concreteness, proverbs exercise various forms of authority. A proverb can serve as "(1) a universal mandate (Prov. 3:5), (2) an ideal-confirming exhortation (Prov. 10:4), (3) a simple nonmoral observation (Prov. 14:10), (4) an ideal-disconfirming warning (Prov. 11:13), (5) an absolute prohibition (Prov. 6:16–17)." Proverbs furthermore accomplish numerous rhetorical functions: "Perhaps the proverb is cited simply for pointed humor,

1. For a survey of the difficulties and possibilities in translating 22:20—and whether it refers to thirty sayings (which are frequently related to the thirty chapters of *Amenemope*)—see Waltke 2005: 219–20n113.

such as the sluggard who is too lazy to raise his hand up to his mouth (Prov. 19:24; 22:13)."[2] We should not miss the huge emphasis on orality that takes shape in all the exhortations to "listen, my son." Oral forms of learning elicit meditation and memorization for the sake of this deep internalization. Most proverbs are not mere platitudes; they are for pondering. However, modern Christians typically pursue forms of certainty that God does not offer in scripture—certainly not in Proverbs, anyway. This quest for certainty may help to explain the modern demise of proverbs in the first place. Our culture tends to prefer either firm answers or else ceaseless self-exploration. Hence proverbs are largely relegated to advertising slogans—hardly catalysts to reflection on memorable, time-worn truths.

Different kinds of parallelism appear in proverbs:

synonymous—in which the two statements say basically the same thing
antithetical—in which the two statements portray opposites
synthetic or constructive—in which the second statement adds to the first

Although these categories are now viewed as too simplistic by more intricate contemporary scholarship, this outline can be useful at a basic level, if not pressed too literally. It should go without saying that no two statements are entirely synonymous unless they are exactly the same. Thus, synonymous parallelism still somehow involves the addition of nuance or difference in the second statement. Antithetical parallelism, meanwhile, cannot involve absolute antithesis without fundamental contradiction. So, as is common in Prov. 10–15, two statements may portray the righteous in one way and the wicked in another, thereby seeming antithetical, but the larger point is actually—dare we say it?—relatively synonymous, since the theme concerns the two ways that people could possibly live and God's invitation to choose life.

Proverbs, in other words, do not map the world in the systematic fashion that modern scholars are used to. Neither are they, for all their concreteness, practical in the sense that Western people expect. For instance, when the biblical proverbs dwell over and over again on the importance of speech, they offer little or no instruction on "*how* to speak well."[3] Scholars now recognize that Proverbs does not focus on the relation between particular acts and consequences, but more richly targets the formation of character that results in certain acts. Proverbs arrived at emphasis on character long before contemporary appeals to virtue theory. The book tries primarily to inculcate a heart of wisdom that not only avoids the disastrous consequences of foolish choices but also pursues ever greater prudence. Proverbs does not directly stipulate what to do or not do in every circumstance.

2. Ted A. Hildebrandt, "Proverb, Genre of," in *Dictionary of the Old Testament: Wisdom, Poetry, and Writings*, ed. Tremper Longman III and Peter Enns (Downers Grove, IL: InterVarsity, 2008), 531.

3. Stuart Weeks, *Early Israelite Wisdom*, Oxford Theological Monographs (Oxford: Oxford University Press, 1994), 159.

Pedagogical Progression

Therefore, Proverbs can seem to contain randomly collected aphorisms that basically provide memorable moralism. Even if the book focuses on character first and foremost, it can be tempting to downplay the coherence and scope of its moral vision, especially if the proverbs mostly appear at random, without larger structuring principles. Recent scholarship contains numerous attempts to discover some kind of organizational pattern(s), but strong demurrals remain.[4]

Theological interpreters could import thought relationships that are purely of our own devising and utterly extraneous to the text's message. The resultant danger would obscure other possibilities that are just as valid or indeed distort the particular meaning(s) of individual sayings. However, since the goal of theological exegesis is not to engage in an endless historical quest for authorial or editorial intentions when these are unrecoverable, or as if they could be disconnected from the scriptural texts themselves, this danger should not preclude considering relationships between the sayings. Aspects of their meaning come to light in this way, for the sayings now reverberate with each other as part of a canonical text rather than being tightly bound by any original *Sitz im Leben*. The occurrence of repeated material (e.g., 13:14 and 14:27) suggests that literary contexts can sometimes be important, regarding distinctive emphases at any rate. Proceeding with cautious openness to connections between sayings, we find small thematic groupings at fairly regular intervals.[5] These may arise due to word connections, moral and theological themes, and so forth. It is difficult, when faced with series of verses on a subject such as speech, to imagine that the collector(s) never gave thought to thematic connections. Their appearance does not mean that groupings are everywhere or that Proverbs ought to be read as offering some kind of linear argument. But thematic clusters do appear, and this adds support to the fuller canonical enterprise.

William Brown discovers pedagogical progression across the proverbial collections in interesting ways. First, the implied reader grows from "the silent son" at the beginning into "his mature counterpart, the esteemed spouse of the 'woman of strength,' profiled at the conclusion."[6] Second, proverbs attributed to Solomon eventually give way to anonymous sayings, the Hezekian collection, and then collections apparently from non-Israelite figures. Third, antithetical proverbs dominate Prov. 10–15 (approximately 84%, with thirty-nine occurrences of *ṣaddîq* ["righteous"] and forty-two occurrences of *rāšāʿ* ["wicked"]), while they diminish in Prov. 16–22 (approximately 21.5%, with ten occurrences of *ṣaddîq* and

4. Waltke 2004–2005 treats the book as highly structured; conversely, Longman 2006 argues for the earlier view that there is relatively little, if any, organization of the individual sayings.

5. For striking examples of how context alters the meaning of proverbs, see 14:20–21 and 22:7–8; Michael V. Fox, "The Epistemology of the Book of Proverbs," *Journal of Biblical Literature* 126 (2007): 683.

6. William P. Brown, "The Pedagogy of Proverbs 10:1–31:9," in *Character and Scripture: Moral Formation, Community, and Biblical Interpretation*, ed. by William P. Brown (Grand Rapids: Eerdmans, 2002), 153.

seventeen of *rāšāʿ*).[7] Fourth, particular themes progress, notably from focusing on the biological family outward toward addressing friends, neighbors, and even national life; from focusing on silence and listening toward preparing for wise, timely speech; and toward tackling wealth and poverty more substantially.[8] By the end, the focus of Proverbs broadens beyond the familial ethos, embracing the cosmos in a fuller ethos that evokes necessary humility[9]—the fear of God. The royal and the familial contexts come together in the address of the royal mother to her son (Prov. 31), and standing behind this royal household is the divine king, who similarly shepherds the creation with parental care.

From this we learn that biblical wisdom is a matter of intricate, deep harmony: between words, actions, and character; between family, neighborhood, community, nation, and even divine rule; between human virtue and other creaturely patterns; between tradition and interpretations of present experience; and so forth. The epistemology of Proverbs is not, therefore, a method or a simple commitment to working out systematically either empiricism or traditionalism. Instead, Proverbs works out in literary form a moral esthetic, which must be perceived in imaginative, dialogical interplay between such entities as tradition and experience or family and nation.[10] Systematic empiricism or traditionalism would adopt one and only one starting point, working out a comprehensive viewpoint from there, into which all other considerations must coherently fit. Such an approach inevitably tries to squeeze square pegs into round holes. But life in the cosmos is not always self-interpreting, on the one hand; while tradition's application to new or complex situations is not always clear, on the other hand. The pursuit of *shalom* requires taking seriously both experience and tradition, both what one sees and what one believes, and reflecting on how to discern their harmony. Proverbs evoke this dialogical interplay by, on the one hand, making tradition memorable and, on the other hand, tying the expression of those beliefs to concrete, observable realities. It is not that truth is continually up for grabs: "Wisdom was given in essence at the start, at least according to Proverbs 8, and only in details and formulations can further knowledge be drawn forth, expanded, and refined."[11] Nevertheless, if humans are hereby put in their place, the cosmos remains a place of joyful discovery, unfolding the beautiful wisdom of God's *shalom* over time.

7. Ibid., 156; and Richard L. Schultz, "Proverbs," in *Baker Commentary on the Bible*, ed. G. M. Burge and A. E. Hill (Grand Rapids: Baker, forthcoming).

8. Brown, "Pedagogy of Proverbs 10:1–31:9," 158–64.

9. Ibid., 177.

10. The esthetic emphasis is nicely developed by Fox, although the claim that Proverbs holds a "coherence theory of truth" probably puts too much weight on the book's adherence to tradition, while not distinguishing carefully between the nature and grounding of truth claims. Fox still importantly demonstrates with examples that "empiricism is irrelevant to most of Proverbs"; "Epistemology of the Book of Proverbs," 671.

11. Ibid., 676.

Seven (Cardinal and Theological) Virtues

Proverbs 10–29 presents coherent divine revelation concerning the moral life, in relatively large collections containing sporadic clusters of themes. So we need an orderly pattern for setting forth the main lines of its teaching, and the Christian tradition provides both positive and negative depictions of the moral life with which Proverbs is concerned. Positively, the church is the primary context within which the family, creation's home for moral formation, can rightly direct a person's life. That direction involves journeying toward virtue. Virtues are developing, deep dispositions resulting in habitual recognition and realization of the good—what one ought to feel, think, and do in particular situations. People are not born with virtues; they are made. This is why Proverbs treats the relative innocence of the young as so unstable—people eventually form character one way or the other.

Cardinal virtues—prudence, justice, fortitude, and temperance—are possible for all humans by virtue of God's creation. They deal fundamentally with living well in this world. Their only biblical citation as such comes in Wisdom of Solomon 8:7: "And if anyone loves righteousness, / her labors are virtues; / for she teaches self-control and prudence, / justice and courage; / nothing in life is more profitable for mortals than these." Given their association with nature and the Greek origins of this scheme, cardinal virtues offer possibilities for civic and philosophical engagement between Christians and those of alternative moral traditions. Yet these virtues are cardinal or principal—those on which moral development chiefly hinges—because they incorporate appropriate desire, not just activity. After falling into sin, humans cannot rightly order their appetites apart from redemption. Nevertheless, particular virtues may be developed to some degree because of the integrity of the cosmos, even apart from integration with the fear of the Lord.[12]

Theological virtues, in contrast, require redemptive grace by which to attain and then pursue genuine faith, hope, and charity. Dealing directly with God, these spiritual realities are "above man," as Thomas Aquinas puts it: "Hence they should properly be called not human but superhuman or divine virtues," for beyond human morality they are forms of participation in the divine life by the Holy Spirit.[13] Theological virtues align us with our true end as God's creatures, but they are not available for our native taking from creation. They result from God's taking initiative to bring us into covenant fellowship, which can render Christian practice of the cardinal virtues distinctive as well.

Negatively speaking, the tradition must condemn the sins into which even virtuous people continue to fall. The root(s) of these sins lie in vices, which function like negative virtues: vices are developing, deep dispositions resulting in habitual failure(s) to realize—and, often, even recognize—the good. Some of these have

12. Most helpfully, see Oliver O'Donovan, *Resurrection and Moral Order: An Outline for Evangelical Ethics*, 2nd ed. (Grand Rapids: Eerdmans, 1994).

13. Thomas Aquinas, *Summa theologiae* 1a2ae Q. 61 (Allen, TX: Christian Classics, 1948).

garnered the misnomer "deadly sins," though they are more appropriately called "capital vices." They are not merely sins but patterns of sin and the dispositions from which these spring: hence "vices." They are not merely deadly concerning their outcome, but in fact serve as the origin(s) from which other vices and various sins spring: hence "capital."

Development of these positive and negative frameworks was not entirely coterminous; there is an array of possible correlations between certain virtues and vices, without exclusive or one-to-one correspondences between any in particular. Although Proverbs had little directly to do with originating these frameworks, still they fit the book's moral teaching. Virtues and vices afford a language within which to examine, structure, and summarize the instruction of Proverbs. Moreover, Proverbs informs these frameworks distinctively and supplements them with unique elements of emphasis and context. Of course, the proof of the pudding for their fittingness vis-à-vis Proverbs lies in the eating below.

Prudence

The first of the cardinal virtues, prudence, has a higher-order function regulating the others. It is cardinal per se, whereas the other three are principal in their particular spheres. Prudence commands action and response by reason rather than whimsical passion, while still respecting the particularity of situations; justice renders what is due in actions related to God and others; fortitude enables right living in the face of difficulty and ultimately death; and temperance restrains the bodily appetites. Prudence "is not to be confused with timidity or fear, nor with duplicity or dissimulation"; to the contrary, it "is the virtue that disposes practical reason to discern our true good in every circumstance and to choose the right means of achieving it. . . . It guides the other virtues by setting rule and measure."[14]

The following survey of the depiction of this virtue in Proverbs—and others to come—does not rely exclusively on any given Hebrew terminology, sifting instead through the various collections for pertinent concepts regarding the theme. A heavy premium placed on quotation keeps the form, not just the content, of the proverbs front and center.

Its value. It should be obvious how strongly the book of Proverbs values prudence. The theme of Prov. 1–9, "Get wisdom!" and its context—the doctrine of the two ways—are repeated endlessly throughout the rest of the book. The antithetical parallelism frequent in Prov. 10–15 reinforces this in literary terms.

Among distinctive expressions of the value of prudence in Prov. 10–29 are juxtapositions of default human thinking with divine wisdom: "There is a way that seems right to a person, / but its end is the way to death" (14:12); "The human mind may devise many plans, / but it is the purpose of the LORD that will be established" (19:21); "Do you see persons wise in their own eyes? / There is more

14. *Catechism of the Catholic Church*, 2nd ed. (Washington DC: United States Catholic Conference, 1997), §1806.

hope for fools than for them" (26:12). Hence, "like a gold ring in a pig's snout / is a beautiful woman without good sense" (11:22). Prudence confers social status: "One is commended for good sense, / but a perverse mind is despised" (12:8); "Wisdom is too high for fools; / in the gate they do not open their mouths" (24:7). This can even overturn social structures: "A slave who deals wisely will rule over a child who acts shamefully, / and will share the inheritance as one of the family" (17:2). After all, parents delight in wise children (23:15–16, 24–25; 27:11; 29:3).

Likewise prudence confers power (21:22; 24:5–6) and wealth. The latter is true negatively in terms of avoiding poverty and positively in terms of enjoying abundance: "The plans of the diligent lead surely to abundance, / but everyone who is hasty comes only to want" (21:5). Thus precious items serve as points of comparison for heightening the value of prudence: "How much better to get wisdom than gold! / To get understanding is to be chosen rather than silver" (16:16); "There is gold, and abundance of costly stones; / but the lips informed by knowledge are a precious jewel" (20:15). Prudence is also sweet as honey (24:13–14) and refreshing as snow (25:11–13).

Illustrations. Moving from the value of prudence to its nature, planning ahead is a key illustration: "A child who gathers in summer is prudent, / but a child who sleeps in harvest brings shame" (10:5; see also 27:23–27). Put the other way, one should avoid being hasty (19:2; 20:25; 21:5; 25:8–10): "Do you see someone who is hasty in speech? / There is more hope for a fool than for anyone like that" (29:20). Here the theme of thinking ahead and avoiding haste merges with speech being a vital domain for prudence. This is true in terms of timing—"A word fitly spoken / is like apples of gold in a setting of silver" (25:11)—and listening, a related form of avoiding haste: "If one gives an answer before hearing, / it is folly and shame" (18:13; also 18:15; 23:6–8 [on paying attention to nuance]; and 23:22–23). Another common illustration of spoken wisdom's situation-sensitive character is this: "Do not answer fools according to their folly, / or you will be a fool yourself. / Answer fools according to their folly, / or they will be wise in their own eyes" (26:4–5). Most of all, prudence demands restraining the amount of one's speech: "When words are many, transgression is not lacking, / but the prudent are restrained in speech" (10:19); "Even fools who keep silent are considered wise; / when they close their lips, they are deemed intelligent" (17:28).[15] Additional verses further contrast mind and mouth: "The mind of one who has understanding seeks knowledge, / but the mouths of fools feed on folly" (15:14);[16] "The mind of the righteous ponders how to answer, / but the mouth of the wicked pours out evil" (15:28; also 16:21).

Prudence entails planning, outside the realm of speech: "Where there are no oxen, there is no grain; / abundant crops come by the strength of the ox" (14:4).

15. Although fools don't do this; see 10:21; 12:23; 18:2; 20:25 plus other verses mentioned regarding haste (25:20; 26:18–19; 27:14; and 29:11).

16. Notice too the singular-plural contrast, which may indicate that broad is the road to folly and narrow the road to wisdom, which only a few find.

Many of the general truisms in Proverbs promote such assessment of opportunities and resources. However, what one avoids is just as important as what one plans, if not more so: giving surety for a neighbor (11:15; 17:18; 20:16; 22:7, 26–27; 27:13); being drunk or gluttonous (20:1; 23:6–8, 17–21; 28:7); committing sexual sin (23:26–28; 29:3; possibly 27:13); and relying on a fool (26:6–11) are all foolish. In short, prudence lies in listening to parents and other wise people so that one fosters greater development in wisdom, along with various forms of self-control rather than foolish self-reliance.

Its acquisition. The acquisition of prudence, as we should expect given the prominence of fearing the Lord in 1:7, involves various dimensions of fearing God (e.g., 28:5). It requires not just avoiding the fool (14:7) but opportunities for evil as well: "The wise are cautious and turn away from evil, / but the fool throws off restraint and is careless" (14:16; also 22:3, 5; 26:17; 27:12). Prudence includes keeping God's law, as we learn from a famous verse that is rarely quoted in this proper context: "Where there is no prophecy, the people cast off restraint, / but happy are those who keep the law" (29:18; also 28:7). The vision usually promoted on this basis—"without vision the people perish"—focuses on human leadership, but actually the verse calls for nearly the opposite: restraint based on divine law. Habtu notes: "It is interesting that here we have a proverb (part of the wisdom literature) that refers to the prophets (who received *revelation*) and to keeping God's *law*."[17]

Such restraint frequently incorporates the mediation of human reproof: "A fool despises a parent's instruction, / but the one who heeds admonition is prudent" (15:5); "Those who ignore instruction despise themselves, / but those who heed admonition gain understanding" (15:32); "A rebuke strikes deeper into a discerning person / than a hundred blows into a fool" (17:10; also 19:25, 27; 22:15; 26:3; 29:15). As in 27:22, several verses acknowledge that fools can thwart the effectiveness of correction. Yet, according to 21:11, people can even learn from awareness of others being corrected: "When a scoffer is punished, the simple become wiser; / when the wise are instructed, they increase in knowledge." Prudence is gained not only from reproof addressing lawless behavior, but also from advice enabling good decisions: "Without counsel, plans go wrong, / but with many advisers they succeed" (15:22; also 19:20; 20:18; 24:5–6). Katherine Dell wryly comments: "This is the best argument for a committee that I have ever heard!"[18]

The prior two paragraphs sketch the contours of a cardinal virtue: on the one hand, virtue is defined and fully realized only in the fear of God; on the other hand, virtue incorporates various means and proximate ends. To the degree that the resulting practices—such as planning, listening, restraining speech, accepting correction, and the like—are possible for all humans as God's creatures, and

17. Habtu, "Proverbs," 783 (emphasis original).

18. Katharine J. Dell, *Seeking a Life That Matters: Wisdom for Today from the Book of Proverbs* (London: Darton, Longman & Todd, 2002), 57.

unfortunately neglected at times by Christian believers, these virtues cannot be defined with sole reference to the fear of the Lord. Of course Proverbs offers no explicit, systematic theory of cardinal virtues, but that theological framework makes the best sense of what the book says about practical wisdom. The fear of the Lord is its proper beginning and the constant orientation of the way to life. Since Proverbs scarcely could have imagined modern forms of atheism or secularity, we could not expect the book to dwell on those alternative paths. Yet its aphoristic treatment of numerous means and proximate ends, as illustrated above, and its recognition that wisdom admits of various stages and degrees and kinds, all support the possibility that some virtues are cardinal rather than solely theological. Thus humans without the fear of YHWH can partially, with different degrees and kinds of attainment, acquire virtue in certain aspects of life—thanks to God's common grace undergirding the cultures of creation. To the extent that cardinal virtues are possible, such people must acquire an element of prudence to regulate them, even if by definition their full integration is impossible without the ultimate orientation of fearing God.

Justice

The second cardinal virtue faces a similar ambiguity between nature and grace. Justice "consists in the constant and firm will to give their due to God and neighbor." Including piety before God, justice in the fullest sense integrates this with responsibility toward neighbors, disposing us "to respect the rights of each and to establish in human relationships the harmony that promotes equity with regard to persons and to the common good."[19] The Old Testament prophets consistently treat idolatry and injustice as inextricably linked. It is now popular to appear communally responsible by decrying definitions of idolatry or depictions of piety that neglect social justice. To be sure, sectors of Protestantism need to recover this biblical truth. However, it is just as true that definitive solutions to social problems involve not only dutiful acts toward neighbors but also appropriate desires. Rightly ordered worship is finally required for realizing justice. Yet that emphasis does not win as many friends or influence as many people in contemporary culture. As with other cardinal virtues, therefore, justice has proximate possibilities tied to nature by common grace, whereas an ultimate, God-centered version is tied to redemptive grace.

Before God. Proverbs asserts the value of righteousness before God on many occasions: "Treasures gained by wickedness do not profit, / but righteousness delivers from death" (10:2); "The wicked earn no real gain, / but those who sow righteousness get a true reward" (11:18); "Crooked minds are an abomination to the LORD, / but those of blameless ways are his delight" (11:20); "To do righteousness and justice / is more acceptable to the LORD than sacrifice" (21:3; also

19. *Catechism of the Catholic Church* §1807.

13:6; 19:1; 20:7; 21:7, 15, 21; 22:8; 24:15–16). Several verses hint at a divine retribution principle; God's sovereignty may even manifest itself via casting lots to resolve disputes (18:18). Other verses speak of the (ideal) king's responsibility for reward and punishment (20:8; 29:4, 14); even so, "many seek the favor of a ruler, / but it is from the LORD that one gets justice" (29:26). Righteousness involves the inside, not just the outside—"The human spirit is the lamp of the LORD, / searching every innermost part" (20:27; also 12:5; 29:27). Ultimately such righteousness reveals itself in action (20:11), not just our good intentions or high self-appraisals, which may explain hints that few are truly righteous (20:6, 9). Of course, wisdom and justice are available to a degree merely by avoiding foolish errors. In the fullest sense, though, "the evil do not understand justice, / but those who seek the LORD understand it completely" (28:5).

Among humans. For this reason, when we examine justice among humans, charity is due to others—neither optional nor supererogatory: "Some give freely, yet grow all the richer; / others withhold what is due, and only suffer want" (11:24); "The righteous know the rights of the poor; / the wicked have no such understanding" (29:7).[20] It is not that the poor are automatically righteous, but in terms of relative tendencies the implication—contra misunderstandings of the claims in Proverbs about retribution—is that they are better off than the rich: "Better to be poor and walk in integrity / than to be crooked in one's ways even though rich" (28:6). Only in this way does Proverbs affirm a preferential option for the poor, but neither does it assume that wealth automatically correlates with divine favor.

Proverbs contains numerous warnings against ill-gotten gain, presuming that this is a frequent source of amassed wealth. We have already seen 10:2 refer to "treasures gained by wickedness"; then there are other texts such as 11:1—"A false balance is an abomination to the LORD"—and 15:27—"Those who are greedy for unjust gain make trouble for their households, / but those who hate bribes will live."[21] Many texts prohibit violence, with 24:15–16 acknowledging that sometimes righteousness can offend the wicked and thereby lead unfortunately to victimization. False witness and unjust rulings constitute another form of human injustice frequently condemned: "One who justifies the wicked and one who condemns the righteous / are both alike an abomination to the LORD" (17:15); "A false witness will not go unpunished, / and a liar will not escape" (19:5); "A worthless witness

20. See 11:26; 14:31; 17:5; 18:23; and 19:7 for critical descriptions implied of those who refuse the poor; see 21:13; 24:11–12; and 29:13 on our common humanity. Additional texts oppose oppressing the poor, such as 22:16, 22–23; 23:10–12; and 28:3.

21. More generally, see 20:14, 17; 22:28; 23:10–12; and 28:24; plus 28:8 against usury. On scales see 16:11; 20:10, 23. On bribes see 17:8, 23; 18:16; and 19:6 for the reigning state of affairs, plus possibly 29:4. According to Longman 2006: 552, there is ambiguity between terms for "bribe" and "gift," as well as between most bribes (which pervert justice) and the possibility of legitimate bribes (which operate within a cultural system to make a way with people). However, if one takes certain passages to be descriptive rather than prescriptive, then descriptions of the success of bribes or gifts need not imply that bribery legitimately exists.

mocks at justice, / and the mouth of the wicked devours iniquity" (19:28).[22] The broad principle of these proscriptions appears in 11:18: "The wicked earn no real gain, / but those who sow righteousness get a true reward."

Once again, a measure of justice for human communities, and righteousness for particular people, is possible through certain basic practices that are available in principle to all. If people do not oppress or commit violence against others, if they do not pursue unjust gain or hoard all their wealth without helping others, then they will be righteous in a legitimate, though limited, sense. If a community has people who embody such righteousness, along with judges and rulers who refuse bribes and seek the truth, then the resulting justice can bring joy to everyone. Such a societal foundation is rooted in the ordered nature of God's good creation. One might explain the logic of Proverbs here by saying that through creational grace God has prepared nature. Sometimes people embody, and communal life reinforces and perpetuates, a measure of justice.

Yet overall Proverbs reflects little optimism about the extent or consistency of such virtue. Without referencing the human fall into sin directly, the book is so pervasively concerned with wicked practices—among the people of God, no less—that its anthropology can hardly be called optimistic. Moreover, righteousness and justice in the fullest sense are defined by giving God his due, not just other people their due. And God searches the heart, not just spoken claims or even outward acts. Therefore, while the fall did not destroy all possibilities of human virtue or communal justice, redemptive grace is necessary to reorient us toward the fear of the Lord, the beginning of wisdom in its robust sense. Since the fall did not destroy the nature prepared by creational grace, it is true that redeeming grace perfects nature so that God's original design might be realized. But the God-directed focus and earthly suspicion evident in the Proverbs material on justice suggest that this formulation needs more bite. Redeeming grace must in some ways transform nature—at least human nature—in order to perfect it. This transformation does not destroy created nature, but deals with the radical effects of sin and enables the full realization of God's original design, which was not a static and safe form of perfection but human growth in goodness along with development of creation's rich cultural possibilities.

Fortitude

Accordingly the next cardinal virtue, fortitude, is necessary for the poor and the righteous to endure injustice they are likely to encounter. Fortitude blends courage with patience: it "is the moral virtue that ensures firmness in difficulties and constancy in the pursuit of the good. It strengthens the resolve to resist temptations and to overcome obstacles in the moral life. The virtue of fortitude enables one to conquer fear, even fear of death, and to face trials and persecutions. It disposes

22. See 12:17, 22; 14:5; 17:26; 18:5; 19:9; 24:23–26, 28–29; 25:18; 28:21; and 29:24; with 18:17 acknowledging the difficulty of judgment.

one even to renounce and sacrifice his life in defense of a just cause."[23] William Mattison rightly points out, therefore, that "what exactly is being praised in the courageous is his dogged pursuit and grasp of the most important goods in life (faith, social justice, fellow citizens, etc.), even in the face of losing important but lesser goods (such as one's health, reputation, or even life). It is not the suffering itself that is praised."[24] Ultimately, the most important good is the fear of God, which is why fortitude is so necessary for overcoming one's vices.

Yet, by implication, fortitude is a key point at which Proverbs is anthropologically suspicious. Lots of people can talk a good game, but the necessity of parental instruction, ongoing guidance, and frequent correction all suggest that Proverbs is realistic about our persistence or lack thereof. This reality concerning the nurture of prudence exemplifies the "unity of the virtues," that attaining one is intertwined with the others. The New Testament frequently contains exhortations to develop wisdom and prayers for the Holy Spirit to grant understanding of the will of God (e.g., Rom. 12:1–3; Eph. 5:15–18; Phil. 1:9–11; Col. 1:9–10; Jas. 1:5–8). In other words, attaining justice requires knowing what to do. But one must follow through on this knowledge. A double-minded person whose pursuit is only partly sincere should not expect to receive wisdom in the first place (Jas. 1:5–8). So, to provide another crucial instance of the unity of the virtues, fortitude is necessary to attain prudence and justice. Further illustrating the point, fortitude is also essential for overcoming the obstacles to temperance, our next virtue.

Specific portrayals of fortitude as such are modest in Proverbs, even though this virtue-fostering dimension is everywhere by implication. The ground of the resistance against temptation mentioned in the *Catechism of the Catholic Church* definition is, to no one's surprise, God: "The name of the LORD is a strong tower; / the righteous run into it and are safe" (18:10). Proverbs recognizes the need to develop endurance of various kinds of suffering and acknowledges the severity of pain: "The heart knows its own bitterness, / and no stranger shares its joy" (14:10); "Even in laughter the heart is sad, / and the end of joy is grief" (14:13); "The human spirit will endure sickness; / but a broken spirit—who can bear?" (18:14). Endurance addresses not just the inner life, but more external circumstances as well: "With patience a ruler may be persuaded, / and a soft tongue can break bones" (25:15); "Like a muddied spring or a polluted fountain / are the righteous who give way before the wicked" (25:26); "The wicked flee when no one pursues, / but the righteous are as bold as a lion" (28:1).

In either type of case God provides diverse aids to sustain us: "A friend loves at all times, / and kinsfolk are born to share adversity" (17:17); "The appetite of workers works for them; / their hunger urges them on" (16:26). Proverbs does not portray fortitude merely as an accomplishment of personal heroism. Building

23. *Catechism of the Catholic Church* §1808.

24. William C. Mattison III, *Introducing Moral Theology: True Happiness and the Virtues* (Grand Rapids: Brazos, 2008), 183.

upon support from family and friends, along with occasionally making virtue out of necessities such as satisfying hunger, this virtue is the realization of how God made us to fit into the cosmos and reflect the divine character. While God's patience takes on a specific shape due to our fall into sin, it reflects more broadly the divine all-sufficiency that God has the freedom to give us the gift of time. Human fortitude ultimately reflects our fear of God above all else, our resting in the divine all-sufficiency, and as a result our appreciation of this gift of time. As we appropriate the variety of divine provisions to sustain us, we develop firmer resolve to hold fast the good that is God.

Beyond patiently resisting evil that threatens, the *Catechism of the Catholic Church* also treats overcoming obstacles as essential. As one illustration of this necessary courage, "To be a partner of a thief is to hate one's own life; / one hears the victim's curse, but discloses nothing" (29:24). Well known for enjoining courage in helping others is 24:10–12:

> If you faint in the day of adversity,
> your strength being small;
> if you hold back from rescuing those taken away to death,
> those who go staggering to the slaughter;
> if you say, "Look, we did not know this"—
> does not he who weighs the heart perceive it?
> Does not he who keeps watch over your soul know it?
> And will he not repay all according to their deeds?

To be sure, this charge could be misused to legitimate extreme action supporting whatever ideology a person wishes to claim. However, the unity of the virtues means that fortitude aligns with prudence, justice, and the like—so one is bound to be wise regarding what God actually enjoins. Proverbs 24:10–12 is not a blank check but instead confronts the person "who knows the right thing to do and fails to do it" (Jas. 4:17).

Finally, fortitude confers on the aged a particular dignity: "The glory of youths is their strength, / but the beauty of the aged is their gray hair" (Prov. 20:29). Older and wiser tend to go together, as a lifetime of enduring and attacking evil in one's life brings results: "Gray hair is a crown of glory; / it is gained in a righteous life" (16:31). One thinks of Paul, able to say toward the end of his life that "I have fought the good fight, I have finished the race, I have kept the faith. From now on there is reserved for me the crown of righteousness" (2 Tim. 4:7–8), hard won given his five lashings of thirty-nine blows each, three beatings with rods, one stoning, three shipwrecks, constant journeys and dangers, hunger and thirst, and anxiety for the church (2 Cor. 11:24–29)—which perhaps precluded his attaining gray hair. By God's mercy most of us will not endure such a litany of hardships. But neither, sadly, will most of us be able to urge others in the same way to imitate us as we imitate Christ. Yet daily some of our brothers and sisters worldwide exhibit dramatic fortitude in the face of persecution, while others enjoy the gray hair that comes with quiet fortitude in a lifetime of persistent faithfulness.

Temperance

Lastly among the cardinal virtues, temperance "moderates the attraction of pleasures and provides balance in the use of created goods."[25] Humans should not be merely instinctual like animals, but should govern their desires by wills in harmony with reason. This does not make the moral life overly intellectual or opposed to emotion, but recognizes that the potential for thinking and communicating about our choices is a crucial distinction between people and other creatures. Therefore these rational capacities must serve as a support structure for the representative vocation to which God calls human beings in the cosmos.

Such temperance requires discipline: "Whoever loves discipline loves knowledge, / but those who hate to be rebuked are stupid" (12:1). Our desires must initially change to the basic extent of welcoming discipline. Thereafter they can change in the very nature of their satisfaction: "The righteous have enough to satisfy their appetite, / but the belly of the wicked is empty" (13:25); "If you have found honey, eat only enough for you, / or else, having too much, you will vomit it" (25:16; for a social context, see 25:17). By contrast, at present "Sheol and Abaddon are never satisfied, / and human eyes are never satisfied" (27:20).

The prudence that accompanies temperance prompts saving: "Precious treasure remains in the house of the wise, / but the fool devours it" (21:20). Lacking temperance keeps us from being prudent: "Prepare your work outside, / get everything ready for you in the field; / and after that build your house" (24:27). Depictions of life without temperance become even more specific when encountering capital vices such as lust and gluttony, so the portrayal of this virtue here can be comparatively brief. For the moment, 25:28 summarizes what is at stake: "Like a city breached, without walls, / is one who lacks self-control."

The New Testament reinforces this. Temperance is a fruit of the Spirit (Gal. 5:22–23), enjoying ultimate position in the list, whereas its lack fosters several works of the flesh (5:19–21). By implication it stands behind James's emphasis on bridling the tongue and ordering desire so as to avoid the spiritual adultery involved in friendship with the world (Jas. 3–4)—another example of which lies in the excessive consumption of the rich (5:1–6). Peter urges, "Therefore prepare your minds for action; discipline yourselves. . . . Like obedient children, do not be conformed to the desires that you formerly had in ignorance" (1 Pet. 1:13–14). We must "live in reverent fear" of God (1:17), and "abstain from the desires of the flesh that wage war against the soul" (2:11), since we had time enough as pagans (4:3). It is a key feature of "false teachers" that they are not self-controlled but

25. *Catechism of the Catholic Church* §1809.

promote unbridled pursuit of pleasure (2 Pet. 2–3). Temperance is also an essential criterion for spiritual leaders in the church (1 Tim. 3:2–5, 8, 11).

One reason for this requirement is that such a leader should be "well thought of by outsiders, so that he may not fall into disgrace and the snare of the devil" (1 Tim. 3:7). The virtue list in 2 Pet. 1 provides an example of a lesser-to-greater argument urging Christians at least to meet, if not exceed, a pagan standard of virtue. In an extreme case, 1 Cor. 5:1–2 is similarly concerned about the church's reputation. So biblical teaching on temperance fits the pattern of cardinal virtues already sketched. On the one hand, as God's creatures all humans can meet some basic standards of self-restraint, sometimes to the relative shame of God's covenant people. On the other hand, the overall assessment of human culture is not optimistic: paganism generally reflects God giving people over to foolish, idolatrous, unbridled pursuit of passions, which become degrading (Rom. 1:24–32). And the situation is not getting better in these last days after the first advent of Christ: people oppose the truth with obvious folly, which can be summed up as loving pleasure rather than God (2 Tim. 3:1–9). Therefore, the grace of God must train us "to renounce impiety and worldly passions, and in the present age to live lives that are self-controlled, upright, and godly," because without a "blessed hope" fallen humans lack the incentive to pursue temperance to the full (Titus 2:11–13).

Faith

From the four cardinal virtues that, in principle anyway, are available to all by virtue of creation, our study now turns to the three theological virtues tied more particularly to redemption. The contours of faith, hope, and charity fill in most fully via divine self-revelation in Jesus Christ. Vital precursors shaping his vocation appear in the Old Testament as God works in covenant with Israel. Plus there may even be loose analogues for these theological virtues operative among pagans. Nevertheless, what ultimately defines trust is not the basic and pervasive human need for it but rather its object—which, for Proverbs, starts and ends with God the Creator. Theologians speak of faith as having objective and subjective dimensions: *fides quae*, those elements we believe, and *fides qua*, the element of personal response by which we trust. *Fides quae* ("the faith") is largely absent from Proverbs in terms of direct claims about God in which people must believe. Formulas such as "the fear of the LORD," though, stake an objective claim regarding the particular God to whom all creatures owe allegiance, *fides qua*.

Upright conduct. Among the relevant Proverbs passages, several associate fear of God with upright conduct: "Those who walk uprightly fear the LORD, / but one who is devious in conduct despises him" (14:2); "By loyalty and faithfulness iniquity is atoned for, / and by the fear of the LORD one avoids evil" (16:6); "Do not let your heart envy sinners, / but always continue in the fear of the LORD" (23:17, with relevant context down through 23:21). Notice the parallelism between fidelity (faith vocabulary) and fear of the Lord, especially since the latter occupies conceptual space similar to faith in the New Testament: fear of the Lord is essential to *both* the beginning of walking the path (whether in terms of wisdom or salvation) *and* each step of its continuation. By implication the fear of God deals with the pious heart from which upright conduct springs: "The sacrifice of the wicked is an abomination to the LORD, / but the prayer of the upright is his delight" (15:8); "When one will not listen to the law, / even one's prayers are an abomination" (28:9).

Humility. Loving the God of Torah from the heart means, as we saw concerning prudence, not pursuing one's own path: "There is a way that seems right to a person, / but its end is the way to death" (14:12); "The fear of the LORD is instruction in wisdom, / and humility goes before honor" (15:33); "All our steps are ordered by the LORD; / how then can we understand our own ways?" (20:24). Humility was not a cardinal virtue for the Greeks, but is prominent in the Christian tradition, which tends to see pride as an idolatrous root of sin, maybe even of the other capital vices. Though not named among the theological virtues as such, humility is vital to a Christian account of the moral life—ingredient in hope and charity while distinctively implied by the concept of faith. Humility has its blessings: "The reward for humility and fear of the LORD / is riches and honor and life" (22:4); "The greedy person stirs up strife, / but whoever trusts in the LORD will be enriched. / Those who trust in their own wits are fools; / but those who walk in wisdom come through safely" (28:25–26). One distinctive mode of operation for the humble person is confession of sin: "No one who conceals transgressions will prosper, / but one who confesses and forsakes them will obtain mercy. / Happy is the one who is never without fear, / but one who is hard-hearted will fall into calamity" (28:13–14).

Besides riches, honor, life, safety, mercy, and happiness, the humble fear of God offers a divine refuge and thereby confidence for oneself and one's children (14:26–27). Freedom from trouble often accompanies great treasure, in which people tend otherwise to place their confidence (15:16). Alongside these blessings of faith Proverbs names secure rest (19:23), strength to bring down strongholds in which others wrongly trust (21:22, 31), avoidance of the trap of fearing others (29:25), and justice from the Lord (29:26; also 16:20). Underlying the typical promise of these benefits is a strong conception of divine sovereignty. The aforementioned text regarding justice, 29:26, juxtaposes God's with the ruler's favor, in which people are tempted to trust. The sphere of God's rule is comprehensive: human hearts or spirits (15:11; 17:3; 20:27), human plans (16:3), the wicked (16:4), the steps of implementation for human plans (16:9; 20:24), and the decision of the lot (16:33). Divine and kingly rule correlate more positively in some places (e.g., 24:21–22); sometimes the king mediates God's justice to the people. But even if he does not, no power can finally gainsay our ultimate need to fear only God.

Wisdom. Yet faith is not equivalent to credulity: "The simple believe everything, / but the clever consider their steps" (14:15). Not only should we avoid believing everything; neither should we trust just anyone: "Like a bad tooth or a lame foot / is trust in a faithless person in time of trouble" (25:19). Obviously we need to avoid trusting in fools. The fear of God instructs in wisdom, not anti-intellectualism (15:33); faith seeks understanding. What is crucial about faith is not its subjective quality, as if it were opposed to reason; rather, its importance lies in linking us to trustworthy objects—in the end, God. Hence we must listen to wise words and apply our minds to divine teaching, growing in readiness to speak such words to others—so that our "trust may be in the LORD" (22:17–21, esp. 22:19).

Hope

Hope and faith are very closely connected, since "faith is the assurance of things hoped for, the conviction of things not seen.... Whoever would approach [God] must believe that he exists and that he rewards those who seek him" (Heb. 11:1, 6). Without frequently using the word, Proverbs therefore addresses hope pervasively, reassuring us that God will indeed bless those who are righteous with life, while those who spurn wisdom eventually fall into folly's deadly traps: "The hope of the righteous ends in gladness, / but the expectation of the wicked comes to nothing" (Prov. 10:28).

Positively. Wisdom is a tree of life by which humans may hope to flourish. "Those who trust in their riches will wither, / but the righteous will flourish like green leaves. / Those who trouble their households will inherit wind, / and the fool will be servant to the wise. / The fruit of the righteous is a tree of life, / but violence takes lives away" (11:28–30). Its focus is the present time: "Hope deferred makes the heart sick, / but a desire fulfilled is a tree of life" (13:12); "the light of the eyes rejoices the heart, / and good news refreshes the body" (15:30). Even so, Proverbs is not naïve in its understanding of retribution. Its understanding of life focuses on temporal experience of blessing but encompasses future promises, even if their meaning and scope remain undefined.

Hope motivates not only pursuit of wisdom, but also its promotion in others: "Discipline your children while there is hope; / do not set your heart on their destruction" (19:18). The vocabulary here refers to the time of simplicity in which young people may still choose wisdom over folly. But the context puts hope's larger range in view as well: if the young people respond well, they may avoid destruction and the parents may rejoice in their flourishing. Wisdom offers to young people the sweetness, like honey, of a divinely granted future (24:13–14). Among other temporal incentives for pursuing wisdom is the opportunity to live in peace, even with enemies (16:7).

Negatively. More than clarifying details of the future, Proverbs concerns itself with denying hope in wickedness, strength, riches, and other deadly alternatives: "When the wicked die, their hope perishes, / and the expectation of the godless comes to nothing" (11:7, in addition to texts already mentioned). Promising that "surely there is a future, / and your hope will not be cut off," in context 23:18 warns against envying sinners or placing one's hope in companionship with gluttons and drunkards. Similarly, "Do not fret because of evildoers. / Do not envy the wicked; / for the evil have no future; / the lamp of the wicked will go out" (24:19–20). Hope cannot be placed wisely in human strength or in the future's predictability: "Do not boast about tomorrow, / for you do not know what a day may bring" (27:1).

Proverbs is not unrealistic about ordinary anxieties: "Anxiety weighs down the human heart, / but a good word cheers it up" (12:25; also 13:12); "A tranquil mind gives life to the flesh, / but passion makes the bones rot" (14:30); "A glad heart makes a cheerful countenance, / but by sorrow of heart the spirit is broken" (15:13); "A cheerful heart is a good medicine, / but a downcast spirit dries up the bones" (17:22); "Like cold water to a thirsty soul, / so is good news from a far country" (25:25). These acknowledgments are important because they reveal that biblical hope is grounded in reality rather than Pollyanna-like escapism.

Eschatologically. Contra Nietzschean critiques of Christianity as world-denying, biblical eschatology recognizes both that good cheer is healthy and that it often needs proximate, not just ultimate, incentives. These proximate incentives—an encouraging word, a tranquil mind that triumphs over anxiety, good news, and the like—have full significance only within a wise life devoted to fearing God. Life must lie at the end, not just in the middle, of the path, and God must eventually smooth out the inevitable inequities of how the wise and the foolish experience life in the here and now.

The ambiguity in Proverbs regarding an afterlife need not weaken biblical eschatology. It can actually strengthen Christian hope by affirming the divine blessing of life even without any precise calendar of future events. The book's efforts to downplay or deny the success of the wicked serve as Exhibit A acknowledging apparent evidence to the contrary, for now at any rate. Proverbs robustly confirms the final value of wisdom without needing to answer every apparent challenge in the interim or ascertain every desired detail about the future. The hope of Proverbs is not irrational but, to the contrary, we must learn that rationality is not entirely based on present experience. Proverbs contains eschatological implications without utterly separating them from particular earthly blessings. The book is not naïve about our lack of guarantees in this present life, and therefore it highlights the ultimacy of fearing God, while nevertheless buttressing that ultimacy with legitimate penultimate incentives: "But strive first for the kingdom of God and his righteousness, and all these things will be given to you as well" (Matt. 6:33).

There is a great lesson in this: we trust in what we do not (yet) see, a reward for those who diligently seek God (Heb. 11:1, 6). Proper hope mitigates the extremes of presumption and despair, which are born of pride. Though we do not currently observe perfect justice, for affirmations of wisdom's value to count requires placing our hope in a God of transcendent justice—justice we may not presently grasp in full. At the same time, Proverbs helps us to observe the many small reassurances that are rooted in God's continual reaffirmation of his design for creation to enjoy *shalom*.

Charity

Hence, finally, we arrive at the pinnacle of the Christian virtues: "And now faith, hope, and love abide, these three; and the greatest of these is love" (1 Cor. 13:13). Augustine treats even the cardinal virtues as forms of love: "This means that our love for him must be preserved whole and unblemished, which is the work of temperance; that it must not give way before misfortune, which is the work of fortitude; that it must serve no one but him, which is the work of justice; and finally, that it be vigilant in its discernment of things so as not to be undermined gradually by trickery or deceit, and this is the work of prudence" (*The Catholic and Manichaean Ways of Life* 15.25, in FC 56.38). In some respects humility is the root of the virtues and charity is the fruit; in another sense charity is the "root and mother" of the rest, according to Thomas Aquinas, since moral life is a matter of loving God and neighbor.[26] In their own ways both humility and charity oppose pride, the fundamental sin that turns our propensity for idolatry in self-serving directions.

The term "charity" guards against unhelpfully broad connotations of the word "love," without conveying a narrow focus on almsgiving or on Christian distinctiveness to the point of being irrelevant for humanity in general: "Charity perfects, rather than destroys or leaves untouched, good natural loves like friendship, parental love, and romantic love."[27] Nonetheless, charity is revealed distinctively and definitively in Jesus, oriented first and foremost to the triune God who redeems us in Christ. Charity involves seeking the good of others in light of God's love for them. Divine revelation is the only source for knowing truly what that good involves.

Obligation. Given the connection in Proverbs between charity and justice, it is our obligation to be generous toward others in need. Acts of almsgiving, therefore, in principle are incumbent upon everyone. Obviously, though, many fail entirely, and all of us fail frequently, to fulfill this obligation. Moreover, many who perform the obligatory outward acts fail to render these alms for the sake of God and neighbor, so that their motivations prevent the acts from being genuinely charitable, even if justice is done.[28]

26. Thomas Aquinas, *Summa theologiae* 2a2ae QQ. 23–27, 161.

27. Mattison, *Introducing Moral Theology*, 292; as well as the worked example of this principle in Alan Jacobs, *A Theology of Reading: The Hermeneutics of Love* (Boulder, CO: Westview, 2001).

28. Wolterstorff's *Justice: Rights and Wrongs* may help us to see how justice establishes certain rights for the poor without necessarily having one-to-one correspondence to specified obligations of charity for particular persons in particular situations. Lurking here is the question of how charity can be both a general duty for the wise and a matter of particular degrees or even supererogation. Part of the resolution to this dilemma may lie in ethics more oriented around virtues (following the pattern of Jesus) than rules. Obligations may play a secondary role in communicating the shape of Jesus's pattern. But they will

Generosity and blessing. Proverbs does not solve every theological and ethical conundrum at this juncture, but instead depicts the blessedness of the generosity involved: "Those who are kind reward themselves, / but the cruel do themselves harm" (11:17); "Some give freely, yet grow all the richer; / others withhold what is due, and only suffer want. / A generous person will be enriched, / and one who gives water will get water" (11:24–25); in a striking metaphor, "Whoever is kind to the poor lends to the LORD, / and will be repaid in full" (19:17; also 14:21, 31; 21:13, 26; 22:9; 28:27). The underlying view of possessions is that, used moderately, they are means to shared joy whereas, used immoderately, they deceive us into pursuing happiness the wrong way: "Better is a dinner of vegetables where love is / than a fatted ox and hatred with it" (15:17). Today's prosperity gospels latch on to the linkage between generosity and blessing without emphasizing equally and adequately the nature of true blessing—not to mention the warnings of Proverbs against latching on to wealth in itself.

Mercy. Help is necessary at times for everyone, and God graciously meets this need through family, friends, and neighbors. However, some are truer friends than others: "Some friends play at friendship / but a true friend sticks closer than one's nearest kin" (18:24). Given the strong dependence on family in the context from which this proverb stems, it contains a remarkable affirmation of friendship! Family members, though, do not always meet our need: "Do not forsake your friend or the friend of your parent; / do not go to the house of your kindred in the day of your calamity. / Better is a neighbor who is nearby / than kindred who are far away" (27:10).

Mercy is not just for loved ones or even other humans, but also for one's animals: "The righteous know the needs of their animals, / but the mercy of the wicked is cruel" (12:10). Charity is a disposition that pervades a life, consistently displayed—or not—across a wide range of interactions. It is not just being kind to friends or superiors through whom one wishes to get ahead. It may require great sacrifice, enabled by fortitude (24:10–12). Charity may not always specify exact duty, but its concern for particular people, as well as justice in general, affects our obligations.

Reconciliation. Another form of mercy is covering offenses: "Hatred stirs up strife, / but love covers all offenses" (10:12); "One who forgives an affront fosters friendship, / but one who dwells on disputes will alienate a friend" (17:9). Alternatively, it can be an act of genuine charity to confront error: "Better is open rebuke / than hidden love. / Well meant are the wounds a friend inflicts, / but profuse are the kisses of an enemy" (27:5–6); "Iron sharpens iron, / and one person sharpens the wits of another" (27:17). Rather than fostering strife or despising our neighbors (also 14:21), we ought to promote the peace and well-being of the community—which may sometimes entail neglecting offenses while at other times requiring gracious confrontation.

---

frequently concern standards of character that people ought to develop, rather than rules for one and only one act appropriate to a given situation.

Pedagogy and prudence. Beyond particular verses enjoining charity, Proverbs embodies loving effort on the part of parents and community leaders to inculcate the pursuit of virtue. The book is loving in both its desired end and its patient implementation, recognizing the initial simplicity and many potential pitfalls faced by the young. The pedagogy is firm yet tender, avoiding the urbane, banal tolerance so tempting for present-day communities. Proverbs is heartily realistic, acknowledging that patience cannot be endless. Past a certain point, people are unlikely or even unable to reform, humanly speaking—so no one should bother casting wise pearls before such swine. Charity does not mean hopeless naïveté about the likelihood of turning people around, which could be dangerous to the wise. Love for the wise and for the community as a whole involves limitations in speaking to the foolish and the self-sufficient.

In other ways too Proverbs cautions well-meaning friends—like Job's!—regarding how they can and cannot help others. "Like vinegar on a wound / is one who sings songs to a heavy heart. / Like a moth in clothing or a worm in wood, / sorrow gnaws at the human heart" (25:20; also 14:10). Therefore, "what is desirable in a person is loyalty" (19:22). Charity must be integrated with prudence: "And this is my prayer, that your love may overflow more and more with knowledge and full insight to help you to determine what is best, so that in the day of Christ you may be pure and blameless, having produced the harvest of righteousness that comes through Jesus Christ for the glory and praise of God" (Phil. 1:9–11).

Seven Capital Vices

By contrast, however, humans are brimming over with selfish folly, with idolatry instead of fidelity to God and with injustice instead of charity. The corresponding vices are misleadingly known as the "seven deadly sins." Films, documentaries, and books now explore this paradigm, though sometimes to celebrate the sins. But the resulting focus on particular acts already distorts what the paradigm intends to address. The capital vices are sinful dispositions from which other sins spring, like roots to flowers or trees. As such they deal with the heart—too closely for anyone's comfort. Thereby they offer a recipe not for legalism or despair, but for the self-knowledge joined to new life in Christ. Accordingly there is no division between cardinal and theological vices; all these vices appear as what they truly are only when we have heard God's word about the disordered desire that results in our current condition. At the same time, each has elements that are recognizably problematic even among pagans.

Precise listings in the Christian tradition are several.[29] For the sake of simplicity and economy, here seven are treated, with vainglory under the heading of pride. It

29. See Jeffrey P. Greenman, "Seven Deadly Sins," in *Dictionary of Scripture and Ethics*, ed. Joel B. Green et al. (Grand Rapids: Baker, forthcoming) and Rebecca Konyndyk DeYoung, *Glittering Vices: A New Look at the Seven Deadly Sins and Their Remedies* (Grand Rapids: Brazos, 2009), for shorter and

is tempting to see seven as involving completion plus hinting at the seven spirits more wicked than the exorcised demon of Luke 11:24–26, which refill the house of the unredeemed sinner.[30] Mere attempts to avoid the deadly sins with sheer willpower never finally suffice; to avoid the underlying vices and not just their outward manifestations, one must instead come to fear the Lord. As Proverbs pervasively makes clear, there are only two ways—there is no agnostic third. One cannot lastingly rid oneself of a vice without turning to virtue, ingredient to which is the fear of God: "Whatever does not proceed from faith is sin" (Rom. 14:23).

Thus pride is usually taken to be the cardinal root of these capital vices.[31] No ordered relationship between the others has won the day. Here we shall proceed in reverse order of Dante, whose circles of hell and terraces of the purgatorial mountain imply that the respective vices descend farther and farther away from the fear of God, while the ascent toward purity must begin with confronting pride. The overall order—lust, gluttony, avarice, sloth, wrath, envy, pride—moves increasingly toward true charity, with everyone exercising their freedom in light of various loves. For Dante the latter three distinctly harm others via love of self; sloth is defective love for God, without one's whole heart; and the former three involve excessive love for creaturely goods relative to God. Of course, the very flexibility of lists from the Christian tradition, concerning both content and order, acknowledges the variety of interrelationships among our disordered desires.

Lust

The present list begins with the "deadly sin" that is subject to the most mockery in contemporary Western culture. The Christian tradition is treated, by many theologians no less, as a source of body-denying prudery (at best) and repression (at worst). No doubt there are unhealthy elements among classic Christian thinkers regarding sexual ethics, yet far from simply despising the body they recognized its integral influence in a person more acutely than many contemporaries do. Precisely our appreciation of physical goods "requires that we not try to use them to satiate our spiritual needs," which drive so much lust as "the habit of trying to engineer my own happiness for myself, on my own terms."[32] Lust flowers from roots in pride.

longer profiles, in addition to Evagrius of Pontus, *The Greek Ascetic Corpus*, trans. Robert E. Sinkewicz, Oxford Early Christian Studies (Oxford: Oxford University Press, 2003); John Cassian, *The Monastic Institutes*, esp. book 5, trans. Jerome Bertram (London: St. Austin, 1999); John Climacus, *The Ladder of Divine Ascent*, trans. Colm Luibheid and Norm Russell, Classics of Western Spirituality (New York: Paulist, 1982); Gregory the Great, *Morals on the Book of Job*, esp. book 16, in Library of Fathers of the Holy Catholic Church 18, 21, 23, 31; Thomas Aquinas, *Summa theologiae* 1a2ae QQ. 49–89, esp. QQ. 61–62 on the virtues and Q. 84 on the vices; and *Catechism of the Catholic Church* §1866.

30. Solomon Schimmel, *The Seven Deadly Sins: Jewish, Christian, and Classical Reflections on Human Psychology* (Oxford: Oxford University Press, 1997), 24.

31. Suitable allowances must be made for pride's various manifestations, including (as feminist theologians rightly note) the despair that stems from failing to meet dominant expectations imposed by others.

32. DeYoung, *Glittering Vices*, 166–67.

Much of the Proverbs material on lust already surfaced in Prov. 1–9. If such texts depict not only physical but also spiritual adultery, that is fitting because the latter too involves dynamics of covenant-breaking self-love. Proverbs does not altogether stop warning of these dangers after Prov. 9: "The mouth of a loose woman is a deep pit; / he with whom the LORD is angry falls into it" (22:14; also 11:22; 23:26–28; 29:3), where the adulteress is an instrument of divine punishment.

Hence loving pleasure can lead to poverty: "Whoever loves pleasure will suffer want; / whoever loves wine and oil will not be rich" (21:17); people dominated by desire wind up spending all day scheming over how to do evil (e.g., 21:25–26; 24:8–9). However, some people counteract such unbridled desire: "The desire of the righteous ends only in good; / the expectation of the wicked in wrath" (11:23; also 11:27 and 13:19). Victory over lust, therefore, lies not in becoming creatures without desire—an impossible task. To the contrary, victory lies in reordering the object, nature, and extent of our desires so that righteousness replaces evil, self-interested scheming. With respect to sex in particular, a healthy marriage can be a crucial component of such reordered desire. Yet people should not be naïve, as many well-intended abstinence campaigns appear to be, about marital sex solving the problem of lust. Proverbs starts sooner, with simple youth needing to hear over and over from parents about the spiritual and earthly dangers of sexual error—an ounce of prevention being worth a pound of cure. Implicit in many of these appeals are other elements of *shalom*, appropriately desired by the righteous person growing in wisdom: a good name, adequate resources, security, social harmony rather than strife, and so forth. Unfortunately, these too can become disordered, as several other vices demonstrate.

It is not good enough, in other words, simply to fight lust with desire for wealth or status. These expedients may prevent self-destructive external acts, but they are unlikely to produce internal transformation by themselves. They point instead to God's design, which we must now undergo new creation to realize. When Augustine was seeking God but torn over his lust, crying "give me chastity, but not yet," eventually he heard a voice telling him to "take up and read" Rom. 13:12–14: "The night is far gone, the day is near. Let us then lay aside the works of darkness and put on the armor of light; let us live honorably as in the day, not in reveling and drunkenness, not in debauchery and licentiousness, not in quarreling and jealousy. Instead, put on the Lord Jesus Christ, and make no provision for the flesh, to gratify its desires." Only in submitting to the Lord Jesus Christ do people really gain freedom from serving fleshly lusts. But the exhortation makes clear that even those who have put on Christ must still choose to live in the light of day—figuratively and literally.

Gluttony

Christian tradition recognizes that vices—like virtues—are linked: "The Fathers believed that the pleasures of the table, in particular, lead inexorably to those of the flesh. Then it's but a few steps farther to jealousy, anger, violence, and the spiritual sloth that destroys the soul. . . . The way to a man's heart is through his stomach. Well, perhaps not to his heart exactly."[33] Gluttony is not as simple as eating or enjoying too much. The acronym FRESH summarizes the variety of errors: "eating fastidiously, ravenously, excessively, sumptuously, hastily."[34] Gluttony embodies pride regarding food, using it to satisfy the soul apart from God. While this may be a matter of binges, comfort food, fast food, and the like, alternatively there could be wrongful asceticism, weight control preoccupation, or devotion to delicacies. Today all of us need to face other uncomfortable questions, for example with respect to our culture's dependence on factory farming, particularly of animals for meat. Undoubtedly this reflects avarice and other vices, but it also hints that our belly is our god (Phil. 3:19): we insist on having it our way, exactly when we want it, without any cost.

Food. Proverbs associates the wicked with such craving: "The LORD does not let the righteous go hungry, / but he thwarts the craving of the wicked" (10:3). According to 20:13, God provides for righteous people who work: "Do not love sleep, or else you will come to poverty; / open your eyes, and you will have plenty of bread." God meets the genuine needs of our bellies. Still, really full satisfaction is found elsewhere: "From the fruit of the mouth one's stomach is satisfied; / the yield of the lips brings satisfaction" (18:20). In other words, this intriguing juxtaposition regarding the mouth locates full delight in righteousness and wisdom, as displayed for instance in timely speech. Meanwhile, more mundanely true satisfaction from food actually requires moderation—neither too little nor too much: "If you have found honey, eat only enough for you, / or else, having too much, you will vomit it" (25:16); "It is not good to eat much honey, / or to seek honor on top of honor" (25:27); "The sated appetite spurns honey, / but to a ravenous appetite even the bitter is sweet" (27:7). How many of us, though, must admit to grabbing extra items of food at parties or the dinner table, with bizarre awareness that we long more to possess them in place of others than to eat them for genuine enjoyment?

Drink. Proverbs confronts these and other follies, such as drunkenness: "Wine is a mocker, strong drink a brawler, / and whoever is led astray by it is not wise" (20:1); "Whoever loves pleasure will suffer want; / whoever loves wine and oil will not be rich" (21:17); "Do not be among winebibbers, / or among gluttonous eaters of meat; / for the drunkard and the glutton will come to poverty, / and drowsiness will clothe them with rags" (23:20–21). Indeed, gluttony easily fosters other vices such as sloth. Proverbs treats the dangers of wine at length:

> Who has woe? Who has sorrow?
> Who has strife? Who has complaining?

33. Aviad Kleinberg, *Seven Deadly Sins: A Very Partial List*, trans. Susan Emanuel (Cambridge, MA: Belknap, 2008), 83–84.

34. DeYoung, *Glittering Vices*, 141.

Who has wounds without cause?
    Who has redness of eyes?
Those who linger late over wine,
    those who keep trying mixed wines.
Do not look at wine when it is red,
    when it sparkles in the cup
    and goes down smoothly.
At the last it bites like a serpent,
    and stings like an adder.
Your eyes will see strange things,
    and your mind utter perverse things.
You will be like one who lies down in the midst of the sea,
    like one who lies on the top of a mast.
"They struck me," you will say, "but I was not hurt;
    they beat me, but I did not feel it.
When shall I awake?
    I will seek another drink." (23:29–35)

The Bible does not require total abstinence from alcohol. Neither does it teach "avoid drunkenness and do what you like." A healthy sense of caution is necessary for avoiding gluttony, whether regarding food or drink.

Some passages recognize the social dimensions involved: "When you sit down to eat with a ruler, / observe carefully what is before you, / and put a knife to your throat / if you have a big appetite. / Do not desire the ruler's delicacies, / for they are deceptive food" (23:1–3). Daniel 1 narrates an example of the spiritual issues related to such delicacies. For Daniel and his friends to eat the Babylonian king's food would signal their acquiescence to cultural captivity. At a more mundane level, the ruler might simply be testing a person's restraint or proclaiming his own largesse, so one should not assume that the delicacies are offered entirely for consumption. Gluttony has other social implications even closer to home: "Those who keep the law are wise children, / but companions of gluttons shame their parents" (Prov. 28:7). In short, while preoccupation with reputation presents several dangers—soon to surface concerning envy, vainglory, and pride—there remains a healthy form of social awareness about perceptions of self-control. Others should perceive us as worshipers of the living and true God rather than of our own bellies.

The New Testament reaffirms this basic teaching: "Anyone unwilling to work should not eat." And the apostle Paul exemplifies avoiding idleness and earning one's keep (2 Thess. 3:6–13). Against excessive scrupulousness and seared consciences alike, "whether you eat or drink, or whatever you do, do everything for the glory of God" (1 Cor. 10:31). Food and drink themselves are divine gifts: "Everything created by God is good, and nothing is to be rejected, provided it is received with thanksgiving; for it is sanctified by God's word and by prayer" (1 Tim. 4:4–5). Because "whatever goes into the mouth enters the stomach, and goes out into the sewer," the real issue is what comes out of the mouth; that is what defiles (Matt. 15:17–20). Food and drink matter insofar as God grants us temporary enjoyment amid the basic necessities of life. Rather than taking the opportunity for grateful worship, though, humans often become idolatrous consumers instead.

Avarice

Like lust and gluttony, avarice deals with misshapen desire—albeit somewhat differently: "Aquinas describes greed's object as money, or whatever money can buy, *considered as useful or profitable*. Lust and gluttony, on the other hand, desire things insofar as they give us physical *pleasure*."[35] So, at the beginning anyway, avarice relates to pleasure more instrumentally. Eventually, and ironically, this form of curvature inward toward the self substitutes money for what it buys. Emblematically the usurer tries to make money from money rather than from labor, with money replacing everything else of value such as friendship or love. The extent of such tragedy renders greed "a sort of spiritual dropsy": "It is characterized by an insatiable thirst for water even though the body is already filled with fluid. Physical and spiritual dropsy are similar also in that the more the afflicted person tries to satisfy his thirst, the more his thirst is stimulated."[36]

In classical understanding, virtues stand between extremes of vice on either side. The virtue opposed by avarice is liberality, freely and artfully using money to meet the needs of others and oneself. Prodigality that wastes money also violates liberality and may even count as avaricious; while lacking a form of attachment to money that leads to careful management, such wastefulness nevertheless reflects excessive desire. Conversely, the stingy person whose spending habits seem prudent may in fact be avaricious too, hoarding money out of misshapen desire for enjoyment in the future or for money itself. Small wonder, then, that "the love of money is a root of all kinds of evil" (1 Tim. 6:10). John Cassian treats Judas's betrayal of Christ as avaricious, learning thereby that "avarice moves us to betray one another's humanness. In so doing, we betray our own humanity as well. One of the more striking illustrations in scripture is Ahab and Jezebel's murder of Naboth to acquire his vineyard. The story concludes with this telling line: 'Indeed, there was no one like Ahab, who *sold himself* to do what was evil in the sight of the Lord, urged on by his wife Jezebel' (1 Kings 21:25; emphasis added)."[37] As with other vices, pride underlies avaricious forms of self-aggrandizement—only to lose the freedom and dignity of the self so prized.

Ill-gotten gain is actually unprofitable. Proverbs confronts avarice variously. First and most obviously: "Wealth hastily gotten will dwindle, / but those who gather little by little will increase it" (13:11; also 20:21); "Those who are greedy for unjust gain make trouble for their households, / but those who hate bribes

35. Ibid., 109.
36. Schimmel, *Seven Deadly Sins*, 188.
37. DeYoung, *Glittering Vices*, 110–11.

will live" (15:27); "Bread gained by deceit is sweet, / but afterward the mouth will be full of gravel" (20:17); "A ruler who lacks understanding is a cruel oppressor; / but one who hates unjust gain will enjoy a long life" (28:16; also 10:2; 11:6; 21:6; 22:16; 28:3, 8). This catena of texts associates wickedness, bribery, deceit, oppression, and usury with get-rich-quick schemes. Many people would be willing to reject most items on that list while simultaneously preferring speedy ways of wealth acquisition over labor-intensive, long-term projects. For Proverbs, however, the fruitfulness of wealth is tied to flourishing in its means of acquisition—only thereby can one flourish with others in its means of enjoyment. We must not, therefore, exonerate ourselves merely for avoiding criminal behavior, lest we gain wealth improperly by a wider variety of means. Improper means do not constitute avarice in themselves, whereas someone using proper means—and even lacking wealth—can likewise be full of avaricious desire. But in the cases quoted above, the improper means manifest the underlying avarice; that is the nature of a capital vice.

The acquisition of wealth involves complex factors. Proverbs acknowledges that sovereign divine blessing brings wealth: "The faithful will abound with blessings, / but one who is in a hurry to be rich will not go unpunished" (28:20); "The blessing of the LORD makes rich, / and he adds no sorrow with it" (10:22). However, there are human factors too that, as we have just seen, are not always positive: "The timid become destitute, / but the aggressive gain riches" (11:16); "Why should fools have a price in hand / to buy wisdom, when they have no mind to learn?" (17:16). Despite what some of these scriptures suggest about God's provision, it remains true from another perspective that people often gain wealth in the wrong ways and the wrong people have it. Moreover, appearances can be deceiving: "Some pretend to be rich, yet have nothing; / others pretend to be poor, yet have great wealth" (13:7).

Wealth benefits those who do not hold on to it too tightly. Proverbs acknowledges the reality that people need money to function in society: "The wealth of the rich is their fortress; / the poverty of the poor is their ruin" (10:15); "Wealth brings many friends, / but the poor are left friendless" (19:4). Proverbs acknowledges wealth's necessity while hinting at irony: "The wealth of the rich is their strong city; / in their imagination it is like a high wall" (18:11); "Wealth is a ransom for a person's life, / but the poor get no threats" (13:8). In the latter case, without attracting kidnappers one would need no ransom. In the former case, beyond perceptive description there is a suggestion of implicit problems—the temptation for the rich is to substitute their wealth in place of YHWH as their refuge. "As for those who in the present age are rich, command them not to be haughty, or to set their hopes on the uncertainty of riches, but rather on God who richly provides us with everything for our enjoyment" (1 Tim. 6:17).

Divine blessing frequently flows in relation to generosity. First Timothy 6:18–19 continues by saying, with respect to the rich, that "they are to do good, to be rich in good works, generous, and ready to share, thus storing up for themselves the treasure of a good foundation for the future, so that they may take hold of the life that really is life." Greater eschatological fullness after the resurrection of Christ, combined with Christianity's marginal position in the Roman Empire, impels the New Testament's relatively greater focus on eschatological treasure. Proverbs, though, sees earthly correlation between stinginess and eventual want, or generosity and blessing: "Whoever gives to the poor will lack nothing, / but one who turns a blind eye will get many a curse" (28:27; also 28:8, 22). The "life that is really life" involves both solidly anchored hope for the future and, oftentimes, enjoyment of God's temporal provision.

This is consistent with the underlying perspective of Proverbs concerning ultimate profit: "Riches do not profit in the day of wrath, / but righteousness delivers from death" (11:4; also 11:6); "In the house of the righteous there is much treasure, / but trouble befalls the income of the wicked" (15:6); "Better is a little with the fear of the LORD / than great treasure and trouble with it. / Better is a dinner of vegetables where love is / than a fatted ox and hatred with it" (15:16–17); "Better is a little with righteousness / than large income with injustice" (16:8); "It is better to be of a lowly spirit among the poor / than to divide the spoil with the proud" (16:19); "Better is a dry morsel with quiet / than a house full of feasting with strife" (17:1); "Better the poor walking with integrity / than one perverse of speech who is a fool" (19:1); "There is gold, and abundance of costly stones; / but the lips informed by knowledge are a precious jewel" (20:15); "A good name is to be chosen rather than great riches, / and favor is better than silver or gold" (22:1); "Do not wear yourself out to get rich; / be wise enough to desist. / When your eyes light upon it, it is gone; / for suddenly it takes wings to itself, / flying like an eagle toward heaven" (23:4–5); "The rich is wise in self-esteem, / but an intelligent poor person sees through the pose" (28:11; also 28:6).

The rhetorical purpose of quoting so many passages is to establish the prominence of the Proverbs theme that riches do not offer ultimate profit. Scholars debate the exact contours of the book's approach to wealth.[38] Perhaps the debate stems not only from preoccupation with unanswerable questions about original authors, settings, and editors, but also from common inability to appreciate the sapiential nature of the material. Proverbs offers myriad sayings with various perspectives, resulting not only in aggregate balance but also in contingent resources for pastoral use. In some settings the value of wealth as a necessary resource and an element of divine blessing should be acknowledged. In other settings emphasis must lie on potential dangers: wealth as a false refuge supplanting God, a means pretending to be an end or pointing merely to proximate ends, or a (mistaken) end that people seek inappropriately or excessively. If contemporary people complain that Proverbs and the Christian tradition criticize earthly goods too strongly, that may reveal our pastoral imbalance more than the tradition's weakness. If,

38. See especially Raymond C. Van Leeuwen, "Wealth and Poverty: System and Contradiction in Proverbs," *Hebrew Studies* 33 (1992): 25–36.

alternatively, contemporary people complain that Proverbs and the Christian tradition are too conservative in valuing moderate wealth as a typical result of hard work, then possibly that reveals more about our political commitments or contingent circumstances and the relative emphases they elicit. Nevertheless, Proverbs contains the resources not for flaccid balance, but instead to address whichever extremes a cultural moment affords. We should not be naïve about the dangerous temptation to interpret Proverbs through bourgeois lenses that justify comforts we hold dear.

God made us to work for money that meets our families' needs and provides moderate delights enjoyed as divine gifts. Yet wealth confronts sinful humans with idolatrous and oppressive dangers. To look ahead: "Give me neither poverty nor riches; / feed me with the food that I need, / or I shall be full, and deny you, / and say, 'Who is the LORD?' / or I shall be poor, and steal, / and profane the name of my God" (30:8–9). Or, in the words of a later echo, "Give us this day our daily bread" (Matt. 6:11).

Sloth

According to Proverbs, divine provision is usually mediated via hard work, with laziness a crucial factor behind much poverty: "A slack hand causes poverty, / but the hand of the diligent makes rich" (10:4); "Those who till their land will have plenty of food, / but those who follow worthless pursuits have no sense" (12:11; also 12:24, 27); "In all toil there is profit, / but mere talk leads only to poverty" (14:23); "The way of the lazy is overgrown with thorns, / but the path of the upright is a level highway" (15:19); "One who is slack in work / is close kin to a vandal" (18:9); "The lazy person buries a hand in the dish, / and will not even bring it back to the mouth" (19:24; also 16:26; 19:15; 20:4, 13; 21:25–26; 24:30–34; 26:14–15; 28:19).

Beyond sometimes factoring into poverty, laziness is also shameful: "A child who gathers in summer is prudent, / but a child who sleeps in harvest brings shame" (10:5); "Like vinegar to the teeth, and smoke to the eyes, / so are the lazy to their employers" (10:26). Ironically, however, lazy people often do not realize their social stigma but actually fall victim to pride: "The lazy person is wiser in self-esteem / than seven who can answer discreetly" (26:16). In the New Testament Paul transcends such description in favor of prescription: "Keep away from believers who are living in idleness and not according to the tradition that they received from us" (2 Thess. 3:6–13).

Yet condemning laziness is not all that Proverbs has to say about sloth. Proverbs does not simplistically correlate all poverty with laziness: "The field of the poor may yield much food, / but it is swept away through injustice" (13:23). We have seen enough regarding oppression elsewhere to realize that Proverbs takes note of systemic sin and structural evil. Beyond this, the Christian tradition defines sloth much more broadly than laziness: "The sin of sloth has two components: *acedia*, which means a lack of caring, an aimless indifference to one's responsibilities to God and to man, and *tristitia*, meaning sadness and sorrow. In its final stages sloth becomes despair at the possibility of salvation."[39] Certainly in Proverbs refusal to work can be recognized as problematic in secular terms. However, the larger issue is refusal to undergo with hope the godly discipline, including work, that fosters wisdom.

This classical paradigm leads to more subtle analysis of contemporary sloth, including the recognition that workaholism can reflect such spiritual laziness, as an effort at distracting ourselves from the difficult demands of transformation. It is not that sloth is primarily a feeling, yet in a sense it is a condition of being primarily bound by our feelings. The classical tradition frequently compared vice to illness and used healing or medicinal metaphors for addressing it. Yet the end of such discourse was redemptive transformation, not the treatment of addiction in ways that readily lend themselves to denial or neglect of personal responsibility.[40] Sloth deals with self-interested refusal of responsibility; sometimes this is merely the flip side of proudly claiming the wrong kind of responsibility:

> Experienced abbots constantly ran into novices who passionately declared themselves to be the greatest sinners in the world. The exasperated abbot had to rebuke those monks for their arrogance. . . . Like the vain in general, the novice chafes against his mediocrity. He craves (unwarranted) attention—be it positive or negative. Instead of improving himself, he proclaims himself incorrigible. He should be sent to work—real, not spiritual, work.[41]

And so the themes of Proverbs become freshly relevant.

Proverbs has spiritual concerns about laziness. As discovered earlier, Proverbs acknowledges the reality of affliction along with the healing value of small joys: "All the days of the poor are hard, / but a cheerful heart has a continual feast" (15:15). We should not try to coerce afflicted people into happiness by way of silly songs or forced laughter or pious platitudes. Neither, though, should afflicted people forever wallow in despair. There remains something consistent with Proverbs in the general platitude that life is ten percent what happens to you and ninety percent how you respond to it. Proverbs associates sloth with appetitive preoccupation: "The appetite of the lazy craves, and gets nothing, / while the appetite of the diligent is richly supplied" (13:4); "The craving of the lazy person is fatal, /

39. Here Schimmel, *Seven Deadly Sins*, 193, summarizes what holds true after the common combination of *acedia* and *tristitia* from separate vices into one. He also makes the interesting claim that "sloth is the most explicitly religious of the seven deadly sins"; whereas the others can be treated without reference to God, sloth actually cannot (197–98).

40. Ibid., 233–34. On theology as medicine in the Christian tradition, see the beginning of Ellen T. Charry, *By the Renewing of Your Minds: The Pastoral Function of Christian Doctrine* (Oxford: Oxford University Press, 1997). On the paradigm of sin as addictive, see Cornelius Plantinga Jr., *Not the Way It's Supposed to Be: A Breviary of Sin* (Grand Rapids: Eerdmans, 1995).

41. Kleinberg, *Seven Deadly Sins*, 34–35.

for lazy hands refuse to labor. / All day long the wicked covet, / but the righteous give and do not hold back" (21:25–26). This preoccupation with unsatisfied desire elicits vanity: "worthless pursuits" (12:11; 28:19); "mere talk" (14:23); lame excuses, such as ignorance (24:12) or a lion outside in the streets (22:13; 26:13); excessive sleep (26:14); and so forth.

The descriptive acuteness of Proverbs requires contextual sensitivity when applied to contemporary culture. Isolated passages about laziness should not be trotted out in ways that glibly reinforce sleep deprivation and workaholism.[42] Ancient wisdom further presumes levels and kinds of physical activity with which many today are unfamiliar—in work or otherwise. Hence we may suffer from sloth in multiple ways—neither working faithfully when working nor resting fully when resting. Yet employer expectations of constant focus and productivity may be dehumanizing as compared to more natural rhythms of labor, so the cultural negotiations concerning sloth are quite complex.

Proverbs treats dimensions of sloth broader than laziness. It remains to make explicit that Proverbs does not just address the issue of work in a spiritual way; broader dimensions of sloth fit into the comprehensive problem of approaching life foolishly. Not only does the book confront excessive, debilitating preoccupation with desire; its confrontation presents a pedagogy that moves the simple youth away from destruction. The broad road is reachable via the easy listening of seductive speech, being in the wrong place at the wrong time, longing for a gang of one's own or an alternative spirituality, and so forth. Proverbs moves vulnerable youth away from this destructive path and through the narrow gate toward wisdom, recognizing the need for its parental promotion along with disciplined embrace. The goal of this pursuit is the easy yoke and the light burden of resting in the fear of the Lord—thereby having all other desires rightly ordered and realizing that our embrace of godly discipline is enabled by grace. "Now for this very reason also, . . . in your faith supply moral excellence. . . . Be all the more diligent to make certain His calling and choosing you; for as long as you practice these things, you will never stumble; for in this way the entrance into the eternal kingdom of our Lord and Savior Jesus Christ will be abundantly supplied to you" (2 Pet. 1:5, 10–11 NASB); "Work out your own salvation with fear and trembling; for it is God who is at work in you, enabling you both to will and to work for his good pleasure" (Phil. 2:12–13).

Wrath

Like lust and gluttony, the next capital vice, wrath, sins against temperance. Passion per se is not the problem—only preoccupation with it (sloth) or inappropriate pursuit of appropriate objects (lust and gluttony) or pursuit of inappropriate objects (avarice: money as an end in itself). Similarly, wrath stems from a passion

42. For spiritual reflections on sleep in our culture, see Lauren F. Winner, "Sleep Therapy," *Books and Culture* (January–February 2006): 7–8.

for justice activated by perceived injustice, which may be real—in which case the problem is a disproportionate response—or unreal. Theological debate continues regarding whether, in cases of genuine injustice, some anger is a legitimate passion or whether any anger is automatically a vice. Ephesians 4:26–27 supports the case for righteous anger: "Be angry but do not sin; do not let the sun go down on your anger, and do not make room for the devil." Still, aside from reaching a position in principle, the practical difficulty would involve knowing the when and how of appropriate anger. Rather than primarily analyzing whether anger is sinful when it arises, we should probably focus on moderating its occurrence and effects. There is biblical support for this practical approach: "A quick scan of a biblical concordance yields a dozen passages, most of them from Proverbs, giving counsel about anger. Interestingly, none of these mentions a single word about the *object* of our anger. The passages on anger's rightful expression can be briefly summarized in the advice, 'Cool it.'"[43]

Violence. To begin our examination of Proverbs, then, are passages treating the violence that often stems from wrath. As mentioned before, this is sometimes a means of obtaining riches (11:16). Yet in other cases it almost becomes a desired end in itself (e.g., 13:2; 24:1–2). The wicked may be violent out of hatred for the righteous (29:10). Frequently they entice their neighbors (16:29), with ambush used as a metaphor for their words (12:6). Twice we are told that "the mouth of the wicked conceals violence" (10:6, 11). However, in the end "the violence of the wicked will sweep them away, / because they refuse to do what is just" (21:7); they may wind up as fugitives (28:17).

Strife. Violence may not be physical, operating metaphorically in terms of strife. "Hatred stirs up strife" (10:12); so too, "a harsh word stirs up anger" (15:1). Some texts focus on instigators into which even the wise can occasionally fall—hatred, harsh words, and the like. But these instigators do not characterize wise people, and several texts focus instead on those who are characterized by folly, often using the image of starting a fire: hot-tempered (15:18a), perverse (16:28), scoffer (22:10; 29:8), gossip (16:28; 26:20–21), greedy (28:25a), and godless (11:9). It should be sobering to realize that indulging wrath quickly places a person among the characteristically foolish (20:3). Therefore, "the beginning of strife is like letting out water; / so stop before the quarrel breaks out" (17:14). Moreover, "like somebody who takes a passing dog by the ears / is one who meddles in the quarrel of another" (26:17). Lovers of strife and lovers of transgression overlap (17:19). The consequences can be disastrous: "An ally offended is stronger than a city; / such quarreling is like the bars of a castle" (18:19). On a more mundane, though no less relevant, level: "It is better to live in a corner of the housetop / than in a house shared with a contentious wife" (21:9; also 21:19; 25:24). How does one avoid strife? "Love covers all offenses" (10:12); "A soft answer turns away wrath" (15:1); "Those who are slow to anger calm contention" (15:18). Finally, "whoever

43. DeYoung, *Glittering Vices*, 124.

trusts in the LORD will be enriched" (28:25)—in contrast to the greedy person stirring up strife.

Slander. Already identified among instigators of strife, and reinforcing these themes, is slander: "Do not be a witness against your neighbor without cause, / and do not deceive with your lips. / Do not say, 'I will do to others as they have done to me; / I will pay them back for what they have done'" (24:28–29). Though false witness against a neighbor seems like an effective weapon (25:18), actually "like a sparrow in its flitting, like a swallow in its flying, / an undeserved curse goes nowhere" (26:2). In fact a backbiting tongue produces anger as surely as the north wind brings rain (25:23). In the end, "lying lips conceal hatred, / and whoever utters slander is a fool" (10:18).

Retribution. The follies of slander and retribution connect since, according to Jas. 4:11–12, the slanderer usurps God's position as Lawgiver and Judge over others, and God does not delegate retribution to nongovernmental people—even when they are genuinely wronged. "Vengeance is mine, I will repay, says the Lord" (Rom. 12:19, quoting Deut. 32:35). "Do not say, 'I will repay evil'; / wait for the LORD, and he will help you" (Prov. 20:22). As Paul picks up in Rom. 12:20–21: "If your enemies are hungry, give them bread to eat; / and if they are thirsty, give them water to drink; / for you will heap coals of fire on their heads, / and the LORD will reward you" (Prov. 25:21–22). Whether or not the apparent shame leads to repentance, meeting the needs of enemies promotes charity. Wrath seems understandable in the face of wrongs undergone, along with the very real vulnerability that wronged people feel. But wrath—even despairing wrath—proudly usurps divine prerogatives while misunderstanding the character of justice. Because God's justice can incorporate mercy along with opportunity for reform, at times it requires considerable patience.

Temper. The broadest opposition in Proverbs to wrath regards a quick temper. "Fools show their anger at once, / but the prudent ignore an insult" (12:16); "Rash words bring sword thrusts, / but the tongue of the wise brings healing" (12:18); "One who is quick-tempered acts foolishly, / and the schemer is hated" (14:17); "Whoever is slow to anger has great understanding, / but one who has a hasty temper exalts folly" (14:29; also 17:27; 29:11); "A violent tempered person will pay the penalty; / if you effect a rescue, you will only have to do it again" (19:19); "Make no friends with those given to anger, / and do not associate with hotheads, / or you may learn their ways / and entangle yourself in a snare" (22:24–25; also 22:8); "One given to anger stirs up strife, / and the hothead causes much transgression" (29:22). From a variety of angles, a quick temper frequently correlates with what is unsavory: folly, wounding, scheming, repeat offenses, on and on.

A king's wrath is compared to a lion's growling in 19:12 and 20:2; thus "whoever is wise will appease it" (16:14). Similarly matter of fact is the description of bribery's effectiveness: "A gift in secret averts anger; / and a concealed bribe in the bosom, strong wrath" (21:14). But Proverbs is not happy with these situations: "One who is slow to anger is better than the mighty, / and one whose temper is controlled than one who captures a city" (16:32). The New Testament's preeminent wisdom text places the same high priority on controlling anger: "You must understand this, my beloved: let everyone be quick to listen, slow to speak, slow to anger; for your anger does not produce God's righteousness" (Jas. 1:19–20); "How great a forest is set ablaze by a small fire! And the tongue is a fire" (3:5–6). Meanwhile, "strife," "anger," "quarrels," "dissensions," and "factions" are prominent among "the works of the flesh" opposed to the fruit of the Spirit (Gal. 5:19–21).

Turning to contemporary culture. "Why are we so angry? Perhaps it is because our culture espouses pride, standing up for one's rights, and combative competitiveness."[44] Yet among pride's various manifestations is fear as well:

> The fear that is born of trusting oneself in pride is opposed to the freedom and peace of trusting God for assurance and love. If we can look only to ourselves for an ally and a source of security when we are threatened, then we would do well to be afraid . . . and angry.
>
> Our bad anger thus shows us to be trying—and failing—to be God. We are wrathful when we can't control things that hurt us and keep them at bay. Our anger is ready to remedy this vulnerability by taking full control of establishing justice in the world and avenging any wrongs against us. Wrath's expression therefore usually involves the assertion of control, even as—ironically enough—we lose control over ourselves when we are angry.[45]

In other words, wrath stems from pride, the opposite of both the fear of the Lord and charity—the beginning and end of wisdom. The God whom we ought to fear is "merciful and gracious, slow to anger and abounding in steadfast love," according to an oft-repeated Old Testament refrain. Pagans can recognize the destructive effects of anger and, at times throughout history, have admired dispassionate people as prudent. In a contemporary culture that lauds authenticity and self-expression, however, people now throw off such restraint and reveal self-preoccupation more than ever. Glorifying violence in terms of self-defense and revenge, our culture then wonders how other forms of violence—both physical and verbal—can run so rampant. In such a situation, prudence is likely to be tied more tightly than ever to the fear of God, since other incentives toward self-restraint do not obtain.

Envy

Much that Proverbs calls "strife" may involve components of envy. The distorted sense of justice behind wrath turns against the other party, in the case of envy, simply for who they are or what they have. Envy, though, is not merely coveting what someone else has, or feeling jealous over what should belong to

44. Schimmel, *Seven Deadly Sins*, 92.
45. DeYoung, *Glittering Vices*, 134.

oneself. Envy is wishing to have what someone else has *and* desiring that they not have it. Envy, in other words, has the neighbor as its object of attack, rather than focusing primarily on an object of desire. Envy is sadly central to the biblical story, almost from the beginning. Since there can be only one God, to desire the fruit of the tree for being "like God" attacked the divine sovereign directly. The narrative soon follows with Cain's murder of Abel, which transpired out of envy over God's approval. Envy deals even more deeply than covetousness or jealousy with who we are on the inside, violating both aspects of charity—love of God and love of neighbor.

Proverbs explicitly confronts envy more rarely than other vices, as we should expect. Proverbs addresses character, not just behavior, yet focuses—given its literary nature—primarily on the resulting social practices and public manifestations such as speech. Thus envy is difficult to confront directly with the kind of advice Proverbs usually gives. Nevertheless, Proverbs does baldly say, "Don't envy the wicked" and "don't envy the rich" (e.g., 23:17–21; 24:1–2, 19–20). Plus, many bases on which people envy others are confronted by material regarding other sins such as lust, gluttony, and greed. The reasons for not envying the wicked or the rich are familiar: their hedonism ironically leads to poverty; they introduce chaos and strife into the social order; and they have no future—even if we do not know exactly how God will deal with them. Proverbs describes envy of the rich as an unfortunate fact of cultural life: "The poor are disliked even by their neighbors, / but the rich have many friends. / Those who despise their neighbors are sinners, / but happy are those who are kind to the poor" (14:20–21). Furthermore, the ways in which the text confronts avarice suggest a basis that likewise confronts envy: "Better is a dry morsel with quiet / than a house full of feasting with strife" (17:1). Verses such as this laud loving harmony in the social order as a divine gift that offers life to the fullest. In so doing they point beyond rejecting avarice or lust or gluttony alone toward avoiding envy as well.

Other verses confront one's attitude toward a neighbor. "Whoever belittles another lacks sense, / but an intelligent person remains silent" (11:12); "The souls of the wicked desire evil; / their neighbors find no mercy in their eyes" (21:10); "Do not rejoice when your enemies fall, / and do not let your heart be glad when they stumble, / or else the Lord will see it and be displeased, / and turn away his anger from them" (24:17–18); "An enemy dissembles in speaking / while harboring deceit within; / when an enemy speaks graciously, do not believe it, / for there are seven abominations concealed within; / though hatred is covered with guile, / the enemy's wickedness will be exposed in the assembly. / Whoever digs a pit will fall into it, / and a stone will come back on the one who starts it rolling" (26:24–27). Read together, these verses suggest that, when struggling with envy, one should keep it to oneself; however, given the tendency for our true feelings to reveal themselves over time, we ought to overcome our envy or else expect it to ensnare us in due course—if not by natural processes, then perhaps due to divine intervention.

The power of this cluster of emotions is apparent comparatively in 27:4: "Wrath is fierce and anger is a flood, / But who can stand before jealousy?" (NASB). The terms are absolute in 14:30: "The life of the body is a healthy heart, / but jealousy is a rot of the bones" (translation from Longman 2006: 306). Jealousy can have a positive connotation in the context of covenant, when God or a married person is appropriately zealous for the loving fidelity of a partner. Here, though, the text is confronting the rotten envy that eats away at one's insides until, more than likely, it surfaces in a way that spreads the danger from oneself to others.

> The only escape from this vice is to find a completely different foundation for our self-worth. Envy depends on a comparative self-value. The worth of the envious—at least from their perspective—is conditional on excelling their competitors. Moving out of envy into love is analogous to making the transition from dating to marriage. The premise of dating includes needing to outdo the competition to win your lover's affection and secure the relationship, while the premise of marriage is that one is working from an already secure relationship into greater and greater love.[46]

In short, if we really fear God in covenant, then the opinions of others should not control us. Too often, though, we try to secure our own place in the world.

Pride and Vainglory

Ultimately, therefore, pride goes before a fall—after the human fall into sin, at any rate. No doubt people mask their ambitions or envy for a time, but an arrogant person manifests pride, and many others who mask their pride eventually find that their mouth reveals it. Augustine acutely recognizes the particular difficulties of overcoming this vice. Regarding riches: "If the mind cannot clearly perceive whether it despises the possession of them, that can be simply tested by giving them away," yet

> how can we live so as to be indifferent to praise, and to be sure of this in experience? Are we to live evil lives, so abandoned and depraved that no one who knows us does not detest us? Nothing more crazy can be suggested or imagined. If admiration is the usual and proper accompaniment of a good life and good actions, we ought not to renounce it any more than the good life which it accompanies. Yet I have no way of knowing whether my mind will be serene or upset to be lacking something unless it is actually absent.[47]

This is why, in the interests of economy, we can treat vainglory together with pride. The two are conceptually distinguishable: pride deals with striving to promote the self in ways the self approves, vainglory with striving to please others. Excellence can be a legitimate pursuit, appropriate for a culture to recognize. In

46. Ibid., 53.
47. Augustine, *Confessions* 10.60 (trans. Chadwick), 215.

our culture, though—and probably in many others—people are more interested in the opinion of others than excellence itself, and this myopia brings vainglory and pride closer together. It is ironic that the lust for authenticity and self-expression can coexist with such a craven need for affirmation. Vainglory can involve (1) seeking praise for something unworthy or (2) seeking praise from a worthless source, but also (3) seeking praise for one's own rather than God's or the neighbor's sake. Pride can involve (1) seeing oneself as the cause of achievements, (2) believing oneself to deserve these even if they come from God, (3) boasting of qualities one actually lacks, or (4) despising others who lack what one has.[48]

Hence striving for excellence does not specify clearly enough either the end or the means of one's pursuits. In Proverbs, "the message keeps coming across that virtue should precede everything else: if it makes a person wealthy then all well and good, but the material rewards should not become ends in themselves."[49] This holds true for social and personal rewards as well: virtue is its own reward only if, in the end, virtue is defined in relation to fearing God. So, however much Proverbs can engage pagan societies with practical wisdom by virtue of cosmic order, in the end it cannot help but point toward the need for redemption because charity is the *telos* of fully realized virtues. It is no accident that classic Christian virtue lists portrayed humility as the root from which charity finally blossoms because pride is idolatry—the first sin.

In our culture of self-esteem this raises objections: "The problem is that without pride there is no individuality—at least, not in the deep sense that one must assume vis-à-vis God. To wish to be unique, to make personal choices—even good and appropriate ones—testifies to the presence of a voice ceaselessly saying 'I' when it is supposed to be saying 'God.' For even when we call upon God to have pity on us, our 'I' does not disappear."[50]

The biblical tradition offers two responses to this concern. First, scripture depicts an alternative account of the self in terms of relations—preeminently to God, then to parents, other family members, neighbors, and still others in the social order. Proverbs, insisting on traditional mediation of divine teaching, promotes a form of social order that inevitably opposes the supposedly autonomous self of modernity. Second, it is not obvious that individuality must disappear in the biblical account. Freedom involves enough context for the "I" to face meaningful choices, which result in (further) self-definition. The "I" must start with givens even to exist as a meaningful subject. Proverbs presumes that fear of the Lord and guidelines of parental or traditional wisdom place the self in a context of freedom for delighting in creation and community—not under enslavement. If the secularist wishes to argue that biblical humility denies personal uniqueness, then a workable account of the "I" without such relations must be offered in its stead. Suggesting

48. Schimmel, *Seven Deadly Sins*, 32–34.
49. Dell, *Seeking a Life That Matters*, 66.
50. Kleinberg, *Seven Deadly Sins*, 138.

that one's uniqueness owes ultimately to the creating and sustaining power of God is not tantamount to denying such uniqueness, but rather undergirds it. Humility is not groveling like a worm but, instead, refusing to "think of yourself more highly than you ought to think," recognizing how particular strengths and weaknesses relate a person to God and others in the community (Rom. 12:3).

God opposes the proud, so the basic scriptural rejection of pride appears frequently in Proverbs: "The LORD tears down the house of the proud, / but maintains the widow's boundaries" (15:25); "All those who are arrogant are an abomination to the LORD; / be assured, they will not go unpunished" (16:5); "Pride goes before destruction, / and a haughty spirit before a fall. / It is better to be of a lowly spirit among the poor / than to divide the spoil with the proud" (16:18–19); "Before destruction one's heart is haughty, / but humility goes before honor" (18:12); "A person's pride will bring humiliation, / but one who is lowly in spirit will obtain honor" (29:23; also 21:2, 4, 24); aligning the fear of God with honor and against pride, "The fear of the LORD is instruction in wisdom, / and humility goes before honor" (15:33); "The reward for humility and fear of the LORD / is riches and honor and life" (22:4; also 28:25; 29:25–26). The severity of the problem of pride is clear: "Do you see persons wise in their own eyes? / There is more hope for fools than for them" (26:12).

Anticipating Jesus's Sermon on the Mount, "Do not boast about tomorrow, / for you do not know what a day may bring" (27:1), this theme of unpredictability echoes against self-important worrying in Matt. 6:25–34 and against the overconfident merchants in Jas. 4:13–17. In both cases self-reliance is deadly, as we saw regarding prudence and its limitations: "Fools think their own way is right, / but the wise listen to advice" (Prov. 12:15); "There is a way that seems right to a person, / but its end is the way to death" (14:12; also 16:25; 28:26); "Who can say, 'I have made my heart clean; / I am pure from my sin'?" (20:9); "All deeds are right in the sight of the doer, / but the LORD weighs the heart" (21:2); "No wisdom, no understanding, no counsel, / can avail against the LORD" (21:30).

Yet Proverbs does not reject every form of seeking honor or social status. The book emphasizes that pride actually brings dishonor, and humility the reverse: "When pride comes, then comes disgrace; / but wisdom is with the humble" (11:2; also 13:10; 15:33; 22:4; 29:23). A healthy community recognizes the wisdom of humble people and disregards fools: "The talk of fools is a rod for their backs, / but the lips of the wise preserve them" (14:3); "Like snow in summer or rain in harvest, / so honor is not fitting for a fool" (26:1); "It is like binding a stone in a sling / to give honor to a fool" (26:8). Meanwhile, "even children make themselves known by their acts, / by whether what they do is pure and right" (20:11); "A good name is to be chosen rather than great riches, / and favor is better than silver or gold" (22:1). There is a difference between pursuing honor solely for oneself, to the detriment of others or denial of divine gifts, and seeking acceptance as a responsible member of a covenant-keeping community. Indeed, Augustine cautions, "Often the contempt of vainglory becomes a source of even more vainglory. For it is not being scorned when the contempt is something one is proud of."[51]

Still, by no means are all forms of honor appropriate to grasp. "Better to be despised and have a servant, / than to be self-important and lack food" (12:9); "The wicked put on a bold face, / but the upright give thought to their ways" (21:29); "Like clouds and wind without rain / is one who boasts of a gift never given" (25:14); "it is not good to eat much honey, / or to seek honor on top of honor" (25:27); "let another praise you, and not your own mouth— / a stranger, and not your own lips" (27:2). In fact, receiving praise is a test of character: "The crucible is for silver, and the furnace is for gold, / so a person is tested by being praised" (27:21). There is a temptation to curry favor with others rather than dealing with truth in love: we must, however, believe that "whoever rebukes a person will afterward find more favor / than one who flatters with the tongue" (28:23). Again, in a healthy covenant community, a form of social approval may follow godly action. But fortitude enough to fear God rather than humans may often be required, at the outset anyway, even in such communities. Strictures against people-pleasing pride apply even to dealings with the most potent earthly rulers: "Do not put yourself forward in the king's presence / or stand in the place of the great; / for it is better to be told, 'Come up here,' / than to be put lower in the presence of a noble" (25:6–7). This advice echoes in Jesus's words: "But when you are invited, go and sit down at the lowest place, so that when your host comes, he may say to you, 'Friend, move up higher'; then you will be honored in the presence of all who sit at the table with you" (Luke 14:10).

After all, appearances can be deceiving. Aside from high-minded theological reasoning behind spurning many forms of social status, there is a more pragmatic reality: "Some pretend to be rich, yet have nothing; / others pretend to be poor, yet have great wealth" (Prov. 13:7). Augustine comments, "The thing really to be afraid of with riches, you see, is pride." He uses the analogy of a bloated wineskin to illustrate the way in which a rich person, relying on riches, may appear to be filled while actually being an empty beggar (Sermon 36.2, in WSA 3/2.174). Meanwhile, the wicked manifest their pride not only in seeking inappropriate social status, but also in being heedless: "The wise are cautious and turn away from evil, / but the fool throws off restraint and is careless" (14:16). Again there is ironic reversal: God has set up the world so as to turn the tables on those who set themselves up as kings. These dynamics of the temporal realm apply spiritually as well: "Already you have all you want! Already you have become rich! Quite apart from us you have become kings!" (1 Cor. 4:8); "so if you think you are standing, watch out that you do not fall" (10:12).

Evidence of humility, by contrast, lies in listening to wisdom. This is already a prominent theme. Beyond texts previously mentioned, note the following: "Fools think their own way is right, / but the wise listen to advice" (Prov. 12:15); "By

51. Augustine, *Confessions* 10.63 (trans. Chadwick), 217.

insolence the heedless make strife, / but wisdom is with those who take advice" (13:10; also 10:17; 15:12, 31; 29:1). Biblical humility therefore does not destroy all individuality or render every form of social status inappropriate. Seeking, at minimum, to avoid disrepute in the covenant community is a legitimate goal. Pursuing recognition as a wise person can be healthy. Deadly pride is involved when people pursue forms of recognition that separate them over against others or deny their need for divine grace—failing to love God and neighbor, serving only themselves. The analogy between the divine and human households reinforces the deadliness of pride: those who refuse to accept correction from earthly friends and parents not only will reject the discipline of God—they already have rejected the discipline of God. Pride is the opposite of the fear of the Lord, and so it goes before an eventual fall. People may develop some preliminary elements of prudence or other cardinal virtues apart from faith, but even this moral progress would require a measure of humility—and we may hope, by God's grace, that such humility will point them to their deeper spiritual need.

Speech Acts

Thus our quick tour of Prov. 10–29 concerning cardinal and theological virtues, as well as capital vices, comes to an end. To be sure, these later frameworks do not correspond one-to-one with the themes of Proverbs. Yet in the main the coherence is strong. Among the cardinal virtues, prudence has regulative pride of place, which holds true within Proverbs. Justice is a crucial concern of this biblical text, given the priority it places upon human flourishing in community. Fortitude is necessary for youths to resist turning their simplicity into folly before wisdom can really take hold and thereafter to act nobly for others or under duress. Though rarely by name, Proverbs calls for temperance in spades. Among the theological virtues, fear of the Lord is a dominant motif roughly synonymous with faith, charting the full course of wisdom's path from beginning to end. Again rarely by name, Proverbs offers hope in God's ultimate vindication of wisdom over folly, though calling for faith rather than sight as to the nature and provenance of that final vindication. Finally, charity is surprisingly intertwined with and essential to justice in the fullest sense to which Proverbs aspires. In other words, some of these virtues are prominent by name in the book and the others by implication. The cardinal virtues tend to be more overt, especially when temperance is viewed in terms of its opposite vices. The theological virtues explicate the normative framework by which wisdom is pursued to the full—fearing the Lord, in hope that this really is the path to life, enjoyed by giving and receiving charity.

Among the capital vices, lust was already an important concern long before Prov. 10, but reiterations of its dangers continue throughout the collections of individual proverbs. There gluttony too plays a prominent role among the disordered passions into which the simple may plunge. Proverbs condemns neither money nor wealth as such, yet is quite attentive to their dangers as ends in themselves—the problem of avarice—rather than God-given means to enjoy the fruit of labor moderately and gratefully. The book confronts mundane dimensions of sloth very directly, offering thereby some practical means—namely, physical work to provide for one's needs and to avoid social stigmas—that are often commended by the Christian tradition for addressing the deeper spiritual problem. Proverbs confronts wrath from numerous angles, whether in terms of epiphenomena such as violence and strife or via exhortations against giving in to the passions and people that reinforce a quick temper. Envy is not directly prominent, but its power is acknowledged and its condemnation is evident by contrast with positive depictions of community life involving family and neighbors. Finally, pride is deadly according to Proverbs, though not in a simplistic sense that forbids appropriate social reinforcement regarding personal development.

What then do these classic frameworks miss with respect to the teaching of Proverbs? The surrounding emphasis, of course, is on two ways, a theme with repeated and varied expressions throughout Prov. 10–29, not in just Prov. 1–9. There are also myriad observations and prescriptions regarding social order, from families to friends to neighbors to kings, as discussed with more focus regarding Prov. 30–31. The chief remaining theme, only partially accounted for within the virtues and vices, concerns speech. Speaking and listening are incredibly prominent throughout the book, in which speech *acts*. That is to say, we are morally accountable for the influence of both our mouths and our ears.

Mirroring complex tensions regarding divine sovereignty and human freedom throughout Proverbs is 16:1: "The plans of the mind belong to mortals, / but the answer of the tongue is from the LORD." The juxtaposition of mind and tongue signals that human character comes to expression in speech: "Out of the abundance of the heart the mouth speaks," according to Jesus (Matt. 12:33–37, esp. 12:34). The juxtaposition of human and divine action expresses a seemingly insoluble tension, from our limited perspective. But in the perspective of Proverbs, human responsibility and divine sovereignty are interwoven in the mix of activity and passivity tied to speaking and listening. In God's providence our real intentions eventually come forth even if we plot otherwise. Of course the answers of others lie within the Lord's ultimate purview as well. We ought to plan prudently, yet acknowledge the limits of human control over results.

Many proverbs align speech with prudence or other virtues. Therefore, needing treatment here are only the leftovers, so to speak—those proverbs addressing speech in categories not yet covered.

Gossip. First of these is the prohibition of gossip. "A gossip goes about telling secrets, / but one who is trustworthy in spirit keeps a confidence" (11:13); "An evildoer listens to wicked lips; / and a liar gives heed to a mischievous tongue" (17:4); "The words of a whisperer are like delicious morsels; / they go down into the inner parts of the body" (18:8, repeated in 26:22); "A gossip reveals secrets; / therefore do not associate with a babbler" (20:19). Most notable in these passages is the character of one who listens to gossip. Its strong temptation is acknowledged in 18:8, but the extent of communal disruption is such that one should avoid even associating with a known gossip (20:19). This could be due either to the principle of bad company corrupting good character (1 Cor. 15:33) or to prudent avoidance of having tales told about oneself or both. In any case, those who give in to the temptation of listening are characterized by evil and deceit (Prov. 17:4).

Lying. Second and obviously related is the prohibition of lying. "Truthful lips endure forever, / but a lying tongue lasts only a moment" (12:19); "The righteous hate falsehood, / but the wicked act shamefully and disgracefully" (13:5); "A truthful witness saves lives, / but one who utters lies is a betrayer" (14:25); "Fine speech is not becoming to a fool; / still less is false speech to a ruler" (17:7); "A false witness will perish, / but a good listener will testify successfully" (21:28).[52] Beyond these gnomic statements—comparing the enduring success of truth and falsity as well as their respective associations—specific forms of lying are confronted. After repetition of the proverb regarding delicious morsels of gossip (26:22), we read:

> Like the glaze covering an earthen vessel
> are smooth lips with an evil heart.
> An enemy dissembles in speaking
> while harboring deceit within;
> when an enemy speaks graciously, do not believe it,
> for there are seven abominations concealed within;
> though hatred is covered with guile,
> the enemy's wickedness will be exposed in the assembly.
> Whoever digs a pit will fall into it,
> and a stone will come back on the one who starts it rolling.
> A lying tongue hates its victims,
> and a flattering mouth works ruin. (26:23–28)

In part the message is that "flattery will get you nowhere." However, the passage also beckons people who are vulnerable to flattery toward awareness of what the speaker's true intentions—and thus the ultimate results—might be: "A man who flatters his neighbor / Is spreading a net for his steps" (29:5 NASB). The prime antecedent of "his steps" is probably the neighbor (as the NRSV translates), but the grammatical ambiguity makes both the flatterer and the neighbor potential victims, because pride goes before a fall. In contrast, parental wisdom presents a repository of hard truths, willing to say what is unpopular rather than flattering youths or shielding them from uncomfortable realities of life. Proverbs practices what it preaches: speech that is timely and truthful, winsome yet not falsely sugarcoated.

Power. A third theme involves affirmations of the power of speech. On the plus side: "A bad messenger brings trouble, / but a faithful envoy, healing" (13:17); "A

52. For a defense of such a translation in 21:28b (over against, e.g., the NASB's "will speak forever"), see Waltke 2005: 163–64nn43–44, 189–90.

gentle tongue is a tree of life, / but perverseness in it breaks the spirit" (15:4); "To make an apt answer is a joy to anyone, / and a word in season, how good it is!" (15:23); "Pleasant words are like a honeycomb, / sweetness to the soul and health to the body" (16:24). The first two texts reflect the two-ways tradition so dominant in Prov. 10–15, contrasting the positive value of speech with negative examples. On the minus side: "Scoundrels concoct evil, / and their speech is like a scorching fire" (16:27); "The crooked of mind do not prosper, / and the perverse of tongue fall into calamity" (17:20). Once again, Jesus shares the realism of Proverbs when he tells us not to cast our pearls before swine: "Do not speak in the hearing of a fool, / who will only despise the wisdom of your words" (23:9). In other words, speaking and listening are two sides of the same coin—character. Over the long haul the quality of one's listening and speaking will fare the same, because each reveals who a person really is. A positive concept of power as appropriate influence is operative, in this case via speech. Granted the corruptive dangers of absolute power and the legitimacy of appropriate suspicion, nevertheless we should not glibly reject the positive influence of truthful communication. After all, biblical strictures against lying presume the appropriate power of human speech within the divine economy.

Social context. Thus, finally, the societal vision of Proverbs (with special connection to Prov. 30–31) highlights distinctive communal contexts of speech. Concerning the home: "If you curse father or mother, / your lamp will go out in utter darkness" (20:20). Meanwhile: "A continual dripping on a rainy day / and a contentious wife are alike; / to restrain her is to restrain the wind / or to grasp oil in the right hand" (27:15–16). Needless to say, Proverbs prioritizes harmony in the household. Whereas one cannot select parents—and Proverbs tends to assume their faithful stewardship of authority—a person can try to avoid selecting the wrong spouse.

Concerning the social order outside the home, Proverbs has a conservative streak: "Inspired decisions are on the lips of a king; / his mouth does not sin in judgment" (16:10). The wise king is portrayed as making such determinations, however, which becomes evident three verses later: "Righteous lips are the delight of a king, / and he loves those who speak what is right" (16:13). More generally: "With patience a ruler may be persuaded, / and a soft tongue can break bones" (25:15). Such advice is appropriate whether the king is wise, in which case the advice centers more on how to contribute wisdom, or tyrannical, in which case caution becomes the order of the day.

Proverbs is not naïve about the power of either speech or authority figures. However, despite the social effects of human sin, there is hope: in listening to parents and others who can foster fear of the Lord, we embrace wisdom and, as many in a community do so, the possibility of *shalom*. At minimum a provisionally stable social order looks forward to full justice and charity, even if the outlines of such a hoped-for society remain ever fuzzy in Proverbs itself. Proverbs prioritizes character; in its program of general education, one need not learn methods of speaking so much as habits to avoid and hopes to cultivate. If one recognizes the power of speech and rejects fiery dangers such as gossip and lying, then communication is an occasion for personal delight and communal edification. In short, these boundaries of divine law mark out the space for joyful freedom.

Keeping in line with this recognition of the power of speech, the goal throughout the preceding discussion of Prov. 10–29 has been to present the proverbs in their own words and thought forms as much as possible. Excessive loads of pious, prosaic abstraction could otherwise obscure their rhetorical effectiveness. At times the commentary is thick with quotation, even catenas of texts. Theological commentary on Proverbs should not substitute second-order discourse for the text itself; most of the time its teaching is clear and compelling enough on its own. Rather, fresh arrangements of such material should enable its beauty and coherence to shine forth: "A word fitly spoken / is like apples of gold in a setting of silver" (25:11).

FINAL WORDS:

Wisdom in Cosmic, Social, and Familial Context

PROVERBS 30–31

Proverbs 30–31 puts a closing bracket around the proverbial collections, corresponding to Prov. 1–9. The two oracles apparently arrive from outside Israel—first "the words of Agur son of Jakeh" (30:1) and then "the words of King Lemuel" (31:1), which he learned from his mother. That these oracles do not present alternatives to YHWH's revelation is evident from Agur's prayers in 30:1–6 and 30:7–9, along with allusions to other canonical books.[1] The oracles actually provide a helpful conclusion that recapitulates major themes of Proverbs, relating wisdom even more closely to the cosmos, the community, and the household as spheres of activity ordered by Israel's God.

Oracles from Outsiders

In fact, Agur's pleading concerns desire for the proper knowledge of Israel's God that is the essence of full humanity. Two confessions of inadequacy (30:2–3) introduce two kinds of rhetorical questions—who and what (30:4). There is a tradition of reading 30:4 as trinitarian. The last question, "What is His name or His son's name? / Surely you know!" (NASB) teases Christian readers regarding Jesus Christ, as do the mention of ascent and descent earlier. Furthermore, the

1. Richard L. Schultz, "Unity or Diversity in Wisdom Theology? A Canonical and Covenantal Perspective," *Tyndale Bulletin* 48 (1997): 301.

verse refers to the wind, associated with the Spirit. In the first instance, the son must be Israel or its king, while of the incarnation it could not be said to the first generations of readers, "Surely you know!" Nevertheless, the verse manifests the logic of revelation that trinitarian theology ultimately fulfills. No mere human can ascend to gain knowledge of God and descend to distribute this to others. Only the name YHWH answers the question, "Who is the creative power behind everything else?" Yet Israel has been uniquely chosen to represent the Creator in the world and, as the divine Son in the fullest sense, Jesus Christ fulfills this vocation. The confessions of inadequacy are balanced by two scriptural counterstatements affirming this divine revelation (30:5–6). The first scriptural adaptation comes from 2 Sam. 22:32 = Ps. 18:31, which in the near context alludes to the name YHWH: "For who is God except the LORD?" The second alludes to Deuteronomy's prohibitions (4:2) against adding merely human words to the covenant revelation. Suspicion of human understanding mixes with strong reliance on God's Word.

Poetic balance becomes even more pronounced in the following sections, especially given their considerable reliance upon numbers. Rejection of false speech and avarice continues famously in Prov. 30:8–9; the poet ardently pursues moral rectitude in these matters according to 30:7. Echoing this is the Lord's Prayer: if all that one seeks is daily bread, then speech will concern prayer, praise, and pleading for forgiveness, not power-grabbing by means of lies and deceit. In 30:10 there is a specific instance of false speech to reject, regarding servants; in 30:11 comes another, regarding parents, before a series of verses connects the underlying pride with both verbal violence and greedy oppression (30:12–14). As these themes expand, avarice and insatiable desire appear unflatteringly as leeches (30:15–16); the proud scorner of parents is depicted as a victim of birds (30:17); and, while mysteries to male-female relationships there may be (30:18–19), the insatiable and incorrigible way of the adulteress accompanies other ways of destabilizing the community (30:20–23).

Positively, on the other hand, we can look at the nonhuman creatures God has made and discover the incredible power of wisdom—even in tiny animals (30:24–28). There are great animals too, of course, to which kings compare in their majesty (30:29–31), but what these actually have in common is wisdom that leads to humility. Folly exalts the self and plots self-interested evil, which only produces communal strife (30:32–33). The point of this quick tour is to show that Agur's oracle tightly interweaves seeking and receiving divine revelation with rejecting certain basic vices: avarice, falsehood and slander, lust, and ultimately pride. The cosmos climactically reinforces the fear of YHWH and the avoidance of foolish vices against which the rest of Proverbs warns. Outsiders long for a harmonious culture of simple virtue arising from knowledge of Israel's Holy One.

The royal status of Lemuel in Prov. 31 affirms even more clearly his status as a foreigner. Nevertheless he learns wisdom from his mother, as the Israelite learns from parents throughout the rest of the book. The content of the teaching is similarly consistent: rejection of lust for women (31:3) and gluttony when it comes to strong drink (31:4–7). A king ought to represent God in defending the powerless and the destitute, providing justice even for them (31:8–9). The famous ode to the "Prov. 31 woman" follows in 31:10–31.

The ode begins with a general affirmation of her value as "far more precious than jewels" (31:10). Proverbs 31:11–12 offers initial reasons for this estimate: her husband trusts her, and she is a boon to him. More detail follows: she is industrious (31:13), she takes clever initiative (31:14), she plans and provides ahead (31:15), she pursues diverse enterprises (31:16), she is strong and works to grow stronger (31:17), and she keeps working rather than quitting at the first convenient moment (31:18). A chiasm (an X shape) in 31:19–20 forms a transition between subunits. Hands reaching out to the distaff in 31:19a match hands reaching out to the needy in 31:20b; hands holding the spindle in 31:19b match yet contrast with the hand opening to the poor in 31:20a. In the aggregate 31:13–19 not only contains the above emphases, but also depicts the generation of income, especially via textiles.

In 31:21–22, as a result, the wife's household is well adorned. As one would expect, her husband has a good reputation among leaders of the land (31:23), and her clothing is desirable beyond the threshold of the household (31:24). Using clothing as a metaphor, 31:25 expresses how the wife's strength enables her to face the future confidently. According to 31:26, the wife is a wise teacher in her own right—and she teaches kindness. The wrap-up in 31:27 reaffirms the wife's provision and industriousness.

The conclusion in 31:28–31 summarizes the praise that the wife receives from her family. Her children recognize her flourishing (31:28a); her husband recognizes her unique excellence (31:28b–29). She is the opposite of the adulteress, not because she is ugly but because her excellence makes her winsome to her husband and in fact to the entire community. Her winsomeness is grounded in her fear of the Lord (31:30). The theme of praise continues in 31:31, where a better translation than many (such as the NRSV) would be, "Extol her for the fruit of her hands" (Waltke 2005: 514). Her works speak for themselves regarding her excellence in the community.

The poem in 31:10–31 is an acrostic, each verse beginning with a successive letter of the Hebrew alphabet. Beyond reflecting the intricacy of beautiful design, this suggests a stylized discourse conveying a climactic point. The ode surely works at a literal level, and therefore—influenced as it is by Lemuel's mother, no less—it has profound implications for assessing the portrayal of women in Proverbs. Many a fundamentalist patriarch runs aground here—or should, anyway—when setting forth a simplistic vision of the postindustrial nuclear family, with no woman working outside the home as the exclusively biblical paradigm. To the contrary, the "Prov. 31 woman" is industrious in multiple senses, even as this household does not neglect care for children. At the same time, the superlatives-with-acrostic character of the ode suggests another level of meaning beyond the literal. While it is important to see the possibility of embodying Lady Wisdom's teachings in flesh and blood, her foil, Dame Folly, promoted not only literal license but also spiritual adultery. Likewise, it seems probable that in Prov. 31 we get a portrait of the ideal partner for the divine husband. The conclusion, regarding works that manifest the fear of the Lord, reinforces this. Thus the person who learns the wisdom of Proverbs will be a boon to others—industrious, taking clever initiative, strong, caring for the needy, planning and preparing, enjoying a good reputation and results, teaching wisdom to others—as well as, ultimately, one who through these works expresses devotion to God. The spiritual interpretation calls God's covenant people to render tangible service.

Order in Society and the Family

Proverbs 30–31 fits the broader emphasis of the book upon harmony between the cosmic, social, and familial contexts of Wisdom. Many passages have previously surfaced regarding these themes. On numerous occasions a feature of the animal kingdom or the cosmos illustrates God's design for human flourishing. Behind this proverbial practice stands commitment to creation as having divine order throughout intersecting spheres of activity even if, as Dietrich Bonhoeffer insists, due to the fall we may not discern this fully without reference to Jesus Christ. We deal not with natural "orders of creation" but with gracious divine "mandates" or "orders of preservation." It remains here to make the cultural implications of such possibilities for *shalom* more explicit.

Proverbs clearly affirms the sapiential value of friendship. Charity is an obligation for all to all, but this does not cancel out particular loves—which are essential both to give and receive. Proverbs does not specify criteria for selecting which neighbors to develop as friends.[2] Instead, as in other areas, the book sets down basic moral parameters within which a more esthetic sensibility is given free reign. These moral parameters include the truism that "bad company ruins good morals" (1 Cor. 15:33) along with the recognition that some are willing to offer friendship for self-interested reasons, not sticking with a person through thick and thin. Communal character operates on local and also larger-scale levels. "When the righteous triumph, there is great glory, / but when the wicked prevail, people go into hiding" (Prov. 28:12); similarly, "When the wicked prevail, people go into hiding; / but when they perish, the righteous increase" (28:28); accordingly, "When the righteous are in authority, the people rejoice; / but when the

2. The relevant term most common in Proverbs can refer to either "friend" or "neighbor," with the best translation sometimes difficult to discern (Longman 2006: 555). The preeminent biblical concern is what kind of neighbor I prove to be toward others—as noted in Luke T. Johnson, *Sharing Possessions: Mandate and Symbol of Faith*, Overtures to Biblical Theology (Philadelphia: Fortress, 1981), esp. 104. Johnson's wise reflections on possessions have implications for charity more generally, recognizing the need for discernment in diverse life circumstances. Bodily actions have symbolic import, manifesting and reinforcing idolatry or faith.

wicked rule, the people groan" (29:2). This notion that communal flourishing runs parallel to communal virtue leads to additional texts about kingship.

Most basically, "righteousness exalts a nation, / but sin is a reproach to any people" (14:34). Thus, in an ideal nation, "a servant who deals wisely has the king's favor, / but his wrath falls on one who acts shamefully" (14:35). The king's favor is compared to "the clouds that bring the spring rain," where "in the light of a king's face there is life" (16:15; also 22:11, 29). Thus, "when a land rebels / it has many rulers; / but with an intelligent ruler / there is lasting order" (28:2); the king's authority is affirmed, yet so are expectations that the king will mediate divine justice to the people and order their lives with wisdom. Hence, "it is an abomination to kings to do evil, / for the throne is established by righteousness" (16:12); "A wise king winnows the wicked, / and drives the wheel over them" (20:26). Social conservatism of this kind is really revolutionary if the king obeys God and leads the nation to do the same. Yet the danger of power in the hands of wicked kings is severe: "If a ruler listens to falsehood, / all his officials will be wicked" (29:12); "Like a roaring lion or a charging bear / is a wicked ruler over a poor people" (28:15; also 25:4–5). Kings are to care for others rather than themselves; they have no legacy without their people (14:28). As with fathers, if kings do not correspond to the divine ideal, then their power is a dangerous bane rather than a blessed boon.

The importance of husband and wife to their household continues the theme: "The wise woman builds her house, / but the foolish tears it down with her own hands" (14:1). More specific regarding the necessity of wisdom for the household's success are texts with the motif of inheritance: "Those who trouble their households will inherit wind, / and the fool will be servant to the wise" (11:29); "The good leave an inheritance to their children's children, / but the sinner's wealth is laid up for the righteous" (13:22). Beyond our own activity, though, "house and wealth are inherited from parents, / but a prudent wife is from the LORD" (19:14). For lasting *shalom* a household needs people of godly character, and this necessity transpires only by divine gift. The godly wife as God's gift is affirmed: "A good wife is the crown of her husband, / but she who brings shame is like rottenness in his bones" (12:4); "He who finds a wife finds a good thing, / and obtains favor from the LORD" (18:22); and "A stupid child is ruin to a father, / and a wife's quarreling is a continual dripping of rain" (19:13). Fox places the latter saying in the theological context of Proverbs:

> What made the contentious-wife sayings sound to the sages like wisdom (rather than like wisecracks or grousing) was that the collective enterprise that shaped the book of Proverbs repeatedly warns about the baleful effects of contentiousness. The large number of verses on this topic—thirty-one in all—shows just how important this issue was to the sages. They knew that disharmony in marriage was grievous because they knew that harmony was precious.[3]

3. Fox, "Epistemology of the Book of Proverbs," 678.

Parallel to the importance of a good rather than contentious wife is the significance of wise rather than foolish children. Indeed, the entirety of Prov. 10–29 begins, "A wise child makes a glad father, / but a foolish child is a mother's grief" (10:1). Moreover, "a wise child makes a glad father, / but the foolish despise their mothers" (15:20); "The one who begets a fool gets trouble; / the parent of a fool has no joy" (17:21); "Foolish children are a grief to their father / and bitterness to her who bore them" (17:25). The value of these relationships even extends for another generation: "Grandchildren are the crown of the aged, / and the glory of children is their parents" (17:6).

Given this priority on wisdom in family relationships and across generations, we should not be surprised to see more affirmations of discipline: "Those who spare the rod hate their children, / but those who love them are diligent to discipline them" (13:24); "Train children in the right way, / and when old, they will not stray" (22:6);[4] "Do not withhold discipline from your children; / if you beat them with a rod, they will not die. / If you beat them with the rod, / you will save their lives from Sheol" (23:13–14); "Discipline your children, and they will give you rest; / they will give delight to your heart" (29:17). From another perspective: "A wise child loves discipline, / but a scoffer does not listen to rebuke" (13:1). These texts raise difficult questions concerning whether to use physical means of discipline today, in light of child abuse and contemporary ethical sensibilities. Read as a whole, the book of Proverbs provides adequate theological and moral boundaries. (1) The importance of discipline as an act of parental love cannot be gainsaid; in this God's loving discipline is our model (3:11–12, reaffirmed in Heb. 12). (2) The selflessness of wise parents—most notably their avoidance of acting wrathfully—should moderate any physical forms of punishment considerably. (3) The priority in texts regarding discipline is not physical punishment but rather verbal correction. Beyond this, getting the youth's attention regarding the importance of the correction is necessary for memory and proper commitment to follow. But of course there may be adequate or even better ways of getting this attention in cultures not oriented to physical discipline, whereas some forms of punishment could actually fail to meet the loving standard of divine discipline in Proverbs.

Difficult issues remain in household texts, including slavery. In 29:19 we read: "By mere words servants are not disciplined, / for though they understand, they

4. This NRSV is a debatable translation. The verse quite possibly refers to youths entering adulthood, so "children" may mislead. There are various views of how to render "according to his way": the NRSV reflects (1) a moral view (but the usual adjectival qualifiers of "way" from such cases are absent); whereas others favor (2) vocation, (3) personal aptitude or destiny, (4) personal demands (if the verse were ironic, as in "don't let a youth have his way, or else"), or (5) status (as in "train a young squire to be ready for what he will become"). Whether the last interpretation is best historically (as Ted A. Hildebrandt, "Proverbs 22:6a: Train Up a Child?" *Grace Theological Journal* 9 [1988]: 3–19, the author of the survey appropriated here, argues), it is important to recognize what *na'ar* probably does not mean—namely, this verse is not about the discipline of young children. If nothing else, its various possibilities reflect the generality and nonpromissory character of proverbs, so we should not rest too much on it—while using the options as an occasion for wise reflection.

will not give heed." Two verses later: "A slave pampered from childhood / will come to a bad end" (29:21). The latter verse is difficult to translate. Dell relates the former verse to the necessity of a master providing an example.[5] Even if this should prove to be incorrect, the verse requires an implicit assumption, namely the genuine wrongdoing of the slave like that of the son in other texts. These two verses therefore establish an obligation to discipline slaves in a sober manner similar to correcting sons. They do not establish the legitimacy of severe, whimsical mistreatment; indeed, the potential for slaves to become heirs (17:2) further establishes their relative dignity. Incentives for slaves correlate with implicit exhortations such as 27:18: "Anyone who tends a fig tree will eat its fruit, / and anyone who takes care of a master will be honored." These are consistent with the household passages in the New Testament (e.g., Col. 3:22–4:1). The reader who expects Proverbs to revolutionize the social context of its original historical setting(s) will be disappointed. Readers will not be disappointed who, more realistically, expect the Bible to moderate abuses and avoid theologically justifying permanently illegitimate practices—thereby making space for subsequent change over the course of history, redemptive or otherwise. Theological exegesis does not entail neglecting historical difference, naïvely transporting textual paradigms into contemporary life without discernment. To the contrary, theological interpreters read scripture with a hermeneutic of trust in the Bible's divine speaker but also with healthy suspicion of the human contexts into and through which God speaks.

What, then, of the obvious patriarchy reflected along the way in Proverbs? Detailed discussion is beyond our scope here. If historical criticism helps at all, then one of its contributions lies in reminding us of differences between Israel's context—along with its surrounding cultural options—and our own. Forms of contemporary patriarchy—for good and/or ill—are substantially different from the possible household arrangements within Proverbs-like settings, especially those dominated by agriculture. Proverbs does not argue for patriarchy but instead assumes elements that are relevant to its context(s).

Theologically we ought to take a cue from Jesus who, in discussing divorce (Matt. 19:1–12 and parallels), illustrates the possibility of taking Israel's salvation history seriously without accepting all of its structures as permanent. The narrative of creation and fall, coupled with proper eschatological sensitivities, suggests that Old Testament texts may involve temporary divine provisions or toleration due to human sinfulness, along with signals of God's permanent intentions. Christ actually intensified the biblical standards for marriage by returning focus to the original divine design.

Proverbs itself says little explicitly about how to place its provisions within that larger context of salvation history. What we can say is that (1) Proverbs heartily affirms traditional Jewish and Christian sexual ethics; (2) Proverbs heartily affirms the importance of parenting children carefully and does not minimize but

5. Dell, *Seeking a Life That Matters*, 89.

if anything maximizes fatherly involvement (in other words, its preoccupation is not patriarchal status but paternal shepherding); (3) Proverbs rarely if ever denies that the shoe could also fit the other foot with respect to gendered material such as contentious-wife sayings; (4) Proverbs heartily affirms the wisdom of women for teaching children and others outside the household; and (5) if we were to follow the book's phenomenological tendencies, we would not treat longstanding, widespread cultural patterns as either utterly irrelevant or absolutely given, nor should we fail to reflect upon the significance of biological differences between male and female. So, on the one hand, when we allow for contextual assumptions and differences, reading Proverbs still allows for considerable cultural fluidity. Yet, on the other hand, reading Proverbs ought to provoke questioning our own cultural prejudices just as much as ancient ones. Proverbs challenges modern men and women alike to rethink notions of the good life in light of the profound importance of parenting along with the blessings of community and the cosmos in the book's worldview. If, following Jesus's pattern with respect to marriage and divorce, we were to dispense with some cultural accretions or toleration of patriarchy while intensifying our commitment to the core divine design, then we would outdo each other in seeking to give of ourselves in faithful love. Undoubtedly that could occur one-sidedly in culturally tragic ways, but it seems preferable to pursue wisdom within Proverbs and the rest of scripture than merely to fixate instead on how to maximize personal freedom or rights.

Proverbs therefore enjoins deeper respect for familial and communal traditions than current Western culture fosters or tolerates. Change is inevitable and necessary, yet not an automatic or unadulterated good. Moreover, we should not lionize change as if there were no cosmic structures or limits, as if culture were infinitely plastic (an ironic metaphor, since plastic hardly seems malleable in many cases). Many debates about patriarchy detour us from bringing the real priorities of Proverbs to bear on our culture—including its dominant patterns, which are found within our churches, not just outside. Traditionalists easily neglect the extent to which the traditional family structure has regularly undergone significant change. Progressives easily ignore the difficulties that drastic change poses for passing on stable forms through which to embody biblical wisdom. Both sides easily miss how the mobility of contemporary people thwarts the rootedness in place and time that is integral to this book's account of moral formation; debates over family structure can miss the main point.

We should not romanticize intact agrarian or small-town communities, whether from the left or the right. Marilynne Robinson's novels *Gilead* and *Home* depict powerfully both their blessings and pitfalls for child-rearing.[6] Speaking of the former, David Lyle Jeffrey writes: "The sub-genre of wisdom literature which Robinson evokes, even recreates in this novel, is distinctively biblical: 'My son, hear the

6. Marilynne Robinson, *Gilead: A Novel* (New York: Farrar, Straus & Giroux, 2004); idem, *Home: A Novel* (New York: Farrar, Straus & Giroux, 2008).

instruction of thy father, and forsake not the law of thy mother' (Prov. 1:8 KJV) is its watchword, a call to attention and recollection of family identity parallel to a larger invitation to instruction, '*Shema, Ysrael*' (cf. Deut. 5:1; 6:4; 9:1, etc.)."[7] True enough, but the latter novel pinpoints the poignant blind spots of such familial identity. Parents easily become guilty of forcing outward conformity or passive-aggressively eliciting pleasantness, failing to foster growth into genuine wisdom. Neither childhood conformity nor parental guilt-complexes embody the vision of Proverbs. All this requires prudence to address, but we must fear the Lord enough to take the Proverbs teaching seriously and attend to these complex factors.

Finally, reflecting upon these social concerns in Proverbs makes explicit once more our overarching theme: the household is an analogy of life in covenant with God. With any analogy there are points at which the parallels break down. Yet this analogy involves participation of the one reality in the other: in other words, the household is not only *like* the spiritual life; the household is a vital analogy because it is *fundamental to* the spiritual life. Rejecting the teaching of Proverbs is therefore akin to rejecting the basis of traditional Christian faith. Karl Barth's reflections are worth pondering:

> The Book of Proverbs, which can be read as a large-scale commentary on the fifth commandment, is not in any sense an unspiritual book. In it we are not prescribed, ordered or commanded, but persuaded and advised and invited to make a personal trial and well-considered decision, and this always with an appeal to the court which stands above the fatherly teacher and advisor. Yet it also cannot be denied that in the Old Testament the problem of the relation of the fifth to the first commandment is concealed under patriarchal modes of thought, and that the spiritual nature of the command, although it is a fact, is not yet manifest as such, but can always go unrecognised.[8]

Barth's concern is to place "honor your father and mother" in a more fundamental context: "We must obey God rather than any human authority" (Acts 5:29). When Jesus remains in the temple, going about his Father's business to the distress of his earthly parents, the narrative (Luke 2:41–52) is not a case of disobedience. To the contrary, the proper orientation of all earthly parenting is to inculcate in children growing wisdom for the sake of freely offered obedience to God. Jesus's actions at age twelve render upon Joseph and Mary the judgment, "Well done!"—whether or not they could recognize this.

The relevance of Barth's claim for Proverbs does not primarily concern patriarchal modes of thought. These are, as noted above, obvious. Moreover, Barth neglects "the fear of the LORD" as a way in which Proverbs itself affirms the

7. David Lyle Jeffrey, "Sharing Wisdom as an Act of Love," in *Christian Reflection: A Series in Faith and Ethics* (Waco: Baylor University Press, 2009), 67.

8. Karl Barth, *Church Dogmatics*, vol. 3/4: *The Doctrine of Creation*, trans. A. T. Mackay et al. (Edinburgh: Clark, 1961), 249.

priority of obeying God over obeying parents. Nevertheless, Proverbs largely treats God and parents on the same side. In this sense Barth rightly recognizes that New Testament narratives about Jesus challenge us to clarify the possibility and priorities of cases to the contrary, when we must obey God rather than even our parents. Even still, in the recognition that Proverbs basically places God and parents on the same side, we find a key for interpreting elements of patriarchy theologically. This key lies in "honor your father and mother" really pointing toward obeying the first commandment, always giving God precedence. The give-and-take of parenting and obeying calls us into an embodied analogy of life in covenant with God. This analogy is not just an abstraction about which we think; it is a reality in which we participate. As with any analogy, not only are there significant points of dissimilarity, but one must also pay attention to the direction from which the analogy begins. Although in our experience the analogy begins with obeying earthly fathers, the reality that gives structure to the analogy begins with the divine Father giving us life and commands.

Such theological ordering, based on ontology over epistemology, protects us from naïvely projecting patriarchy, as we understand it, backward onto God and outward onto society. The proper order begins not with whatever we know of human fathers in our culture or even personal experience, subsequently interpreting scripture about God as Father in that light. To the contrary, the proper order begins with scripture regarding God as Father and subsequently clarifies—or chastens—human concepts of fatherhood in light of the analogy's back-and-forth movement. Of course, the analogy starts to operate immediately once we use language concerning God as Father. But such a hermeneutical circle may be virtuous rather than vicious as God disciplines our speech over time. In this process we will learn far more about how men *and women* ought to parent children than about human fathers or gender dynamics, since the divine analogue with which we start is asexual and—depending on what we mean—nongendered.

What Proverbs ultimately teaches about parenting is the tremendous privilege involved in imitating God at a creaturely level. We participate in bringing forth, providing for, protecting, and nurturing life on behalf of God, so that each precious child grows into a wise person who offers free obedience and joyful discovery back to the Creator. This self-offering brings delight to family and neighbor, who watch youth respond to the heritage they have received by developing their particular gifts. Even those who never become parents may participate in this joy through various modes of teaching and caring. Yet there is nothing quite like parenting itself for learning the fear of the Lord, as one comes to learn more experientially about the dynamics of God's covenant life. The blessed Trinity is so gracious that the very fellowship of Father and Son in the Spirit spills over into parenting of covenant children, who in turn may enjoy parenting of their own. At each level of this reality lies tremendous mystery beyond which we cannot penetrate, leading us to fear the One whose wisdom began it all. At the same time, eliciting our faith in seeking to understand, there remains a common element: the giving and receiving of love.

ECCLESIASTES

INTRODUCTION

NOTHING IS REALLY NEW OR LASTING (UNDER THE SUN)

Ecclesiastes 1:1–11

> The sun rises every morning. I do not rise every morning; but the variation is due not to my activity, but to my inaction. Now, to put the matter in a popular phrase, it might be true that the sun rises regularly because he never gets tired of rising. His routine might be due, not to a lifelessness, but to a rush of life. The thing I mean can be seen, for instance, in children, when they find some game or joke that they specially enjoy. A child kicks his legs rhythmically through excess, not absence, of life. Because children have abounding vitality, because they are in spirit fierce and free, therefore they want things repeated and unchanged. They always say, "Do it again"; and the grown-up person does it again until he is nearly dead. For grown-up people are not strong enough to exult in monotony. But perhaps God is strong enough to exult in monotony. It is possible that God says every morning, "Do it again" to the sun; and every evening, "Do it again" to the moon. It may not be automatic necessity that makes all daisies alike; it may be that God makes every daisy separately, but has never got tired of making them. It may be that He has the eternal appetite of infancy; for we have sinned and grown old, and our Father is younger than we.[1]

Whose words? "The words of the Teacher," 1:1 announces, raising several questions about how these words relate to the divine Word in scripture.

1. G. K. Chesterton, *Orthodoxy* (Garden City, NY: Doubleday, 1959), 60.

First, what about the indirectness that follows? There is no straightforward plunge into narrative (as in Genesis or Job) or divine blessing and worship (as in Psalms) or a sermon from Moses (as in Deuteronomy); these are not "the proverbs of Solomon." The most we can say is that, as in Jeremiah and Amos, "the words of . . ." introduces collected sayings. The fact of their collection already hints at editorial presentation and, since this is now a scriptural text, canonical evaluation of the material.

Second, what is the identity of "the Teacher"? Is the Hebrew term *qōhelet* a proper noun or a title? The construct form "words of" followed by a noun has the above parallels and others, such as Neh. 1:1, where a specific person is narrated in Israel's salvation history: "The words of Nehemiah son of Hacaliah. In the month of Chislev, in the twentieth year, while I was in Susa the capital." Yet the noun in Ecclesiastes is unknown as a proper noun, but is related to a verb—for "calling" or "assembling." Thus *qōhelet* designates a function or occupation; since no other proper noun is provided, it is sometimes handy to refer to this speaker as "Qoheleth." He is not likely speaking in front of a gathered community as a contemporary preacher or professor would, so renaming Qoheleth "the Preacher" or "the Teacher"—though frequently tempting—misleads. The end of the book (12:9–10) clarifies the sense in which Qoheleth taught: whether or not he assembled an audience, as a wise man he assembled and arranged proverbs. The best name for the book's main voice is therefore "the Sage," a person of wise character whose skill in reflecting upon life gets preeminently put to use in writing, apparently behind the scenes.

Third, how do these words relate to Solomon? Are he and Qoheleth one and the same figure? In 1 Kgs. 8, Solomon assembles the leaders of Israel for the sake of dedicating the temple. Moreover, Ecclesiastes immediately identifies the Sage as a son of David and king in Jerusalem. Hence it was natural for ancient Jews and Christians to see King Solomon as the author. The Latin title "Ecclesiastes" is directly borrowed from the Greek *ekklēsia*, which could designate nothing more than an assembly (stemming from *qōhelet*). But of course *ekklēsia* calls to mind the church as well. On this reading Solomon typifies Jesus Christ, drawing together people "from the ends of the earth to listen to . . . [his] wisdom" (Matt. 12:42; Origen, *Commentary on the Song of Songs*, prologue, in Ancient Christian Writers 26.39–46, 51–52).

Origen influenced early Christians to see Proverbs, Ecclesiastes, and Song of Songs in terms of a pattern for becoming wise unto salvation. For the beginning of the Christian pilgrimage, Proverbs is Solomon's book of "the most basic religious instruction," regarding "good conduct." At the end, Song of Songs is Solomon's book of "the most sublime religious achievements," regarding "the mystical contemplation of divine things." Ecclesiastes stands in the middle, pertaining "to those whose religious instruction is already significantly under way, but who have yet to attain the highest goals of that instruction. It is the next to last stop in the project of learning to love." A parallel structure appears in Dante's medieval

Commedia with its threefold organization according to *Inferno*, *Purgatorio*, and *Paradiso* (Christianson 2007: 38–39): first the conversion by which one begins the journey away from hell; then the purgation by which one ultimately becomes fit for paradise and the vision of God. Whatever one makes of the Song of Songs, the first two stages highlight real progression: the wisdom of Proverbs sets a person on the path of fearing the Lord; the Sage in Ecclesiastes purges us of naïve and wrongful earthly attachments, advancing that holy fear.

Despite these insights, the classic "Jesus is the Ecclesiast" approach works against the tendency to see these words as those of an aging, repentant Solomon. If part of the point of Solomonic authorship is his autobiography—Ecclesiastes offering the reflections of a king for whom wisdom had to become more than worldly skill, via the school of self-imposed spiritual hard knocks—then it is hard to press the parallels to Christ very far. Indeed, the text itself works against directly Solomonic authorship. For one reason, Ecclesiastes lacks the proper noun "Solomon" provided directly in Proverbs. For another reason, the text presents Qoheleth in the third person, not only at the beginning and the end but also in the middle—at 7:27. For a third reason, there are apparently hints of criticism regarding Solomon's successors (e.g., 2:19).[2]

It is not necessary to settle authorship as a historical question. Rather, discerning the text's self-presentation has implications for how its message works with the Solomonic persona. Solomonic authorship, though not necessarily impossible, threatens to obscure the indirectness *and the canonical filter* through which we gain access to *and evaluation of* the Sage's words. This filter also grants perspective on Solomon himself as the paragon of human wisdom. If Solomon wrote the book, then he certainly did so with a great deal of self-critical awareness and not always as a positive christological figure. The vocation of the Sage vis-à-vis the Messiah, in some cases, is to depict the fall from which we are redeemed, not just the paragon of redemption. The proof of the pudding on this score becomes clearer as the book's quest advances, particularly in Eccl. 7.

Fourth, then, how do these words relate to Jesus? Little in Ecclesiastes points explicitly to Christ, as if these words and the Sage's persona were typical of the Son of God or his most direct address to the church. Yet not all divine speech in scripture occurs via prophetic oracle in which we hear, "Thus says the Lord." The Bible also takes up human words—in this case, with all their traces of our experience and struggle—for us to weigh them and be prodded by them as we pursue the fear of the Lord (12:9–14). These words can teach wisdom precisely because of their earthy—even edgy—character. In other words, the best way to read this Old Testament book christologically is to take seriously the full depth of its portrayal of human experience—warts and all. We can see more clearly what it means for Jesus Christ to be our wisdom only when wisdom's worldly

2. Moreover, the overwhelming majority of Old Testament scholars find the Hebrew wording, grammar, and style to reflect those of a much later period.

paragon—no less than the biblical Solomon—gets taken down a notch or two: "Jews demand signs and Greeks desire wisdom, but we proclaim Christ crucified, a stumbling block to Jews and foolishness to Gentiles, but to those who are the called, both Jews and Greeks, Christ the power of God and the wisdom of God" (1 Cor. 1:22–24).

All is hebel. Ecclesiastes 1:2 continues the verbal indirectness, with "says the Teacher," while announcing the book's most prominent term: *hebel*. Its virtual restatement in 12:8 forms an inclusio, sandwiching the body of the book inside. In English its most frequent translation, or cultural association anyway, is "vanity" (e.g., RSV, NRSV, NASB). But possibilities abound: "meaningless" (NIV, TNIV); "[absolute] futility" (Holman Christian Standard Bible); "utterly absurd";[3] "[utterly] enigmatic" (Bartholomew 2009: 104–7); and so forth. Such translations present to readers the fruit of skilled interpreters' labor. Yet they threaten to obscure a basic metaphor and a key question, as well as a long history of interpretation.

The basic metaphor is vapor. We can see its importance by noting the connection with "chasing after wind" (1:14; 2:11, 17, 26; 4:4, 16; 6:9). The metaphorical concreteness is further evident with *hebel* applying "under the sun." Ironically, then, the "breath" most fundamentally associated with the word vanishes quickly in a haze of abstract translations, all with negative connotations. The key question likewise vanishes: whether the meaning of *hebel* is the same in every case throughout or instead involves nuances that sometimes call for different terms.

To be fair to translators, they face a virtually impossible task. Nevertheless, readers need to become familiar with a complex history of interpretation in order to situate the word properly within a context of linguistic and churchly actions and reactions. Christianson 2007: 140 summarizes this history in five stages. First, the *contemptus mundi* ("contempt for the world") reading—popularized by Jerome—suggested that since everything earthly is vanity, the book points toward the love of God and our future heavenly home. Second, from Martin Luther and other Protestant (especially Puritan) commentators, is the opposite approach, which rejects the use of Ecclesiastes to call for asceticism and instead highlights the book's calls to earthly joy. Navigating the tensions between these two stages frames the chief challenge of theological commentary. The third through fifth stages, from the Renaissance through early modernity to the present, manifest more fragmentary appeals to particular expressions from the book, chiefly oriented around its preoccupation with death. Reflection on death resonates with the focus on human experience that characterized these ages, of concern to all people, not just Jews and orthodox Christians. But the challenge remains to move beyond resonating with the poetry and memorable prose—to understand how the affirmations of joy in Ecclesiastes relate to its *hebel* motif and thereby to discern what theological message emerges from all this material on facing death.

3. Michael V. Fox, *A Time to Tear Down and a Time to Build Up: A Rereading of Ecclesiastes* (Grand Rapids: Eerdmans, 1999), 159.

Jerome, whose Latin translation of the scriptures dominated Western culture for centuries, did not follow early Greek translators who understood *hebel* as vapor. Instead he went with the Septuagint's Greek rendering (*mataiotēs*) and thus introduced the abstract *vanitas* to render *hebel*. While the Latin *vanitas* could include less negative meanings such as "unsubstantial" or "lacking in permanence" within its semantic range, the meanings "useless," "futile," or "illusory" came to dominate.[4] The early Christians struggled with this reading: "If everything that God made is very good, then how can everything be vanity—and not only vanity, but even vanity of vanities?" (Jerome, *Commentary on Ecclesiastes* 1.2, in Corpus Christianorum: Series Latina 72.252 and Wright 2005: 194). Augustine and others answered this with respect to humanity's fall into sin and God's resulting curse on creation. Yet, though acknowledging the beauty of God's creation as such, Augustine asserted that "corporeal beauty is the lowest beauty" (*Of True Religion* 21.41, in Library of Christian Classics 6.244–45), quite apart from the fall that also factors into vanity. This sort of thinking appears strikingly in Origen, who equates vanity with the material body (*On First Principles* 1.7.5, in ANF 4.264). The appropriate response to this situation would be asking God to "turn my eyes from looking at vanities" (Ps. 119:37). The true message of Ecclesiastes tells these readers, "Set your minds on things that are above, not on things that are on earth" (Col. 3:2).

Luther, however, believed that such classic readers taught "contempt of things that have been created and established by God. Among these is St. Jerome, who by writing a commentary on this book urged Blesilla to accept the monastic life. From this source there arose and spread over the entire church, like a flood, that theology of the religious orders or monasteries."[5] The affirmation of ordinary life became a badge of Protestant identity and tremendously influenced the development of the modern West. Amid all these options and opinions regarding *hebel*, what should we make of the *contemptus mundi* tradition in a commentary that takes seriously the church's classic heritage? About *hebel*, as with so much else, seeking too much clarity is like chasing after wind. However, what can we say with some confidence, especially in relation to the rest of scripture?

First, *hebel* is probably one among the many allusions in Ecclesiastes to Genesis: in this case, to Abel. The fleetingness of his godly young life seems absurd, like much that the Sage ponders. Cain too may be present in Ecclesiastes, with an echo in the verb for buying (*qānâ*) in 2:7. So is Adam, whose name names our species.

> The names of the two brothers are heavy with portent: Permanence and Impermanence, Possession and Ephemerality. Koheleth sees that in a profound way the history of *adam*, humankind, mirrors the history of the younger brother Hevel/

4. Kathleen A. Farmer, "Piety or Heresy?" in *Reflecting with Solomon: Selected Studies on the Book of Ecclesiastes*, ed. Roy B. Zuck (Grand Rapids: Baker, 1994), 225.

5. Martin Luther, *Notes on Ecclesiastes*, trans. J. Pelikan, Luther's Works 15 (St. Louis: Concordia, 1972), 4.

> Abel, who enters the biblical narrative only to die. His death is nonsensical, as is every murder. But is his life then meaningless, entirely absurd? The one thing we know about Hevel/Abel is that he offered the best of his flock as a sacrifice that brought God pleasure (Gen. 4:4). And is not just that the point of human life, to give some pleasure to God, to make our work in this world holy by offering something of it to God?[6]

Second, strongly negative translations of *hebel* generate inconsistencies. Farmer notes: "Only one verse (the last verse in the book of Proverbs) separates Prov. 31:30 from Ecclesiastes in Christian Bibles. But ironically, some modern English versions (such as the NIV and New American Bible), which recognize that *hebel* means 'fleeting' in Prov. 31:30 ('beauty is fleeting'), translate the same word two verses later (in Eccl. 1:2) as 'meaningless' and 'vain.'"[7] Of course there is no need to adopt a monolithic translation policy of always using the same word. However flexible *hebel* in Ecclesiastes may be, though, value remains in having some translations signal the word's presence with the same English gloss, especially given nearly constant repetition throughout the book. Mere vapor hovers somewhere in the background, even if presenting causes or manifestations vary in particular contexts.

Third, there are New Testament echoes to consider. Paul speaks in Rom. 8:20–21 of God's subjecting creation to "vanity" (*mataiotēs*) with a view to its redemption. James 4:14 refers to our lives being like "mist" (*atmis*) that vanishes quickly. Making this connection clear, among others, is the Codex Vaticanus translation of Eccl. 9:9 with *atmos*. "Meaninglessness" would be too strong in Rom. 8, while fleetingness is clearly the key concern of Jas. 4. So far, we have reasons for taking *hebel* in a less negative sense than many usually do.

Fourth, however, almost half of the thirty-two *hebel* occurrences outside Ecclesiastes deal with idols, so in some cases the transitory nature of life is not the key issue. Despite the despairing tone in a number of passages, whatever this condition is, "'vanity' does not mark a world *without* God; it marks a world *subjected by* God."[8] In the words of Ellul 1990: 53, "Smoke or mist diffuses; *it has no result*: it is not nothingness!" This emphasis on divinely ordained (lack of) results is especially important in light of another major theme in Ecclesiastes, profit, which is announced by way of a question in 1:3. What causes the lack of results to render everything *hebel* is human preoccupation with turning life toward one's permanent advantage: in short, idolatry. Thus Rom. 1:21 becomes relevant, describing idolatrous pagans: "For though they knew God, they did not honor him as God or give thanks to him, but they became futile in their thinking, and their senseless minds were darkened." The word for futility stems from the same family as the vanity of Rom. 8, highlighting misuse of God's good creation as the

6. Ellen F. Davis, *Proverbs, Ecclesiastes, and the Song of Songs*, Westminster Bible Companion (Louisville: Westminster John Knox, 2000), 168–69.

7. Farmer, "Piety or Heresy?" 226.

8. William P. Brown, *Ecclesiastes*, Interpretation (Louisville: Westminster John Knox, 2000), 125.

root cause of cultural malaise. Ecclesiastes does not deny but in fact underscores the goodness of God's earthly gifts. Yet the book simultaneously situates that goodness within a more comprehensive framework of remembering the Creator: if people fasten on to the gifts themselves for the sake of personal advantage, in hopes of permanently holding on to their claims, then in such an idolatrous state God-given disappointment is bound to result. Moreover, the Sage's narrative of his failed quest for profit indicates that sometimes we cannot figure out how to gain advantage in the first place. It is impossible not just to know how to keep it for long, but also to guarantee how to produce it.

Fifth is the subtle distinction between the *hebel* theme and the central message of Ecclesiastes itself. If we believe the canonical commentary on the book in Eccl. 12, then the central message has to do with fearing and obeying God from youth onward. *Hebel* is a motif that spells out the setting within which people are called to fear God, clarifying the genuine and false incentives for doing so. The ungraspable nature of vapor—sometimes merely fleeting, at other times seemingly meaningless—applies to the effects of the cosmos on misshapen, idolatrous human lives. The repetition of the term in Hebrew construct form adds emphasis—hence literal translations such as "vanity of vanities" often give way to adverbial renderings, for instance "utterly enigmatic" or "absolutely futile." And "all" is *hebel*: everything in the book's purview—namely, the cosmos that God created, as 1:3 reinforces—has this ungraspable nature. Even so, important as *hebel* is, its significance lies in encouraging us to remember our Creator. As Eccl. 12 makes clear, that remembrance does not reject earthly goodness but interprets it.

In the end, attempts to provide a single, definitive translation for *hebel* are the equivalent of chasing the wind! Frequently the Sage's frustration lies in impermanence; on other occasions in apparent absurdity or perhaps even meaninglessness. The traditional "vanity" translation, despite its potentially misleading connotations, remains commendable precisely because it requires explanation. Its cultural associations provide a measure of unity to the book and its interpretation, while its lack of clarity elicits further commentary. Behind vanity, the root metaphor of vapor can hover ethereally in the background without alternatives such as "absurd" or "meaningless" overly determining audience reactions. If, thereafter, we seek a less poetic word to convey the connotations of *hebel* along with the connected metaphor of chasing after wind, then "ungraspable" might be the best candidate. The theological thrust of the Sage is that sometimes earthly life remains outside intellectual grasp; at other times it challenges our emotional hold on ourselves; and always it thwarts any full sense of spiritual accomplishment or predictive control. There is no guaranteed way of using wisdom to turn life toward lasting advantage.

This reading of *hebel* accounts for the strengths of both the *contemptus mundi* tradition and Luther's critique. The tradition is correct that Ecclesiastes is spiritually purgative for misplaced love of this world, helping us to recognize all the complexity and tragedy of life "under the sun." Luther's critique forces us to speak more clearly and energetically of the goodness of the divine gifts in creation, to match the material in the book. The underlying compatibility of these emphases lies in understanding the good purpose of the divine gifts: they are to bring *temporary* delight as they lead toward grateful praise of our Creator and thereby toward true and *permanent* joy. Vanity arises from humans seeking to gain lasting joy on their own apart from God, by turning temporary delights under the sun into idols.

Inside the narrative frame. In moving to 1:3, we arrive more directly at the words of the Sage himself, away from the "frame narrator" who, having introduced Qoheleth, now disappears from view for a while. The listener recognizes the element of quotation noted in 1:1–2 but, contra many critical and populist readings, cannot be expected to insert a minus sign negating the divine truth of everything from 1:3 onward. Simply because now the words of the Sage become the direct focus does not mean either that an editor rejects Qoheleth as a cynical skeptic until rescuing his orthodoxy in 12:9–14 or that God gives us a book with a thoroughly secular perspective until revealing its apologetic rationale at the very end. The frame does not cancel out everything in between, as if the listener would be only semihooked throughout 1:3–12:7 (or 1:12–12:7), expecting the rug to be pulled out from under the book at its conclusion. After all, the frame narrative expresses harmony between its final evaluation (12:9–14) and the rest of the Sage's material. If an editor thought this would pull the wool over orthodox eyes, then he was either naïve on the one hand or else contemptuous of his readers' intelligence on the other.

The reader is set up for shared intellectual and spiritual struggle, not blunt rejection of the Sage's reflection. From 1:3 onward the Sage matches this substance with style. The somewhat monotonous rhythms of the world play out in the book's lumbering repetitions, such as the *hebel* theme or the profit question. Our feeling that we cannot fully grasp the message is fitting in light of 1:2–3: depending on expectations, the reading of Ecclesiastes itself elicits cries of "*Hebel! Hebel!*" along with the admission that we are unsure of exactly what we have gained. This blend of style and substance plays out via incessant words in the poetry of 1:4–11.

Before that 1:3 introduces three more key terms or themes. First, *yitrôn* ("gain, profit, advantage") appears nine times in Ecclesiastes (1:3; 2:11, 13; 3:9; 5:9, 16; 7:12; 10:10, 11) yet nowhere else in the Old Testament. As a rhetorical question, 1:3 implies the answer "none," although the question form (similarly posed in 3:9 and 5:16) keeps the reader hanging a bit. Second, *ʿāmāl* ("toil") can neutrally designate labor, but frequently carries a negative connotation, which the context surely supports here. The power of the rhetorical question lies in the contrast between juxtaposed elements: What *benefit* is there in our *burden* of labor? Third, "under the sun" is the Sage's most infamous refrain next to the *hebel* formulas. Strictly speaking, like *yitrôn* it occurs nowhere else in the Old Testament, while frequently in Ecclesiastes (twenty-nine occurrences).[9] The basic sense of the phrase

9. Relative synonyms—"under heaven" (2:3; 3:1) and "upon/on earth" (5:2; 7:20; 8:14, 16; 11:2)—do appear outside the book, though.

focuses on the Sage's terrestrial, empirically focused perspective, referring to the sun for poetic effect and possibly alluding to its oft-wearying heat. The sun also highlights the passage of time, involving both a measure of change season by season and considerable monotony day in and day out.

For the most part the Sage is not addressing human advantage, including eternal matters, comprehensively. Rather, he restricts his focus to the ebb and flow of temporal gain. Thus, while the question may evoke memories of Jesus's query, "What does it profit them if they gain the whole world, but lose or forfeit themselves?" (Luke 9:25), in itself Eccl. 1:3 does not yet point to the Son of Man coming in eternal glory (Luke 9:26). At this point the Sage registers only the apparent zero sum of the temporal life, and—creating a deficit—death haunts because we do not know clearly what comes after. Life and immortality come to light in the gospel (2 Tim. 1:10); whatever hints of divine judgment and blessing the Old Testament gives, only in Jesus Christ does an eternal alternative to gaining the whole world come fully into view. Augustine rightly alludes to this Ecclesiastes text when discussing how the rich ought to live, connecting it with 1 Tim. 6:18–19: "They are to do good, to be rich in good works, generous, and ready to share, thus storing up for themselves the treasure of a good foundation for the future, so that they may take hold of the life that really is life" (Sermon 61.111, in WSA 3/3.147). Yet at this point the Sage, not trying to reach Jesus's stage of the argument regarding treasure in heaven, deals only with a theme that appears in 1 Tim. 6:17: "Command them not to be haughty, or to set their hopes on the uncertainty of riches." The poetry that follows in Eccl. 1:4–11 deconstructs the human drive for lasting earthly profit, but this is as far as it goes for now—providing the canonical setup for clarity about the future that comes only later.

Generations come and go. This initial deconstruction of profit motives occurs implicitly, through poetic descriptions of the cosmos that precede explicit allusions to human life. Whether the "generations" of 1:4 refer to humans or nature, in context the verse introduces the earth's stability in contrast with human fragility. Hence Gregory of Nyssa points out the vanity of a landowner seeking to gain more and more and to hold on to it forever. The earth is God's, not ours; God is the one who gives it duration—for the sake of all, not just a few (*On Virginity* 4, in NPNF^2 5.349). This may not resonate with very many contemporary Westerners, but as a son of a farmer I can attest to land's hold over people. When it is the source of one's basic livelihood, this hold is understandable. Even still, the value of earthly ownership must remain relative, to acknowledge the coming and going of generations under God.

For Christians rooted in biblical and creedal tradition, the final clause, "the earth remains forever," is potentially discomfiting. After all, the Bible frequently affirms that only the word of God remains forever: "All flesh is like grass" (1 Pet. 1:24–25, quoting Isa. 40:6–8). Moreover, the Almighty God is Maker of heaven and earth; therefore the earth is not eternal, but comes into being *ex nihilo* ("out of nothing," by way of divine speech). Hence there has been much debate over the meaning of *ʿôlām* ("forever") and whether the Israelites had a concept of eternity. In context the text is trying to say that the earth remains "as long as we could think of," without contradicting the biblical creation story on which Ecclesiastes depends. If the earth remains for an inconceivably long time, of course, that is due to its origin and sustenance in the divine Word abiding forever. Positively, humans ought to trust and desire the eternal God; negatively, we ought to learn that the earth itself is indifferent to us, with numerous people coming and going, seeking gain and either coming up empty or else learning that they cannot take it with them.

Sunrise . . . sunset. The parallel to 1:5 in Ps. 19:4–6 reminds us that the sun's travels speak volumes about God's glory: "Their [the heavens'] voice goes out through all the earth, / and their words to the end of the world. / In the heavens he has set a tent for the sun, / which comes out like a bridegroom from his wedding canopy, / and like a strong man runs its course with joy. / Its rising is from the end of the heavens, / and its circuit to the end of them; / and nothing is hid from its heat." But God's glory is not the surface agenda here, which is the apparent monotony of creation's orderly cycles. These represent human life in terms of "one damn thing after another," as the saying goes. If nothing truly new happens in creation, then by definition there can be no lasting profit or advantage for humans to gain—God's glory becomes clearer when the cosmos reminds us of our finitude.

The ceaseless cycles of the cosmos are not merely allegories or analogies for human life, but realities within which God places us. In other ways too, the poetry manifests careful craftsmanship. For example, in Eccl. 1:6 several repeated participles build suspense before the wind is identified as the subject. The north-south direction complements the east-west movement of the sun in 1:5, demonstrating the completeness of cosmic order (Longman 1998: 69–70).

The dominance of repetition appears again in 1:7, which avoids more economical ways of making the point in favor of repeating "streams" and "flow." By this time 1:4–7 has cited the four fundamental elements of the ancients, as Ibn Ezra saw: earth, fire, wind, and water (Longman 1998: 70). Several words, particularly for motion, have occurred numerous times. The text is not only reinforcing cosmic monotony, but ultimately underscoring that humans fit into the cosmos rather than controlling it.

This distinction is important in relation to the biblical doctrine of creation. The repetitive cosmic order bears potential for monotony when humans ponder how to master the universe. Our Maker is "the Father, the Almighty"; we are not to be captains of our own fate. The Sovereign is a loving Father whom we can trust to provide what is truly best—accomplishing divine purposes in the world and drawing us as apprenticed children to participate in those accomplishments. The other side of the potential monotony, then, is the reliability we take for granted. Tsunamis, hurricanes, and so forth are exceptions that prove the daily rules on which humans rely. The Sage leaves this aspect of the truth out of the equation in the present passage, in order to establish first of all that finite goods do not satisfy infinite longings. But this initial truth does not negate the very real grace underlying creation's narrative.

"I can't get no . . . satisfaction." The Sage does not emphasize the gracious character of created order here, because his rhetorical aim is even more unsettling. Whether we should translate "all things are wearisome" (NRSV) or "all words are wearisome" (NRSV margin), 1:8 manifests the ongoing focus on the insatiability of human desire. Acknowledging this truth requires no denial of the goodness of the cosmic order, if anything affirming that order as the divinely imposed set of limits within which humans learn to receive God's gifts. Christina Rossetti uses the Sage's language to express this other side of the coin:

> Experience bows a sweet contented face,
> Still setting to her seal that God is true:
> Beneath the sun, she knows, is nothing new;
> All things that go return with measured pace,
> Winds, rivers, man's still recommencing race:—
> While Hope beyond earth's circle strains her view,
> Past sun and moon, and rain and rainbow too,
> Enamoured of unseen eternal grace.
> Experience saith, "My God doth all things well":
> And for the morrow taketh little care,
> Such peace and patience garrison her soul:—
> While Hope, who never yet hath eyed the goal,
> With arms flung forth, and backward floating hair,
> Touches, embraces, hugs the invisible.[10]

In 1:8 human desire fits within the cosmic cycles by means of the body: the eye and the ear become vehicles through which our longings likewise become monotonous. There is a sense in which God created us for the regular, temporary fulfillment of desire, as we learn from our need to eat (6:7–9). Unfortunately, though, most humans are unable to rest in the experience of "unseen eternal grace" mentioned by Rossetti, instead finding the regularity of the cosmos to elicit feelings of weariness.

Nothing is new under the sun. Because cosmic repetition extends into the realm of human activity by the time we reach 1:9, the claim that "there is nothing new under the sun" creates irony for the Sage's subsequent claims that he surpassed all previous kings of Jerusalem (1:16; 2:9). Of course at times "the LORD creates something new" (Num. 16:30), as the incarnation dramatically attests. Yet, left to itself, the natural realm knows nothing truly and dramatically new apart from supernatural grace, even though grace usually works through rather than against or apart from nature. God's activity in Jesus Christ serves as the exception proving the rule: the rest of history turns on that pivot, in which all other candidates for

10. Christina Rossetti, *The Complete Poems of Christina Rossetti*, ed. R. W. Crump (Baton Rouge: Louisiana State University Press, 1986), 2.251.

relative newness find their true meaning.[11] However new someone's achievements or attributes seem to be, in the end they are measured by the stature of the fullness of Christ (Eph. 4:13) and whether they enhance or inhibit such faithfulness to God the Creator.

Modern people find it tempting to claim that we have invented all sorts of new things and that the newer is always better. The Sage is not silly enough to deny the powers of human invention, especially given the litany of royal achievements soon to follow. From the standpoint of ultimate human advantage, however, inventions come and go; even claims to improvement have a "been there, done that" character, as incessant offers of software upgrades demonstrate. The apparent paradox in the rhetorical question of Eccl. 1:10—can people really claim to know that something has never been before, since they are always new to the scene?—challenges what level of genuine progress lies within our ceaseless inventiveness. Ellul 1990: 153 notes: "Making such a statement requires tremendous pride, unless its author is expressing a message from the one who knows everything, because he is outside everything—the one whom time does not limit. Humanly speaking no possible assessment of science exists."

There is irony in the dazzling array of new technologies: this panoply gives the impression, on the surface, of endless variety and limitless possibilities—making the problem of boredom in relation to the natural world increasingly acute. The contemporary person is tempted to mock: if only the Sage had our gadgets, then the monotony would not be so wearisome. Yet our greater opportunities for distracting entertainment correlate with lesser interest in particular moments and therefore a decreasing sense of happiness. Plus technological capacity depends more than ever on the regularity of God's created order. Below the surface veneer we remain as dependent as the simple farmer on the underlying reality of the cosmos: "The more things change, the more they stay the same."

This should not foster fatalism, warns Augustine the great predestinarian (*City of God* 12.14, in FC 14.268–69)! The biblical view of history does not contain endlessly returning earthly cycles alone. Nor does this poetry present the Sage's last word on the subject. Whatever we say about history's relation to the mind of God, this passage—an exercise in introductory question-raising—does not exclude its linear drive toward Jesus Christ. Instead, human achievement and its cosmic context are spheres of repetition manifesting certain limits. Whether 1:11 refers most directly to people or things, to inability or unwillingness to remember, it subtly but effectively concludes a broadside against human pretension. It does not even mention the present, but only the past and the future—thus foreshadowing what will occur to the Sage's readers who are part of the cosmos (Krüger 2004: 52, 55)! They cannot control their legacies. In the words of Milan Kundera:

11. Much of what the New Testament designates "new" clusters around the incarnation; Carl B. Hoch Jr., *All Things New: The Significance of Newness for Biblical Theology* (Grand Rapids: Baker, 1995).

> Yes, suddenly I saw it clearly: most people deceive themselves with a pair of faiths: they believe in *eternal memory* (of people, things, deeds, nations) and in *redressibility* (of deeds, mistakes, sins, wrongs). Both are false faiths. In reality the opposite is true: everything will be forgotten and nothing will be redressed. The task of obtaining redress (by vengeance or by forgiveness) will be taken over by forgetting. No one will redress the wrongs that have been done, but all wrongs will be forgotten.[12]

Or so a strictly empirical perspective could suggest. Ecclesiastes gives permission to describe phenomena as they are "under the sun," acknowledging the element of truth therein without making such a perspective ultimate and leading to the nihilism Kundera explores.

Many commentators place the first structural division in Ecclesiastes before or after 1:3, for literary reasons connected to the frame narrative. What the present commentary highlights by treating 1:1–11 together, however, is the thematic continuation of the introduction. The speaker(s) come on scene in 1:1–2, and the major rhetorical motif announces itself in 1:2. But the driving question that so often elicits the rhetoric of *hebel* appears in 1:3, and this question stings with full force only after we have labored through 1:4–11. The Sage's reintroduction in 1:12 affirms this reading.

The Solomonic overtones initially lead the reader to expect traditional wisdom. But 1:2 throws us off balance, and 1:3 turns us toward the cosmos—"under the sun"—with unexpected results. Whereas wisdom theology should laud the value of living in harmony with creation's order, in 1:4–11 empirical observation suggests something else. If everything is subject to ceaseless cycles and nothing is genuinely new, then it is impossible to find genuine wisdom in creation when it is divorced from salvation history. The alternatives are stark, highlighted in Kundera's novel *The Unbearable Lightness of Being* as it reflects on Friedrich Nietzsche's myth of eternal return.[13] Without salvation history, either one takes human history to consist of endlessly recurring cycles, in which case acting is a heavy burden with drastically important consequences—or else history is a one-shot deal and human existence is unbelievably light, with no lasting consequences: "Let us eat and drink, / for tomorrow we die" (1 Cor. 15:32). No doubt this typology of heaviness and lightness is simplistic upon further reflection, for, with endlessly recurring cycles, one is likely playing out a script already written, so choices are not that heavy after all. And, in the case of "the one who dies with the most toys wins," choices become quite a bit heavier upon realizing just how limited our earthly time really is. Taken with this potential heaviness, the Sage sets up queries about acting to maximize "profit"—whatever *yitrôn* might be—for as long as possible. In the long

12. Milan Kundera, *The Joke: The Definitive Version Fully Revised by the Author* (New York: Harper, 1993), 294.

13. Milan Kundera, *The Unbearable Lightness of Being*, trans. Michael Henry Heim (New York: Harper & Row, 1984).

run, of course, if this poetic introduction were the entirety of his thought, then *hebel* would pervade with the strongest possible negative meaning.

Yet elsewhere the book hints at a longer-term perspective, involving divine judgment with which to make limited sense of human action. Read in that light, this passage remains consistent with God promising to take care of us via the rhythms of the cosmic order. God does not provide a context in which to "make a name for ourselves" (compare Gen. 8:22 with the Babel narrative in Gen. 11). Human activity is not meaningless, nor is human inactivity appropriate; between fatalism and hubris lies fear of God. But we must allow Ecclesiastes to draw us toward its conclusion in due course. For the moment, Qoheleth poetically raises a question that initiates a pilgrimage of reflection, and commentary should not run ahead of the Sage's pace.

PART 1

A QUEST FOR "BETTER"

Ecclesiastes 1:12–6:9

At 1:12 comes another beginning. Now the Sage reflects by way of personal narrative rather than poetry. The concerns of 1:1–11 pertain to every human; the mode of engagement is universal, open to anyone willing to search the cosmos for broad patterns. Now the Sage's undertakings in the following sections, while similarly pertaining to everyone, have more particular modes of pursuit, frequently open only to people of enormous power or means. The scope of 1:1–11 opens inquiry to everyone's experience; the scale in 1:12–6:9 often circumscribes the possibilities of pursuit, so that the king functions as a paragon whose experience others must trust. This allows for greater-to-lesser arguments, of an "if even the king" type, thereby touching everyone. Even so, this affects the way people are drawn into the text's implied situation(s). With the power of "I" in Ecclesiastes, most cannot directly identify.

Some commentators despair over the structural coherence of Ecclesiastes, whereas others find an intricate structure therein. The present commentary seeks middle ground. Jennifer Koosed compares the book's structural elements to a decomposing body, fitting the Sage's preoccupation with death.[1] Each time it seems that a fully coherent structure lies within scholarly grasp, one or more factors cause this to unravel. The book's form fits its meaning. Taking this intriguing notion

1. Jennifer L. Koosed, *(Per)mutations of Qohelet: Reading the Body in the Book*, Library of Hebrew Bible/Old Testament Studies 429 (New York: Clark, 2006).

(laden with excessive postmodern theory all around) in a different direction, one wonders if Ecclesiastes actually mirrors the Sage's life narrative—beginning with a quest in clearly delimited stages; eventually turning to repeated musings on key themes along with aphoristic wisdom as the best available possibilities; and continually raising the stakes, regarding God and death, joy and knowledge, until concluding with the most intense yet elusive material. The Sage's reflections die off as he reaches the height and kinds of profundity available to humans. While Ecclesiastes does not proceed via linear argument the way modern Westerners might expect or impose as interpreters, themes and motifs have accumulating effects as they recur. In some cases, literary markers sufficiently determine textual units. In other cases, though, literary markers are open to multiple possibilities for thematic connections and development. The overall effect is a looping or lumbering one, in which the text steps forward to explore territory before doubling back to take another path, only to revisit earlier areas from new angles. Units accordingly vary not only in size but also in the scope of the issues they raise or the scale of their contribution to the movement of the whole.

Other than the so-called frame narrative, the division of the book into two halves (→6:10–12) provides the only overarching structure within which more particular units fit. The first half narrates the Sage's quest. Conclusions often suggest what is "good" or "better" (the Hebrew word is the same), yet their uptake is quite modest. Such disappointment prepares for the second half to raise the question, "Who knows?"

Wisdom Offers No Permanent Gain (1:12–18)

> "Soon the sun will set"—is *that* prophecy? No, it's merely an assertion of faith in the consistency of events. The children of the world are consistent too—so I say they will soak up everything you can offer, take your job away from you, and then denounce you as a decrepit wreck. Finally, they'll ignore you entirely. It's your own fault. The Book I gave you should have been enough for you. Now you'll just have to take the consequences for your meddling.[2]

In 1:12–18 there is a schematic narrative of the Sage's quest, put in terms of a search for wisdom. After this general overview of human activity, subsequent sections explore the details.

Reintroducing the Sage. The first verse of the section restates the Sage's Solomonic identity as "king over Israel." There are good reasons for wondering whether this is Solomon's actual self-reflection or instead a portrayal adopting his persona for effect. The perfective verb in 1:12 may place the kingship in the past; although not conclusive, this seems most consistent with the following narrative and would

2. Benjamin the Hermit, a character in Walter M. Miller Jr., *A Canticle for Leibowitz* (repr., New York: Eos, 2006), 173.

thereby signal a post-Solomonic author. The wisdom paragon's tragic quest makes the Sage's case as poignantly as possible. Despite Solomon's powerful position, the resulting lessons are universal. Perhaps for this reason the Revised Common Lectionary uses 1:12–14 to frame selections from Eccl. 2 as its only material from Ecclesiastes, apart from 3:1–13 for New Year's Eve. While the book contains numerous powerful passages, it is understandable that the heart of its churchly reading would orbit around the Solomonic narrative, for Christians must wrestle with this paragon to understand the vocation of Jesus Christ. The story of Solomon proves that even the wise person who has everything cannot escape the common human fate: frequent vexation followed by death. Wisdom only forces us to face this fate more honestly. In this respect Solomon serves as a tragic antihero who dramatizes human limitations and thereby the shape of the need that Jesus meets. No human climbing toward God, even when started by way of wisdom, will enable us to make complete sense of providence or to transcend death. At the same time, redemption does not destroy all human wisdom but nullifies its present form in order that we may have "the mind of Christ" (1 Cor. 1–2). Though wisdom quests of human initiative come to naught for seeking wrongly, Jesus Christ is the antitype of Solomon by embodying Wisdom's ultimate fulfillment. This stems from divine initiative and constancy rather than merely human ego.

Introducing the—unhappy?—quest. This quest on which the Sage reports through the end of Eccl. 2 is announced in 1:13. The idiom emphasizes the internal, holistic nature of the struggle, as opposed to a purely intellectual exercise. The writer "gave his heart [*lēb*]" to the search. This "heart" (*lēb*) and "wisdom" (*ḥokmâ*) point again to Solomon, who received these from God (*lēb* in 1 Kgs. 3:9, 12 and *ḥokmâ* in 2 Chr. 1:10, 12). Yet here Solomon's application of these seems too self-important. Certainly the contrast is stark between Ecclesiastes, with the overwhelming frequency of its "I" language, and Proverbs, in which the speaker—even during personal address—passes on wisdom as a received tradition. Seeking for wisdom is ambiguous since, as Job 28 asks rhetorically and repeatedly, where shall it be found? In itself and as such, wisdom is unavailable to humans, but seeking via fear of the Lord is worthwhile. God rewards those who diligently seek him (Heb. 11:6), though it seems that no one ever does (Rom. 3:11, echoing Ps. 53:1–3). Solomon embodies this ambiguity: it was right to use his divine gift; however, eventually the sapiential quest became all about himself.

With the divine delegation of an "unhappy" (NRSV), "miserable" (Holman Christian Standard Bible), "evil" (*raʿ*) business to humankind, we face a recurring struggle in this book. The NIV and TNIV domesticate the verse with their translation "heavy burden," for *raʿ* often if not generally has moral or tragic overtones, at least designating calamity. On the surface the apparent reversal of Gen. 1–2 regarding God's "good" creation, so influential in Ecclesiastes, is shocking: this verse attributes the tragic business to divine giving. But that prods deeper reflection. It is usually noted that the Sage calls God *ʾĕlōhîm* rather than YHWH, the covenant name by which Israel knows the Creator. So this verse remains within the framework of what the Sage can observe, outside the perspective of Israel's salvation history. Without further revelation, how can it appear otherwise than tragic to be curious about divine purposes for human action? Where shall the requisite wisdom be found? The point, then, is that the divine gifts of creation are meant to be enjoyed as matters of stewardship rather than possession. God does not transfer title of the universe to humans, and therefore we do not receive independent epistemic access to sovereign divine purposes. The kind of wisdom worth having comes by faith, not by sight.

Limiting the perspective. The next verse summarizes these initial thoughts again in terms of *hebel* and its descriptive partner, chasing after wind. If this summary in 1:14 and the proverb in 1:15 are follow-up descriptions of preliminary conclusions, then they further constrain us not to take 1:13 too strongly as an absolute conclusion, but to interpret the divine gift canonically as a genuine gift. Here is not sheer absence, but inability to grasp what is present: "'Enigmatic' expresses this more clearly than proposed translations such as 'meaningless' or 'absurd,' which close down the very struggle that the reader is being called to engage in" (Bartholomew 2009: 124). Here God is not acting reprehensibly but rather humans engage in fruitless striving. The possibility remains open that the extent of the apparent tragedy depends on our forms of pursuit, not simply what God has given. Thus 1:13–15 manifests the limitations of a *king* undertaking *limitless* inquiry into *everything* based only on *what he can see*: from that perspective God occupies the seeker with a hopeless task—one that seems cruel, and in which the human may fall into evil, but not one that is evil per se. It would be unlikely for the Sage to contradict Gen. 1–3 baldly, given its constant use throughout the book; instead he creates tension with which we must wrestle, between the proximate goodness of creation and the ultimate goodness of God, as well as between reason and faith. Foreclosing the tensions, by reading final answers too quickly, would eclipse rather than interpret this portion of the text. However, a glimpse at the solution lies in recognizing that God may sometimes give gifts that humans do not want—but it is nevertheless good for us to learn our place.

Learning the limits of wisdom. Ecclesiastes 1:16–18 repeats the pattern of 1:13–15: initial reflection, followed by a statement about the vanity of pursuing wisdom, followed by a supporting proverb. The initial reflection in 1:16 is one of several occasions on which the Sage talks to himself, with the idiom involving speech "in my heart." The content of the speech expresses silly arrogance, since at the forefront of the reader's mind the only king over Jerusalem prior to Solomon was David! A relevant biblical paradigm is the rich fool, who builds bigger and bigger barns while isolating himself from the surrounding community with which he might share his wealth. He likewise talks only to himself (Luke 12:13–21). Conversely, by nearly universal acclamation, one of the most self-reflective treatises in Christian history is one of the greatest: Augustine's *Confessions*. What is the difference between Augustine and the Sage? Augustine's reflections are prayerful, whereas Solomon's here are not; Augustine's reflections are indeed confessions in a twofold sense, regarding his own sin and God's transforming grace, whereas Solomon boasts. The one who genuinely seeks wisdom ought to ask God and not be double-minded (Jas. 1:5–8); any other wisdom quest chases after wind, as Eccl. 1:17 concludes.

A bit of the wistful yet grateful spirit seen later in Augustine lurks in this report reflecting back on the quest, and such a narration of actual experience is biblically useful. Were Solomon dismissed as simply a rich fool, Ecclesiastes would hardly present compelling limitations upon genuine human wisdom. Even so, it will hardly work to deny the tragedies of the Solomonic saga in readers' minds or the self-preoccupied tone of the textual persona. The argument of Ecclesiastes succeeds because of both genuine wisdom *and* dysfunction in the paragon to whom the book draws attention. Solomon must be both tragic and typical of Christ, not just one or the other.

The proverb in 1:18 is heavy on repetition, conveying the vexation of the search. Again, its fruitlessness comes from seeking knowledge without the more important self-knowledge that leads to repentance and the love of God.[3] To search for true wisdom means first seeking after God, receiving divine grace instead of finding some interpretative key for mastering the universe outside the self. There is no pleasure in wisdom per se, not of the kind we often tempt ourselves to seek at any rate; such a pursuit only comes to grief for refusing to accept limitations.

These verses speak powerfully to those affected by the various movements dubbed the Enlightenment. The Sage sounds like a modern person in his focus on the "I," the self. One glimpses here the Judeo-Christian influence upon Western culture, not only subsequent to Augustine but even preceding him in biblical figures who dialogued with God—Abraham, Moses, Job, David, and the like. Knowledge of God and knowledge of the self are intertwined, so divine revelation enables listening to our lives. Yet the great danger is sliding into solipsism, starting with what the self can know from its own resources. Rather than responding to divine revelation, many modern forms of self-preoccupation are obsessed with humans as subjects and mired in epistemology. When God's gift of the intellect seems only burdensome, as in this section of Ecclesiastes (though not the whole book), the burden lies in recognizing that knowledge is power and that we do not have it.

Achievements Offer No Permanent Gain (2:1–26)

> The closer men came to perfecting for themselves a paradise, the more impatient they seemed to become with it, and with themselves as well. They made a garden of pleasure, and became progressively more miserable with it as it grew in richness and power and beauty; for then, perhaps, it was easier for them to see that something was missing in the garden, some tree or shrub that would not grow. When the world

3. Augustine, *The Trinity* 4.prologue (trans. Hill), 152–53.

> was in darkness and wretchedness, it could believe in perfection and yearn for it. But when the world became bright with reason and riches, it began to sense the narrowness of the needle's eye, and that rankled for a world no longer willing to believe or yearn. Well, they were going to destroy it again, were they—this garden Earth, civilized and knowing, to be torn apart again that Man might hope again in wretched darkness.[4]

The Solomonic self-portrayal continues throughout Eccl. 2. The initial section, 2:1–11, announces a focus on pleasure, whereas 2:12 returns to the nature of wisdom. On the surface, this produces at least two sharply distinct units, with the possibility of a further break around 2:18 or 2:24—before or after toil becomes prominent. However, the approach taken here finds Eccl. 2 to narrate a quest for a unified object, with the chief distinction between 2:1–11 and 2:12–26 concerning the mode of pursuit. The object pursued is status, and wisdom always hovers in the background as the know-how for establishing a reputation that lasts. The Sage emphasizes that he does not leave wisdom behind when testing pleasure (2:3, 9), and in fact pleasure is under scrutiny as a realm of achievement, whereby to demonstrate that one has life figured out. The effects of death unify 2:12–17 with 2:18–26, and both consider how wisdom might establish any lasting legacy via one's toil. The Sage does not bluntly pursue hedonism or workaholism. He tests pleasure and work as modes of human achievement—as status symbols.

Personal Narrative (2:1–11)

Exploring the Solomonic self. Ecclesiastes 2:1 introduces the narrative reflection once again with "I said in my heart" as the idiom. However hedonistic the Solomonic actions to follow, they result from deliberate choice, not loss of control. Many contemporary readers are used to controlling their own destinies. But who, or how many, in Solomon's time would have possessed the opportunity to choose such exploration? Even in our own day legions of people cannot opt to test pleasure on any significant scale. Thus the text, under the surface, confronts many of us with the reality that we live like kings—if indeed the ensuing Solomonic choices seem run of the mill.

The apostle Paul sarcastically confronts the Corinthians with the barb, "Quite apart from us you have become kings!" (1 Cor. 4:8). Poking at their inflated self-assessments, this also highlights their refusal to be "fools for Christ." Few Christians are called to sacrifice certain comforts as professional missionaries, and family life, as Paul makes clear in 1 Cor. 7, alters the extent to which many can devote themselves single-handedly to advancing Christ's kingdom. Even so, it is unlikely that the gospel should make no difference to cultural status or lifestyle for lay Christians. A surfeit of worldly goods places many today squarely in the

4. Thoughts of Brother Joshua, a character in Miller, *Canticle for Leibowitz*, 285.

Solomonic position, rather than identifying us with the likely majority of the text's earlier audiences.

Luther notices a parallel quest on a smaller scale:

> It is as though he were saying: ". . . I shall create ease and tranquility. . . ." Often dinner parties are arranged to create a happy atmosphere, with foods and entertainment intended to make the guests happy. But usually it comes out just the opposite way, and only seldom does a good party result. Either there are gloomy and somber faces present, or something else upsets all the arrangements, especially when there is such deliberation and planning about how much fun it will be. By contrast, it often happens that someone happens upon a most joyful dinner party by accident, that is, by the gift of God.[5]

The way to experience genuine pleasure is not to pursue it; or, in Jesus's terms: "Those who want to save their life will lose it, and those who lose their life . . . for the sake of the gospel, will save it" (Mark 8:35).

Testing laughter. Hence 2:2 reverses 1:17–18: there wisdom failed because it restricts pleasure; here pleasure fails because it makes no sense. Moreover, in 1:14–15 human actions seem meaningless, whereas here pleasure accomplishes nothing. In the Christian tradition, critique of laughter can go too far: Basil the Great concedes the presence of Prov. 15:13 ("a glad heart makes a cheerful countenance"), but insists based on Eccl. 2:2 and 7:6 that body-shaking laughter beyond a cheerful smile is dangerous. According to him, the Gospels give no indication that our Lord Jesus, while experiencing bodily emotions necessary for humanity, ever laughed (*The Long Rules* 17, in FC 9.271). Yet in Ecclesiastes the critique regards not laughter as such but folly and/or ambition as its context. Jesus could scarcely have been rejected for "playing the pipe" (Matt. 11:17), namely partying with sinners, if he were unwilling to identify with the hearty laughter enjoyed during table fellowship. Legitimate warnings against frivolity must not degenerate into rejecting the divine gifts that wisdom literature celebrates. Laughter is not the best medicine, if sought for ultimate healing—so Eccl. 2:2. But a valuable, temporary salve it can be, according to both Proverbs and Ecclesiastes.

Wisely pursuing folly? Ecclesiastes 2:3 makes clear that Solomon tried to apportion the right amount of folly wisely—irony indeed. Micah 6:8 famously outlines what is good for humans: to do justice, to love mercy, and to walk humbly with God. In Ps. 90 figuring out how to apportion our days on earth requires divine teaching instead of the independent human exploration portrayed in the present context. The Sage echoes our fall into sin by deciding that he must know both wisdom and folly experientially. While here the folly may not simply be evil, still the Sage pursues knowing the good apart from divine terms.

Echoing Genesis with forbidden fruit. Such independence is all the more striking in light of 2:4, with its echoes of divine creation language from Gen. 1–2. Since

5. Luther, *Notes on Ecclesiastes*, 29.

emphasis falls on the Sage's "I" making these accomplishments, he has come even closer to the fall in Gen. 3; Solomonic self-absorption stands in stark contrast to the Lord's making Solomon great in 1 Kgs. 1:37. One cannot help thinking of Nebuchadnezzar's boasting in Dan. 4—and its terrible immediate consequences, in which the Lord literally made him live like an animal for a time. As echoes of Gen. 1–2 accumulate, the Sage's Solomonic "I" attempts to re-create Eden—usurping God's place. Once we pursue moral autonomy—the "knowledge of good and evil"—humans become all the more vulnerable to deception regarding what is truly desirable, whether God really desires what is best for us and whether we can make it forever on our own. We become self-aware to an extent that such nakedness frightens us. The good news is that Nebuchadnezzar's story did not end brutishly; after God humbled him, his reason returned and he praised the king of heaven (Dan. 4:37). While we do not know how Solomon's story finished, by the end of Ecclesiastes the Sage unambiguously focuses on the Creator—once certain pursuits of reason have left him.

The plurals in Eccl. 2:5 further emphasize magnificence. Perhaps given the context, Gregory of Nyssa is not far off, then, to find the vineyards leading to excessive wine:

> Who in the world does not know that once wine immoderately exceeds what is necessary, it is tinder for licentiousness, the means to self-indulgence, injury to youth, deformity to age, dishonor for women, a poison inducing madness, sustenance for insanity, destruction to the soul, death to the understanding, estrangement from virtue? From it comes unjustified mirth, lamentation without reason, senseless tears, unfounded boasting, shameless lying, craving for the unreal, expectation of the impracticable, monstrous threats, groundless fear, unawareness of what is really to be feared, unreasonable jealousy, excessive bonhomie, the promise of impossible things. (*Homilies on Ecclesiastes* 3, in Hall 1993: 67–68)

As many Christians emerge from requiring teetotalism over the past few decades, it is sad but true that the other extreme easily reappears—not drunkenness necessarily, but a kind of excess with which Solomonic slackness and folly correlate. It is tempting to dismiss Gregory's concerns as overscrupulousness, the worst version of the *contemptus mundi* tradition. But Gregory never rejects the divine gift; he confronts a lack of moderation, self-indulgence of a sort that reduces self-restraint across the board. Thinking we have enough to spend lavishly on wine, humans are likely to view constant acquisition of the various pleasures described here as an accomplishment and a mandate for excess. The point is not that the Sage descended entirely into folly, now appealing to wisdom only ironically. Easy to miss is the strategic pursuit of achievement and status that fundamentally underlies this use of pleasure. Understanding that wisdom sometimes refers merely to skill explains how the Sage could genuinely claim *ḥokmâ* and not violate strictures against drunkenness, yet still be off the spiritual rails. The Sage uses pleasure in pursuit of greater wisdom. But he fails to recognize the moral problem with the self-preoccupation involved, and he becomes vulnerable to emotional highs and lows that reflect no other reality than a culture of drinking.

Creating oneself and enslaving others. It is not that God denies all pleasures; the scene set in 2:6 could readily involve divine blessing, as in contexts like Ps. 1. Yet Ecclesiastes emphasizes human construction and cultivation, even relative to divine creation; in this setting nostalgia for "the garden" may be telling. What is problematic, again, is not the physical realities or activities themselves but the active "I" and "myself" language exhaustively surrounding the verbs—without divine praise. In 2:7 we hear the frequent early refrain, "more than any who had been before me in Jerusalem." Apart from the irony in this claim, its focus is not pleasure per se, but providing for pleasure as a way of measuring accomplishment. Solomon is more modern, or moderns are more perennial, than we think when it comes to temptation: toys function as status symbols, with which to convince ourselves—by convincing others—of our worth. Contemporary society knows plenty about hedonism without ambition, but the Sage was not vulnerable to that problem in this particular quest.

The issue of slavery surfaces in 2:7, which is no surprise. Gregory of Nyssa writes at length that only "such a gross example of arrogance in the matters enumerated above"—an opulent house and the like—could lead a human "to think himself the master of his own kind": "This kind of language is raised up as a challenge to God" (*Homilies on Ecclesiastes* 4, in Hall 1993: 73)! Gregory's sharp criticism is noteworthy since usually he is exceedingly kind toward Solomon, whom he sees as repentant (Christianson 2007: 159). But not here: thus the Christian tradition, though far from unanimous given complicated circumstances, certainly had resources for rejecting slavery earlier than the nineteenth century.

> He who knew the nature of mankind rightly said that the whole world was not worth giving in exchange for a human soul. Whenever a human being is for sale, therefore, nothing less than the owner of the earth is led into the sale-room. Presumably, then, the property belonging to him is up for auction too. That means the earth, the islands, the sea, and all that is in them. What will the buyer pay, and what will the vendor accept, considering how much property is entailed in the deal? (Gregory, *Homilies on Ecclesiastes* 4, in Hall 1993: 74–75)

Accordingly, our passage calls into question not the value of human beings or gardens or trees, but the extent to which we can own any of these gifts of God. The Sage held slaves to further needlessly his proprietary interests, whereas—whatever one makes of the modern issue of private property rights—in the biblical view no one does more than serve as a steward for the true owner, God.

Clarifying further the deconstruction. Regarding 2:8 Gregory continues with deconstruction of gold: in itself it has little value, apart from what it can purchase. Although it can buy something like clothing, this is only because of value that humans assign; even then many people with lots of gold cannot purchase goods that enable them to live genuinely healthy lives (*Homilies on Ecclesiastes* 4, in Hall 1993: 76–77). Despite this litany of pleasures, their predominant connection with status is clear, for even the reference to Solomon's sexual exploits (2:8) is not spelled out in terms of extreme hedonism, but rather appears alongside his taxation policies(!), leading into another recital of self-importance (2:9).

Confirmation of this point appears in the insistence that his wisdom remained. Thus he did not plunge into the heedless hedonism today associated with the word, but instead a calculated hedonism of accomplishment. While the text reflects exaggerated self-importance, there is also a degree of truth. Especially in association with wisdom, after all, Solomon was the greatest of Jerusalem's kings. In the simultaneous accuracy (to a degree) and inadequacy of such a phenomenological assessment there is a cautionary tale. Sometimes, when we craft and then believe our own press, a narrow form of accuracy can obscure more important truths. So, at the human level Solomon and Nebuchadnezzar made their various choices, often skillfully. Without any other perspective transcending "under the sun," however, ultimately such assessments distort, leading to delusions of wrongful grandeur. Narrating Solomonic achievements solely at the human level engenders "more than any who were before me" comments without mention of divine grace. The entire logic of the Sage's striving and comparing is misleading, even if particular statements have grains of descriptive truth.

Finding pleasure in toil, treating pleasure as toil? According to 2:10 Solomon came to see not just his toil as pleasurable—God's design, in a way—but any pleasure as legitimate reward for this toil. The experiment of satisfying his eyes comprehensively contradicts other scriptural texts. Numbers 15:39 commands not following our lusts and treats fringes on garments as preventative reminders of divine commandments. Psalm 131:1–2 expresses the humble trust absent from the Sage: "O Lord, my heart is not lifted up, / my eyes are not raised too high; / I do not occupy myself with things / too great and too marvelous for me. But I have calmed and quieted my soul, like a weaned child with its mother." First John 2:15–17 confronts lust and pride together: "Do not love the world or the things in the world. The love of the Father is not in those who love the world; for all that is in the world—the desire of the flesh, the desire of the eyes, the pride in riches—comes not from the Father but from the world. And the world and its desire are passing away, but those who do the will of God live forever." Didymus the Blind appeals to Matt. 5:8: pursuing purity in heart means that we shall "see" God, who ought to be the true orientation of our vision (*Commentary on Ecclesiastes* 44.17, in PTA 25.215 and Wright 2005: 212).

In Ecclesiastes irony is present once again: pleasure as "reward" (*ḥēleq*) suggests that the king's wisdom and great works have relatively little value in the end, especially since he probably could have had pleasure without great works (2:1–2). Such is the conclusion of 2:11, which distinguishes between *ḥēleq* ("portion," rather than "reward") and *yitrôn* ("profit")—the latter of which, in agreement with

1:3, the Sage found lacking. There may have been value in the works themselves, possibly even in their immediate possession,[6] but no long-term gain.

Gregory of Nyssa offers the image of writing on water: we focus on the act, rather than the effect, as the only object of interest (*Homilies on Ecclesiastes* 4, in Hall 1993: 84). So Solomon anticipates modern consumer culture: workaholism and a kind of hedonism go hand in hand. People swing back and forth between being caught up in the activity of work itself and momentarily consuming its effects—the products it obtains. Eventually they construct their very identities around the labor of refining both pleasures, as David Brooks's *Bobos in Paradise*[7] details so hilariously and as Radiohead's song "Fitter Happier" criticizes so sarcastically. Living like kings, they fail to heed the Solomonic testimony that such a life is not all it's cracked up to be.

Another way in which this passage holds up a mirror to our culture concerns wine, women, and song. Treatment of women in 2:8 is more or less derogatory, with the extent depending on how one understands the word rendered "concubines." The esthete is male. Has the supposedly enlightened modern West changed very much? For all its flaws, the enactment of Prohibition sought to address the social chaos by which alcohol disadvantaged women. Contemporary male esthetes may refine their discourse in certain settings, but we all know what happens when liquor flows in other settings where speech may flow freely. Furthermore, it is not clear that the so-called sexual revolution has actually liberated women rather than reinstating tyranny with new social forms. More than ever, men pursue whatever their eyes desire (2:10), acting as if a hard week's work entitles them (2:11). The world of Ecclesiastes is male dominated. But subtle undercurrents in such passages render that situation problematic.

Tragic social consequences should not surprise us, for they are natural companions of idolatry. And idolatry is in view, as the incessant litany of the self's activities ironically parallels the portrayal of the cosmos in Eccl. 1.[8] In the Old Testament prophetic writings, idolatry and injustice go together, hand in bloody glove—as they should, since they counterfeit that for which God made us, namely charity. Augustine's distinction between "enjoyment" and "use" remains apposite: the earthly gifts described in 2:1–11 are indeed *goods* if used ultimately for the sake of enjoying God, their giver; unfortunately, our gaze easily fixes onto them till we enjoy them purely for their own sake—purely for *our* own sake, we think, thereby supplanting the Creator with the creature. Since "the world and its desire are passing away" (1 John 2:17), this self-interest is unenlightened; we actually serve the goods—idols—on which our gaze fixes. In the context of Eccl. 2:1–11 we must not miss the subtlety by which people thus ensnare themselves, not in

6. That is true if one takes *'āmāl* as "possession" rather than "toil," but this is unclear.

7. David Brooks, *Bobos in Paradise: The New Upper Class and How They Got There* (New York: Touchstone, 2000).

8. Elsa Tamez, *When the Horizons Close: Rereading Ecclesiastes*, trans. Margaret Wilde (Maryknoll, NY: Orbis, 2000), 47.

rank hedonism, but in refined pursuit of status via pleasure. The lust of the flesh and the lust of the eyes wrongly become the pride of life.

Perceptive Reflection (2:12–26)

The chronicle of self-reflection continues, now turning in 2:12–26 from narrating actions and accomplishments toward reflecting on such experience.

Transition. The transitional character of 2:12 is apparent, partly due to the verb (*pānâ*) shared with 2:11. Whereas 2:1–11 concerns pleasure and 2:12–26 concerns wisdom, in another sense the overarching theme remains the same: assessing the legacy of human efforts to gain lasting status. In 2:1–11 pleasure is the temporary reward, though not an enduring legacy, of work; in 2:12–26 wisdom's value is likewise limited. Wisdom offers the temporary reward of avoiding folly, yet the ultimate result is the same. Both the wise and fools die; neither can control their legacies. Indeed, not even the process of the work itself is altogether free of vexation (2:23), while its products provide no truly permanent gain in light of death. This recurring theme is a crucial component of *hebel*: the transitory nature of earthly goods and gains for which humans grasp. Received as provisional gifts, these bring blessing as a means of enjoying God, their giver; clutched tightly with hopes of permanence, they bring vexation.

Ecclesiastes 2:12 announces the scope of subsequent reflections: 2:12a introduces wisdom and folly, the focus of 2:13–17; and 2:12b introduces the successors treated in 2:18–21. Conclusions affirming that all is *hebel* further delineate subunits in 2:13–15, 16–17, 18–19, 20–21. Ecclesiastes 2:22–23 finally works toward a more general conclusion, summarized in 2:24–26. In 2:12b—whatever we make of its exceedingly difficult grammar—one cannot help but think of Rehoboam. Unable to break out of his father Solomon's pattern, he only intensified its self-destructive ways. When the people pleaded with him for less labor and taxation after Solomon's death, Rehoboam consulted elders for advice, and they advised him to answer the people favorably. But younger friends told him to insist that his little finger was thicker than his father's waist: whereas Solomon scourged them with whips, he would scourge them with scorpions. As a result the Davidic dynasty began to crumble (2 Chr. 10:1–11:4).

Wisdom's value in view of death. Ecclesiastes 2:13 could minimally suggest that the Sage examined a parallel between wisdom and folly, light and darkness. But more likely the verse goes further, affirming wisdom's actual value: wisdom enables people to see where they are going, as light enables them to use their eyes effectively, according to the proverb in 2:14. This effectiveness is temporary, for death happens to everyone. To reinforce the reality of this fate, in 2:14 the subject and verb stem from the same root. One's fate is not always death in Ecclesiastes, but the two are contextually connected in each case; death is the ultimate example of human subjection to contingency. Nevertheless, despite death's leveling, asymmetry remains underneath the surface: all humans have eyes, whether or not their use is effective vis-à-vis light or darkness. Darkness is the absence of light, says Gregory of Nyssa, as evil is the privation of good (*Homilies on Ecclesiastes* 5, in Hall 1993: 88). Hence even the fool has capacities for judgment (eyes) but misdirects them (not finding light to make the eyes effective). The Rehoboam story illustrates both sides of the coin: on the one hand, wisdom's relative value is clear in Rehoboam's folly of listening to younger friends rather than elders; on the other hand, wisdom's limited legacy is clear in Solomon's lack of proper influence over the character and decision of his son, which cost the family dearly. The fool cannot see what is real—even death, about which the wise have to be clearheaded. The fool may bump into realities momentarily, but cannot see what, if any, permanence they have.

Twice in 2:15 the Sage talks to himself, questioning whether wisdom has any value in light of death. He answers that this quest for gain via wisdom is likewise a matter of *hebel*. Wisdom offers a paradigmatic instance of how *hebel* functions: the vanity is not absolute meaninglessness, but relative in terms of temporary value, which tempts us to pursue too much. As 2:16 suggests, neither the wise person nor the fool has a permanent legacy. Despite surface tension with Prov. 10:7 ("the memory of the righteous is a blessing, / but the name of the wicked will rot"), the Sage's conclusion is not flatly unorthodox. In fact, it is consistent with Ps. 49:10–11:

> When we look at the wise, they die;
>   fool and dolt perish together
>   and leave their wealth to others.
> Their graves are their homes forever,
>   their dwelling places to all generations,
>   though they named lands their own.

Hatred for life? Obviously, however, to fade from lasting memory troubles the Sage greatly (2:17), whereas the proverb concerning the blessed memory of the righteous is more optimistic about covenant fidelity in the community. Again the Sage uses the word *ra'* (1:13); he experiences the limited value of human activity as deeply tragic, at minimum. Is it "evil"? Once more, the Sage's approach remains empirical. On this phenomenological basis he cannot adopt the Israelite tendency toward open-ended hope in a God-given future. This hope could take on either personal or corporate dimensions, but neither would appear likely based on observation alone.[9] Israel's salvation-historical situation is absent from Ecclesiastes, except insofar as its post-Solomonic division and disasters lurk by implication. Thus, at this stage of the quest, the Sage states explicitly that death—for everyone—sets the limit of what we can perceive about personal destiny (2:14). For just this reason the Sage is quite vexed because, contrary to

9. For a review of literature on postmortem possibilities in the Old Testament, see Bartholomew 2009: 141–43.

our culture, he also accepts the teaching of Genesis that death—as we now face it, anyway—is unnatural.

The strength of this statement needs the context of other, more positive texts such as Eccl. 9:4–5: "But whoever is joined with all the living has hope, for a living dog is better than a dead lion. The living know that they will die, but the dead know nothing; they have no more reward, and even the memory of them is lost." Therefore 2:17 uses "hate" to state "a relative contrast in absolute terms (see the use of 'hate' in Gen. 29:30–31; Deut. 21:15; Luke 14:26)" (ESV Study Bible note on 2:17). By analogy, when Jesus tells us to "hate" father and mother, he does not mean we should not love them; he means that we should love them as a way of loving God, our supreme good. So the Sage does not simply hate earthly life. At moments he makes a strong statement to that effect, rhetorically leading us to acknowledge that life thwarts aspirations to grasp something eternal. But this life is also better than nothing, the context within which God leads us to the eternal life for which we long. The proper theological conclusion is not to hate life but rather to acknowledge its relative value in light of the vexation that transpires under the sun. This vexation can result in unhealthy despair or else recognition of the ultimate purposes for which God gives life in the first place.

Successors toiling wisely? Ecclesiastes 2:18 explicates the tragic situation of 2:17 in terms of the king's legacy in the hands of successors. As 1 Tim. 6:7 puts it bluntly, "We brought nothing into the world, so that we can take nothing out of it." Athanasius argues that this can provide backhanded incentive for virtue: since we are going to leave behind our goods regardless, we may as well choose to leave them behind for good reasons now (*Life of St. Anthony* 17, in FC 15.151). Dependence on the virtue or lack thereof in one's successors signals that the pursuit of lasting earthly gain is misplaced. Again Rehoboam and others lurk in the background of the Solomonic narrative (Eccl. 2:19). This provides an example of the dual meaning of *ʿāmāl*, designating both the toil itself and possessions, the results of one's toil. For the Sage, lack of control over the legacy of the product casts a threatening shadow over pleasure in the process. The refrain "who knows?" suggests inability to make predictive decisions amid that process. The wisdom vocabulary describes the manner of the toil, possibly via hendiadys ("toiled wisely"); the verse implies that wisdom, whatever else it might entail, cannot consist in applying masterful knowledge of the likely future.

A worst-case scenario. After yet another *hebel* miniconclusion, 2:20 shifts into a worst-case scenario: a wise person giving his portion to one who did not toil for it (perhaps, by implication, to one who could not or would not have done so?). The Septuagint and the Vulgate wrongly rendered "despair" with "renounce," helping to foster the view that Solomon repented (Longman 1998: 104). But the piel infinitive construct *lĕyaʾēš* is interesting in a different way, apparently suggesting that humans can exert control over emotions, causing their own despair. If so, then once again the unorthodox conclusions here are not absolute. In contrast, the Sage offers via Solomon one possible take on the dangers of thinking one has everything. The Sage runs up against the way of the world—but part of the scenario involves his own reaction. He realizes he caused his own despair regarding the apparent uselessness of toil under the sun by longing to make its results impossibly permanent.

The scenario playing out in 2:21 seems not to involve normal inheritance, since no "son" is mentioned (Longman 1998: 104). A stranger inherits; this appears tragic and perverse. Krüger 2004: 71 notes: "At this point a critical reader can ask in retrospect whether the 'great deeds' of the king (vv. 4–8) were possible only because of what he had inherited from *his* father"! Irony is dripping: the Sage complains about successors, yet given the royal context of the persona, he was once a successor himself. Before Solomon could complain too long about Rehoboam, he would have to reckon with his own mixed reception of David's legacy. Of course, this opens its own can of worms, since the familial relationships involved in each case were complex.

So we reach the darkest hour of the section, casting a shadow not just on the products of toil but even over the process itself: 2:22 is a negative rhetorical question, with linkwords recalling tragic verses from earlier ("work" from 1:13; "pain" and "vexation" in reverse order from 1:18). The mood is bleak: the Solomonic autobiography reaches a tragic stopping point. So vexing is the lack of permanent outcomes that toil itself robs humans of rest. Yet it is possible to read elegiac hints of self-criticism between the lines. The Solomonic quest fails not solely because of external conditions under the sun, but also because of human pursuit gone wrong. If loss of rest is due to toil's contamination with wrongful expectations, then a change in perspective might enable the audience to gain from the Sage's failures. The wise person catches on that one cannot catch the wind.

Carpe diem *as God's gift.* Gain, as 2:24 makes clear, is not a matter of humanly produced advantage but instead emerges "from the hand of God." The first part of the verse remains under expert dispute, either fitting into the "nothing better than . . ." pattern of other texts with the *carpe diem* motif (3:12–13, 21–22; 5:18–20; 8:15; also relevant are 4:4–6; 9:7–10; 11:7–10) or else asserting that humans produce nothing good. Either way, the verse supports the rhetorical question of 2:25, asserting that without God humans cannot find joy. *Carpe diem* means "seize the day," and in one respect these verses—and their several echoes in the rest of the book—support the pursuit of food and drink and work as divine gifts. But we cannot seize them; we can only receive from the hand of God. Use of *ṭôb* in the "nothing better" phrase closes the loop with 2:3, in which the Sage stipulates that he pursued "what was good [*ṭôb*] for mortals to do under heaven." Accordingly, though the Sage clearly struggles with God's apparent distance from humans and resulting inscrutability, nevertheless "the gulf between God and humans is bridged in these instances that speak of humans receiving and enjoying God's gifts," with the joys of table fellowship in the background.[10] Luther found

10. James Limburg, *Encountering Ecclesiastes: A Book for Our Time* (Grand Rapids: Eerdmans, 2006), 34.

in 2:24 the point of the entire book: "Solomon wants to put us at peace and to give us a quiet mind in the everyday affairs and business of this life, so that we live contentedly in the present without care and yearning about the future and are, as Paul says, without care and anxiety (Phil. 4:6)."[11]

Modern people live in an era suspicious of gifts, as Ellul 1990: 252–53 highlights. Ecclesiastes 2:24–26, however, does not allow Christians to accept the view that a gift cannot be given. Some claim that a gift always creates bondage via an economy of expected exchange: the worry is all too common that a supposed gift or an invitation obligates us to reciprocate. Thus, on this view, no such thing as a gift really exists; life is an endless treadmill of what is done to us and what we must do in return. Ecclesiastes, of course, does not lack guidelines for receiving the Creator's gifts well. But these expectations are for the sake of joy and rest, offering freedom from the self-imposed, debilitating grasp for human mastery that never ends. They establish a form of reciprocity in which humans can be free from poisonous forms of obligation that render a gift no gift. In other words, God's gifts are gracious, and grace liberates us for fulfilling our only obligation, than which there is nothing better.

However one translates 2:25, it makes God our ultimate provider, with the nature of these gifts unfolding further in 2:26. If "sinner" is taken in the usual sense, then the basic thrust is moral dualism, reaffirming a genuine connection between wisdom and pleasure. In that case God's grace to those who remain sinners (as a fundamental category) is temporary; God sustains them for a time, but eventually their harvest transfers to someone good. Here the difficulty concerns the *hebel* conclusion; why would a sinner be given a chance to express this perspective on toil? Hence, alternatively, many take these religious terms in a secular way, as a statement about divine arbitrariness. "Sinner" does not tell the truth, but is a label only. On this view, the Sage complains ironically that some please God while others are out of luck before the deity.

Faced with this conundrum, theological interpreters could find a way forward in either direction, but contextual factors tentatively support a moral notion of "sinner." First, both sets of descriptions apply to toil: "wisdom and knowledge and skill" in 2:21 now give way in 2:26 to "wisdom and knowledge and joy" for one who pleases God. In the sinner's case, although the application of wisdom and knowledge remains from the setup in 2:21, joy gives way to gathering and heaping. The "gathering and heaping" manifest human initiative all the way down. This is joyless folly, because the sinners receive divine gifts without acknowledging them. They gather and heap without considering the source of their bounty. Second, "sinner" is indisputably moral in 8:12 and arguably so in 5:6. Third, then, the king portrayed in 1:12–2:26 landed himself in vanity, toiling only for another, and this helps to clarify 2:26. While that successor inevitably followed in established footsteps (2:12), whether these would be wise or foolish is unpredictable (2:19),

11. Luther, *Notes on Ecclesiastes*, 7.

and in any case the bounty would be undeserved (2:21). If, as an undertone in 2:21 suggests, the immediate successor is a bit of a lout, then the possessions will transfer again anyway (2:26). Actual benefits would eventually go to a successor who could enjoy them restfully. Constituting a sinner, in this context, is not primarily Torah observance, but refusal to receive divine gifts as such. The term is moral, but not in a legal or moralistic sense. Rather, the verse reinforces the overall thrust of the personal quest narrative. Therefore, the conclusion that "this also is vanity and a chasing after wind" refers to joyless gathering and heaping, not the whole of 2:24–26. Limitation on the scope of this verse's conclusion is not really surprising; when previous *hebel* clauses are examined more closely, the extent of their reference varies. As a result, the apparent problem with the moral interpretation dissolves; the sinner's *hebel* conclusion is not a complaint about divine despotism, but instead an acknowledgment of his own foolish chase.

The major thrust of the passage is therefore consistent with the aforementioned group of texts sharing *carpe diem*, "nothing-better-than" motifs. Human achievements, viewed as temporal opportunities for application of wisdom and acquisition of joy, are gifts of God. They cannot contribute permanent profit in the face of death, due to the impermanent experience of pleasure (the focus of 2:1–11) and the merely temporary control people have over their legacies (the focus of 2:12–26). We need to grasp God's earthly gifts while we can, but only for the momentary provision that they are. In an intellectual autobiography, contrasting the death of scholar Mircea Eliade with the suicide of Ricoeur's own son, Paul Ricoeur writes: "This death, which left a work behind it, made even more cruel that other death that seemed to have left nothing at all. I had yet to learn that, by equalizing all fates, death invites us to transcend the apparent difference between work and nonwork."[12] Such is the spirit of Eccl. 2, which makes the space for later revelation about resurrection.

Such *carpe diem* passages seem curious in relation to those surrounding them, such as 2:1–23, where God is never explicitly mentioned. Readers tend to privilege one or the other, or else to see in their juxtaposition an insoluble tension. It is assumed that there are divine gift passages and *hebel* passages; either they are incoherent or else one set is ironic, its meaning controlled by the other. Yet, although both divine gift and *hebel* voices need to have their say, here 2:24–26 offers a preliminary last word. Since both divine gift and *hebel* voices speak within 2:24–26, this is not just another set of verses but instead serves as a provisional conclusion for the quest so far. The theme of divine gifts is not a matter of revelation suddenly intruding from the outside or the Sage slavishly quoting orthodox tradition with a wink, for the empirical approach has not disappeared altogether. Tension persists, but not merely juxtaposition of perspectives: the hand of God

12. Paul Ricoeur, "Intellectual Autobiography," trans. Kathleen Blamey, in *The Philosophy of Paul Ricoeur*, ed. Lewis Edwin Hahn, Library of Living Philosophers (Chicago: Open Court, 1995), 51. My thanks to Jon Laansma for noticing it.

providing these quotidian enjoyments is what the Sage "saw" (2:24). Revelation bears out in reality, even if the scope of this preliminary conclusion remains quite modest. Seeing is believing: seeing that temporal gifts are good, but earthly gains are scattered and provisional, helps us to place our trust in the Giver rather than the gifts themselves. The peek at salvation history in 2:26 introduces a longer-term perspective, shaping current decisions in view of God's judgment, as the Sage king should have done.

Everything Must Be Suitable for Its Time (3:1–15)

> But the mercy of the world is time. Time does not stop for love, but it does not stop for death and grief, either. After death and grief that (it seems) ought to have stopped the world, the world goes on. More things happen. And some of the things that happen are good. My life was changing now. It had to change. I am not going to say that it changed for the better. There was good in it as it was. But also there was good in it as it was going to be.[13]

The provisional conclusion of 2:26 is followed by a completely different type of text beginning in 3:1. The Byrds recording "Turn! Turn! Turn!" widened the audience for this next passage in the 1960s, and *Time* magazine commercials kept the song alive decades later. In original context, the poem of 3:1–8 hardly constitutes an appeal for world peace after the fashion of the song. It leads, instead, to prosaic recapitulation in 3:9–15 of questions with which the Sage has been working, resulting in summary affirmations of divine sovereignty over human activity.

Poetry (3:1–8)

The spectrum of approaches to the poem presents three broad options: (1) the Sage is a determinist, describing times that God has inflexibly set so humans cannot alter them; (2) the Sage is an opportunist, presenting times of decision that those familiar with Greek might term "*kairos* moments" (as in the Septuagint here); or (3) the Sage is not a determinist, though favoring an ordered life in which one aligns oneself with proper timing given providential direction.

A time for everything. Significantly emphasizing divine sovereignty is the use of "under heaven" rather than "under the sun." This passage is primarily descriptive rather than prescriptive; these are activities that occur on earth, whether they should or should not occur at different times. Yet, on at least some occasions in the book, time establishes a proper human response, as in 10:8–11.[14] Thus it is not surprising to read in 3:1 that there is a time for every activity—the strange noun

13. The narrator in Wendell Berry, *Jayber Crow: The Life Story of Jayber Crow, Barber, of the Port William Membership, as Written by Himself: A Novel* (Washington DC: Counterpoint, 2000), 296.

14. For careful development of this theme, see Richard L. Schultz, "A Sense of Timing: A Neglected Aspect of Qoheleth's Wisdom," in *Seeking Out the Wisdom of the Ancients: Essays Offered to Honor Michael*

ḥēpeṣ ("matter")—under heaven. The activity is human and intentional, not just general and cosmic, which becomes even clearer once the subsequent catalog of activities depicts human decisions among various temporal options. While time limits possibilities for gain (3:9), 3:1 suggests that within the span of human life a full set of options presents itself.

The poetry forms an interlude, mirroring 1:3–9, although this time the statement comes first, and a question comes last. The large-scale regularities of the cosmos now give way to the particular temporal changes affecting ordinary lives. The pairs are carefully structured; via a merism in which parts count for the whole, they involve not just the respective poles but everything in between. The initial two are first positive, then negative (3:2); the next four first go negative, then positive (3:3–4); another set of four are first positive, then negative (3:5–6); a twosome return to negative before positive (3:7); finally, we get one pair each (positive first, then negative first; 3:8). The intricate design makes a subtle statement about God's providential ordering of human affairs. Our activities may seesaw back and forth, but God is never threatened by chaos. The comprehensiveness of the design appears in the total number; seven groups of four combine the number of completion or perfection with the cardinal points of the heavens, treating human time in terms of cosmic order (Krüger 2004: 76).

Gregory of Nazianzus notes that, though these verses call for balance and for limits on the proper timing of theological activity, nevertheless we are to pray without ceasing throughout all our activities (*Against the Eunomians: Theological Oration* 1[27].5, in Library of Christian Classics 3.130–31). Likewise, today is the day of salvation; one should not wait for a more advantageous time. At the same time, as Tertullian notes, by implication the passage makes room for slow growth in human lives, to parallel the processes of the cosmos (*On the Veiling of Virgins* 1, in ANF 4.27–28). In the juxtaposition of these two comments we find the necessary perspective on God's timing: remembering our Creator is a matter of constant urgency yet, almost paradoxically, this God responds patiently to our cries, leading us one step at a time. Ecclesiastes 3 affirms the intricacy and comprehensiveness of the divine plan while hinting that humans cannot know the proper timing all at once. Bonhoeffer reinforces this point:

> It is part of the great naïveté or, more accurately, folly of ethicists to overlook this fact willfully, and to start from the fictional assumption that human beings at every moment of their lives have to make an ultimate, infinite choice; as if every moment of life would require a conscious decision between good and evil; as if every human action were labeled with a sign, written by divine police in bold letters, saying "Permitted" or "Prohibited"; as if human beings incessantly had to do something decisive, fulfill a higher purpose, meet an ultimate duty. This attitude is a misjudgment of historical human existence in which everything has its time

V. Fox on the Occasion of His Sixty-Fifth Birthday, ed. Ronald L. Troxel, Kelvin G. Friebel, and Dennis R. Magary (Winona Lake, IN: Eisenbrauns, 2005), 257–67.

(Eccl. 3). . . . It is the presumptuous misjudgment of this creaturely existence that must drive a person either into the most mendacious hypocrisy or into madness.[15]

In contrast to the sober freedom Eccl. 3 ought to elicit, instead the passage has become a source of easy platitudes and Christian kitsch. Though the passage can be reassuring with respect to divine sovereignty, skipping straight to "he has made everything beautiful in its time" (3:11 NIV) makes its message trite. By contrast, genuine comfort lies in the obvious but potentially startling truth: the Bible actually addresses all moments of our lives, including ordinary—and tragic—ones. Given views of God we sometimes have, it may astonish us to find poetry like this in scripture—not only comprehensive in dealing concretely with our lives, but also frustratingly indirect. With literature of this kind God invites not detailed philosophical inspection but rather personal expression and careful reflection. These words, as Pete Seeger proved, express and generate feelings about our place in the world. Such poetry is deliberately open-ended, not denying the dramas of small choices in which today really is the day of salvation, but resisting treatment of wisdom as a blueprint with full guarantees concerning earthly outcomes.

Birth and death, planting and uprooting. The activities mentioned in 3:2 evoke memories of 1:12–2:26. There is a temptation to see their comprehensiveness right from the start with the pair of being born and dying, although giving birth is another possible reading. Symmetry of activity and/or passivity does not settle the issue, because dying, while an active verb, is really a passive activity. Or at least it should be; whatever the difficulties, life is precious in the Sage's eyes. Even at his most despairing moments, he laments life and gives no thought to taking his own ("a living dog is better than a dead lion"; 9:4). Either way the entire life cycle is at stake. Though we are dependent upon God for life and reminded of this by each birth and each death, the latter half of 3:2 dignifies humans as stewards of creation. We fulfill our identity as divine image-bearers in part by planting and uprooting—by having a subsidiary responsibility, under God, for the life of other creatures.

Killing and healing, breaking down and building up. Both animate and inanimate objects are covered in this series of beginnings and endings. Whereas the activities in 3:2 are either inevitable and/or properly beyond human choosing, 3:3 presents the first possible, and the chief, moral dilemma of the poem. If, as the exegesis hints so far, the Sage is neither a determinist nor an opportunist, then what should readers make of a "time to kill"? Exodus 20:13 states flatly, "You shall not kill," with "murder" (e.g., NRSV) an interpretative translation that presumes some killing is justified based on the rest of the Old Testament. So, does the time for killing in Eccl. 3:3 likewise presume the legitimacy of capital punishment and/or just warfare—situations in which killing is appropriate or even necessary? Interpretation

15. Dietrich Bonhoeffer, *Ethics*, trans. Reinhard Krauss, Charles C. West, and Douglas W. Stott; ed. Clifford J. Green; Dietrich Bonhoeffer Works 6 (Minneapolis: Fortress, 2005), 365–66.

of this verse depends on the framework with which one approaches the passage as a whole—deterministic or not, descriptive only or also prescriptive, and so forth. If one follows the present commentary in taking a nondeterministic line, seeing moral implications in the passage, then the verse could offer small confirmation of the church's historic tendency toward acknowledging the potential existence of (carefully circumscribed) situations of justified killing. In that case its witness would reflect, in another literary form, the practices implied within the Torah and Old Testament narratives. However, the wider dogmatic and historical issues are sufficiently complex, and the exegesis here sufficiently contested, that in and of itself 3:3 proves little.

The latter half of the verse assumes an appropriate life cycle beyond the human realm. The implication is that human constructions, whether buildings or institutions of various kinds, should not be expected to live forever. These projects are worthwhile, but in the course of time some of them may become damaged or damaging. Then they need tearing down, which is consistent with the prohibition of nostalgia in 7:10: "Do not say, 'Why were the former days better than these?' / For it is not from wisdom that you ask about this." Rather than clinging to the past, sometimes we need to go out with the old and ring in the new.

Weeping and laughing, mourning and dancing. Ecclesiastes 3:4 shifts to covering a range of emotions. Some words and a grammatical omission may appear for consonance and assonance, agreements in sound. This signals that our exegesis should not be overly technical regarding theological abstractions, when the text may primarily manifest poetic intentions instead. As usual, though, there is comprehensive coverage: both personal and public expressions appear in 3:4. Without going too far in confronting the *contemptus mundi* tradition (→1:2), this passage implies no lesser legitimacy for laughing than mourning. Moreover, mourning lacks here the self-reflexive and spiritually focused sense that gives it priority in the Sermon on the Mount. There, the focus of mourning concerns sin—our poverty in spirit. Here, various concerns—not least, death (3:2a, 3a) and change (3:2b, 3b)—make mourning appropriate.

Throwing away and gathering stones, embracing and refraining. Ecclesiastes 3:5 moves deeper into social interaction. The last clause could include various situations of embracing, not just sexual ones. Unlike some earlier clauses, the actions are mutually exclusive: one either embraces or refrains from embracing at any given time. In the first clause, the referent of casting away and gathering stones is debated. Rabbinic midrash takes the metaphor as a sexual reference, and so do patristic Christian commentators; Augustine appeals to 1 Cor. 7, suggesting that now after Christ's advent is the redemptive-historical time for gathering stones, avoiding embrace if possible (*On Marriage and Concupiscence* 14, in NPNF[1] 5.269). The fathers also provide allegorical interpretations about embracing wisdom (e.g., Gregory of Nyssa, *Homilies on Ecclesiastes* 7, in Hall 1993: 116–17). This array of interpretations displays the text's poetic range. But the passage does not differentiate between redemptive-historical eras. So, whether the reference is sexual or commercial/agricultural or otherwise, the point holds for humans in general, across the ages: there are times when both sets of activities are appropriate. In light of the later reference to quarrying stones (Eccl. 10:9), a construction project involving a house or field is probably at the root of the metaphor in 3:5a while, as Bartholomew 2009: 164–65 notes, a house might provide the place for the embracing of 3:5b. On this basis we may consider the interaction between the building activity of 3:3b and the social activity of 3:4b. Sometimes our focus should be on the work, and other times on the play; keeping time for both adds up to a well-ordered life, in any era. Redemptive history may then help us to discern particular times for each, and the nature of the work to pursue.

From seeking and losing to war and peace. Ecclesiastes 3:6 focuses on possessions, and again in the aggregate all possibilities are covered. Ecclesiastes 3:7a continues to address possessions, and part of the reason we should not hold on to them too tightly is because we are not their ultimate owners. Sometimes the best stewardship involves mending, whereas at other times the fabric must be torn to start anew.

Ecclesiastes 3:8 addresses emotions and their larger social consequences. Once again the verse could seem morally jarring. Even if one grants the necessity of war in a fallen world, in light of occasionally justified killing (→3:3), what about hate? The text does not specify other people as the object, while the rest of scripture does suggest that hate is appropriate with respect to sin: "I hate the company of evildoers, / and will not sit with the wicked" (Ps. 26:5); "You [the Messiah] love righteousness and hate wickedness. / Therefore God, your God, has anointed you / with the oil of gladness beyond your companions" (45:7); "The LORD loves those who hate evil; / he guards the lives of his faithful; / he rescues them from the hand of the wicked" (97:10); "I will not set before my eyes / anything that is base. / I hate the work of those who fall away; / it shall not cling to me" (101:3); "Through your precepts I get understanding; / therefore I hate every false way" (119:104; also 119:113, 128, 163). The old canard about "hating the sin and loving the sinner" fits these texts, respecting that hatred, like vengeance, is proper only to God in judgment. Psalm 139:21–22, however, speaks of hating those who hate the Lord and counting God's enemies as ours. Still, in context the hatred is not violent emotion leading to vicious behavior; to the contrary, it is personal, prayerful alignment with the will of God in judgment. The only sense in which we properly hate the wicked involves prayerfully anticipating judgment in God's time and refusing to cavort with God's enemies as if we were simply friends and their opposition to God were no barrier between us. It is never appropriate to hate God's image-bearers in themselves and as such, or to appoint ourselves as their moral superiors aside from divine grace. But it is necessary to hate evil in such a way that those persistently characterized by opposition to God leave us distraught until we take into account the end of their behavior (73:17, 27).

It is clear that Eccl. 3:1–8 primarily describes the world, not directly authorizing what to do. God's ideal world would not have war, killing, hate, and so forth, as these were not originally the dynamic of creation. Coupled with the despairing rhetorical question of 3:9, this could suggest a deterministic and thoroughly descriptive interpretation, according to which the Sage just reports the news. At minimum the concluding rhetorical question precludes an opportunistic approach. Yet the element of human decision in the *ḥēpeṣ* of 3:1 and in many activities throughout 3:2–8, along with the preoccupation of the rest of the book with knowing the future or lacking perfect timing (e.g., 11:1–6), favors the view that God's sovereignty establishes rather than excludes the need for good timing. Precisely the awareness that some times are better than others, but humans frequently struggle to discern them, causes the anguish in 3:9: "What gain have the workers from their toil?" Hence a moderately prescriptive interpretation is best: the Sage favors an ordered life in which, when possible, one acts at the time made clear by divine wisdom. On the occasions when discernment is difficult, we must rest in the times being established "under heaven"—even, perhaps, the times to be confused as well as the times to act with conviction—for, as suggested earlier, God does not grant our desire for permanent gain from our toil to lie within our own control. That is the subject of the ensuing prose.

Prose (3:9–15)

Restating the inquiry. As just noted, 3:9 implies that humans cannot consistently gain the knowledge whereby to profit from good timing. This question surfaced earlier, framing the initial inquiry in 1:3. Likewise 3:10 repeats elements from Eccl. 1, especially 1:13b. First-person singular forms start to dominate again, down through at least 4:8. Thus it is possible to see 3:10–22 correcting the king's earlier secularism by considering providence, and 4:1–12 supplementing the king's earlier individualism by considering community (Krüger 2004: 83). Yet the tone seems downcast: God seeks to keep us busy without offering profit. Thus these passages are not so much remedies as continuing reflections. The Sage narrates his quest somewhat inductively, so that readers endure the fits and starts of his inner journey. The answer to the question of 3:9 remains pessimistic when posed in absolute terms: he cannot figure out the times sufficiently to establish lasting profit, and so 3:10 implies frustration with God's limitations. Later the rest of the book holds out hope of enough wisdom to handle this reality without self-destruction. It is worth trying to make the most of opportunities—though one cannot, and should not attempt to, preclude all risk or figure everything out.

Understanding our restlessness. Ecclesiastes 3:11 is oft sentimentalized, with God making everything "beautiful" in its time. A better translation is "appropriate" or "fitting"; the esthetic dimension of this divine work is not to inspire romantic fancies. Yet "everything" is fitting, a strongly positive affirmation. God's work must be assessed comprehensively, with everything from beginning to end in view. In the Sage's current estimation, though, God remains a bit of a taskmaster by setting *ʿôlām* within human hearts without revealing the divine plans in the full sense desired. People thus find themselves always searching. The translation of

ʿôlām is contentious: should it be rendered "eternity" or "world" or "course of the world" or something else still? Given usage in the rest of Ecclesiastes, "eternity" is preferable so long as it is not overloaded with a rigidly philosophical definition. A temporally relevant meaning, pro or con, is natural following 3:1–8, and the word "eternal" fits nicely with God's activity in 3:14. Accordingly, 3:11 affirms that appropriate timing exists, "but still" (not "so that"; see Bartholomew 2009: 167) humans cannot comprehensively find it. Although the Sage is provisionally frustrated by this, the rest of the book will gradually reorient his quest and reconcile him to the divine decision.

Augustine's famous confessional prayer comes to mind quickly: "You have made us for yourself, and our heart is restless until it finds its rest in you."[16] Human desire to make sense of life in the universe expresses itself religiously. However, if religion—activity from the human side—is all there is, then we are chasing after wind. People are not capable of satisfying the fullness of this divine desire themselves. Once again Ecclesiastes has Gen. 1–3 in the background: Gen. 1 early in the verse, leading us to link divine creation with providential sustenance of the world; Gen. 2–3 in the latter part, limiting inquiry in ways that humans then transgressed (Krüger 2004: 87). God configures humans to be eternity-seeking not so they despair over earthly futility in itself, but so that restless hearts might rest in their ultimate Good alone—at the pace made possible by divine revelation.

Restating the carpe diem *conclusion.* To avoid sentimentality, we must admit that the Sage's tone includes resignation, despite positive affirmations in 3:12–15. Is *carpe diem* the best humans can do? That would be anesthesia in place of what we really yearn after: fuller involvement with God's plans in the world, and especially knowing how to handle monotony. The repetition of 1:9 in 3:15, along with the suggestion that *God* is the one who brings everything back around again, is hardly concern for the eternal existence of souls or large-scale metaphysical affirmations. The repeated claim is simple: there is never anything new under the sun. This does not mean that there are no occasions for joy, but that God's gifts must be enjoyed for what they are, while they last. Trying to turn them into permanent gains means trying to usurp God's sovereignty, not fearing him.

Such fear is not cravenness about divine inscrutability and/or determinism. In contrast to the frequent (and resigned) query "who knows?" 3:12 underscores what the Sage does know, supporting both joyful and moral living (for "do good" in a moral sense, →7:20). Legitimate joys include bodily delights that, as Bonhoeffer notes and 3:13 manifests, are not merely means to some superspiritual end.[17] Parallels to 2:24 are strong; here it is perhaps even clearer that humans do not control such delights but depend instead on divine gifts. It is fitting therefore to view the end of the passage as a confessional retort to the worries of 3:9–11. The

16. Augustine, *Confessions* 1.1 (trans. Chadwick), 3.
17. Bonhoeffer, *Ethics*, 187.

divine sovereignty and repetition of 3:14–15 cannot denote awful determinism. The divine activity is enduring and purposeful, with earthly repetition transpiring due to God's orchestration of patterns of creaturely freedom. If everything were deterministic, then whether humans fear God would hardly matter to the divine purpose.

The future is not utterly alien, but this holds true only if God patterns it after elements that have gone before. Hence the past is not utterly lost, but this holds true only if God preserves its integrity in preparation for what is to come. The Sage occasionally expresses what it means for humans to be stuck in a disconnected present. His statements are not necessarily false, only limited—having the character of juxtaposed perspectives difficult to integrate. However, human aspiration for eternity constitutes indirect evidence for our divine placement within a larger narrative framework of meaning. The quasiconfessional affirmations in 3:12–15 can hold true while we *also* acknowledge that human ability to discern divine plans remains very limited (3:11).

Is There a Time or Place for Justice? (3:16–22)

> He might be living somewhat better
> Had you not given him of Heaven's light a glitter;
> He calls it reason and, ordained its priest,
> Becomes more bestial than any beast.[18]

Places of injustice? The subject shifts in 3:16 ("moreover I saw") to the question of injustice, but the form of this question remains tied to time and eternity. Ecclesiastes 3:17 repeats a phrase from 3:1, reaffirming "a time for every matter." Now, though, place becomes an issue in addition to time. An acute problem for God's sovereignty over the flow of time is not just the prevalence of injustice, but its presence in the very context designed to counteract it. Poetic description of wicked courts does nothing to make them more appealing.

A time for judgment? Despite this conundrum, 3:17 tries to reclaim the divinely backed confidence from the preceding verses by recalling the significance of divine judgment. It is not necessarily that the Sage escapes the earthly problem by switching the subject to the afterlife. Instead, to speak in his heart brings up an interim statement for further consideration (also 1:16; 2:1, 15). Accordingly, the Sage ponders the operation of God's judgment, probably through historical times for the various matters, which accord with the empirical focus in general and the vocabulary of sight in this passage. Succeeding verses countenance the possibility that death, at a minimum, brings the comeuppance that mitigates any actual gain for the wicked. The rhetorical question at the end of 3:22 may indicate

18. Mephistopheles, in Johann Wolfgang von Goethe, *Faust: A Tragedy*, 2nd ed., trans. Walter Arndt, ed. Cyrus Hamlin (New York: Norton, 2001), 10.

openness to divine judgment and life after death, although the tone suggests that one could hardly be certain.

Animal behavior? The frame for 3:17 involves the Sage speaking in his heart, so that personal reflection—neither predominantly empirical nor confessional—is at issue. Such self-reflection recurs in 3:18, which considers the divine setting apart of human beings. "Testing" is usually positive, so here God's intention is for our best. Unfortunately, the testing elicits only the conclusion that humans are beastly toward each other, in seeming contradiction of our distinctiveness as divine image-bearers. As is frequently the case, especially in these early chapters of Ecclesiastes, we must not run too far with the surface words or claims. They provide an interim report on Qoheleth's thinking as the drama of his quest unfolds—not a settled conclusion. Here the point is more poetic than propositional, given the assonance present (*šĕhem-bĕhēmâ hēmmâ lāhem*). Sinclair Ferguson pointedly comments that in a dog-eat-dog world, "If we behave like animals we end up sharing their final destiny."[19]

Dust to dust? Ecclesiastes 3:19–20 follows with a stark, empirical version of this conclusion: people and animals share the breath of life and its loss in death, so there is no profit for humans. To all appearances, people simply go from dust to dust. Again, taking the words at face value would entail a theological conflict with Gen. 1–3, to which the Sage alludes. But the literary context clarifies that the text presents serial possibilities; the Sage turns over various observations and ideas in his head. Perhaps, on reflection, God will ultimately judge everyone; or perhaps God sovereignly shapes history so as to reduce human grandeur, for indeed we are subject to death just like animals. This latter conclusion is all that one can say for certain on an empirical basis. The importance of this section lies precisely in its vagueness; prematurely replacing this indecisiveness with final canonical conclusions would blunt its rhetorical force. We need to recognize how the world looks for people apart from divine revelation. For that matter, even people with divine revelation still must reckon with the equalizing force of death. And there is also the injustice routinely seen among the living, notably in places of judgment. Humans are beastly to each other; on empirical grounds, how can anyone be sure that divine judgment will eventually remove the gains of the wicked?

Who knows? Additional help in understanding the Sage's considerations comes from translating 3:21 without the usual emendation. If the proper reading is, "Who knows the spirit of man, which rises upward, or the spirit of the animal, which goes down into the earth?"[20] then 3:21 further reflects the back-and-forth uncertainty of the passage, hardly asserting an unorthodox or cynical conclusion. No doubt the passage has pessimistic elements, emphasizing in preceding verses

19. Sinclair Ferguson, *The Pundit's Folly: Chronicles of an Empty Life* (repr., Carlisle, PA: Banner of Truth, 2000), 20.

20. Richard L. Schultz, "Ecclesiastes," in *Baker Commentary on the Bible*, ed. G. M. Burge and A. E. Hill (Grand Rapids: Baker, forthcoming).

the likeness between animals and humans. Since the possibility of their common fate has been asserted with such force, however, 3:21 can pull the punch by acknowledging uncertainty. Who really knows, based on what is seen (3:22a)? At minimum the attitude is one of doubt rather than what is seemingly reflected in the NRSV, namely outright rejection of human distinctiveness: "Who knows whether the human spirit goes upward and the spirit of animals goes downward to the earth?" On either rendering we ought to make sense of this verse in relation to 3:11. The Sage has already affirmed the presence of "eternity" in human hearts. Against the idea that he would now rescind this affirmation skeptically, 3:11 also contains the insistence that human knowledge is divinely limited. Far from contravening 3:11, therefore, 3:21 applies its concluding point about human limitations to our inabilities to resolve questions of injustice and divine judgment. Accordingly, 3:21 asks its rhetorical question about human knowledge in terms consistent with 3:11 rather than cynically dismissing orthodoxy. Such a position leads better into the resulting conclusion of 3:22. To rejoice in "work," not "profit" from it, is the human allotment from God. Beyond that, no one under the sun can bring humans to see what comes after us, whether potential judgment or animal survival or anything else.

Humans cannot even know themselves as they would like, since empirically they cannot investigate the possibility of an afterlife. Christian interpreters need not agonize too long over problematic theological implications on the surface of this text, because there are no firmly asserted conclusions. It explores possibilities and reflects the level of clarity—or not—that we can attain from sight and speech "under the sun," unaccompanied by revelation. We should not miss the irony that the Sage pursues rational exploration as far as it can go—only to discover that, on such a basis, humans get no further than the irrational animals from which they wish to distinguish themselves. For rationality—the distinct human power to muse on observations—to have real meaning requires divine revelation.

The evidence regarding a time and place for justice remains ambiguous apart from Jesus Christ. What is unambiguous is the sting of death. Though Paul taunts death as having its sting removed in the resurrection (1 Cor. 15:51–58), nevertheless he acknowledges the sting for humans alienated from God by sin. In Christ alienation may no longer be fundamental, but sin persists within us for a time: we are *simul iustus et peccator* ("simultaneously justified and still sinful"). Accordingly, even for those who will be victorious—having received revelation of our future in Christ—there presently remains an element of struggle with death.

This is true even of Jesus's life. He who bore all the sorrows and temptations we face likewise stood in the place of justice only to see wickedness initially triumph; like us "he was oppressed, and he was afflicted" (Isa. 53:7). He faced the fear of an excruciating death head-on, to the extent of appearing to sweat blood: "Who could have imagined his future?" (53:8). However, in faith he expected to "prolong his days" (53:10), to "make many righteous" (53:11), and thus in his resurrection he found "a portion with the great" (53:12). This full divine embrace of the fallen human condition now sheds new light on our future (2 Tim. 1:10), but the curse of that condition lingers real for the time being.

Justice and the Community (4:1–16)

> The answer was near at hand; there was still the serpent whispering: For God doth know that in what day soever you shall eat thereof, your eyes shall be opened: and you shall be as Gods. The old father of lies was clever at telling half-truths: How shall you "know" good and evil, until you shall have sampled a little? Taste and be as Gods. But neither infinite power nor infinite wisdom could bestow godhood upon men. For that there would have to be infinite love as well.[21]

The transitional character of 3:16–22 becomes clearer upon moving into Eccl. 4. The subject of justice and injustice remains on the table, but the perspective shifts away from focusing on time and death toward interrogating the social implications.

Oppression and Envy (4:1–8)

The lonely despair of the oppressed. In 4:1 references to oppression (*ʿāšaq*) are repeated several times so that the rhetorical force is overbearing. *Hinnēh* ("look") can convey mournful resignation; in none of the passages concerning oppression does the Sage lift a finger of resistance or directly ask others to do so (3:16; 8:9, 10). Yet the odd repetition of "with no one to comfort them" not only conveys despairing resignation but also subtly condemns other members of the community for doing nothing to alleviate the condition of the oppressed. God's judgment may help in the future, but even God seems absent now. Ellul 1990: 83 rightly catches the force of what is missing in light of the rest of the passage: the oppressed have no *person* to comfort them, whereas "abstract comfort in such a situation would amount to still another illusion, or vanity."

The ironic despair of an observer. Ecclesiastes 4:2–3 follows with statements of despair about life, even stronger than in 2:17. These claims are almost absurd, since those who have not lived are only meaningful as those who have not *yet* been—who therefore have lives still ahead, despite all the inevitably attendant suffering. Thus the Sage's judgments favoring death are not quite as straightforward as they seem—anticipating 9:4, where "a living dog is better than a dead lion." Moreover, parallels to Job 3:3–5 and Jer. 20:14–18 are important, reflecting the possibility of godly believers giving vent to great despair. Hence, in context, the Sage's hyperbole offers another biblical incentive to express freely our frustrations with the way of the world. Moreover, it is ironic that only someone living could experience and express the conviction about being better off nonexistent; Eccl. 4:3 deconstructs itself.

21. Thoughts of Dom Paulo, a character in Miller, *Canticle for Leibowitz*, 234.

At the same time, the Sage's despair is not born of direct suffering; his is not the "How long, O Lord?" of a martyred soul crying out under God's altar (Rev. 6:9–10). It is instead born solely of observation. The structure of these verses contains the activity of observation or reflection in Eccl. 4:1–2, 4, 7, 15; "better than" statements in 4:2–3, 6, 9, 13; and *hebel* statements in 4:4, 8, 16. Both sides of the picture—*carpe diem* and human frustration—are apparent to the Sage's eye, as previously. But consistently missing are references to God, which must wait until Eccl. 5, along with positive resolution of the problem(s) of injustice, as the *hebel* statements indicate. The Sage becomes discouraged merely as a spectator, for thereby he does not take God into account. This both shapes our use of these statements and evokes sympathy for young adults who become flummoxed about the problem of evil even before their personal suffering ever grows acute. Here and elsewhere the Bible itself offers empathetic recognition of their experience, while refusing to leave them permanently in that condition.

Foolish and envious despair. Ecclesiastes 4:4–6 moves beyond evil deeds of oppression and lack of comforters to address motives with which humans in general pursue their work. The alternatives are stark: either envy results in successful, though excessively strenuous, work (4:4, 6) or else folly results in self-destructive lack of work (4:5). The proverb in 4:5 fits hand in glove with Prov. 6:10–11: "A little sleep, a little slumber, / a little folding of the hands to rest, / and poverty will come upon you like a robber, / and want, like an armed warrior." In recognizing the frequent tendency—sometimes in the same life—toward either workaholism or laziness, the Sage foresaw the cultural outworking of late modern capitalism long before it arose!

In Eccl. 4:4 we read of envy, not just jealousy, with the king from Eccl. 1–2 serving as an illustration: he compares his success against others before him, not motivated purely to become a good ruler but instead to outachieve everyone else. His desire is not predominantly positive regarding an object but negative against other subjects. With this envy and the pride from which it springs, the seven deadly sins are out in full force. The fool in 4:5, by contrast, is guilty of sloth. Beyond sheer laziness he wallows in the spiritual mire, accepting the inevitable malaise of human envy and simply giving up in place of joining the cutthroat competition. But he does not pursue the divine rest of 4:6, thus languishing too in the end result of the deadly sequence (lust) or its predecessor (gluttony), as suggested by sarcastic hyperbole regarding consumption.

Alongside the despairing elements in this passage are repeated references to two as opposed to one (4:3, 6, 8, 9, 10, 11, 12, 15). The obvious theme is the value—even need—of companionship. Ecclesiastes 4:6 puts this companionship in the context of the Sage's larger-scale message. On the side of companionship is quietness or rest; on the opposite side are toil and chasing after wind. Accordingly an earlier interpretative emphasis is confirmed: the Sage values processes of human work while confronting foolish tendencies toward seeking everlasting profit from them. Whereas previously he challenged the prospects for such profit, now he confronts the envy underlying and spoiling the very process of toil itself. Each is associated with chasing after wind. The form of argument in 4:6 is recognizably parallel to Proverbs: *x* (wisdom) is "better than" *y* (folly—even if it is industrious folly).

Miserly despair. Ecclesiastes 4:7–8 describes the miser so often produced by such envious striving. On Bonaventure's reckoning, "Having treated of the vanity of malice, he now deals with the vanity of *avarice*" (2005: 196). Once again the rich fool described by Jesus comes to mind. The toil of such a fool is ceaseless because he is insatiable. If moments of self-awareness break into his uninterrupted striving, then he realizes two ironies, one immediately and the other eventually. The eventual tragedy is that the toil benefits no one else; it precludes interaction with others, and the fool cannot control his legacy (as in Eccl. 2). The more immediate tragedy is that the toil precludes even personal pleasure. If genuine pleasure lies in blessings like table fellowship—eating and drinking and so forth—then it cannot be had solo, without sharing. The unsatisfied eye of 4:8 is in the singular (on the most likely text-critical reading, at any rate), and the passage as a whole prepares to celebrate companionship in 4:9–12 while being suspicious of loneliness. The concern has shifted—from controlling a selfish legacy through a worthy heir to confronting the senselessness of a working life without companions.

Companionship and Wisdom (4:9–16)

At 4:9 the tone changes, completing the transition of 4:7–8 and positively extolling the value of two over one through 4:12. Ecclesiastes 4:13–16 extols wisdom, albeit wistfully: *hebel* returns by the end, along with the sour note that a wise young king from humble origins will not last too long. In other words, though wisdom promotes sticking together, humans tend instead to develop a herd mentality and fight with each other. The envy observed in 4:4 is endemic to human culture most of the time. Wisdom's victories under the sun are unfortunately temporary.

The blessings of the threefold cord. Ecclesiastes 4:9 begins this section by making explicit the connection in 4:6: rewarding[22] toil aligns not just with quietness but also with companionship. In fact, contrary to the tendencies of modern society, rest and companionship relate. People often presume that others slow down their climb to the top in a dog-eat-dog world or merely hang on to enjoy the victory spoils. Friends are accessories, with relationships pursued on self-interested and therefore temporary terms. Family obligations are to be undertaken only once a person is well established, financially and otherwise—having taken the time to have fun first. If more than anecdotal confirmation of these claims is necessary, then a recent sociological study of young adults will suffice.[23] The witness of Eccl. 4, along with biblical wisdom literature generally, is countercultural on this score. The restless hearts of our culture will ultimately be satisfied only in God, of course;

22. The word is not *yitrôn*, so the Sage's denial of profit remains intact.

23. Christian Smith and Patricia Snell, *Souls in Transition: The Religious and Spiritual Lives of Emerging Adults* (New York: Oxford University Press, 2009).

but, penultimately, humans need community. And the community that people currently seek—shorn of obligations, particularly familial ones, while protecting self-interest—only reinforces the despair also profiled in Eccl. 4. Humans cannot overcome envy on their own, and otherwise they cannot find true community or face oppression with hope.

Ecclesiastes 4:10–12 provides a reason for needing companionship, in the form of a scenario: the setting is a journey, on which one might fall (4:10), or need warmth at night (4:11), or be attacked (4:12). Peter Chrysologus notes that Christ sent out disciples two by two (Sermon 170, in FC 17.280), fitting the recommended pattern. In a milieu filled with platitudes and plaques, marriage is not the immediate subject of these verses. Companionship (*ḥābēr*; 4:10) is the major issue; such a comrade "can also be sought by someone who has no son or brother" (with regard to 4:7–8; Krüger 2004: 99). Beyond exegetical integrity, this recognition is practically important if the church is to welcome single people wholly into God's first family. Many of us can attest to the agonies produced by churchly confusion over which authentically biblical family values to perpetuate, and how to do so. Contemporary Western capitalism, with proliferating technologies that advance certain forms of communication and mobility, detaches people from thick communal structures. No doubt the family needs strengthening as a result, but so do other forms of friendship and companionship, not least those into which the church calls us. Bonhoeffer rightly distinguishes *Christian* community from familial and companionable bonds that, however important, are not constituted entirely by our being "in Christ."[24] Based on Eccl. 4, we must celebrate all varieties of human relationship that God gives us, without treating them all the same.

Granted this text's reach beyond weddings, it would be churlish on the other hand to preclude all marital appropriations of 4:9–12. Doubtless not all ancient marriages centered on biblical friendship, although without some complexities of modern romance they may have done better than we think. Nevertheless, there is no reason that today's marriages cannot ground themselves in this way. Such a reality might counter many falsehoods of romantic love that dominate the contemporary scene. Moreover, since Gen. 1–4 stands prominently in the background of Ecclesiastes, it is appropriate for the Sage's words to have secondary resonance regarding marriage: two are better than one since it is not good for a man to be alone, without a God-given helper (Gen. 2:18–25); these two lying together surely could embrace more than sexual intercourse, but not necessarily less. Bonaventure 2005: 198 recalls even the aged King David receiving the warmth of a young woman in 1 Kgs. 1:1–4.

Lurking tragically behind the scenes, the story of Cain's envious murder of Abel highlights the need for the right companionship to offer real safety. The positive

24. Dietrich Bonhoeffer, *Life Together and Prayerbook of the Bible*, trans. Daniel Bloesch and James Burtness; ed. Gerhard Ludwig Mueller and Albrecht Schoenherr; Dietrich Bonhoeffer Works 5 (Minneapolis: Fortress, 1996).

ideals of Eccl. 4:9–12 do not appear in isolation. The emphasis on solidarity provides the counterpoint to the tragedies of 4:1–8: "In order to withstand and overcome a society dominated by the logic of 'save your own skin' and 'all against all,' it is not advisable to be alone; one must seek the company of others—in this case, not only in order to eat and drink and share the enjoyment of work but to get a better wage, pull each other up, ward off the cold, and face an enemy attack."[25] The Sage does not laud the ideals of companionship as romantic abstractions capable of soothing angst-ridden postmodern adults, who long for community when their individual entertainments lag. The Sage writes of real dangers and relational provision for dealing with them.

Theological readers find additional intrigue in the threefold cord not easily broken. In the first instance, this makes no reference to the divine Trinity or to the three theological virtues of faith, hope, and love; it is apparently traceable to an ancient Sumerian proverb. Before leaving the cord entirely there and then, however, we ought to contemplate its contextual function in light of two points: (1) the dominance of the numbers one and two suddenly being interrupted by this number three; and (2) the gnomic character of such a proverb permitting extensions of a principle into other contexts. The teaching of 4:7–12 concerns God creating humans for personal relationship and mutual support. Finding faith, hope, and love to be a referent of the threefold cord is difficult because virtues are only indirectly personal; they are dispositions or character traits, not agents themselves. Such a reading is at or beyond the text's broadest reach, drawing merely upon the language of the proverb in general, largely shorn of this particular context.

Yet hearing a divinely placed echo of the Trinity is not fanciful. To be sure, such an echo could not be heard by many earlier generations that encountered the text, becoming possible only with further unfolding of the drama of redemption. But that does not preclude its advance placement by the Lord of all history. If the number three sounds a jarring note in a text capable of making its point with ones and twos, then one ponders why the affirmation of human companionship includes this image rather than stopping with the prior material.

Concerning the Trinity, Richard of St. Victor's proposal is intriguing, that human love between only two can become self-enclosed, stopping with the *erōs* of desire for another person and failing to open outward toward sharing the joy of *agapē*, of self-giving charity.[26] Thus God's love brings a third dynamic into the relation, for instance, children into a family. By analogy—and only analogy, which of course breaks down eventually—if God is love then God's being involves not self-enclosed, shared egoism but mutual indwelling in fullness. This fullness is sufficient to overflow fittingly, into creation of the cosmos and interaction with its human stewards. We need companionship because God made us for fellow-

25. Tamez, *When the Horizons Close*, 72.

26. Richard of St. Victor, *On the Trinity* 3.11, in *The Twelve Patriarchs, the Mystical Ark, Book Three of the Trinity*, trans. Grover A. Zinn, Classics of Western Spirituality (New York: Paulist Press, 1979), 384–85.

ship, first with God and secondarily with each other. It is appropriate for our lives to signal—though only in a creaturely image—the communicative nature of the Creator. God's life involves companionship; so ideally does ours, even if love for humans is what we are to do rather than what we simply are. The reality with which 4:9–12 deals, that it is not good to be truly alone (4:8), stems from our Maker. So it is not unreasonable, confronted by the heightening from two to three in this particular text, to ponder that.

The curse of fickle kings and communities. Ecclesiastes 4:13 shifts to another "better than" proverb, providing a mininarrative scenario over the next few verses. The unit is transitional; it could be included within a unit stretching to 5:9, in which 4:13–16 and 5:8–9 frame exhortations about approaching God (in 5:1–7) with "critique of expecting too much from a king" (Krüger 2004: 101). But the more important thematic connection involves the "better than" sayings and the focus of Eccl. 4 on what we need from others—hence the structural approach taken here. In either case, themes interweave with various, loose repetitions of certain elements.

The scenario introduced in 4:13 asserts that a region is better off when led by a poor (lower class, not from the nobility) yet wise youth than by an old king who is foolish because he no longer accepts advice or correction. Wisdom often goes with age in wisdom literature, but here again the Sage can present empirical evidence that precludes any absolute rule—or at least an exception that proves the general rule. Numerous times already, preoccupation with status accompanied significant dangers. Moreover, everyone knows from observation the mysterious difference between some who grow old gracefully and others who prove the adage, "You can't teach an old dog new tricks." When age leads to preoccupation with control over a legacy, displacing the wisdom to know that one cannot know it all, the social and political consequences can be disastrous.

New Testament revelation completes the other side of the picture. While respecting the value of age (in the concept of leadership by elders, for instance), the text portrays the Holy Spirit gracing young and old alike (e.g., Acts 2:17). Therefore, otherwise dangerous, even "foolish" advice can be given to Timothy: "Let no one despise your youth, but set the believers an example in speech and conduct, in love, in faith, in purity" (1 Tim. 4:12). By the Spirit, young people can grow into wisdom—the goal of wisdom literature in the first place.

Despite countering the expected correlation of age and wisdom, the Sage does not run entirely counter to wisdom's conventions, as his appreciation of the value of advice demonstrates (e.g., Prov. 11:14; 15:22; 20:18; 24:6). The syntax of Eccl. 4:14, continuing the surprising scenario that demonstrates the importance of listening, is difficult: who, in the first line, is the one coming out of prison to reign? The old king is the nearest antecedent, but the young and poor king is the most natural one—given not only the mention of poverty (albeit with a different word) but also the linkage of "youth" in 4:13 and 4:15. The contribution of the second line to the story is murky, depending on translation decisions. In any case

4:15–16a depicts a youth gaining an initial following, while 4:16b acknowledges that the masses are fickle. There the syntax is again problematic; so the youth in view may be a third party, who supplants the original wise youth (the second king), or there may be continuation of the original youth's story (the second king supplanting the first).

All the possible versions of the story have the communal rejoicing in the youth end fairly quickly, and this is another instance of *hebel.* Neither age nor political power automatically correlates with wisdom or popularity. These cautions prevent excessive enthusiasm being generated by the preceding pro-community verses. Two may be better than one, but human threefold cords prove fickle. They readily place too much hope in a leader, only to switch allegiances at the instant when that leader disappoints. Even leaders who have grown old and gray during apparent success can become addled by self-importance—with David and Solomon perhaps rivaling each other to serve as Exhibit A.

Bonaventure's spiritual interpretation (2005: 204) is right to highlight the illustration of Jesus Christ: he came from humble origins to gain quick popularity, only to see that momentum can be very fleeting. The audience is also free to ponder several Old Testament figures such as Joseph, David, and Solomon. The text does not fixate on any one of them, but broad parallels to their life stories surely surface: Joseph gaining rule after prison, David from poverty, and so on. In general, history is littered with the scenario: young liberators lead revolutions only to outbid the previous colonizers in their oppressive measures. Solomon may not have been a postcolonial hero turned goat, but he epitomizes a ruler who started well and aged poorly.

Hence 4:13–16 resonates with the plight of many in today's world. Western readers unfamiliar with ancient monarchy may initially feel distant from the text, but conversely the scenario of people choosing to follow a leader (4:15–16a) seems more relevant to contemporary democracies than many might expect of the ancient world. Not only does promising leadership go bad as with Solomon, but also "Qohelet is presumably getting at the fact that even when the good is provided, people cannot be relied on to embrace it. This is truly the nature of a fallen world—it is not that there are not solutions and salvation but so often humans do not want the good, do not want salvation" (Bartholomew 2009: 199). It would be dangerous to overstate the claim, but the Old Testament tends to find parallels between the spiritual state of the king and the nation—however complex the cause-and-effect relationships might be in any given case. There is a limited sense in which we tend, over time, to get the leaders we deserve.

American readers who lived through the 1970s may remember talk of a "misery index," as political candidates debated whether people were better off than four years earlier. One might say that in the descriptive political theology of 4:13–16 a misery index operates: the young upstart emerges from prison and/or poverty to supplant an aging failure; yet before long there is dissatisfaction with the youth too—possibly because he failed to fulfill legitimate expectations he himself created.

The normative implication seems to be that for wise leadership to flourish, a wise community is necessary. Otherwise people may not recognize opportunity when they have it, let alone foster conditions within which wise leaders could emerge in the first place. In several ways, therefore, Eccl. 4 bears out the truth of an Akan saying: "One person alone cannot build a town."[27]

God's Economy: Fulfilling Vows (5:1–7)[28]

> Fear God. Honour the king. (1 Pet. 2:17 KJV)

In terms of grand themes, Eccl. 1–2 interrogates experience and Eccl. 3–4 takes on time. Ecclesiastes 5–6 confronts still another element that makes the world go round: money. To be sure, thematic overlap occurs, including the aforementioned connections between 4:13–16 and 5:8–9. Nevertheless, although the political focus does not entirely disappear, in Eccl. 5 a newly economic element comes on the scene. In addition, 5:1 contains the first directly hortatory material of the book.

The first command. Thematic continuity with preceding verses, though, occurs with this admonition to listen; God's word is even more important than the human advice mentioned in 4:13–16. To avoid the sacrifice of fools includes rejecting frivolous festivals that mix piety with partying. The contrast with "listening" is important: in 1 Sam. 15:22 the Lord delights more in those who hearken to his voice—obey—than those who offer sacrifices. Provocation for that statement is King Saul's protesting too much about sacrifice, when he plundered the Amalekites in disobedience to God. God's ultimate desire for heartfelt obedience echoes elsewhere too: "Wash yourselves; make yourselves clean; / remove the evil of your doings / from before my eyes; / cease to do evil, / learn to do good; / seek justice, / rescue the oppressed, / defend the orphan, / plead for the widow. / Come now, let us argue it out, / says the LORD: / though your sins are like scarlet, / they shall be like snow; / though they are red like crimson, / they shall become like wool. / If you are willing and obedient, / you shall eat the good of the land; / but if you refuse and rebel, / you shall be devoured by the sword; / for the mouth of the LORD has spoken" (Isa. 1:16–20); "As for you, O house of Israel, thus says the Lord GOD: Go serve your idols, everyone of you now and hereafter, if you will not listen to me; but my holy name you shall no more profane with your gifts and your idols" (Ezek. 20:39; also Mic. 6:8 and Ps. 40:6–8). Indeed, hearing and obedience are virtually synonymous in the Old Testament. Hence those who

27. Tewoldemedhin Habtu, "Ecclesiastes," in *Africa Bible Commentary*, ed. Tokunboh Adeyemo (Grand Rapids: Zondervan, 2006), 790.

28. NRSV verse numbers are used throughout this commentary. In the Hebrew text, 5:1 is 4:17, with the result that English verse numbers throughout Eccl. 5 are one number higher than their Hebrew counterparts.

guard their steps, as enjoined by the Sage, sacrifice to God primarily via obedience instead of empty ritual.

The application of divine transcendence to human speech. Ecclesiastes 5:2 applies an ongoing theme to establish a reason for guarding one's steps. God is in heaven and you are on earth: as a finite creature, you cannot brag or predict as if controlling your life. Hence Jas. 4:13–17 enjoins verbal modesty about one's plans; in Ecclesiastes this extends even to religious plans (5:4). Saul continues to provide a notable contrast: he took upon himself the right to determine the best course of action. He was not ignorant, at a mundane level, of what God told him through Samuel. He knew therefore that he was doing evil if measured strictly by that standard. But he thought he knew better, posturing about a way to satisfy religious duties while simultaneously attending to personal advantage. It is naïve to treat folly as literal ignorance of evildoing; biblically, folly is a moral category. It confronts our practical atheism, the tendency to live *as if* God did not exist, whatever our professed beliefs. The fools of Ps. 14 and Ps. 53, who say in their hearts that there is no God, are citizens of Israel, the covenant community. Theirs is not the modern, supposedly absolute, version of atheism, but rather an inward disposition that may not even come to public expression—except in unjust acts that are heedless of divine judgment. Such practical atheism provides an ironic undercurrent below the textual surface of the Sage's quest: if folly rejects what you hear from God in favor of what you think you know, then some of the Sage's own prior speech comes under criticism. Yet, for the Sage merely to parrot orthodoxy without admitting his questions would not be honest before God either. According to Eccl. 5:2, it would be foolish to think that one could get away with fooling God in such a fashion.

Gregory of Nyssa reflects on this verse regarding the doctrine of God:

> He shows, I think, by the relation of these elements to each other, or rather by their distance, how far the divine nature is above the speculations of human reason. For that nature which transcends all intelligence is as high above earthly calculation as the stars are above the touch of our fingers, or rather, many times more than that.
>
> Knowing, then, how widely the divine nature differs from our own, let us quietly remain within our proper limits. For it is both safer and more reverent to believe the majesty of God to be greater than we can understand, than, after circumscribing his glory by our misconceptions, to suppose there is nothing beyond our conception of it. (*Answer to Eunomius's Second Book*, in NPNF[2] 5.260)

Divine transcendence restrains our speech, but should not be exaggerated—as critical scholarship frequently does—to belie the emphasis of 5:1 on listening to the present divine instruction or of 5:2, 4–6 on being aware of divine judgment. The Sage's point in emphasizing divine transcendence is to encourage genuine remembrance of the Creator.

The folly of many words. Ecclesiastes 5:3 may quote a proverb, since its beginning is not perfectly apt to the subject at first glance. However, dreams, attractive as forms of divine revelation, could make humans vulnerable to endless quandaries over interpretation, making life toilsome. Or the thought might be more general, about excessive toil affecting our sleep. Regardless, in a tiresome way fools multiply words when it comes to religion, as James Limburg notes:

> The most well-known public prayer that Jesus has given to followers is the Lord's Prayer, which is very short (Matt. 6:9–13). But Jesus also taught that there is a time for private prayers (Matt. 6:6), and these prayers may indeed be lengthy, as Jesus exemplified in his prayers in Gethsemane (Mark 14:32–42 and parallels).
>
> "God is in heaven, and you upon earth; therefore let your words be few" (5:2). It can be that, in our own situations, we tend to reverse the practice of Jesus. There are overenthusiastic clerics and worship leaders who love to pray at great length in public, and there are also interminable litanies and liturgies that test the patience and piety of even the most faithful believers. On the other hand, the practice of disciplined private prayer is often a difficult one to maintain.[29]

God knows the difference between prayers that babble on like paganism and those that reflect genuine faith.

The folly of unfulfilled vows. Fools are identified (5:4–5) as those who do not pay a vow to God, at least not quickly. Against the view that this section emphasizes divine arbitrariness or distance is its stock Old Testament teaching; Deut. 23:21–23, for instance, similarly teaches that it is better not to vow than to delay fulfillment. In Matt. 23:16–22 Jesus likewise confronts religious game-playing. Our first impulse is probably to mock the Pharisees and make excuses for ourselves. But the relative frequency of such biblical teaching indicates that practicing religion in terms of momentary bargaining with God is all too common. Caesarius of Arles highlights the theological implication: "Above all, we must fear lest someone believes so strongly that he will receive God's mercy that he does not dread his justice. If a person does this, he has no faith. Likewise, if he dreads God's justice so much that he despairs of his mercy, there is no faith. Since God is not only merciful but also just, let us believe in both" (Sermon 12.5, in FC 31.71–72).

Ecclesiastes 5:6 extends the prohibition of foolish vowing, implying another operational description. It is true that vows are not explicitly mentioned, and one can certainly sin more broadly with speech (Jas. 3). Yet vocabulary appears from Deut. 23:21–23, which, as just noted, deals with vows. Some were apparently making vows but reneging when the priestly collector came, appealing via the terminology of *šĕgāgâ* to the Old Testament distinction between ignorant or unintentional and intentional sins (Lev. 4; Num. 15:22–31). The latter had no atoning sacrifice whereas the former could be handled by cultic means. Ironically, divine anger attaches to those who claim ignorance—appealing to a possible sacrifice—instead of admitting failure. In the Sage's eyes, honesty is the best policy—calling folly what it is and casting oneself entirely on God's mercy. But

29. Limburg, *Encountering Ecclesiastes*, 71.

better still would be avoiding these vows in the first place. Proper timing comes into play again, as we must act neither too quickly (Eccl. 5:2) nor too slowly (5:4).

It may be odd to imagine a religious bill collector; the lack of relevant historical-critical background depicting this "messenger" exacerbates the oddity. However, it should give pause to consider the differences in social context that lie on the textual surface. In many contemporary cultures it offends against a right to privacy for others to know one's religious duties or commitments, let alone the financial situation. But in biblical times exclusion from the community, in principle anyway, occurred on account of greed (1 Cor. 5:9–11; 6:9–11), which implies considerable attention to people's spending possibilities and habits.[30] Narratives in Acts support this reading. Ananias and Sapphira were guilty of lying in the first instance. Yet they were tempted to do so because they could gain religious currency by offering gifts of property. In many contexts today, by contrast, one might gain greater religious currency by consuming—the only occasion when we let others see into our financial lives comes when we show off our goods.

The fear of God, not money. The Sage warns the maker of the foolish vow against divine anger. The verb for the resulting destruction (*ḥibēl*) sounds like *hebel*, which itself appears explicitly in 5:7. The dreams and foolish verbosity referenced in 5:3 qualify for such "vanity," and so does the idolatry that *hebel* can convey. The preeminent form of idolatry that concerns Ecclesiastes is self-centeredness, which can manifest itself via trying to appear more pious than we actually are. This *hebel* reference is less expansive than others; it lacks the "all"-type language usually found, which makes quite clear that the Sage does not view all religious duties as vanity (Krüger 2004: 110). The language of fearing God finally becomes explicit; obviously the concept has been lurking throughout the section.

Ecclesiastes 5 hinders treating the conclusion of Eccl. 12 as utterly incongruous with the rest of the book. Here are more moderate uses of *hebel* than previously, a strong parallel with Deuteronomy, the language of fearing God, the lack of "I"- and sight-language, plus thematic resonances with *carpe diem* passages and 9:7–12:7. Given all this, the rejection of enigmas (*hebel*) as associated with folly (5:7) tempers the import of the Sage's musings elsewhere (Bartholomew 2009: 208–9). The Sage is keenly sensitive to misuse of wisdom as a tool for trying to manipulate rather than fear God. Seen in the light of Eccl. 12, this makes it even clearer that the Sage affirms rather than rejects orthodox, traditional wisdom—shaping its use to foster genuine rather than counterfeit fear of the Lord.

Ellul 1990: 275–76 wisely reflects on the meaning of this "fear-respect": "Being conscious of something of infinite seriousness: recognizing and approaching the Wholly Other." This cannot be pure terror, for even approaching such a one

30. This first struck me while hearing a talk that eventually expanded into Brian S. Rosner, *Greed as Idolatry: The Origin and Meaning of a Pauline Metaphor* (Grand Rapids: Eerdmans, 2007).

"presupposes a desire, a will, a hope, and an anticipation"; otherwise it would hardly be worth the risk (see also Prov. 1:1–7)! The goal behind the risk is not that fearing God would lead to happiness as an external means to a separate end: "Rather, the person who fears God experiences happiness because this fear itself *is* the presence of God. For the person who experiences it, this fear gives assurance of the Lord's presence. . . . Those who tremble in God's presence *are* in his presence." The fear of God is the goal; as Eccl. 5:7 demonstrates, few other words are necessary.

While the Sage speaks of Elohim rather than YHWH, nevertheless God is in the temple addressing the community. This passage therefore applies to God's covenant people. Its connection between divine address and human response should end the contest many people today sense between emphasizing proclamation of scripture and pursuing justice or authentic communal life. Extremes are surely possible in either direction. Yet focusing on biblical teaching need not produce theological eggheads with no regard for active faith. According to 5:1–7, biblical teaching instigates faithful activity; the passage integrates the hearing of the word with wise deeds, as does Jas. 1:19–27:

> You must understand this, my beloved: let everyone be quick to listen, slow to speak, slow to anger; for your anger does not produce God's righteousness. Therefore rid yourselves of all sordidness and rank growth of wickedness, and welcome with meekness the implanted word that has the power to save your souls.
>
> But be doers of the word, and not merely hearers who deceive themselves. For if any are hearers of the word and not doers, they are like those who look at themselves in a mirror; for they look at themselves and, on going away, immediately forget what they were like. But those who look into the perfect law, the law of liberty, and persevere, being not hearers who forget but doers who act—they will be blessed in their doing.
>
> If any think they are religious, and do not bridle their tongues but deceive their hearts, their religion is worthless. Religion that is pure and undefiled before God, the Father, is this: to care for orphans and widows in their distress, and to keep oneself unstained by the world.

How then does all this material relate to the subject of money, which becomes fully explicit only in Eccl. 5:8? The very fact that minds run toward the story of Ananias and Sapphira demonstrates that religious vows enter an economic realm. Sometimes this is explicitly true, with vows that have direct implications for finances. Even other cases, though, address exchange: whether people (a) serve God in order to get something or (b) genuinely give obedience for God's own sake. Earlier Ecclesiastes called into question the contemporary cynicism about whether gifts can truly be given without leaving people mired in economies of obligation (2:24–26). Here the Sage calls *us* into question, regarding whether we really give to God or instead seek to gain advantage. We should not be deceived: God is not mocked (Gal. 6:7–10).

Earthly Economies: Seeing Wealth, Sleeping Well (5:8–6:9)

> The sermons, mostly, were preached on the same theme I had heard over and over. . . . We must lay up treasures in Heaven and not be lured and seduced by this world's pretty and tasty things that do not last but are like the flower that is cut down. The preachers were always young students from the seminary who wore, you might say, the mantle of power but not the mantle of knowledge. . . . They learned to have a very high opinion of God and a very low opinion of His works—although they could tell you that this world had been made by God Himself.
>
> What they didn't see was that it is beautiful, and that some of the greatest beauties are the briefest. . . .
>
> The world-condemning sermons were preached to people who, on Sunday mornings, would be wearing their prettiest clothes. . . . The people who heard those sermons loved good crops, good gardens, good livestock and work animals and dogs; they loved flowers and the shade of trees, and laughter and music; some of them could make you a fair speech on the pleasures of a good drink of water or a patch of wild raspberries. . . . And when church was over they would go home to Heavenly dinners. . . . And the preacher and his family would always be invited to eat with somebody and they would always go, and the preacher, having just foresworn on behalf of everybody the joys of the flesh, would eat with unconsecrated relish.[31]

The economic metaphors of the early verses in Eccl. 5 now lead into more direct discussion of money. After the opening imperative in 5:8–9, a chiastic structure unfolds (Krüger 2004: 118):

5:10–12	proverbs
5:13–17	negative cases ("evil")
5:18–20	positive cases ("something good")
6:1–6	negative cases ("evil")
6:7–9	proverbs

The Sage repeatedly lodges the value of wealth in the opportunities it affords for simple, God-given pleasures: eating, drinking, and so forth. Additional warnings appear, however, concerning the power of wealth to lead people astray.

Politics and Injustice Go Hand in Hand (5:8–9)

Returning to the concerns over government from 4:13–16 and injustice from as far back as 3:16–22, 5:8–9 continues addressing the audience directly as in 5:1–7. At a technical level, these are possibly the two most difficult verses to interpret in all of Ecclesiastes. The scene shifts away from the temple and into provincial society. Bureaucracy is at issue: higher officials watching over lower ones. The

31. The narrator in Berry, *Jayber Crow*, 160–61.

first question concerns whether this is a cause for injustice or rather its cure. One could translate "do not *be frightened* . . . a higher one *watches* over . . ." and see bureaucracy as the cure; or one could translate "do not *be surprised* . . . a higher one *protects* . . ." and see bureaucracy as the cause of injustice (Krüger 2004: 114). This latter approach seems more likely, since it runs truer to the Sage's skepticism regarding human justice. T. M. Moore's paraphrase captures the connection of the skepticism with 5:1–7: "What can a man expect when all throughout the land are people playing games with God?"[32]

The next question concerns how to take 5:9 and the significance of the king vis-à-vis agriculture. The verse could extend the theme of 5:8, with the king serving as the highest oppressor. Or, given the possible affirmation of "advantage" (*yitrôn*) that is denied elsewhere in the book, the verse could reverse the negative course, by offering a hopeful concession: sometimes a king can forestall the unjust bureaucracy below him or be helpful even in spite of this. The difficulty could also be solved if 5:9 is ironically quoting a slogan or referring to an ideology, but we have no evidence with which to establish such a claim.

Because commentators despair of a confident solution on text-critical, literary, or historical grounds, this provides a particularly useful test case for theological exegesis: can we find a way to read this text as having a divine message, which we can discern with conviction despite the absence of clarity from the immediate contextual details? Canonically, although kingship became God's will for Israel, the story of its introduction is ambiguous. While Israel's ultimate destiny involves a monarch, it asked for a king on spiritually dubious grounds. Contrary to its wishes, the shepherd God desired would be unlike any other earthly king. Yet, even at best, Israel's kings had moments as oppressors, which Solomon—so relevant to the present book—exemplifies. It is therefore no rejection of divine monarchy in Jesus Christ, or of human rulers being divinely appointed (Rom. 13:1–7), to read Eccl. 5:9 negatively. If anything, such an approach heightens the contrast between the ultimate divine will and the current realities to which the Sage gives careful attention. Thus, remaining consistent with the rest of the book, the Sage does not view *yitrôn* as a present human possession or possibility; potential gain gets swallowed up by the king's cultivation of his own interests. Were the verse depicting an ideal king protecting property rights, it would surely come with a wink in light of episodes such as Ahab's seizure of Naboth's vineyard in 1 Kgs. 21. Throughout the Old Testament, farmers are associated with the poor and oppressed, victims of the powerful. In many places and many ways, this holds true today. A canonical reading therefore prefers a negative interpretation of both Eccl. 5:9 and 5:8: earthly kings tend to oppress the peasants they rule. At the same time, the canon protects against becoming too antimonarchical or cynical as a result, because the rest of scripture places Israel's kingship within the

32. T. M. Moore, *Ecclesiastes: Ancient Wisdom When All Else Fails: A New Translation and Interpretive Paraphrase* (Downers Grove, IL: InterVarsity, 2001), 44.

overall plan of God and reaffirms the divinely instituted need for governmental authority.

Ecclesiastes 5:8 can then be read with reference to Jesus Christ, the exceptional instance of the commonplace reality it describes. Its exhortation not to be shocked at injustice parallels those of John, in which Jesus tells his followers not to be amazed if the world hates them (e.g., John 15:18–16:4; 1 John 3:13). For Jesus, the one in whom we find justice and righteousness (1 Cor. 1:30), who came not to be served but to deliver the oppressed, death on the cross was ironic but not shocking. It is paradoxical but true that Christ underwent such a common tragedy of injustice to the ultimate degree, in order to subvert the system; its time is limited. There is insight in alternative interpretations of Eccl. 5:8–9, that the Bible makes space for human government's real, though limited and provisional, work to mitigate injustice. But scripture never views the divine legitimacy of the political realm as achieving human advantage that endures; governmental contributions are cyclical and temporary.

Satisfaction and Wealth Don't Go Hand in Hand (5:10–12)

Moving into a proverbial mode, 5:10 could teach simply that money itself cannot satisfy; for satisfaction people need what money buys. But it could also go further, suggesting what we know to be true from the rest of scripture: insatiability prevents satisfaction even with what money can buy. The end of 5:10 is ambiguous too, either a rhetorical question affirming wealth ("who loves wealth without gain?") or a statement introduced by an indefinite pronoun criticizing wealth ("whoever loves wealth is without gain"). The latter interpretation—appearing in Gregory the Great's translation, "he that loves riches shall not reap fruit thereof" (*Pastoral Care* 3.20, in NPNF[2] 12.46)—is more likely, given the *hebel* clause at the very end and the proverbial character of the verse.

Ecclesiastes 5:11 finds another downside of money: the goods it buys are conspicuous, attracting companions who want to consume them. The supposedly powerful owner of the wealth becomes a mere spectator of its use. In 5:12 there is another proverbial reason for this. Whether a laborer eats little or much—this deals not just with money but with what it buys—he or she sleeps well. The rich, though, cannot sleep due to their abundance: "It is said that in a country of sharp contrasts, no one can sleep. The poor—the majority—do not sleep because they are hungry, and the rich do not sleep because they know it."[33] As John Chrysostom notes, food can prevent sleep due either to its lack or its excess; but those who lack food at least get some sleep due to fatigue stemming from labor (*Homilies concerning the Statues* 2.23, in NPNF[1] 9.352). Many in the West, by contrast, are all too familiar with ways that excessive food can hinder rest and create vivid dreams. A complementary truth frequently appears elsewhere in Ecclesiastes: enjoyment of

33. Tamez, *When the Horizons Close*, 82.

a good meal is a gift from God. However, the enjoyment lies primarily in the table fellowship, not merely the food consumption itself. Lavish meals should not be routine, even if the routine should be festive. Acknowledging the sweet sleep of the laborer need not romanticize poverty or reinforce oppressive systems; it may be God's good, interim gift to the marginalized.

"You Can't Take It with You" (5:13–17)

Other factors besides food can prevent the rich from sleeping, such as worrying about how to acquire more (5:10) or keep what one has (5:13). At 5:13 the text moves from proverbs into negative cases, introduced by the Sage's stock phrasing: a "grievous" evil he has seen "under the sun." In this case one hoards wealth, yet loses it in some unspecified misfortune, so that there is nothing to leave his son as an inheritance anyway (5:14). In 2008 many homeowners watched their primary investments drastically decline in value due to the nearly impenetrable machinations of markets and perceptions of those with whom they have no interaction: let this be a lesson about what we can or cannot control! The Bible often rings true, even for sophisticated modern people.

In 5:15 comes the punch line, echoing Job 1:21 and echoed in 1 Tim. 6:7: we come into the world naked and die without pockets. We can take nothing with us at death so, as Jesus teaches, we had better store up treasure in heaven. First Tim. 6 has multiple resonances with Ecclesiastes. Pauline teaching is criticized for relative acquiescence to the system of slavery (e.g., 1 Tim. 6:1–2). Yet under no circumstances should people imagine that "godliness is a means of gain" (6:5). However unpopular the stance of the New Testament epistles about honoring masters, and however utterly unjustifiable slavery is (and was), still we must not allow craving for revolution to obscure the difference between gain and contentment. Paul does not exhort us to be content whatever our circumstances because social injustice is unimportant; he allows for slaves taking freedom when they can get it (1 Cor. 7:21). But whatever our circumstances, something is still more important: in contentment lies true gain (1 Tim. 6:6), as the Sage likewise teaches. Having the basics needed for survival is enough for contentment (6:8); beyond this, desire brings great dangers in tow (6:9–10). Many wealthy do-gooders actually despise the poor for whom they advocate, while simultaneously being in danger of romanticizing them in other ways. People are neither automatically righteous nor entirely powerless because they are poor. They may indeed be divinely privileged in one sense: if it is more readily possible for them to recognize and attain true contentment. In that sense scripture preferentially associates the poor with righteousness (→Prov. 10–29 on "justice").

Anything aside from such genuine gain amounts to "toiling for the wind" (Eccl. 5:16, which may not introduce another evil but instead emphatically extends the point). This plight gets more description in 5:17: darkness (earlier associated with folly), vexation, sickness, and anger. Particularly poignant is the image of a miser eating in darkness—in that case unable even to see the fruits of his wealth. Compare this ironically with 5:11: wealth either attracts envious consumers, so that rich people can only watch as their bounty gets swallowed up, or else they repel other people, so that as lonely misers they cannot even see their own consumption. Either way, there is no point in living for money, because you can't take it with you and it can hinder communal joy in the here and now.

Coda: God Occupies Us Well (5:18–20)

Before running too far down the path of rejecting earthly goods, though, the Sage pulls back. In 5:18 he affirms a personal conclusion (what he himself has seen) regarding what is good: it is appropriate to eat and drink and see successful results from toil (manifest in goods).[34] Such, again, is one's allotment apportioned by God. Consistent with the previous section, it is not necessary to hold extensive property in order to enjoy the modest consumption the Sage envisions.

Ecclesiastes 5:19 addresses those who possess sufficient wealth to eat, warning about the possibility that God will not grant enjoyment. Liturgically the church remembers "the gifts of God for the people of God," acknowledging that blessing is never a result of solely natural causes. Possession may be nine tenths of the law, but it is inadequate for enjoyment apart from divine grace. The consumption here is partitive: eating from what we possess rather than all we possess (Krüger 2004: 123n25). Regarding wealth, the Sage is not so much a man of extremes going back and forth as a seeker of the mean between extremes, along with the right mode of its pursuit.

Ecclesiastes 5:20, recalling the theme of God's keeping people occupied, is one of the most revealing verses regarding commentators' overall stances toward the book. This time the theme expands a bit: God keeps us occupied with gladness of heart. Read tragically, 5:20 has God distracting some people from facing reality by giving them enjoyment via wealth—and they are the lucky ones, whereas the rest get nothing at all except harsh circumstances. Read comically, 5:20 teaches that God generously uses the frequency of these joyful interludes to preserve us from taking ponderous questions too seriously. If the sleep of (even or especially poor) laborers is a joyful gift, then the reality described by 5:20 is, in principle, possible for most people much of the time. Thus the comical reading commends itself as the most likely observation of the Sage (note the empirical frame in 5:18), not to mention the most canonically consistent portrayal of God, whose characteristic action throughout Ecclesiastes is giving. It is not that these three verses are glib. But, on balance, they positively set forth the parameters of divine *gifts* (5:19), with 5:20 portraying God as a gracious Lord rather than a conniving tyrant.

34. Remember that "toil" can address the process or the product. Here, since the second occurrence of the term refers to process, the first probably refers to the product.

Yet Humans Remain Occupied with Appetite (6:1–9)

Joining 1 Tim. 6 as a crucial New Testament passage connecting with Eccl. 5–6 is 1 John 2:15–17. Not just love of money, but also love of "the world"—all that people try to buy with money—is dangerous. These dangers take concrete shape through three tempters, the world, the flesh, and the devil, with the latter typically working through the former two: "the desire of the flesh, the desire of the eyes, the pride in riches." Goods themselves are not sinful; the problem is inordinate desire and pride in acquiring or possessing or consuming them. The crucial issue is that "the world and its desire are passing away, but those who do the will of God live forever." Ecclesiastes 6:1–9 addresses this temporal character of worldly goods, acknowledging the difficulties they create for ordering our desires rightly.

Does God withhold enjoyment? Ecclesiastes 6:1 introduces the matter with formulas that are now standard, until the last phrase: the evil observed under the sun "lies heavy upon" humans—a qualitative translation. A quantitative interpretation is also possible—it happens frequently. Both are surely true, for the problem according to 6:2 involves well-off people whom God does not enable to eat from—metaphorically, to enjoy—their abundance. Given the ascription of divine agency, it almost appears as if God is to blame, preventing these folks from enjoyment by withholding the power to do so. Such is an instance of probably the most difficult theological conundrum within this book: God's sovereign determination not to allow certain people to enjoy their wealth is termed "evil." Already several passages have seemingly jeopardized the Sage's orthodoxy in this way (e.g., 1:13; 2:17; 3:10; 5:18–20).

It is important to remember a key factor from many other texts: the Sage reports and then reflects on what he observes. Surely he saw—for we too see—people unable to enjoy wealth even when they have it. While in many cases the lack of enjoyment is traceable to moral causes—Hollywood stars and athletes come to mind—others remain inscrutable to outward observation. Moral dimensions may be present, but we cannot always discern them. The Sage is unafraid to name this elephant in the room of God's mysterious providence. It would be inconsistent with the reserve that Ecclesiastes advocates elsewhere, though—its awareness of human finitude—to conclude thereby that God is a whimsical despot. The Sage raises questions but nowhere comes to such a despairing conclusion himself. No, his only answer is that God is simply inscrutable at times: we cannot know enough to say in troubling cases that God is tyrannical; the Sage remains on the lookout for evidence suggesting otherwise.

We must not miss parallels between 5:18–19 and 6:1–2 (Bartholomew 2009: 235). There is good . . . there is an evil. God gives wealth and possessions . . . God gives wealth, possessions, and honor. God enables everyone to enjoy in 5:18–19 . . . whereas God does not enable those in 6:1–2 to enjoy. In the latter case, a stranger enjoys; in the former case, and this is the crucial point, God enables humans to accept their lot—to enjoy whatever one has, assuming enough to meet basic needs. "Wealth, possessions, and honor" appear in 2 Chr. 1:11–12 regarding what Solomon did not ask God for—but received anyway (Bartholomew 2009: 232n2). One has to wonder whether Solomon ultimately enjoyed what he received! Wisdom offers no long-term guarantees, at least if one casts aside the fear of God.

Does long life count without enjoyment? In exaggerated fashion 6:3 then expands the description of troubling scenarios in view. Even someone who lives to a ripe old age and has one hundred children—hyperbolic proverbial blessing—may lack enjoyment as well as proper burial in the end. A stillborn child would be better off (note parallels to Job 3:11–16; 10:18–22). The force of this statement echoes in Paul's comment: "If for this life only we have hoped in Christ, we are of all people most to be pitied" (1 Cor. 15:19). This surely commends an eternal perspective that comes into focus more clearly long after Ecclesiastes. Yet it also indicates that much in earthly life is worthwhile. The grounds for sacrificially giving up goods in service to Jesus Christ finally lie in the truth of his resurrection (15:58). In canonical perspective, the Sage adds a more proximate consideration, hanging the value of earthly life not on possessions or status per se, but on the end of enjoyment that these means can bring. Genuine enjoyment comes only from God, putting worldly desires in the proper context, namely that they are always passing away. When sermons against worldliness go wrong, as suggested in the epigraph for this section, their error does not stem from calling for an eternal perspective. Instead, they mistakenly equate an eternal perspective with absolute rejection, rather than careful assessment, of the delight that worldly goods bring. The goods are not evil, but they are only provisional means for grateful enjoyment of God, so that they quickly pass away. Since no one can absolutely reject them, to call for that simply leads people into failure, despair, and corrective overindulgence. To use the language of the epigraph, people therefore need to understand consecrated rather than unconsecrated relish.

Ecclesiastes 6:4 describes the stillborn child's subjection to *hebel* and darkness, a recurrent motif. It is striking that Paul refers to "one untimely born" and to vanity in the course of teaching on the resurrection (1 Cor. 15:2, 8, 10, 14, 58); indeed, he also echoes Ecclesiastes by referencing a proverb on eating and drinking (15:32) and sharing Genesis as a backdrop. Lacking knowledge the stillborn child, according to Eccl. 6:5, has more rest than the restless rich person. There may be an allusion to Gen. 5:28–29, where old and overworked Lamech finds hope in the birth of Noah (whose name means "rest"): "Out of the ground that the Lord has cursed this one shall bring us relief from our work and from the toil of our hands" (noted in Bartholomew 2009: 236). By contrast, the Sage finds no guarantees in the birth of a son who might inherit. Next Eccl. 6:6 continues the hyperbole but alters the problem: now turning life into *hebel* is lack of any goods with which to pursue enjoyment—even within an absurdly long life, quite apart from the possibility of an heir.

Can anyone desire rightly? Returning to proverbs for closing the section, 6:7 is blunt: humans toil in order to consume, and this basic appetite ("for the mouth") is never satisfied. If God made us this way—so that no amount of acquisition or achievement could remove need for the next meal—then by implication we ought to live for the present moment rather than abstractions about long lives or legacies. Chicken soup is not for the soul; it is merely for the body, and this reality returns day by day, again and again and again. Regarding the merely temporary satisfaction of earthly goods, at this basic level there is no difference between a wise person and a fool (6:8a): both must eat. Thus, 6:8b concludes that one must not automatically glamorize the poor. Even if they know how to find proper enjoyment, they may lack any basic goods with which to put this knowledge into operation. Poor people cannot enjoy the sweet sleep of the laborer if they starve. Accordingly the provisional satisfaction of earthly goods cuts both ways: it commends the wisdom to recognize the limitations of any satisfaction, but it also underscores that there are genuine needs that people must satisfy.

Hence the proverb at the beginning of 6:9 contrasts seeing with searching, suggesting that a bird in the hand is worth two in the bush. To have joy in the present, however fleeting, is better than wandering around in search of something else to which desire can attach. Luther refers to Aesop's fable about "a dog snatching at the meat in the mirror and thus losing the morsel in its mouth" (mentioned in Longman 1998: 175). With this realistic restraint of desire, at the end of 6:9 the proverbs have come back around to parallel 5:10–12. Also here is the last appearance of the full form of the *hebel* phrase that includes the chasing after wind. In fact, this concludes the first half of the entire book, even marking the halfway point in terms of numbers of verses. The themes of the second half will not be altogether new, but focus will shift away from inquiries into means of enjoyment or ultimate advantage. Having isolated what is best ("nothing better than") under the sun, now the book will evaluate possibilities for knowing how and when to pursue these provisional joys. In considering this question of knowledge more intensely, the Sage keeps human finitude firmly in view. Since part 1 discovered nothing "better" than fearing God, part 2 finds only one answer to the question, "Who knows?"

TRANSITION

SUMMARY OF PART 1 AND INTRODUCTION TO PART 2

Ecclesiastes 6:10–12

Having just signaled in 6:9 a major conclusion, in 6:10–12 the Sage moves from part 1 into part 2 of his treatise. The chief point of 6:10 concerns divine sovereignty and human finitude. God is the one who names, the ultimate act of creation. Such vocabulary refers to God creating the stars in Ps. 147:4 and Isa. 40:26, with compelling juxtapositions of God's personal care and awesome power. Humans are unable to dispute with God, who is stronger than we are—and why would we want to? Adam named other animals but not the events of history. To know what human nature is, here, means recognizing finitude and hence limitations. Self-knowledge is partly knowing what we cannot know. Sounding superficially parallel to Immanuel Kant, this constitutes another of the Sage's protomodern elements—anticipating modernity in his very preoccupation with epistemology. Nevertheless, getting to human finitude from the reality of divine creation requires a very different route than starting with Kantian exploration of human possibilities or epistemological abstractions. The Sage knows what he cannot know because he believes that God names things, not just by virtue of the failure of his human starting points.

The rhetorical question in 6:11 denies that humans profit from multiplying words about these complex matters. As 6:12 suggests, no one can reliably foretell the future and therefore no human can tell others how to live a better life now (in the sense of gaining permanent, decisive advantage). However, the rhetorical question in 6:12 has a positive as well as negative answer: not humans, but God. God knows what is good for mortals, so the words of Ecclesiastes are worthwhile inasmuch as they direct us toward divine revelation. The simplicity of that revelation—having to do with eating, drinking, and modest enjoyment instead of scheming for ultimate advantage or lasting legacies—may surprise us. But, rather than assuming that divine revelation must be interpreted so as to give us a grand scheme, we should instead welcome the rest and simplicity of the life God offers.

The expression comparing human life to a shadow (1 Chr. 29:15; Job 8:9; 14:2; Ps. 144:4) conveys its fleeting nature. Thus translating *hebel* in this verse as "transitory" seems redundant. Yet if *hebel* involves some apparent absurdity in this case, it stems primarily from the finite, ephemeral character of human life. Hence many of the darker possible translations take *hebel* too far into utter meaninglessness. The problem in Eccl. 6:12 is not the absence of goodness, but the difficulty of gaining human knowledge regarding what is good—especially, as the final question indicates, concerning the future. Our lives seem "enigmatic" or, properly understood, "vain," but this is problematic only if we try to advance beyond our station, multiplying words in attempts to understand what we cannot (6:11).

As a result, 6:12 nicely puts together where we have come from and where we are going. No one can tell human beings how to strategize with certainty for control over the good life—not even Solomon with all his varied experiences and vast wisdom. Not wisdom, not pleasure, not achievement, not their careful combination—nothing can fully and lastingly satisfy under the sun—for time and death happen to all, whereas injustice happens to so many so often. Humans easily get confused, seeking after money rather than the enjoyment it could buy, and spending this on ourselves while seeking more and more instead of enjoying its small gifts with companions. If the point has now been made that no human can say *what* is best to do on some grand scale, then the question yet to be fully explored is *when* one can know how to act on a smaller scale—even provisionally—and *why* our knowledge in this regard is so minuscule. How does one handle not knowing? Can wisdom offer any way at all to address that condition?

PART 2

WHO KNOWS?

Ecclesiastes 7:1–12:7

Having downsized expectations regarding the accomplishments of human wisdom in 6:10–12, Ecclesiastes launches into a series of proverbs. The attentive reader notices a series of repeated terms: *ṭôb* ("good" or "better"; eleven times); *ḥākām* or *ḥokmâ* ("wise" or "wisdom"; six times); *lēb* ("heart"; five times); *kĕsîl* ("fool"; four times); and *ka'as* ("sorrow" or "anger"; three times). Overall the key issues are wisdom and death. In the face of strongly negative statements in preceding verses, here the Sage confirms that some things are better than others. But still these earthly advantages are temporary; even at its best wisdom cannot outrun death.

Proverbs are pithy generalizations, such as "a stitch in time saves nine" or "a penny saved is a penny earned." They offer wisdom for relating general principles to specific situations, but not woodenly. So "a penny saved is a penny earned" does not imply that one should always save and never spend; surely there are situations to the contrary (although erring on the side of saving may be better in the current economy). Today's proverbs are not passed down orally through family contexts; old wives' tales and the like are dying out under the onslaught of an image-driven culture. Today's proverbs instead come from Madison Avenue; typically they are less literate (even when clever) while inclined to undermine the values promoted by ancient proverbs such as we see in the Bible.[1]

1. So Ellen F. Davis, "Preserving Virtues: Renewing the Tradition of the Sages," in *Character and Scripture: Moral Formation, Community, and Biblical Interpretation*, ed. William P. Brown (Grand Rapids: Eerdmans, 2002), 183–201, esp. 198.

However much the Sage questions traditional wisdom, he shifts toward more imperative forms, second-person discourse, and proverbs starting with 7:1—another clear sign of a new major section that, while emphasizing how much we cannot know, nevertheless does not dismiss wisdom altogether.

Proverbs on Wise Living in the Face of Death (7:1–14)

> We are violently propelled into the world with blood and pain and few of us will die with the dignity for which we hope and for which some pray. Whether we choose to think of life as an impending happiness broken only by inevitable grief and disappointments, or as the proverbial vale of tears with brief interludes of joy, the pain will come, except to those few whose deadened sensibilities made them apparently impervious to either joy or sorrow.[2]

The value of a good name. The beginning of 7:1 says that a person's good name lasts longer than perfume, the probable referent of oil or "precious ointment." "Precious" is actually *ṭôb* ("good"), so there is a wordplay with the start of the sentence. One thinks of the expensive oil with which people are anointed for burial. In the famous case of Jesus's anointing, the woman's good name has in fact outlasted the smell of the costly perfume (John 12:1–8). If the second half of Eccl. 7:1 initially puzzles us in affirming the day of death over the day of birth, then that is probably because many today have life free and easy. But this is our problem, not the text's, as subsequent verses clarify further our need to learn from those who die about attending to our own death. Church fathers such as Didymus the Blind, by contrast, viewed this statement positively because death means the end of having to endure evil, since we are with Christ (*Commentary on Ecclesiastes* 196.22, in PTA 16.3–5 and Wright 2005: 249). Rabbis, meanwhile, saw the positive thrust of 7:1 to lie in rejoicing at a good death of someone who lived well; at birth there is greater peril because no one knows how the person will live (*Midrash Qoheleth* 7.1.4), whereas at death we can celebrate someone who has finished well. Proverbs 22:1 offers a parallel: "A good name is to be chosen rather than great riches, / and favor is better than silver or gold."

The words "reputation" and "oil" sound alike in Hebrew, an example of wordplay that may have led to the chosen image. Ellul 1990: 78 heightens the resonance of the image with *hebel* as well: "We have a terrible irony here, confirmed by other texts. What is special about perfume? It smells good, gives a pleasant impression, but . . . it evaporates quickly! If you leave the bottle open, soon you have nothing left! Fame is similar: it also evaporates quickly and dissipates. Perhaps less quickly than perfume, but similarly; it does not last." Thus the value of a good name is significant but relative; the Sage cannot affirm it absolutely, given what he says

2. Thoughts of Adam Dalgliesh, a character in P. D. James, *The Private Patient* (New York: Knopf, 2008), 276.

elsewhere about memory and legacies. Even so, "thanks be to God, who in Christ always leads us in triumphal procession, and through us spreads in every place the fragrance that comes from knowing him. For we are the aroma of Christ. . . . [Yet] who is sufficient for these things?" (2 Cor. 2:14–16). In this way seeking a good name in the community characterizes and appropriately motivates the wise. Christians know that good names are neither their native accomplishments apart from grace nor fixed possessions until they have finished fighting the good fight and running the race. At the day of death, though, such good names can be treasured crowns to cast at the Savior's feet. And, in the meantime, they can bear witness, letting our light shine so that others will glorify Christ (Matt. 5:13–16).

The value of considering death. Ecclesiastes 7:2 resonates with the beatitude: "Blessed are those who mourn, for they will be comforted," as noted by Evagrius of Pontus (*Scholia on Ecclesiastes* 55.7.2, in Sources Chrétiennes 397.156). Among such people there is no "moral superficiality," according to Didymus the Blind (*Commentary on Ecclesiastes* 197.19–198.22, in PTA 16.7–11 and Wright 2005: 249). If people take this to heart, moral seriousness can drive them to Jesus Christ, seeking clearer answers than the Sage gives about the ultimate meaning and possibility of fearing God. Is such seriousness inconsistent with *carpe diem* passages? Not necessarily, if God is the one who turns our mourning into dancing (Ps. 30:11), whose anger is momentary while his favor is lifelong (30:5). Not necessarily, if the context for seizing the day is fear of God, while the context for going to the house of mourning is gaining the sobriety with which to do so. Not necessarily, since these are proverbs (so are the *carpe diem* texts, involving "better than" sayings), not resulting in contradiction but rather juxtaposing true though limited perspectives.

The value of vexation? Another apparent tension occurs between 7:3 and 5:17–20. Earlier *ka'as* was clearly negative (e.g., "vexation"), whereas here it may refer to sorrow rather than anger; such is the solution adopted by many from Luther onward. Or instead this may be another example of the Sage's surface absurdities, which are not fundamentally contradictory relative to their contexts. The troubled face makes the heart well because it sometimes reflects reality. John Chrysostom reminds us that even feasting can evoke sorrow or anger due to envy; for instance, we go to a party and come home sulking about how much more others have than we do. Alternatively, at the house of mourning we can mourn even for our enemies, since everyone faces death (*Homilies concerning the Statues* 15.5, in NPNF[1] 9.440).

Honestly facing reality is better than distracting ourselves to avoid it (the way fools use the "house of mirth"; 7:4). If God gives small pleasures with which to avoid brooding, that is one thing; but using these constantly to avoid facing death, that is another. Commentators who insist that these verses fundamentally contradict others in Ecclesiastes fail to recognize the importance of their proverbial character. Their literary juxtaposition with more positive sayings elicits reflection from the audience on how the various perspectives relate to particular situations. To insist, for instance, that 7:4 is merely poking the wisdom tradition in the eye, advocating obsession with death, forecloses the very inquiry that incorporation of a proverb should evoke.

The value of avoiding fools. In 7:5 the fools are plural whereas the wise one is singular, subtly suggesting that not many humans get the balance right. "Enter through the narrow gate" (Matt. 7:13): while the Christian tradition's occasional ambivalence toward music, given its expressive power, can be overdone, the end of Eccl. 7:5 contrasts a wise person carefully speaking words with fools casually singing. Ecclesiastes 7:6 continues to portray the frivolity of the fools with wordplay between "thorns" (*sîrîm*) and "pot" (*sîr*). Their laughter is short-lived, followed by destruction—though noisy while it lasts (Didymus the Blind, *Commentary on Ecclesiastes* 203.3, in PTA 16.19 and Wright 2005: 251). Obviously the fools' laughter fits within the category of *hebel* at the end of the verse; so too, probably, the need to live in light of death—as described from 7:1 onward—seems enigmatic.

The value of endurance. Lest wisdom get too big for its britches based merely on avoiding fools, 7:7 casts doubt on its constant success. "Oppression" may refer more specifically to extortion; regardless, both the stick (7:7a) and the carrot (7:7b) can thwart wisdom's operation. Even wise people find themselves susceptible to bribes unless they are vigilant, since everyone is subject to craziness under oppressive circumstances. Thus 7:8 prizes the end over the beginning. People need to endure in their wisdom over the long haul. Reference to patience versus pride "in spirit" finds an echo in another of Jesus's Beatitudes: "Blessed are the poor in spirit, for theirs is the kingdom of heaven" (Matt. 5:3). Unless broken before God, humans are too resourceful at servicing their own pride; one cannot rest securely until a matter is over because of this relentless possibility for human self-assertion.

The need to avoid vexation? In 7:9 attention turns from pride back to anger or vexation, which often results. The same word, *kaʿas*, appears here as in 7:3, where it is commended. Whatever the nature of the wordplay, blatant contradiction in meaning is unlikely within the span of a few verses. The Sage—and his editor(s), if such there be—show far too much evidence of literary sophistication to handle a problem so carelessly. Indeed, in 7:7–12 the Sage examines the flip side of several coins from 7:1–6. It is not that he affirms exact opposites, but he shades in contours of meaning. In what sense is "the day of death" better than "the day of birth," given the apparent tragedy involved? In what sense is "vexation" better than "laughter"? And so forth.

So the vexation forbidden in 7:9 involves deep-seated "anger" and foolish nostalgia preventing wise life in the present. Not being "quick in your spirit" to become angry indicates a degree of internalization. Moreover, speed is another part of the problem, so room may remain for legitimate dimensions of anger (→Prov. 10–29 on "wrath"). After all, avoiding the love of money does not preclude all uses of money. Of course the analogy is inexact, as are all analogies. (But before treating money as inherently less dangerous than any and all forms of anger, we should think twice.) Nevertheless, even if righteous anger is possible, Jas. 1:19–20 echoes the call for slowness to anger, since "your anger does not produce God's righteousness." The temptation is great to nourish anger so that one is ready to lash out at any moment. But the wise person is sufficiently realistic—even vexed rather than laughing (Eccl. 7:3)—to take setbacks in appropriate stride, with a patient spirit (7:8). The Sage insightfully recognizes that so-called wisdom can lead to a faulty sense of entitlement, to unhealthy pride supplanting godly patience. His deconstruction of faulty wisdom offers true wisdom via the back door.

The need to avoid nostalgia. The nostalgia criticized next results from angry, wrongly entitled, impatient folly, backhandedly contradicting the claim that "there is nothing new under the sun." Not just the triumphs but also the tragedies of any contemporary scene have come and gone before. If the end is better than the beginning, then if one errs, it should not be on the side of nostalgia for the past. Nostalgia only reveals the current focus of one's vexation. Now, since other places in the Bible are not free of decline narratives, this cannot mean that we may never criticize an aspect of the present. And we must oppose false prophets who promise only positive trends for the future. On occasion scripture calls for a return to a former state: "But I have this against you, that you have abandoned the love you had at first. Remember then from what you have fallen; repent, and do the works you did at first. If not, I will come to you and remove your lampstand from its place, unless you repent" (Rev. 2:4–5).

Yet it is easy for people of a certain disposition to move beyond legitimate lamentation or critique regarding cultural losses into selective whitewashing, becoming lopsided in leaving out the deficiencies of the past. Having no certainty regarding the future and (foolishly) believing that we control the past in memory, we grasp for its glories and neglect its foibles—perhaps the very foibles that, via laws of unintended consequences, have elicited the present worries. Past glories, if indeed that is what they were, merit gratitude to God. But such glories are, like everything, temporal pleasures rather than permanent benefits. As a child of a family farm, I confess particular vulnerability to nostalgia. A once-intact communal way of life is now going the way of all flesh in America's heartland. Aspects of this tragic transformation merit moral disapproval—even resistance. But it will do no good to ignore mistakes of family farmers and their communities along the way, or to repristinate yesteryear, or to imagine that any culture ever remains completely static; somehow one must pursue a new mode of existence in which some farms are sustainable. Amid the tragedy lurks a hidden form of opportunity. In any case, family farmers hardly need romantic academics, or their own children who have moved away, to read Wendell Berry and wax eloquently nostalgic about a life they lack the fortitude—or even the divine call—to choose or sustain for themselves. Ecclesiastes confronts the folly of such smug hypocrisy, because nostalgia clutches earthly realities—selectively remembered along selfish lines—too tightly, thinking that one has chased down the wind and now can hold on to it.

The advantage of wisdom. The next verse, 7:11, positively connects wisdom with an inheritance that the nostalgic may have received: wealth. In fact, wisdom is a matter of profit or advantage, *yôtēr*, which elsewhere throughout the book is denied to humankind; yet one thinks again of Solomon, who asked for wisdom rather than riches and received both. According to 7:12, wisdom shades people with protection, like having the money to meet their needs can do. Despite our nervousness, the Sage is unflinchingly honest with his empirical perspective. He observes both money and wisdom having this preservative function, and says so. It hides no dangers of the love or excessive amounts of money to acknowledge the obvious. By implication the Sage also affirms earthly life as worth preserving—regardless of what a few isolated statements could otherwise convey (particularly 2:17; 4:2–3; 6:3–6). Of course, earlier worries about the love of money (5:8–6:9) imply related dangers about the quest for wisdom: if one seeks to control the future for the sake of lasting personal advantage, then disappointment is likely. Even so the end of 7:12, with its clause affirming life, acknowledges relative superiority for wisdom over money; wisdom is slightly less subject to loss via the external forces that can take life itself.

The advantage of considering God's work. The goal of pondering God's work, then, is not changing but going along with it (7:13, which restates and clarifies 1:15). Thus the Sage concludes his proverbial material on wisdom and death for the time being, looking ahead to consider wisdom vis-à-vis righteousness. Wisdom attempts not to alter God's sovereign purpose, but to take careful stock of one's situation in light of what can and cannot change. God's work is not morally crooked but sufficiently jumbled—to human gaze—that one cannot develop a master plan or straight path toward attaining grand goals. God "makes crooked" to keep humans in their place—but this is grace, not tyranny. Hence, according to 7:14, days of good call for a response of good (probably something like joy) while days of evil (or adversity) call for acknowledging the divine purpose behind them—whatever it might be. The word "find," picked up from 3:11, now becomes important (7:24, 26, 27, 28 [three times], 29), as does the parallel to 6:12 regarding what "will come after them" and the inclusio formed with 7:1 by the repetition of "good" and "day." The wisdom that comes from considering God's work brings the possibility of joy, but does not allow us to find out the future in the present as if to conquer life for ourselves.

Musings on Retribution Theology (7:15–29)

> What then? Are we any better off? No, not at all; for we have already charged that all, both Jews and Greeks, are under the power of sin, as it is written:
> "There is no one who is righteous, not even one;
> there is no one who has understanding,
> there is no one who seeks God.
> All have turned aside, together they have become worthless;
> there is no one who shows kindness,
> there is not even one."

"Their throats are opened graves;
they use their tongues to deceive."
"The venom of vipers is under their lips."
"Their mouths are full of cursing and bitterness."
"Their feet are swift to shed blood;
ruin and misery are in their paths,
and the way of peace they have not known."
"There is no fear of God before their eyes." (Rom. 3:9–18)

Turning from death, the text now considers possible connections between wisdom, righteousness, and apparent success in life. Some of the book's most jarring and curious statements appear in these musings.

Giving Up Self-Interested Striving for Perfection (7:15–22)

Succeeding in spite of retribution problems. Signaling a turning point in 7:15 is the now familiar vocabulary of "seeing." The Sage claims to have seen it all—including the failure of so-called retribution theology, according to which God directly or indirectly recompenses goodness with blessing and evil with tragedy (→Prov. 3; Eccl. 8:10; 10:5–7). Here the Sage's empiricism[3] raises objections: he has seen righteous people perishing in their righteousness and wicked people prolonging life in their wickedness. The "in" prepositions establish only that the righteous are perishing *in spite of* their righteousness, not necessarily *because of* it, and similarly for the wicked: otherwise the following verses' emphasis on the extent of righteousness or wickedness makes little sense.

There is a striking entry in the guest book of one Otto Salomon:

In a time of great decisions
May 1942
Ecclesiastes 7:15
Dietrich Bonhoeffer[4]

Bonhoeffer's exhortation apparently concerns not lingering too agonizingly over decisions when unable to foresee the outcome. This becomes all the more compelling when the next verses, 7:16–17, infamously tell us, "Do not be too righteous,

3. The word "empiricism" is contested, most recently by Bartholomew who opts instead for describing Qoheleth's epistemology as "autonomous." However, "autonomy" sounds theologically loaded, overwhelmingly critical of the Sage. It is potentially misleading too, since it does not specify *how* the self goes about knowing. "Empirical" is an adequate descriptor when not presuming the nuance of Enlightenment debates. It makes the general claim that the Sage begins with observation and builds with reflection upon its results. We need to use a word laden with connotations of "sight," given how dominant that vocabulary is in Ecclesiastes.

4. Dietrich Bonhoeffer, *Conspiracy and Imprisonment, 1940–1945*, trans. Lisa E. Dahill; ed. Jørgen Glenthøj, Ulrich Kabitz, Wolf Krötke, and Mark S. Brocker; Dietrich Bonhoeffer Works 16 (Minneapolis: Fortress, 2006), 288.

and do not act too wise; why should you destroy yourself? Do not be too wicked, and do not be a fool; why should you die before your time?" Notice the obvious parallels in structure: two imperative (technically, jussive) verbs, each followed by a "why?" question. The end of 7:16 is probably better translated "why shock yourself?" or "why should you be surprised?" given how that verb is used elsewhere in the Old Testament (e.g., Ps. 143:4; Isa. 59:16; Dan. 8:27—as noted by Krüger 2004: 139).

These clues, combined with adequate attention to context, help to sort through the interpretative options.

1. Neither the *pretense* of righteousness nor simple *self-righteousness* can be at issue, despite the strange verbal construction.[5] These options make little sense of 7:17 (people do not try to pretend or estimate themselves to be fools), and it would not likely surprise such people if the pretense failed.
2. Interpretations that find *ironic cynicism* here fail to give the Sage his due for making a serious point. He is trying to address the problem of apparent injustice raised in 7:15 and its implications for how one should live.
3. The *degree* of righteousness or *effort* is not likely at issue either, per se, because it is unlikely that 7:17 commends seeking a certain level of wickedness. Moreover, folly at least (if not wickedness) seems to require a different form or lack of effort, breaking the symmetry.
4. The key, then, is the *motivation or calculation of teleology* behind pursuit of righteousness, in view of injustice. Within this framework, issues of self-righteousness and excessive effort can then take on proper, secondary relevance. Righteousness is not a quantitative strategy for success, as if just getting enough would ensure profit. Yet the flip side is partially true: there are foolish degrees and forms of wickedness that typically have deadly consequences. So, as usual, the Sage tempers but does not reject traditional wisdom. He clarifies that wisdom offers no guaranteed outcomes, except for vexation if one pursues it with a profit motive and preservation if it protects a person from disastrous folly. In this way the Sage is consistent with a later sage Jesus Christ, who enigmatically enjoins, "I am sending you out like sheep into the midst of wolves; so be wise as serpents and innocent as doves" (Matt. 10:16).

No doubt many who use righteousness as a strategy for success are self-righteous (and accordingly self-deceived), overestimating—to speak from personal experience—the importance of being earnest. The Sage hardly has to commend wickedness or folly, since he is quite clear throughout the book about our ability to achieve this normally. He therefore does not run afoul of Rev. 3:16, our Lord's rejection of the lukewarm Laodiceans. The Sage is presuming, not prescribing,

5. The Sage could have used a more straightforward verb for being righteous, rather than *hāyâ* plus a predicate adjective.

a level of failure. A degree of wickedness is inevitable; what one must avoid is folly—which lacks a qualifying adverb like the other categories have in Eccl. 7:16–17. This suggests that folly is more fundamentally avoidable. Remember the empirical nature of the Sage's contribution: in terms of how things go under the sun, avoiding folly or extreme wickedness can prevent dying early. Undoubtedly, however, there are imbalances of justice between the righteous and the wicked in this life, so wisdom cannot guarantee one's destiny simply by virtue of a certain level or form of righteousness. Regarding 7:18, therefore—"it is good that you should take hold of the one, without letting go of the other; for the one who fears God shall succeed with both"—it is better not to see an affirmation of moderation between two extremes. The recommendation does not concern holding on to a bit of both righteousness and wickedness, but rather both pieces of advice in 7:16–17. Earthly calculation supports neither excessive righteousness nor folly in any form. Thus, in fact, 7:18 offers a sound reading strategy for the juxtapositions and tensions within Ecclesiastes or even the wisdom corpus as a whole. Fearing God rather than calculating and trying to control one's advantage is the proper approach; in this way, distinguishing the fear of God (7:18) from so-called righteousness (7:16) is not as odd as it first appears. To the contrary, the reference to the fear of God buttresses the interpretation of 7:16–17 offered above, because it clarifies that the issue is not moderation of righteousness but rather the motivation for its pursuit. God is in heaven and we are on earth; that is the fundamental perspective.

Seeking wisdom yet lacking righteousness. Lest such distinctions appear too sharp or idealistic, 7:19 reaffirms the mundane value of wisdom. Referencing rulers recalls Solomon, wisdom's earthly paragon. How wisdom's strength connects with the wise people is not spelled out in the first phrase. This again keeps humans from overconfidence about their wisdom. In a postmodern age when talk of wisdom is everywhere, we need healthy reserve about prospects for obtaining it and knowing when people have it. This point is reiterated concerning righteousness in 7:20, where the Sage flatly states that no one is righteous on earth.

Kî at the beginning, translated "surely" in the NRSV and left out by the NIV, could be rendered "for" to suggest that 7:20 is the reason for 7:19—the wise must rule *because* there is no one righteous. That seems odd in view of the relatively close connections between wisdom and righteousness throughout much of scripture (not to mention elsewhere in Ecclesiastes). One could therefore take the word, in the sense of "surely," as introducing a qualification: yes, wisdom is great, but *surely* no one is actually righteous enough to attain it fully. If no one is really righteous, then the sting of apparent injustice in 7:15 recedes a bit, and the element of implied asymmetry between 7:16 and 7:17 is confirmed. That is, the apparent injustice of inadequate retribution is only relative, since no one is really righteous enough to merit divine blessing (addressing 7:15). Some wickedness is inevitable, but avoiding folly is a worthwhile pursuit out of self-preservation

(7:17). Beyond that, no one can gain sufficient righteousness to control their own destiny the way God does (7:16).

How categorical is the opening statement of 7:20 (that no one is righteous), vis-à-vis the second phrase (referring to one who does good and never sins)? Much of Rom. 3:9–20 stems from Psalm quotations, but in that text Paul may also provide the only New Testament quotation of Ecclesiastes: "There is no one who is righteous, not even one; / there is no one who has understanding, / there is no one who seeks God." Hence it is tempting for some, who interpret Paul's statement categorically, to view righteousness in terms of absolute perfection, which no one can attain. Nevertheless, whatever one makes of Romans, it is better to take Ecclesiastes less categorically, not as an assertion that no people are righteous in any sense. Instead, the text claims that no one possesses absolute righteousness—doing good without ever sinning. Solomon's dedicatory prayer in 1 Kgs. 8:46 sounds almost alike—"if they sin against you—for there is no one who does not sin"—supporting this interpretation. Early Christians were right when they eventually recognized that such teaching excludes Pelagianism, the view that, after humans fell into sin, it remained possible to choose righteousness by nature rather than grace (Augustine, *On Nature and Grace*, in FC 86.27–28). Contra Pelagianism, Eccl. 7:20 does not stop with asserting that *in actuality* no mere human never sins. In rhetorical context it makes this observation precisely to deny even the *possibility* (after the fall) that anyone would never sin. Such is an impossibility apart from grace—God taking on humanity personally in Jesus Christ, identifying with our predicament: "Indeed, I was born guilty, / a sinner when my mother conceived me" (Ps. 51:5).[6] Niebuhr's famous witticism, that original sin is the one empirically verifiable Christian doctrine, holds true in the Sage's observation.

Sinning with speech. The next two verses provide a case study to prove that everyone is caught in sin. Agreeing with another wisdom text, the Sage appeals to the tongue: "All of us make many mistakes. Anyone who makes no mistakes in speaking is perfect, able to keep the whole body in check with a bridle" (Jas. 3:2). Ecclesiastes 7:21 advises a thick skin or even a tin ear so as not to hear what inevitably happens—badmouthing from one's servant. Lest this thick skin make a person smug and unforgiving toward such a servant—as if there could be no reason for what is overheard—7:22 ensures that no one misses the point of 7:20 by turning the tables. There is a broad parallel with the parable of the unforgiving servant (Matt. 18:21–35): first one encounters a relatively small, commonplace infraction, then the unexpected reversal. For, says Eccl. 7:22, in your heart of hearts you must acknowledge that you have yourself badmouthed others—and this in the plural, not the singular! From the heart the mouth speaks (Matt. 12:34–37); yet, ironically, according to the Sage this same twisted heart knows deep down of its own guilt, even when the mouth is tempted to point the finger at others.

6. Mentioned by Gregory the Great, *Forty Gospel Homilies* 39 (trans. Hurst), 365.

Giving Up Wisdom's Striving for Total Understanding (7:23–29)

Another series of verses spells out deeper implications of this inquiry into wisdom and righteousness; "all this" beginning 7:23 refers both backward and forward, acting transitionally. The section holds together via catchwords for "wisdom" (7:23, 25) and "knowledge" (7:25, 27, 29), "seeking" (7:25, 28, 29) and "finding" (7:26, 27 [twice], 28 [three times], 29). The first test occurs in 7:23–24, with the second in 7:25–29.

Testing human wisdom. In another irony 7:23 insists that during the first test the Sage discovered the limitations of wisdom by means of wisdom. His search was not diverted by other means, nor did it altogether preclude uses for wisdom. Instead, wisdom crucially involves knowing its own limits, as well as ours in attaining it. With Solomon lurking in the background of the Sage's persona even here, his paradigmatic function confirms these limits of biblical wisdom (Gregory of Nazianzus, *On Theology: Theological Oration* 2[28].21, in NPNF^2 7.296). Ecclesiastes 7:24 parallels Job 28, taking to significant "depths" this theme of wisdom being unfathomable (also Prov. 1:20–33). God's knowledge is so high that we cannot attain or fathom it (Ps. 139:6, mentioned by Athanasius in *Letters to Monks* 1.2, in NPNF^2 4.563). Seeking wisdom to know God involves a bittersweet yes and no: "For the joy of what we have discovered is no greater than the pain of what escapes us; a pain, I imagine, like that felt by those who are dragged, while yet thirsty, from the water, or are unable to retain what they think they hold, or are suddenly left in the dark by a flash of lightning" (Gregory of Nazianzus, *In Defense of His Flight* 2.75, in NPNF^2 7.220). Physical images for desire are particularly appropriate in light of the earlier teaching in Ecclesiastes about our inevitable, repetitive, insatiability as creatures (esp. 1:8; 4:7–8; 5:10–12).

Testing human wisdom, again. Ecclesiastes 7:25 introduces the next test with verbs that foster this sense of desire, through accumulated repetition. The Sage drags it out. When many modern readers discover what this inquiry involves, they become all the more uncomfortable. Ecclesiastes 7:26 piles up images once more, this time in service of describing the seductive woman, a stock type against which wisdom literature warns. In itself these observations are unobjectionable, even useful. Those who please God avoid seduction that ensnares, while those fundamentally defined as "sinners" do not escape. Questions arise, however, in connection with 7:27–28, where the Sage's most fundamental wisdom seems to involve the nearly absolute unrighteousness or folly of humanity, mixed with the relative superiority of men over women. At first glance the cumulative portrait is misogynistic, with the question being to what extent this is so.

Ancient commentators often interpreted the text spiritually, so that sin or heresy is more bitter than death. But this does not really solve the problem, merely moving the misogyny to choices of metaphors. Plenty of other ancient voices, though not all, reflected their own misogyny in their comments.[7] Without simplistically conforming to modern sensibilities, can theological considerations assist in handling this text responsibly?

Other biblical texts do not portray women as lagging behind men in capacity for righteousness or wisdom. Moreover, of the tricky texts remaining (e.g., 1 Tim. 2:13–14), some bear a strong relationship to Gen. 1–3, as does Eccl. 7:25–29. We must therefore discern in what ways the narrative of creation and fall applies. Sometimes a particular homiletical use is in view, as in 1 Tim. 2, when Eve's deception is paradigmatic for dangers facing the Ephesian women. At other times, the fall is universally shared by all of God's image-bearers in Adam—as in Eccl. 7:29: "See, this alone I found, that God made human beings straightforward, but they have devised many schemes." None of these texts treat women as intellectually or spiritually inferior to men. Meanwhile, numerous other biblical narratives depict women favorably in faithfulness and certain forms of leadership (think of Deborah or Jesus's and Paul's circles). Thus 7:25–29, whatever it means, cannot turn elements of misogyny into canonically faithful, authoritative teaching. Of course, it is expedient to note how often the Bible records perspectives it does not endorse, with a nearby example involving the speeches of Job's friends.

This makes a first possible interpretation tempting: to accept that the text before us is misogynist yet the Sage is simply wrong. However, that would be too simple. To be sure, an interesting element of quotation is involved, so that parallels to Job's friends are not altogether inappropriate. In 7:27 the intriguing addition of "says Qoheleth" provides a singular (apart from the book's beginning and end) reminder of editorial presence representing third-person discourse. This makes it likely that an element of irony lurks underneath the surface, with editorial tongue firmly in cheek. Yet it is unlikely that 7:26 refers to all women in general as a class of dangerous seductresses. The text refers with an article to a definite woman or type of woman, not to everyone. And, whether or not misogyny was widespread in the ancient world, the Sage's affirmations of marriage in 4:9 and 9:9 would not sit well with denigration of women. Furthermore, given nearby parallels to Proverbs, it would be odd for this text to present a fundamental contradiction of the female potential reflected in Prov. 31.

One can take this last point further as incentive for a second solution: to treat the women spiritually as helping to personify wisdom versus folly. The word "bitter" (*mar*) in 7:26 parallels Prov. 5:4, where beyond the literal level Dame Folly is portrayed. Quite possibly, therefore, the Sage gives his own testimony; he is the sinner ensnared, at least on the metaphorical level, who did not find wisdom. Conversely, it is not necessary for such interpretations to preclude literal references to women as well. It seems unduly ethereal for Ecclesiastes (or Proverbs, for that matter) to treat righteousness and wickedness entirely as abstractions

7. For troubling examples see Longman 1998: 206, though this should be balanced with Christianson 2007: 212–13.

without addressing embodied life directly. If Eccl. 7:26 functions at least partly as stock wisdom advice about a dangerous type of woman, that would actually be consistent with a promarriage agenda. Ellul 1990: 200–201 provocatively suggests that if woman per se were a snare, then it would have been impossible for the Sage not to find her in 7:28, since she would have found him! Furthermore, "Why is a bad woman (*when* she is a trap and a chain) worse than a bad man? I believe we can see the same logic at work concerning the word: it is the highest good, but precisely because of that, when it is perverted, it becomes a worse evil: sin. Similarly, in the case of woman: she should be what Qoheleth expects her to be: wisdom, and, even more remarkably, reason."

As intriguing as such an approach might be, it fails to account for all of the details. For one, the text from 7:15 onward tends to emphasize wisdom's practical availability, at least to the point of avoiding disastrous folly. If woman were primarily personifying wisdom here, then would she be entirely elusive (except for the bitter one)? A related consideration is the emphasis on inscrutability beyond the basic wisdom just mentioned. If woman were primarily personifying wisdom, then what is the man's role in the figure? Hence, almost exactly opposite of associating women (ideally) with wisdom runs a third approach: to emphasize inscrutability, such that the (male) author can scarcely comprehend any human, but certainly not women. It is true that this passage is not high on human self-understanding, and 7:28 speaks explicitly only of finding or finding out one man and no women in a thousand. So, the argument goes, the proportions are such that no real misogynist insult is made. But in view of 7:26 and 7:29 this interpretation hardly seems adequate to the charged atmosphere. It will not do to reduce the Sage's death-dealing complaints to the equivalent of locker-room banter, a sidetrack comment that well-meaning Western, male, married scholars could imagine themselves making. The Hebrew text of 7:28 may more technically read "but not one woman among them all," yet the lack of uprightness seems to be present given the implications of 7:29, reducing this interpretation to special pleading.

Instead, the interpretative key proposed here is that the number one thousand begs the reader to think yet again—ironically—of Solomon and all his women: seven hundred wives and three hundred concubines. The persona has faded into the background but never announced leaving the scene. Solomon is guilty of the error against which 7:26 warns; he gives in to seduction that turns him away from divine wisdom toward other gods. If we stop at this juncture, then some of the scandal is already gone, but it might still appear that women are generally dangerous in contrast to the occasional exception among men. However, we can go further. Solomon's aura as the paradigm for wisdom already lurked in 7:23. If any would qualify as the one man in a thousand, he would be the one. In fact, though, he is the paradigmatic foolish sinner turning aside after women! So 7:28 is thickly laced with irony. The supposed paragon of the wisdom tradition falls into its most blatantly criticized form of folly—over and over. No woman among his one thousand enhanced his wisdom, but each embodies its deconstruction.

If by this point the text is not a protofeminist one, then at the very minimum it does not at all tip the balance in favor of men. Their champion has gone down. Someone—the Sage or his literary executor—cannot resist hinting in 7:27 that these words come from the Solomonic persona with tongue firmly planted in cheek: "Not even Solomon can serve as our example, mediator, or as a promise for the future! Again in this passage, Qohelet doubtlessly prepares us for Jesus' words: 'even Solomon in all his glory' (Matt. 6:29 RSV)" (Ellul 1990: 203).

The passage's deconstruction of Solomon drives toward the conclusion in Eccl. 7:29: all of humanity has fallen from creaturely righteousness. Wisdom may offer preservation from disastrous folly, but its paragon figure—for all his grand achievements—failed to attain even this most basic goal, violating persistently the wisdom tradition's most basic rule. The "wisdom" that Solomon found, as he strayed from fearing the Lord, led away from righteousness. In Genesis (e.g., 5:2) both men and women are *'ādām* and were made upright. Nonetheless, they "sought out many [of their own] devices," perhaps an allusion to Gen. 6:5 given a common underlying root: "The LORD saw that the wickedness of humankind was great in the earth, and that every inclination of the thoughts of their hearts was only evil continually." The appeal of Eccl. 7:29 to Genesis concerns what is common to men and women, not distinctions in their relations to the fall. This common human contribution is excessive reliance on our own reason, independent of God, as 7:23–25 anticipates.

It is not explicitly clear to what extent *hebel*, the ungraspable enigma of life, stems from the fall, as distinct from finitude. Augustine rightly saw that this text opposed Manichean dualism according to which good and evil are deadlocked, for "God made humanity upright." Our finitude is a gift. And the current struggle is temporary, in light of creation's original goodness, which signals the future triumph of our great God. The Pelagians may have worried rightly about moral laxity, but the ardent search of the Sage in Eccl. 7 suggests that beefing up the efforts of present human nature offers no solution. Under the sun, "this alone I found," namely that our fallenness thwarts even wisdom's most basic tactics for avoiding folly. Consistent with this picture are the following implications for *hebel*, which have floated beneath the surface of our study and can now be summarized explicitly.

Fallenness involves, at least in part, wrongful attempts to transcend our finitude in the first place. Thus, apparent absurdity—even idolatry—ensues when transitory beings try on their own to gain an eternal perspective or mastery over their lives. Accordingly, it will be difficult to untangle the causal connections between finitude and fallenness in many instances. Although they are distinct as matters of theological principle, they are now difficult to separate in the ways they affect human life. When therefore we try to understand what *hebel* means in Ecclesiastes—let alone in life—viewing it only as a function of either finitude or fallenness would be unwise. Negative views of Qoheleth, and strong interpretations of *hebel* as absurdity or utter meaninglessness, tend to neglect the Sage's affirmations of creaturely goodness in contrast with human fallenness. Positive views of the Sage, and weaker interpretations of *hebel* as transitoriness, tend to neglect the ambiguities of creaturely finitude and how it becomes epistemically bound up with our fallenness. Humans were always made for limits on our knowledge and its resulting power; after the fall, these limits appear frustrating instead of occasioning rest in the Creator. Taking the end of Eccl. 7 seriously helps us to read the book in proper relation to redemptive history, recognizing that after the fall our very desire to sort out *exactly* what *hebel* means threatens to transcend divinely set limits upon human wisdom.

The Sage's overall claim is that wisdom does not deliver comprehensive understanding or ultimate righteousness; in theory it could, however, keep a person from outright, self-destructive folly, of which sexual sin is a preeminent case. Ecclesiastes 7 manifests additionally that reflections on personal righteousness eventually point beyond the self, to communal relations and larger questions of justice. This is true early in Eccl. 7 (7:1–2, 4–5, 7, 9, 11–12) and later (7:15, 21–22, 26–28); soon this trend will reappear in Eccl. 8. But as for the mysteries of the universe, they are reserved for God (8:17).

Reflections on Wisdom and Authority (8:1–9)

> But the mind is like a dog chained to a post. When he runs he thinks he is going faster than the wind, though he only goes in circles and does not know it.[8]

Wisdom brightens the faces of a few. Ecclesiastes 8 echoes Eccl. 5, again investigating the interface between wisdom and various forms of authority. However, whereas Eccl. 5 focused on divine authority, Eccl. 8 now addresses human authorities. Ecclesiastes 8:1 asks, "Who is like the wise man? / And who knows the interpretation of a thing?"—perhaps better, "Who is truly wise?" taking *kî* as emphatic. In an absolute sense the answer is no one (the end of Eccl. 7). But this is not to say that wisdom offers no help. Getting on with governing authorities serves as a test case over the next few verses; several key words from 8:1 reappear in 8:2–9. At the end of 8:1 the description of wisdom's value, in terms of brightening the face, bears similarities to the blessing in Num. 6:24–26:

> The Lord bless you and keep you;
> the Lord make his face to shine upon you, and be gracious to you;
> the Lord lift up his countenance upon you, and give you peace.

Wisdom illuminates slightly how to deal with rulers. In terms of the details regarding how wisdom brightens a person, 8:2–3 is difficult. The general point is

8. David Schäfer, a character in Michael O'Brien, *Sophia House: A Novel* (San Francisco: Ignatius, 2005), 341.

that the king's courtiers cannot definitively use wisdom to get ahead. They need instead to be cautiously obedient—thus wisdom provides more pedestrian help with keeping one's wits when facing the king. Still, several ambiguities remain. When is the king's authority in view versus God's—or the two together? Does 8:2b refer to oaths made *before* God or *by* God? Does this clause provide the basis of 8:2a or begin anew an admonition leading into 8:3? Should the start of 8:3 be translated, "Do not be terrified; go from his presence" (as in NRSV) or, "Do not hurry away"?

The advice may be to leave the king's presence in order to obey quickly, or to leave when your advice has been rejected in order to hide your anger. These very ambiguities offer a theological opportunity, quickly clarifying that courtly wisdom is not a straightforward matter of knowing how to get ahead. The irony of the text's advice being unclear, in light of the knowledge we presently have anyway, suggests a different interpretative outcome than selecting from the options above. Rather, wisdom literature generates paradigms for thinking through a situation. Wisdom helps with the self-restraint necessary in tricky circumstances, but cannot remove risk altogether. It illuminates the potential courses of action and plausible outcomes, yet ambiguity persists. Our lack of clarity about authorial intentions, in God's providence, can sometimes open up the reading experience to a different kind of spiritual development.

Rulers have godlike power. Ecclesiastes 8:4 highlights what is at stake in the test case: the word of the king is, functionally, law. Certainly this was true before the Magna Carta, and it remains the case to a considerable degree. Christianson 2007: 202 details historical examples of explicitly political application from this text, calling for support of monarchs in power. To be sure, the text tends toward the politically conservative. Missing are themes from Proverbs regarding the ruler's obligation to care for the poor, listen well for advice, and so forth (e.g., Prov. 16:10, 13)—although one verse operates on a rather small scale to expect too much. Because of the connection between obedience to government and obedience to God (especially with the oath bringing in divine authority from Eccl. 5:1–7), people often recognize similarities between 8:2–4 and Rom. 13:1–7, where we read: "Let every person be subject to the governing authorities; for there is no authority except from God, and those authorities that exist have been instituted by God. Therefore whoever resists authority resists what God has appointed, and those who resist will incur judgment." A parallel with Job 9:1–12 is all the more obvious: "He [God] snatches away; who can stop him? / Who will say to him, 'What are you doing?'" Fear God and honor the king.

If, on the other hand, governmental supremacy involves receiving a delegated share in divine sovereignty, then already some theological checks and balances appear by implication: there is important asymmetry between *fearing* God and *honoring* the king. Romans 13:3–4 spells out a general assumption behind that chapter's support for governing authority: rulers are divinely instituted for judging evil and approving good. Moreover, Eccl. 8:4 describes empirically what *is*, not necessarily what *always ought* to be. Still further, 8:3 prohibits involvement in an evil matter, which cuts both ways: it could align the king's authority with the divine, but alternatively it can hint at the ultimate need to "obey God rather than any human authority" (Acts 5:29). Finally, is there not a suggestion, toward the end of the section, that the king lacks ultimate power to harm us? No mortal can control the wind or the future (Eccl. 8:8); only God can.

Wisdom and obedience work together. Accordingly, 8:5 calls for obedience—whether merely to the king or additionally and ultimately to God remains ambiguous. In this way one avoids evil; the interpretative question concerns whether this evil involves actions or consequences. Since the king is involved, the refusal of conspiracy prevents both in some sense: the passage obviously emphasizes royal power, so consequences are at stake; more canonically, conspiracy against the Lord's anointed one is generally an evil action. Emphasis upon wisdom in 8:6–8 addresses how to handle the ambiguities of 8:2–4, but could also imply that sometimes there are difficult decisions about obeying the king. In those cases the wise person may not know what to do by rule, but instead must recognize in the heart what is the right time for a particular action. Numerous Old Testament narratives dramatize the basic principles: Joseph and Daniel exemplify wise men at court, while Ezra 7, Neh. 2, and Esther provide paradigmatic cases of knowing the time for principled rather than subversive action in tricky circumstances.

Wisdom has limited power, yet so does the king. Exploring the principles more broadly, 8:6 recalls Eccl. 3 by reiterating the possibility of a time corresponding to beautiful or fitting matters. This cannot help but evoke divine, not just human, authority as the subject of concern, with humanity in general facing the flow of time. The latter part of 8:6, weakly rendered "the troubles of mortals" by the NRSV, speaks more literally of "the evil of humanity," possibly picking up this phrase from Gen. 6:5 in the flood narrative (→Eccl. 7:25–29). Before becoming unduly optimistic about wisdom, we need another reminder that perversity weighs humans down. Ecclesiastes 8:7 reiterates other limitations of human knowers, who are finite, not just fallen. Then 8:8 reestablishes still more human limitations, picking up elements from previous chapters. Humans cannot restrain the wind; they only chase it. Nor can they control the day of death or ensure that they avoid war. There may be another wordplay with respect to *rûaḥ*, doubling as "wind" and the human "spirit," which emphatically makes the point about no one having power over death—except God. This is particularly poignant for the king, whose power is therefore not unlimited, no matter what 8:3b–4 initially suggests (*šlṭ* ["power"] is repeated from 8:4, with a negative sense, in 8:8). God has not consigned us to be subjects of potential tyrants, as if monarchic conservatism were the only word spoken here. Kings have their share in human limits too; the assertion at the verse's end makes this matter all the more pointed, to the effect that wickedness is no guarantee of deliverance. Accountability hovers over even the king.

To sum up: power can (not: must) have tragic consequences. Ecclesiastes 8:9 closes the section with a standard formula concerning the Sage's observation and reflection. These formulas operate transitionally, prompting the reader to look ahead. This concluding note acknowledges that some humans exercise power over others, which can be tragic or downright evil. The object of the evil more likely refers primarily to the oppressed instead of the oppressors, though the ambiguity might be purposeful. Regardless, we should not quickly expand this statement into an assertion that all human power-relations are inevitably and only tragic. The Sage observes plenty of abuses of power, but likewise some of the communal blessings he lauds (e.g., 4:9–12) involve asymmetrical power-relations or actions undertaken on behalf of others.

Ambiguities between divine and human authority in Ecclesiastes reflect divine design: God establishes the human authorities over us. Yet, observing how often power goes awry and how careful those near human leaders must be, the Sage acknowledges again how fallen human culture is and how limited human expectations for governmental accomplishment must be. Any political theology tempted to overemphasize either staying with the status quo as divinely given or else seeking revolution to promote divine justice must grapple with the Sage's various observations.

Observations Regarding (In)Justice (8:10–17)

> Then shall I find stability and solidity in you, in your truth which imparts form to me. I shall not have to endure the questions of people who suffer from a disease which brings its own punishment and want to drink more than they have the capacity to hold.[9]

Justice delayed . . . Building on the transition in 8:9 ("all this I observed"), this section extends the Sage's observations with respect to wisdom and authority. Interpretation is not simple, especially given the textual problems in 8:10. A helpful starting point recognizes a problematic connection (in light of the *hebel* formula at the end) between the wicked and the holy place. Most likely, the misdeeds of the wicked are forgotten in the city where they went to the holy place while persisting in their wickedness. In other words, this refers to the same hypocrisy depicted in 5:1–7. The *hebel* conclusion is jarring since initially one might think it good for the wicked to be forgotten. Thus some insert or see in *kēn* ("praise") a subtle reference to the righteous, with their deeds being the ones that are forgotten. Others emend the verb slightly to read "praised" (e.g., NRSV), suggesting that the praise of the wicked is what counts as *hebel.*

There are more satisfying alternatives, though. The forgetting recalls the problem of memory and what God does or does not do with the past, so that justice becomes impossible because the deeds of the wicked no longer surface in anyone's mind; in this way, they escape. The forgetting could also be coterminous with

9. Augustine, *Confessions* 11.40 (trans. Chadwick), 244.

the coming and going in the holy place, so that the very ability of the wicked to circulate freely in the community is evidence of absurd neglect concerning their deeds. Relevant but often neglected is the next verse, in which judgment delayed is incentive denied, regarding righteousness. Apparently in 8:10 the community neglects to deal swiftly with the wicked, soon forgetting to construe them as such or to see much of a problem. This neglect fosters further wickedness (8:11), to the point that the Sage sees the wicked prospering routinely (8:12).

In any case, 8:10 raises a twofold problem for retribution theology, the traditional connection between deeds and consequences (→Prov. 3; Eccl. 7:15; 10:5–7). First, it becomes difficult to believe that a personal Creator upholds this connection, ensuring the moral order of the universe, when wicked people die happy. Not to get their comeuppance in this life makes the wicked seem, to all appearances anyway, as if they have "gotten away with it." Second, this is all the more galling when the wicked circulate freely and hypocritically in the holy place, showing themselves at divine worship without rendering obedience. Relevant parallels are close at hand today: celebrities so routinely commit misdeeds that we become numb. Unless they perpetrate something newly salacious, from this numbness they gain opportunity to operate at will. Soon enough, however, these celebrities die, and a torrent of eulogies pours out as if their misdeeds were of no consequence and such "great persons" were moral heroes. You might think that a particular example is in mind, identifiable if you could pinpoint the time of this writing. But that is a fool's errand, since the case studies are largely interchangeable and several come to mind just in the last couple of weeks. In any case, while these celebrities are usually not brazen, regular churchgoers, they still fit the current bill of spirituality in contemporary culture, thus fulfilling the thrust of 8:10. Their treatment as moral and spiritual heroes, or at least as admired "beautiful people" irrespective of behavior, not only suggests the ineffectiveness of retribution theology but also dumbs down the very definition of goodness in the culture.

. . . is justice denied. That point becomes even clearer in 8:11. Humans are sufficiently perverse that, when they see people apparently getting away with evil for a time, they follow suit. Implications affect not just human society but also divine governance. Another possible allusion to the fall in Gen. 1–3 interrogates the prima facie excess of divine patience: since neither Adam and Eve, nor humans since, died instantaneously, does God wrongly make space for oppression? One often hears a statement such as Eccl. 8:11 being treated as an absolute principle governing every criminal mind and legitimizing the quickest, fullest extent of punishment. Yet, if virtue in divine patience (e.g., 2 Pet. 3:9) makes room for repentance even though this also makes room for evil, then it is possible to see here a principle that remains true with limited application. As a truism of wisdom, the principle generally holds but does not cover all criminal motivation: many evildoers are enticed further by an apparent lack of speedy punishment, or at least enabled to descend further into wickedness. Meanwhile, the principle does not mandate that punishment must always be "to the fullest extent of the law": neither evildoers nor observers

should conclude that because God's judgment is not empirically obvious it does not exist. The principle in Eccl. 8:11 demands some kind of execution and speed of retribution, but does not weigh in on contemporary debates over the nature of punishment or God's justice.

Beyond the cosmic and cultural implications, John Cassian addresses 8:11 to the Christian life: if we do not deal vigorously with evil thoughts early on, then the more they fester, the more our hearts have opportunity to pursue their fallen tendencies (*Conference* 2.11.4, in Ancient Christian Writers 57.92). Ecclesiastes 8:11 describes more explicitly the subtext of 8:10: because the deeds of the wicked are forgotten rather than addressed, not only are their evil tendencies given free reign, but those of others are also fostered. Ecclesiastes 8:12 asserts an orthodox corollary: no matter how often wicked people seem to get away with evil, still it is better to fear God.

Justice and injustice observed. Ecclesiastes 8:13 illustrates again the back-and-forth nature of the Sage's considerations. Initially a shadow correlates with brevity, particularly due to its earlier use in 6:12, but this makes for exceedingly awkward syntax. Alternatively, shadows lengthen toward the end of a day, so the point might be that, unlike this lengthening, the days of the wicked will run quickly to their end (Longman 1998: 220). That would limit cases in 8:12a of long wicked lives, moving back toward a bit of retribution in 8:12b–13. But not so fast—on still another occasion 8:14 observes the contrary: such retribution does not happen in *every* case. Taking any of the Sage's statements too categorically, we are likely to get whiplash. Yet the tenor of much critical scholarship, reveling in supposed contradictions, misses the obvious point: if distinctions between righteousness and wickedness were utterly impossible, with these terms simply designating "what the deity arbitrarily likes" and "what the deity whimsically dislikes," then it would be impossible for the Sage to question retribution theology as he does. The interrogation entails the meaningfulness of the terms, despite questioning any simplistic retributive expectations.

The Sage actually observes what is all too often the case: sometimes on earth wickedness gets its due, but oftentimes not. Gregory the Great attributes this to benevolent divine motives we might not suspect at first: "God doubtless so ordains it of his inestimable mercy, that both scourges should torture the just, lest their doings should elate them, and that the unjust should pass this life at least without punishment, because by their evil doings they are hastening onward to those torments, which are without end" (*Morals on the Book of Job* 5.23.44, in Library of Fathers of the Holy Catholic Church 23.85). Augustine's understanding is complementary:

> For, if he visited every sin here below with manifest penalty, it might be thought that no score remained to be settled at the Last Judgment. On the other hand, if God did not plainly enough punish sin on earth, people might conclude that there is no such thing as Divine Providence. So, too, in regard to good things of life. If God did not bestow them with patent liberality to some who ask him, we could

> possibly argue that such things did not depend on his power. On the other hand, if he lavished them on all who asked, we might have the impression that God is to be served only for the gifts he bestows. In that case, the service of God would not make us religious, but rather covetous and greedy. (*City of God* 1.8, in FC 8.29)

These factors are not foremost in the Sage's mind at this juncture. The words "on earth" rather than "under the sun"—only here and in 8:16—may distance these goings-on somewhat from divine work (Krüger 2004: 161). Yet the Sage's inability to speak in 8:14 of God's hand in the middle of the apparent injustice does not nullify the above explanations. The larger concern to uphold the fear of God (8:12–13) without minimizing the inscrutability of providence is consistent with the factors Gregory and Augustine introduce. They agree with the Sage that God does not want humans to grasp providence fully, lest we try to manipulate its workings to our advantage (8:17) and fail to fear. They also agree with the Sage that God does not want earthly goods to have either ultimate value or no value at all (8:15).

Simple joys commended. Having emphasized human malfeasance yet once more, the Sage provides in 8:15 the expected swing back in the opposite direction: not only commendation of enjoyment as a coping mechanism, but also its reaffirmation as God-given. One cannot pursue enjoyment through wisdom as if there were a guaranteed deeds-results connection; that would be overly righteous. Wisdom mostly prevents premature death, opening up opportunities to receive provisional enjoyment when the right circumstances pertain.

Wisdom limited regarding divine and human work. Working toward a conclusion, 8:16 describes the Sage's questing still another time. The new element on this occasion concerns lack of sleep. Terminological similarities with the book's early chapters mean that what keeps most people up at night is probably work rather than reflection. Ecclesiastes 8:17, however, speaks of human toil to seek out the work of God—the Sage's work of wisdom, as it were. Over and over verbs pile on to narrate such a quest—for that which humans cannot attain, despite the Sage's ironic and impossible claim to achieve observation of *everything*. Such hubris is considerable since the Sage's epistemology necessarily leaves out creation and redemption (Bartholomew 2009: 293).

What happens on earth due to humans is distinct, though not separate, from the larger framework of divine providence that shapes what happens under the sun. God's work itself may actually involve placing limits on human knowledge. In 8:17 there is a preliminary conclusion regarding the theme dominant since 6:10–12: the limits of human knowing. In the meantime, and again in Eccl. 9–12, various forms of reflection unfold concerning how to pursue living wisely in light of such limits. Thus here is another of the book's recurring transitions, in which themes or subthemes accumulate, overlap, and then roll back over each other.

These particular verses are important for one of the time-honored quests in the study of Christian doctrine. The relation between divine sovereignty and human freedom constructs a nexus of complicated issues. It is proper to seek coherent understanding of biblical truth on these subjects. From the perspective of Ecclesiastes, however, expectations regarding the extent and clarity of that teaching should remain modest. Anything approaching a comprehensive model of providence is unlikely. The incarnation of God in Jesus Christ is instructive. We reason from it, not to it, in order to appreciate the close personal fellowship between God and humanity. In this way we can describe aspects of divine-human interaction that the Bible so often narrates. But we cannot really *explain how* God could take human beings into the very divine life or how such a person as Jesus Christ would experience earthly life. The church embraced the necessary modesty in its creedal formulas by largely using negative language to relate our Lord's divine and human natures (without mixture, without separation into two persons, and so forth). Any model of divine providence and human action must similarly respect our epistemic limitations. This holds true for not only what a model of providence depicts, but especially how it applies in reading the times: "When I applied my mind to know wisdom, and to see the business that is done on earth . . . then I saw all the work of God, that no one can find out what is happening under the sun. However much they may toil in seeking, they will not find it out; even though those who are wise claim to know, they cannot find it out." Those who are truly wise, in fact, know better than to claim too much.

More on Wise Living in the Face of the Future (9:1–10:20)

> Hast never come to thee an hour,
> A sudden gleam divine, precipitating, bursting all these
> bubbles, fashions, wealth?
> These eager business aims—books, politics, art, amours,
> To utter nothingness?[10]

At this transitional point within part 2 of Ecclesiastes, repetition of "all this" in 9:1 could point backward or forward—or in both directions. The statement signals the crux of surrounding reflection, namely, that the Sage is taking to heart God's providential grasp of the righteous and wise, along with human ignorance. In 9:1–6 and 12:1–7 there is emphasis on death as the human fate. In between, short passages exhort enjoyment in the present (9:7–10; 11:7–10), framing material on the uncertainties of the future plus the corresponding strengths and weaknesses of wisdom (Krüger 2004: 165). Yet the outline presented here takes a slightly different form, to emphasize that the concluding chapters have distinctive features within the book as a whole. The book's culmination in 12:8–14 deserves a major heading in its own right, offering summary interpretation within Ecclesiastes

10. Walt Whitman, *Leaves of Grass and Other Writings*, ed. Michael Moon, Norton Critical Edition (New York: Norton, 2002), 232. Thanks to Tim Larsen for mentioning it.

itself. The imperatives in 11:1 and 12:1 unify the prior section (11:1–12:7), in which the Sage unfolds his overall conclusions and resulting advice. By contrast, Eccl. 9–10 continues to meander somewhat, after the provisional conclusion of 8:17, with reflections appearing in various literary forms. Style perhaps matches substance in that readers find multiple, but not infinite, possibilities unfolding for the text's message.

Two Things Are Certain: Taxes and . . . (9:1–6)

What everyone, and no one, knows. In 9:1 the Sage gives his heart to examine the righteous and the wise, along with their deeds, which are in God's hand. Less clear is how the phrase "whether . . . love or hate" connects to this examination, and where to break up the thoughts between 9:1 and 9:2. It seems most sensible to have one object of not-knowing: "everything that confronts" the human. Accordingly, the prior assertion is that all human deeds—whether love or hate—are in God's hands.

What then of 9:2? Its basic thrust is clear. A series of paired opposites—righteous and wicked, clean and unclean, and so forth—covers everyone with the fate of death. There are, however, two odd features: the initial phrase, given the solution to 9:1 just adopted, which strengthens the emphasis on everyone and everything; and the extra word, *ṭôb* ("the good" without "the evil"), floating in the middle and interrupting the pairs. There may be good reason to emend the text, seeing this as an accidental later addition. Alternatively, "good" is an important category in Ecclesiastes and may deserve special emphasis here. The overall point stands regardless: scrutinizing providence may prove fruitless, but death is a sure thing.

The abrupt syntax at the end of 9:3 reinforces the focus on death. The rest of 9:3 (again) appropriates Gen. 6:5 regarding the preflood generation: human hearts are continually full of propensity toward evildoing. This need not entail absolute depravity, as if humans never do any good acts in any sense. But it does approximate total depravity, according to which evil affects all human hearts throughout all the kinds of choices that make up their lifetimes. Against Pelagianism at the very least, humans cannot pick themselves up by their moral bootstraps and achieve goodness that ensures profit before God (Eccl. 7:19–20). The allusion to madness adds a neglected dimension to portrayals of human depravity in the Christian tradition: humans are not merely sinful in the sense of self-absorption. In fact they are so sinful as to misunderstand their own best interests, falling into folly—out of step with the created order, even to the point of craziness. Evangelistic appeals must surely confront selfishness in order to direct people toward their need for God, but we must also highlight the sense in which sin leads away from genuine self-interest. This would give greater balance to subsequent understandings of the Christian life as well. A house must be not only swept clean of evil spirits, but also newly filled with goodness to prevent their return (Matt. 12:44–45). We tend to neglect that new life in Christ graces us to grow in living wisely, in harmony with God's created design. Rules and self-sacrifice pertain, since the Bible instructs us about what virtuous people do and do not do in pursuing charity. But redemption is not about God being a cosmic killjoy, taking away earthly pleasures with a don't-do list. Becoming a "fool" for Christ aligns life with what is truly rational for human flourishing; it should not drive a person insane.

What hope earthly life offers in itself. Indeed, 9:4 swings back in a positive direction, valuing earthly life with a striking proverb. Its force is lost on modern Westerners for whom dogs are "man's best friends." The dog was an unclean, despised animal in the ancient Near East. Yet even a living dog is better than a dead king of the beasts. So, despite the twin fates to which all humans are subject—death and sin, which are related in the Genesis text upon which Ecclesiastes draws—the living have hope.

Ecclesiastes 9:5–6 explains the hope, which goes beyond not being dead yet: because living people know they will die, they can amend their ways. Remembrance of the dead is long gone, so they have no possible recompense to pursue anymore. The word for recompense may appear due to assonance with the word for remembrance, while the dead not knowing anything involves sarcasm. So we should not make too much positive hay out of 9:5, as if it encourages the living to change their behavior for the sake of how people will remember them. The incentive is more modest, that the living still have a share in what happens under the sun (9:6): true enjoyment remains possible—but not the sort of legacy that the Sage precludes elsewhere. Ecclesiastes 9:6, while connecting back to 9:1 with the reference to human love and hate, heightens the contrast with the living: the dead have already enjoyed their full portion from God. The juxtaposition of the living and the dead concerning earthly fates does not preclude the possibility of resurrection, but more locally and less ambitiously protects the value of earthly life from being jeopardized by the deadly fate and the present madness of 9:1–3. Thus 9:4–6 contains no ultimate Christian hope, but a real though provisional earthly one.

Therefore, "Carpe Diem" . . . (9:7–10)

Eat your bread and drink your wine. In light of that hope 9:7 echoes prior passages (esp. 3:12–13; 5:17–18; 8:15), urging enjoyment. These *carpe diem* passages build in intensity; here we have no "better than" motif but instead more absolute claims. The view that these merely provide an anesthetic, or distraction, runs up against strong statements about divine approval. As this subsection shifts toward direct address, with imperatival forms, enjoyment is divinely approved, even mandated. To be sure, the apparently blanket approval of human action is jarring, leading many commentators to panic and search desperately for limitations. But the context supplies all we need: the Sage commends the same modest enjoyments as earlier, while all previous prohibitions of folly and exposures of hedonism still pertain. The *carpe diem* texts intersect with, and embrace without trumping, the *hebel* conclusions.

For reassurance that earthly delights figure within God's blessing, even serving as explanatory metaphors, consider: "You prepare a table before me / in the presence of my enemies; / you anoint my head with oil; / my cup overflows" (Ps. 23:5); "You cause the grass to grow for the cattle, / and plants for people to use, / to bring forth food from the earth, / and wine to gladden the human heart, / oil to make the face shine, / and bread to strengthen the human heart" (104:14–15). The Israelites were actually commanded to celebrate festivals unto the Lord: "The LORD your God will bless you in all your produce and in all your undertakings, and you shall surely celebrate" (Deut. 16:15). These events involved not just food and drink, but rest from work and therefore time spent with people enjoying each other (e.g., "great gladness" in 2 Chr. 30:21, 23). New Testament affirmations of basic earthly goods have already been mentioned (e.g., 1 Cor. 10:31; 1 Tim. 4:4; 1 Tim. 6; cf. Eccl. 1:3; 2:18–19; 5:13–17). To these we can add eschatological images in Revelation (and Old Testament passages such as Isa. 25, with which that final book is consistent); Paul's exhortation to let no one "condemn [us] in matters of food and drink" (although these are but shadows of the ultimate reality in Christ; Col. 2:16–17); and Jesus's sharing the joys of table fellowship to the point of being called "a glutton and a drunkard" by his opponents (Matt. 11:19). Christ brought up this allegation himself, only to dismiss any impropriety with the insistence that "wisdom is vindicated by her deeds."

Church fathers tend to interpret verses in Ecclesiastes about food and drink in relation to the Lord's Supper. While an immediately spiritualizing leap toward a eucharistic reference would do no justice to the Sage's affirmation of the goodness of creation, the Eucharist is still pertinent. We celebrate "the gifts of God for the people of God," not only remembering Christ's death and embodying the church's present unity but also anticipating the eschatological banquet. At that time, "the LORD of hosts will make for all peoples / a feast of rich food, a feast of well-aged wines, / of rich food filled with marrow, / of well-aged wines strained clear" (Isa. 25:6). Hence, the Eucharist celebrates our Lord making significant the ordinary table fellowship that the Sage lauds. This avoids separating common grace entirely from redeeming grace. It is no accident that, in texts such as Matt. 22:1–14, weddings and other festival banquets illustrate the divine work (Ellul 1990: 109–11). Ecclesiastes 9:7 is another text to which Bonhoeffer correctly refers when exhorting us to affirm joy as God does, instead of treating the body merely instrumentally as a means to some spiritual end.[11] Bread and wine figure in the preeminent festivity of God's people because redemption upholds and transforms ordinary life, sanctifying even the most basic staples of our diets for divine use. God takes what seems mundane as grounds for celebration; true celebration is not out of the ordinary, but makes it extraordinary.

11. Bonhoeffer, *Ethics*, 187.

Let your garments always be white. The white garments of 9:8 fit naturally with comfort in a hot climate, for which oil combated harmful effects on the skin. They also symbolize purity and joy, which can go together in cases such as weddings. The temptation to see baptism and chrismation here—ritual celebrations initiating our covenant life with God—is inevitably hard for Christian commentators to resist. As with the Eucharist in 9:7, the verse is not directly about such spiritual realities. However, its indirect pointers still underscore that the sacraments take up material elements and social practices in God's service, to signify the transcendent use of earthly realities. We take care of our bodies not solely or primarily for creaturely comfort, but for the sanctification of our lives—that they might "always" (a jarring word if this verse were solely mundane) flourish under divine approval.

Enjoy life with your wife. Ecclesiastes 9:9 helps to cast the end of Eccl. 7 in the proper light. Women should be prized. *Hebel* is repeated—in the context of divine giving!—as the arena for this admonition. A beloved spouse is one of the chief joys in the earthly portion God gives. Meanwhile, work is not the antithesis of enjoyment. Noting parallels between 9:7–10 and Shiduri's advice in the Old Babylonian version of the *Gilgamesh Epic*, William Brown nevertheless highlights that the biblical Sage's perspective is distinctive: Ecclesiastes affirms work as a God-given, simple joy.[12] The rest of scripture similarly treats work as a blessing (Paul's insistence in 2 Thess. 3:6–13 that one who refuses to work should not eat is seen in Prov. 6; →Prov. 10–29 on "gluttony" and "sloth"). Tragic though some elements of work may seem, it is integral to creation, not a consequence of the fall. The curse in Gen. 3:17–19 does not involve God destroying or fundamentally remaking the original creation. Instead, God altered the human relation to integral features of the cosmos and culture. As with marriage, therefore, work is not a curse imposed in response to the fall, but a created blessing newly affected. Exiled from the garden temple, humans no longer find work to be solely a venue of creative freedom and joyful discovery, developing cosmic and cultural potential under God. Instead of exercising that kind of stewardship (1:28–31), humans now face struggle in mastering the cosmos as a food source (3:17–18) and the deadliness of death constraining freedom and joy (3:19). But Christians should no more despise work than marriage.

Whatever your hand finds to do. Ecclesiastes 9:10 forbids reading 9:1 deterministically or fatalistically: freedom entails taking advantage of opportunities. *Memento mori* ("remember your death") anticipates what it means to remember your Creator: we are all headed to Sheol, the realm of the dead, far too soon from our current perspective. So *carpe diem*: we ought to seize the day, working and thinking and knowing while we can. Gregory the Great's comment is

12. William P. Brown, "Calvin and Qoheleth Meet after a Hard Day's Night; or, Does Ecclesiastes Have a 'Protestant' Work Ethic?" in *Reformed Theology: Identity and Ecumenicity 2: Biblical Interpretation in the Reformed Tradition*, ed. Wallace M. Alston Jr. and Michael Welker (Grand Rapids: Eerdmans, 2007), 88–89.

apposite: "So death itself will be defeated when it comes, if we always fear it before it comes."[13]

Accomplishment comes "not by might, nor by power, but by my spirit, says the LORD of hosts" (Zech. 4:6). "Cooperation" is a dangerous word, taken literally, when it comes to human activity vis-à-vis the divine, because it loses the preeminence of God's initiative. Yet, however mysteriously, God's power generally works through our activity (Phil. 2:12–13). Thus, Luke 16:10 promises, "Whoever is faithful in a very little is faithful also in much; and whoever is dishonest in a very little is dishonest also in much," while 19:17 affirms, "Because you have been trustworthy in a very small thing, take charge of ten cities."[14] God increases the gift of responsibility for those who respond to divine initiative, who put their hand to the plow when by grace they find something to do.

The statements about Sheol need not preclude some kind of afterlife, given potential hints elsewhere in the book. In this passage, though, the Sage gives full voice to his tragic side; most Old Testament references to Sheol concern those under divine judgment, whereas this makes it the destiny of everyone (Bartholomew 2009: 305). The Sage's statements portray the apparent *certainties* from our current, empirical perspective; this verse does not weigh in on other possibilities. Similarities are frequently noted between Ecclesiastes and the *Gilgamesh Epic* yet, although these words sound alike, the epic's advice could amount to little more than "let us eat and drink, / for tomorrow we die" (1 Cor. 15:32)—according to which eating and drinking becomes everything, blown out of proportion. However, just because the Sage does not say everything in every verse, we should not assume that pagan, hedonistic resignation captures his perspective. Ecclesiastes commends these pleasures in moderation that reflects the influence of divine judgment, even without clearly foreseeing the ultimate basis on which that judgment makes sense. Since the Sage can reach such a nuanced perspective on human joys without revelation about resurrection in Christ, Ecclesiastes can help to engage pluralistic civil arenas. Some teaching on cardinal virtues and capital vices commends itself with the book's logic regarding how to handle human limitations and earthly fragility under God. Still, in the end this message drives us toward humility and the necessity of theological virtue.

. . . Since the Time of Death Is Unpredictable (9:11–12)

The exhortations end in 9:11, returning to the Sage's observations. This verse does not deny what often happens: the race can go to the swift, the battle to the strong, and so on. But there is no guarantee of those results, since "time and chance happen to them all." Thus, "the 'righteous' are distinguished precisely by the fact that their action is *not* aimed directly toward their own prosperity. By contrast, the 'swift' run and 'heroes' fight with the direct intention of winning

13. Gregory the Great, *Forty Gospel Homilies* 20 (13) (trans. Hurst), 156.
14. Bonhoeffer, *Ethics*, 295.

the race or battle" (Krüger 2004: 175). The claim about chance is not a denial of earlier claims about divine providence, but instead an empirical description of how causes apparently relate to effects among changeable creatures (Bonaventure 2005: 340). In some cases, of course, divine intervention also happens—as suggested by the parallel in Zech. 4:6 (mentioned above) and the story of David and Goliath (mentioned by Didymus the Blind, *Commentary on Ecclesiastes* 282.1, in PTA 24.41–45 and Wright 2005: 265).

Concluding this subunit, 9:12 reasserts that humans are like animals in being subject to death—in the same way we subject the animals to death. While humans alone are the *imago Dei*, as "rational animals" we share mortality with the beasts. Hence the rich fool (Luke 12:20) again illustrates what can happen: sudden loss when, to all earthly appearances, his time had not yet come (Athanasius, *In Defense of His Flight* 15, in NPNF^2 4.260). To be sure, such tragic times need not occur due to direct divine intervention; the text points to sudden snares, whatever their immediate cause. Neither money nor any other earthly stratagem is failsafe.

God's favor is not for the skillful as measured by worldly wisdom (1 Cor. 1:18–31); getting this point across frequently requires providence to reverse expected fortunes. Better than "seize the day," to capture the theme, is "receive the day"[15]—as God's gift to the world.

A Case Study and Proverbs on the Relative Value of Wisdom (9:13–10:4)

Next a series of short proverbs offers facets of wisdom. It looks as if the Sage incorporates previously existing material. In some cases the juxtaposition of wise and foolish people is prominent, whereas in other cases the preoccupation is with authority.

Another case study. In 9:13–15 a poor wise man could save his city without powerful weapons—from possibly sudden disaster, as envisioned in 9:12, since the word used there for "net," *mĕṣôd*, also designates "siegeworks" in 9:14. But this poor sage would get the chance only if the king discovered him. As with the end of Eccl. 4, this scenario turns our minds backward to the story of Joseph and forward to the story of Jesus—the type and the antitype of the lone wise man.

The point of the Sage's tale is that *both* wisdom *and* chance or opportunity are required. It is not clear whether the poor man saved the city and was subsequently forgotten, or instead never got remembered in the first place. Because human beings look on the outside, David almost didn't get the chance to slay Goliath. Yet God looks on the heart and made a way. Another relevant case happens later in David's story, with the wise woman of Abel, who averted the city's destruction by Joab. She protected the heritage of YHWH by being one of those "who are peaceable and faithful in Israel" (2 Sam. 20:19). By God's grace, these figures,

15. Dorothy C. Bass, *Receiving the Day: Christian Practices for Opening the Gift of Time* (San Francisco: Jossey-Bass, 2001), as cited in Bartholomew 2009: 308.

Joseph, and Jesus were eventually remembered in the necessary ways, partly due to desperate circumstances. This should encourage us that, while wisdom offers no earthly guarantees, our times are still in divine hands.

Lessons about wisdom's strength and weakness. Within the present earthly scenario in Ecclesiastes, though, the discouragement of 9:16 follows naturally: yes, wisdom trumps power, but it must be heeded. Despising the poor is not unknown, even in Proverbs, so we should not overdo contrasts between these books on retribution theology.[16] Despite wisdom prevailing only if it gets a hearing, and in relation to poverty wisdom often being ignored, nevertheless its quietude (depending on whether the focus concerns the hearing or the speaking) can be a virtue (Eccl. 9:17). Calmness helps the public to listen carefully rather than foolishly drowning out wisdom with noise. A community can be rescued or endangered by even one person (9:18) so that, however useful wisdom might be, its results are never guaranteed. In marked contrast to the poor sage of 9:15, here in 9:18 the Sage can go back to Genesis for a foundational case in which one sinner destroys much good.

Fools: the fly in the ointment. So in 10:1 we encounter the proverbial fly in the ointment. The association of perfume with death is ironic, since one of the most likely occasions for its ancient use would have involved a dead body (consider the story of Jesus). The perfume epitomizes the *ephemeral, vaporous* nature of *good* things. Ecclesiastes 9:16a and 9:18a contain "better than" statements; yet 9:16b and 9:18b–10:1a qualify potential optimism; and 9:17 and 10:1b present the two sides of a realistic middle ground. The thrust of the passage is that wisdom can succeed with receptive people but, since a little leaven pervades an entire lump of dough, wisdom rarely gets the audience it deserves.

Ecclesiastes 10:2–3 presses the negatives: trying to educate a fool is basically useless, so if the elite are foolish, the rest of the people are really in trouble. Inclining to the right concerns either good fortune or power, while to the left lies misfortune (10:2). Given Gen. 48:12–20 (Jacob blessing Joseph's sons) and Matt. 25:31–46 (the sheep and the goats), an ethical antithesis, supporting the proverb's chief point, also breaks down along lines of good/right, bad/left. Either the fool says that everyone else is foolish or simply manifests his or her own folly (Eccl. 10:3). The ambiguity is handy, because a crucial manifestation of folly lies in saying that everyone else is a fool.

Calm before a ruler's storm. Ecclesiastes 10:4, then, is transitional, shifting to direct address for introducing a series of proverbs on authority. Beginning in 10:5, these proverbs return to third-person description. Resonating with Prov. 16:14 ("the king's wrath is a messenger of death, / and whoever is wise will appease it"), the exhortation of Eccl. 10:4 is tricky in the details: "Do not leave your post

16. See especially Richard L. Schultz, "Unity or Diversity in Wisdom Theology? A Canonical and Covenantal Perspective," *Tyndale Bulletin* 48 (1997): 271–306; Raymond C. Van Leeuwen, "Liminality and Worldview in Proverbs 1–9," *Semeia* 50 (1990): 111–44; idem, "Wealth and Poverty: System and Contradiction in Proverbs," *Hebrew Studies* 33 (1992): 25–36.

[better: 'place']"—physically, or metaphorically and socially? How does this relate to 8:2–3? "Calmness will undo great offenses"—whose, and how? There seems to be wordplay between "anger" (actually, "spirit"), "leave," and "undo" (Bartholomew 2009: 322). Beyond recognizing verbal cleverness, we should capitalize on the ambiguities: "It can be read (1) as a call for opportunistic behavior toward the ruler *and* (2) as a critique of such an attitude—*or* (3) as a call for 'civil courage.' . . . Like 8:1–9, through its ambiguity 10:4 provokes the readers to multiple readings that stimulate them to reflect critically on the advice of the text, instead of following it without question" (Krüger 2004: 183). Calmness can undo or prevent great shortcomings, yours and/or your opponent's; but such calmness can also make space for mistakes (presumably, those of your opponent). Conceivably, though, maintaining a viewpoint calmly could even prevent what one opposes. Wisdom evokes this sort of effort to discern the various possibilities for applying a rule of thumb to a situation.

More Proverbs on Wisdom and Authority (10:5–20)

Folly before a ruler. Ecclesiastes 10:5–7 continues wrestling with the issue of 10:4—folly and authority—though 10:5 introduces a new scenario with a preamble on observing evil under the sun. The evil concerns a serious error going out from the ruler of 10:4—the same term for inadvertent sin (*šĕgāgâ*) used earlier (→5:4–6): "The Hebrew word here normally designates a mistake that comes about through negligence, forgetfulness, or by accident" (Longman 1998: 242). The error does not necessarily belong directly to the ruler, but may simply occur in his presence. Ecclesiastes 10:6 spells out the error: fools get promoted while the rich are snubbed; 10:7 then restates the error in catchy form. These verses reflect a kind of elitism with which some contemporary readers will not be familiar. The apparent implication that the rich are generally more capable of leadership is not simply the assumption of retribution theology (→Prov. 3; Eccl. 7:15; 8:10), but also a frequent basis of cultures ancient and modern. The Sage can speak proverbially within such a frame to make his point, without thereby teaching that this elitism achieves a divinely favored ideal.

Skill without guarantees. Dealing with an oft-mentioned example (e.g., Ps. 7:15; Prov. 26:27), Eccl. 10:8 introduces connected deeds and results. Though the other contexts imply retribution, the Sage does not make the outcomes absolutely certain. Digging a pit, only to fall into it, recalls other devious schemes against fellow humans, such as Haman's ironic gallows from the book of Esther. As Esther's story demonstrates, behind the proverbial scenes, both court intrigues and divine intervention may be interwoven together yet mysterious or even unseen to outside observers. Retribution may well be in play, but not necessarily always or obviously.

Meanwhile, breaching a wall may have the purpose of stealing. Even though the rest of scripture offers support for such a moral, retributive reading, again the Sage's scenario could encompass accidental outcomes, fitting the broader query about the usefulness of wisdom vis-à-vis the future. In the case of the snake, the outcome is a tragic possibility but by no means obviously expected. The verse parallels Robert Burns's famous observation that "the best laid schemes of mice and men go often askew"—implying a subtle critique even of retribution theology.

Longer term results are not the sole issue, since 10:9 worries about what can happen in the middle of a deed. The truth is that wisdom's skill offers no absolute guarantees for either the results or the process of toil. Ecclesiastes 10:10—though linguistically very difficult—qualifies this pessimism in light of wisdom's relative advantages. Technical difficulties aside, the meaning is broadly evident: if the ax ("iron") used in 10:9 is blunt, then extra strength is necessary for the effort required. Perhaps the irony should not be lost on us that, in God's providence, the linguistic ax of the verse has turned out to be blunt, spawning lots of extra effort by commentators, whereas wisdom—at least for theological purposes—may lie in sticking with the main point. At the end of 10:10, profit or advantage (*yitrôn*) and wisdom are connected, surprisingly so given the rest of Ecclesiastes. The implication is that a wise person prepares by sharpening the ax. Ironically, however, such a person faces greater danger if something goes wrong (Bartholomew 2009: 324). Incidentally, the manual labor involved in the scenario qualifies the prior elitism.

Before getting too excited about expert wisdom, 10:11 revisits the timing or chance or opportunity for wisdom to do its work. The same word, *yitrôn*, about which the Sage is usually pessimistic yet unusually positive in 10:10, reoccurs: denied. If the snake bites precipitously, the charmer might merely lack the expected wages. However, it is tempting to see a more biting subtext.

Words, wisdom, and folly. Ecclesiastes 10:12–15 prolongs the seesawing between positive and negative when contrasting wisdom and folly, especially in relation to speech. In 10:12 the theme of self-consumption returns regarding the fool. It is not entirely clear whether wise words bring favor to the wise person herself or to others—yet both themes are surely present elsewhere in scripture, even inextricably linked, as in Eph. 4:15–16, 25–32:

> But speaking the truth in love, we must grow up in every way into him who is the head, into Christ, from whom the whole body, joined and knit together by every ligament with which it is equipped, as each part is working properly, promotes the body's growth in building itself up in love. . . .
>
> So then, putting away falsehood, let all of us speak the truth to our neighbors, for we are members of one another. . . . Let no evil talk come out of your mouths, but only what is useful for building up, as there is need, so that your words may give grace to those who hear. . . . Put away from you all bitterness and wrath and anger and wrangling and slander, together with all malice, and be kind to one another, tenderhearted, forgiving one another, as God in Christ has forgiven you.

God makes us companions to bless each other, so that part of "redeeming the time" (Eph. 5:15–16) involves making the most of opportunities to edify others in speech.

Ecclesiastes 10:13 describes foolish speech once more; by referring to the speakers indirectly (not as "fools," but via "the words of their mouths begin in foolishness"), the verse indicates that speaking foolishly is an all-too-pervasive human tendency, running from "beginning" to "end." In addition to the obvious merism of these parts embracing the whole, there is also a hint of an advancing process, with folly resulting in evil madness. The next verse implies that for any human to claim confident knowledge of the future (by multiplying words) would be tantamount to folly. The tension between the opportunity for fools to talk on and on (10:14a) and their self-destruction (10:12b) is a matter of timing; self-consumption requires time to chew. In the meantime the fool blunts the effectiveness of the wise (who also can be consumed or affected by foolish talk; →9:16–18).

The subunit closes in 10:15 with the fools growing tired because they get lost as they wander home from work. So, however critical the Sage can be regarding wisdom's profitability, he never befriends folly. A common spiritual interpretation takes the city in 10:15 to be celestial (e.g., Bonaventure 2005: 372–74). Of course the reference can include journeys that are rather more mundane. Yet spiritually loaded vocabulary is present, such as the "grace" of 10:12, and the principle can surely have a more narrow and important application. The fool's incompetence hints not merely at being out of human favor but ultimately at being out of divine favor.

Rulers with consequences. Ecclesiastes 10:16–17 may allude to the reproaches found in Isa. 5:11, 22: Woe to "you who rise early in the morning / in pursuit of strong drink, / who linger in the evening / to be inflamed by wine!" and to "you who are heroes in drinking wine / and valiant at mixing drink!" A young ruler is not necessarily an advantage, for he may not be a crafty outsider—as earlier in Ecclesiastes—but a profligate reveler instead. The NRSV renders the term *na'ar* as "servant," which is possible, yet Solomon is called a "little child" with this word in 1 Kgs. 3:7 (Bartholomew 2009: 325). Either way, there is a proper time for feasting—in preparation for heroism, not excessive partying. But the imperfect verb may depict a frequent (hence inappropriate) practice of feasting.[17] This text does not exclusively depict the spiritual contrast between the city of man and the city of God (Augustine, *City of God* 17.20, in FC 24.76–77). Even so, Jesus Christ embodied the moderate, virtuous feasting that appropriately enjoys God's gifts within the framework of mission—surely emblematic of a noble king.

Practical wisdom, summing up. All things being equal, it is better for rulers to be efficient in getting what they need to feast, as opposed to being lazy (10:18–19). Sloth does not put or keep a roof over one's head (10:18). Food and wine bring laughter and delight; since they have their moments, money has its place in buying them (10:19). But such royal treatment is not an unadulterated good. This ambiguous power of wealth restrains the potential elitism of 10:5–7. Money makes the world go round, but does not automatically lift up particular people

17. Tamez, *When the Horizons Close*, 128.

or the common good. The paradoxes persist in this concluding subunit, as 10:20 is ironic for Ecclesiastes itself! While the book does not simplistically revile the noble (even subtly distinguishing between royalty—most dangerous—and the rich), it obviously harbors and actually expresses subversive thoughts. Undoubtedly the saying "a little birdie told me" could apply with considerable understatement to aspects of the Sage's political ideology.

The rhetorical strategy involves repeated back-and-forth movement that renders problematic any manipulation of the world by means of traditional wisdom: "What is intriguing in this chapter is that abandonment of the biblical doctrine of the two ways always generates another two ways" (Bartholomew 2009: 328)—fraught with idolatrous potential. To put the thesis more cautiously, if the superiority of wisdom over folly becomes disconnected from the basis of righteousness in the fear of God, then the resulting focus on instrumental skill leaves would-be sages mired in aporias, for skills do not guarantee successful outcomes. The only earthly guarantee—that sheer folly somehow undoes itself eventually—threatens to leave these sages paralyzed, since it does not provide enough incentive to escape undecidability. Soon enough 11:1–6 confronts this irony by ruling out excessive caution on the other side of the coin.

Proverbs on Acting without Certain Knowledge (11:1–6)

> The storms of incoherent events tear to pieces my thoughts, the inmost entrails of my soul, until that day when purified and molten by the fire of your love, I flow together to merge into you.[18]

Direct proverbial exhortations continue from 10:20 into Eccl. 11, but the subject matter changes. While wisdom requires circumspect speech, especially pertaining to authorities, it should not create paranoia. Lack of certainty about how to navigate the future is not meant to paralyze. Thus we encounter a series of proverbs on how to act without the firm knowledge that humans desire.

Casting bread upon the waters. Ecclesiastes 11:1 famously exhorts: "Cast thy bread upon the waters: / for thou shalt find it after many days" (KJV). The metaphor is unclear. To put tongue in cheek, what good would waterlogged bread be when found again (Longman 1998: 255)? Focusing on the bread, the image of giving suggests itself. In that case the theme is meeting the needs of the poor, eventually receiving back from the community what one contributes to others. This is thoroughly in line with pervasive biblical teaching. Moreover, such an interpretation is popular in church history and similar to a positive spiritual interpretation of the parable of the dishonest steward: "Make friends for yourselves by means of dishonest wealth so that when it is gone, they may welcome you into the eternal homes" (Luke 16:1–13, esp. 16:9).

18. Augustine, *Confessions* 11.39 (trans. Chadwick), 244.

However, this subject seems to change too abruptly from Eccl. 10:20 to be primary. Alternatively, the image of maritime trade suggests itself when we focus on the waters. In that case the theme is risking the necessary capital for accumulating wealth. One cannot expect to outwit the lack of predictive knowledge by doing nothing unless the risk reduces to zero. Then the outcome would indeed be certain: "Nothing ventured, nothing gained." Confirmation that the metaphor's primary context is maritime trade comes from the more appropriate translation—with all due respect to the KJV's poetic history of effects—"send . . . upon the waters."

Bread is a basic staple of life, and its appearance as the verse's commodity signals just how seriously the Sage takes lack of knowledge about the future. The trader is not playing with house money, but having to jeopardize the very foundations of his livelihood. If the venture fails, he does not eat. For the Sage, Ellul 1990: 190n29 claims, the bread indicates that "the only source of wealth he accepts is agriculture." This may protest too much, yet the sympathy of Ecclesiastes with the peasant farmer is apparent over against royalty (at least) and (possibly) the mercantile class. The gifts of God to enjoy are basic: food, drink, one's spouse, others in the community, and hard work. The process of toil is worth more than the long-term product. To be sure, there are dangers in romanticizing the agricultural life. In the book's earliest contexts, no doubt many farmers were poor enough to be at risk for life and limb, scarcely enjoying God's basic gifts. This remains true today throughout much of the world. Culturally elite admirers of Wendell Berry (→7:10) should exercise caution lest they celebrate a fantasy they have never experienced. Small communities can be spiritually and not just financially impoverished, like anything else. That said, however, they typically are—or at least remained, until their current crises[19]—*communities*. And that is worth a lot, in the Sage's view.

Confirmation comes in 11:2 that the bread-sending metaphor's initial home is in business. The issue of lacking future knowledge becomes explicit. Accordingly one's investment strategy should involve diversification. The x or x + 1 motif is common in wisdom literature, frequently for cataloging sins, though here it just conveys the impression of a sizable number. No doubt, there are tradeoffs: with more investments come more headaches (2:23) and potential claimants on one's money (5:11). As so often in Ecclesiastes, each portrayal of a situation, along with the corresponding advice, is sound—all things being equal. But none of the advice can be taken to isolated extremes.

Sooner or later, one must invest in spite of these risks. This principle may require considerable patience ("after many days") and in context hardly supports the grasping individualism that characterizes contemporary economic life. Both risk (11:1) and risk management (11:2) have communal contexts. In light of such interaction, the basic principle applies beyond business: one does not live forever or possess sufficiently exhaustive knowledge to wait until the coast is clear. What

19. E.g., regarding the American Midwest, see Richard C. Longworth, *Caught in the Middle: America's Heartland in the Age of Globalism* (New York: Bloomsbury, 2008).

God has given to do, we should do now (Jas. 4:17)—even if there is no way of knowing exactly how to predict or control the results (4:13–16), so that only "if the Lord wills, we shall live and also do this or that" (NASB). "Investing" oneself in charity may align more with the spirit of this text than many forms of economic life that harm others in the community (5:1–12).

Clouding the picture. Ecclesiastes 11:3 may be an ironic rejection of techniques such as astrology and divination (Krüger 2004: 193). If so, then we must not quickly dismiss its relevance. Robert W. Jenson's comments are apt:

> We late moderns and postmoderns do not inhabit a secularized world; quite the contrary. The West now lays open before the church's mission in much the same condition as when the missionaries had to cut down its sacred oaks and prove their case by combat with demons. The chief mode of damnation from which the mission has now to rescue our sisters and brothers is superstition, the fear of nameless and named powers that are neither Creator nor creature, that project our wants on infinity without ever quite getting them there, and from which middle position they haunt us dreadfully.[20]

In any case, the juxtaposition of images creates a jarring contrast for wisdom. Full clouds drenching the earth with rain have an aura of inevitability. But one cannot know the precise moment at which this will occur. Meanwhile, trees are heavy enough that they inevitably lie where they fall, yet the side on which they land often seems random. Thus, too much fixation on prediction leads to inaction (11:4). The literary relationship—clouds appear (11:3a, 4b), while the wind blows (11:4a), quite possibly against the trees (11:3b)—shows that order is more apparent in the text than in the creation. Evoking the wind adds further irony, since it is very difficult to observe, reminding us of what we cannot control. We know only its effects, after the fact—it does not offer predictive value for any significant length of time in advance.

Sowing seed, not knowing. Ecclesiastes 11:5 extends this comparison, on analogy with a developing fetus. Again, humans cannot know in advance what they are dealing with. No matter how much is understood scientifically, still there is mystery to the giving of life. Technology may afford relatively reliable capability to discern a child's sex, plus a vast array of exaggerated claims about what we will soon know—or even determine—genetically. But everything important to the Sage remains unpredictable in the womb: namely, a person's character. Remembering the apparent reason why the day of death is better than birth (7:1)—only then is the outcome on this important score finally set.

According to the latter half of the analogy, seeking to know the future pursues the work of God. No particular theory of divine sovereignty is in play. Rather, it is evident *that* God works, but not necessarily *how* or *why*. We usually cannot

20. Robert W. Jenson, "For Us . . . He Was Made Man," in *Nicene Christianity: The Future for a New Ecumenism*, ed. Christopher R. Seitz (Grand Rapids: Brazos, 2001), 85.

specify at what level of detail God determines or intervenes, but only that everything as a whole is subject to divine providence. For the Sage this is enough, in light of human finitude. The history of Christian theology has seen its share of dogmatic debates overreaching themselves, on providence along with many other subjects (→8:13–14, 16–17). However, a wealth of recent scholarship suggests that Christian doctrine at its best offers a distinctive consensus respecting both divine sovereignty and human freedom.[21] In the incarnation of God in Jesus Christ, the fully divine second person of the Trinity, the Son of God, unites himself with the fullness of human nature. Unless God took the initiative, humanity could not be saved. Unless Jesus Christ lived the fullness of human nature faithfully, people would be left untouched by his redeeming work: in the words of the patristic adage, "What is not assumed [taken on] is not healed." This offers not simply an abstract model for preserving the integrity of both divine initiative and human responsibility, but actually the concrete paradigm in which the drama of redemption finds its center. Christ not merely demonstrates but in fact culminates the way God works in history: bringing humanity into fellowship.

Divine providence and human action are therefore noncompetitive according to a Christian point of view. Because God is not just one being among beings, but gives to everything else the gift of being, God's action is not occurring on the same plane as creaturely actions. Hence divine sovereignty and human responsibility are not—as a general rule, anyway—competing causes within a single nexus. They are instead biblical affirmations about what transpires at different levels of causal explanation. They can be true simultaneously, operative in various modes. The Sage's reserve about such realities may in fact leave space for a deeply Christian perspective to unfold later on, in the fullness of time (Gal. 4:4).

In Eccl. 11:6 all of life comes into purview: morning and evening. The overall outcome is surprisingly positive: you do not know which will *prosper* or whether even both will be *good*. At first glance it is tempting to believe that the verse calls for unceasing workaholism. To the contrary, "this or that" makes clear that morning and evening are distinct; interludes for rest are appropriate (Krüger 2004: 195). Besides, the images are open to interpretations beyond a narrow focus on work. There could be a mixture of the biological and the botanical involved with, for example, the sowing of seed.

Psalm 1 applies such images to the outcomes of righteousness and wickedness under divine providence. The righteous "are like trees / planted by streams of water, / which yield their fruit in its season, / and their leaves do not wither. / In all that they do, they prosper" (1:3). Yet, "the wicked are not so, / but are like chaff that the wind drives away" (1:4). The reason is that "the LORD watches over the way of the righteous, / but the way of the wicked will perish" (1:6). The Sage cannot make his confession so clearly as long as he keeps examining the full range of present evidence "under the sun." But nothing in the Sage's perspective

21. See various works by Kathryn Tanner, William Placher, and Colin Gunton, among others.

rejects the ultimate truth of Ps. 1. In the end, the Sage commends the fear of the Lord in light of divine judgment (Eccl. 12). The supplementary canonical point of passages such as Eccl. 11 concerns the proximate situation before the ultimate judgment. No one can gain the sort of wisdom by which to make full sense of how God runs the universe. And no one can gain the sort of wisdom by which to calculate the odds for controlling earthly success. Wisdom lies in respecting our epistemic and spiritual limitations. The fear of God actually lies, therefore, in casting our bread upon the waters with faith about some kind of return after many days, rather than always counting chickens before they hatch. The believer holds that God will reward the righteous and punish the wicked, but exercises faith precisely in accepting uncertainty over the nature, timing, or earthly implications of divine justice.

In an essay entitled "The Politics of Long Joy," Alan Jacobs helpfully spells out a perspective on Christian cultural engagement that is consistent with these verses:

> Perhaps the chief problem with the "culture wars" paradigm that governs so much Christian action and reflection, in the North American context anyway, is that it encourages us to think in terms of trophies rather than testimonies. It tempts us to think too much about whether we're winning or losing, and too little about the only thing we ultimately control, which is the firmness of our own resolve.[22]

Jacobs then quotes 11:6. In this proverbial wisdom the Sage provides much more than business advice. Though this unit follows the stark recognition that money makes the world go round, its larger context involves the Sage's very modest interest in money when compared with the foundational joys that a bit of money is necessary to buy. Hence the Sage offers an expansive paradigm for respecting the status of human activity before God, for reflecting awareness of our finitude within all the hustle and bustle we call culture.

Summing Up: Wisdom for Youth (11:7–12:7)

> The pillars of wisdom are these: humility, powerlessness, poverty, loneliness, sickness, rejection, and abandonment.
>
> Those are sad things.
> Yes, they are.
> It is a hard saying.
> There is a secret joy in it.
> I cannot accept this entirely, Pawel. It is too dark.
> It contains pain, but a passing pain.
> Man was created for joy! . . . He was made to dance!

22. Alan Jacobs, "The Politics of Long Joy," in *Books and Culture*, www.christianitytoday.com/bc/columns/rumorsofglory/070112.html.

> Yes, and to know in his marrow that he is a creature. That he is not God.
> But he rejoices in this knowledge. He dances for love of it.
> Does the dance come before this knowledge?[23]

A number of words (e.g., "good," "many days," "clouds," "rain") connect 11:1–6 to this next section. The imperatives continue, in 11:8 and following. The direct address becomes more specific, though, as youth are referenced in 11:9 and again in 12:1. The material takes on a summative character, not in the narrow sense of woodenly repeating what has already been said but in the broader sense of working toward a final conclusion, presenting a manifesto or mandate for action.

Advice (11:7–10)

The sweetness of seeing the sun. Ecclesiastes 11:7 states the value of life (apart from work!), and 11:8 the value of long life. The motif of the eyes in 11:7 helps to round out the Christian tradition with respect to sight. The *visio Dei*, the vision of God or "beatific vision," is a dominant way in which classic Christians speak of the ultimate end for human life. "Blessed are the pure in heart, for they will see God" (Matt. 5:8). What Moses longed for, all Christians long for; what Moses saw only with a glimpse, from behind, hidden in a cleft of a rock, we hope to behold more fully in the face of Jesus Christ (John 1:18). Even when the fall is finally overcome, no one will be able to see God in ways that eclipse human finitude (1 Tim. 1:16–17). In the words of hymn writer Walter Chalmers Smith:

> Immortal, invisible, God only wise,
> in light inaccessible, hid from our eyes,
> most blessed, most glorious, the Ancient of Days,
> Almighty, victorious, thy great name we praise.

Recognizing the very real ways in which human attachment to creation and culture can turn our eyes away from Jesus, "the pioneer and perfecter of our faith" (Heb. 12:2), Christian tradition tends to be suspicious of earthly sight, associating it with lust (1 John 2:15–17)—asking that God would instead "help us to see 'tis only the splendor of light hideth thee."

Yet Ecclesiastes treats human sight pervasively, many times gratefully. In 11:7 seeing the sun is not a metaphorically minimal affirmation of physical life; there is sweetness involved. "O taste and see that the LORD is good; / happy are those who take refuge in him" (Ps. 34:8). God made us to delight in the gift of creaturely life, with all that puts before our eyes—rightly enjoyed. It is a backhanded reminder to many that modern people have lost meaningful connection with the simplicity of what God has made, if we cannot think of very frequent occasions

23. Dialogue between Pawel Tarnowski and David Schäfer, characters in O'Brien, *Sophia House*, 412.

on which we savor seeing the sun. (Here I must register a complaint about the dehumanizing effects of windowless offices, along with a confession that in an era of electric light none of us really have a concept of how important the sun was in prior generations.)

The reality of dark days. Ecclesiastes 11:8 tempers the affirmation of life's value with a note of realism. The initial exhortation maintains the view that life is precious, for humans ought to rejoice in all the years we are given. Nevertheless, we must remain cognizant that many dark days come along the way. The Sage's exhortations to joy are apparently not inconsistent with acknowledgments of *hebel*—both appear here, together. Indeed, *hebel* in this case shades toward absurdity or apparent paradox, functioning as a middle term between the propriety of rejoicing in all of life and the reality of many dark days. It is difficult to know precisely what is meant by the reference to dark days: there could be the problem of old age and the opportunity to muse on the past or focus on dying; yet there could also be an exhortation to remember that one will die and to live well in light of that. Given the poetic element, reducing these interpretative possibilities down to one may demand too much specificity from a metaphor. Regardless, the Sage announces in 11:8 the themes of his concluding remarks: "rejoice" (11:9–10) and "remember" (12:1–7). Previously the *carpe diem* theme tended to follow *hebel* observations, creating apparent tension using positive affirmations; now it frames the observation of dark days, pointing via memory toward a measure of resolution. Now it remains good to see the sun; in a minor key the dark days merely round out the truth so that we will take God seriously.

The inclination to rejoice. In apparent conflict with the rejoicing of 11:9, other biblical literature (e.g., Num. 15:39, noted in →Eccl. 2:10–11) warns against following one's heart and eyes. Thus, as we might expect, this positive exhortation creates considerable discomfort in the Jewish and Christian traditions. But, in light of the near context and its place within the book, the passage must underscore the possibility of following one's heart and eyes without committing spiritual adultery. Obviously caution is called for; the end of the verse recognizes this with its reminder of divine judgment. The Sage realizes what he is saying and puts the necessary guardrail in place.

Though such assessments are not the focus of the present commentary, we may reject the temptation to see the end of 11:9 as a later interpolation, correcting excessive earlier zeal for youth. Commentators sometimes manifest a decided lack of literary or theological imagination. Have we not, by now, found numerous occasions on which the Sage indisputably labors to state both or all possible sides on a matter? Is biblical theology so inflexible that it cannot handle the need for nuances or checks and balances to ward off extremes? A richly textured, carefully crafted theology of Ecclesiastes is much more probable than a worried editor making minor corrections via late additions, when major subtraction would be necessary to assuage the worries! To be sure, some of critical scholarship's blunt trauma follows the classic tradition's occasional panic at the texts' earthiness. Respect for the tradition entails teachable dialogue, not slavish imitation; at times, with respect to wisdom's bold celebration of creaturely life, so-called precritical exegesis unfortunately could not believe what it was seeing in the text. But the modern reactions regarding supposedly incompatible perspectives are overreactions, lacking the doctrinal nuance to embrace—or even allow for—the tensions inherent in classic faith. Probably many scholars—though beyond this generalization we should not stray—fail to allow the Sage to nuance his quest back and forth because they are unfamiliar with forms of faith that can make room for troubling observations and questions. They may also find it hard to believe that affirmations of creation's goodness cohere with its merely penultimate value.

To a degree, God's judgment lies in people dying. Our lives being temporary, losing further opportunity for joy—and facing that loss—is judgment already. The pattern in these verses goes back and forth: first, a call to joy; then, a call to sobriety. Hence 11:9 closes by acknowledging that somehow divine judgment will address human lives at the end. The Sage cannot see the afterlife, but he can see the need for it. Since earthly joys are gifts of God throughout Ecclesiastes, the Sage may imply that failure to enjoy while alive entails divine judgment as well. Certainly that is true if we follow mistaken inclinations and seek satisfaction in the wrong way. The call to sobriety at the end of 11:9 is not a sour note, for 11:10 quickly underscores that we cannot enjoy life if we sit around vexed about what we cannot control or understand. The youth who follows this instruction will not brood excessively in the heart (where the Sage has done so much of his own speaking in this book, especially early on). So also this youth will put away evil, *ra'*, from the flesh. Nuancing how to enjoy life, this may address pain, not sin, in the first instance. Nevertheless, given the end of 11:9 and the word's frequent meaning elsewhere, sin is also precluded.

Hebel frequently concerns transience, of which 11:10 provides yet another example. The fleetingness of youthful vitality (however we translate the disputed noun at the end of the verse) prompts these exhortations. They do not deny *hebel* but prevent magnifying it to an extent that precludes joy. The Sage begins to sum up by strategizing about how to manage life in a context of vanity. This four-verse context illustrates the impossibility of full management, though, by revealing the impossibility of an exact definition. In 11:8 *hebel* has an aura of absurdity; in 11:10 it focuses on impermanence. What seems problematic about creaturely finitude can subtly shift depending on the context. Better than thinking too long and hard, therefore, is rejoicing and remembering.

Aging and Apocalypse (12:1–7)

Remembering your Creator. Though creation themes are prominent throughout, 12:1 provides the book's only explicit reference to God as Creator apart from the beginning and ending frames. "Creator" (*bārā'*) sounds quite like a word for "grave," and possibly the audience would expect a term connected to death anyway—the *memento mori* theme once again. To remember one's Creator is, in part, to live with the right consciousness of death—and accordingly the preciousness of life (11:8). Remembrance is not mere calling back to mind, but active contemplation by which the object shapes the subject. The appeal to youth addresses not just a particular age group; all of us face possibilities for resetting the course of our lives. Søren Kierkegaard latches onto the spirit of the text when he appeals to Jesus's saying: "Truly I tell you, unless you change and become like children, you will never enter the kingdom of heaven. Whoever becomes humble like this child is the greatest in the kingdom of heaven" (Matt. 18:3–4).[24] Consistent with the Sage's warning against nostalgia, we should not dwell on past failures in light of our impending demise, as if there were no opportunity for change. To the contrary, awareness of death's inevitability and constant possibility impel change now. The childlike, humble trust to which Jesus calls everyone positively corresponds to the youthful awareness of finitude enjoined in Ecclesiastes.

Ellul offers two other poignant comments. First, "Every time you take yourself to be a creator (even as an artist!), you become a destroyer, an annihilator" (1990: 181). Celebration of artistic creativity, as an integral component of humans imaging God, can go to extremes, obscuring the dissimilarity: God the Creator speaks nothing into existence (so to speak), whereas human makers rearrange preexisting materials. This is true even for ideas; after all, there is nothing new under the sun! Once we ignore that humans "create" by rearranging, we more easily deny the materials their proper integrity and simply use them for our own ends, more readily justifying whatever means deemed necessary. Soon, for instance, we change meat from a divine gift into a necessary delight, growing animals in factorylike ways so as to "create" the most efficient economy possible. Second, though, "It is false to say we turn toward our Creator when we take no more pleasure in life. We no longer make reference to God—only to our fear of suffering and death, so that God becomes opium or compensation, like an artificial limb" (Ellul 1990: 282). Remembering the Creator is therefore a principle of moderation, as in 11:9: there, rejection of human arrogance and self-seeking; here, acceptance of God's material gifts. Not just any mean between two extremes will do; the appropriate focus of youthful delight should be the tangible gifts repeatedly referenced in Ecclesiastes as coming more directly from God—food, drink, other people, meaningful work, and by implication the natural world.

Realizing what's coming. This theme of youthful remembrance unfolds via an extraordinary allegory of the end of . . . something, structured by "before" in 12:1, 2, 6. The initial "before" in 12:1 summarily personalizes the evil days of advanced years described in 12:2–5, before 12:6–7 chronicles death. Among the

24. Søren Kierkegaard, "Remember Now Thy Creator in the Days of Thy Youth," trans. David F. Swenson and Lillian Marvin Swenson, in *Edifying Discourses* (Minneapolis: Augsburg, 1945), 3.80.

possible levels of meaning are (1) relatively literally, a description of a funeral or else the onset of a powerful storm; (2) more metaphorically, a representation of the human body and its decline; and (3) still more allegorically, a depiction of the dramatic end of a community.

Ecclesiastes 12:2 has prophetic gloom: the sun and the moon and the stars are darkened often in apocalyptic imagery (e.g., Ezek. 32:7; Joel 2:31). Furthermore, clouds return after rain—the focus is unrelentingly dark. "After a rain a clear sky usually follows. Therefore, when the twirling of the clouds comes after a rain, it is a sign that there is not to be a return of rejoicing and joy" (Bonaventure 2005: 401). In Jer. 13:16 a looming cosmic catastrophe likewise offers incentive to turn away from haughtiness and back to God. Of course, the near referent of terms such as the "sun," in Ecclesiastes, has to do with death depriving a person of the light of life. But the very order of creation (so prominent in Eccl. 1) is threatened here.

Ecclesiastes 12:3 has groupings: the first two male, the second two female; the first and third lower-class servants, the second and fourth upper-class. If the focus is social, then 12:3 is representatively comprehensive for a community. If the focus is physical, then obvious candidates suggest themselves: loss of eyesight and teeth is in view at the end, weakness of limbs at the beginning. It seems more difficult to construe 12:3 in terms of a funeral or storm at the straightforward level. The mention of grinders being few readily depicts teeth falling out, but could seem incidental or even strange in other scenarios.

Ecclesiastes 12:4 also deals with bodily orifices, ears in particular. Ironically, an aging person can both struggle to hear (when the sound of grinding is low) and hear too well (suffering restlessness due to sounds as tiny as those of a bird). A social/apocalyptic understanding is possible too, for people seem to be "closing up shop" due to nervousness, hiding quietly at home rather than boisterously enjoying music in the public square. Both hearing and voice (the female singers) are affected; terror may even be silencing lament. In theory this could address either a cosmic event or a more mundane one such as the aforementioned funeral or storm.

Ecclesiastes 12:5 moves back outside the house. There is fear of heights and of travel. There is limited movement (the grasshopper drags along). There is loss of sexual appetite. The NRSV euphemistically translates "desire fails," obscuring reference to the caperberry, an aphrodisiac. Humans go to their eternal home—a euphemism that goes unexplained—while mourners go about the streets. There may be associations with white hair, depending on how one takes the verb related to almonds. It is hard to read 12:5 only apocalyptically, despite the grasshopper (or locust) often serving as an apocalyptic sign. Mourners suggest that not all humanity meets its demise at once. Ellul 1990: 286 fastens onto the almond tree as a sign of hope. It blossoms in spring (with birds singing in 12:4), symbolizing hopeful activity. Moreover, "almond tree" (*šāqēd*) and "watchman" (*šōqēd*) are quite close, appearing elsewhere in a play on words: "The word of the Lord came to me, saying, 'Jeremiah, what do you see?' And I said, 'I see a branch of an *almond tree*.' Then the Lord said to me, 'You have seen well, for I am *watching over* my word to perform it'" (Jer. 1:11–12). Even amid signs of decline, one cannot avoid signs of hope; put another way, the death of a particular person is a "limited catastrophe"—tragic, but not the end of the world for everyone (Krüger 2004: 203).

Ecclesiastes 12:6 describes death itself, with valuable objects destroyed or rendered useless. The "silver cord" and "golden bowl" may pertain to a candle or lamp. The "pitcher" and "wheel" may involve a cistern: a jar and the pulley that lifts the jar out of the well. Death is the cessation, in that case, of light and water.

Returning to earth. Thus begins the poem's climax, having moved away from describing old age as such in 12:1–5. Death is complete in 12:7, which makes another—very clear—allusion to Genesis (2:7 and 3:19). Augustine's musings turn to the unity of the human race, somehow implied here (Letter 143, in FC 20.156). The unity does not lie in "spirit" treated as a common originating substance. Yet each human *does* share a common origin and, to some degree, end. We return for judgment to the God who made us. The Sage builds on the Genesis narrative, assuming a unified humanity facing death and God.

The "spirit" need not technically designate part of a human being, certainly not just a religious domain. Animals share it; God gathers the spirits of both animals and humans in Ps. 104:29 and Job 34:14. Human uniqueness does not necessarily lie in "spirit," but in the cultural history that grows up around our efforts to take pleasure in the days God gives (Eccl. 12:1–6). Nevertheless, wrongful spirit-matter dualism cast aside, the Bible tends to speak of the human in twofold terms: that which is physical (dust) needs the animating breath of God. Moreover, human identity transcends the temporary survival of its present physical substrate—the spirit returns to God who gave it, whereas the dust returns *as it was*. Humans have transformed in history what God made, which must have some kind of eternal significance. The Sage cannot say much more than that—and, on purely empirical grounds, neither can we. Yet there is a hint in 12:7, picking up from the judgment in 11:9, of something after life "under the sun."

These lines reverberate through the ending of a later classic, *Pilgrim's Progress* (Christianson 2007: 229). Another famous literary allusion stems from Henry James's *The Golden Bowl*.[25] Anyone who actually plods through the entire novel, worthy as it is, may be guilty of the excessive righteousness condemned in Eccl. 7. Such a reader notices general themes relevant to Ecclesiastes—duties to family and community, complexities of upper-class social situations, destruction of naïveté (which can be almost willful), the need for risky wisdom—whether or not these influenced the novelist: "In James' novel, the golden bowl is an emblem of our hope for a *perfect* union of human consciousnesses in love. And yet, the bowl has a crack in it, for the perfect union is impossible in a flawed world."[26] At first

25. Henry James, *The Golden Bowl* (New York: Penguin, 1987).

26. Bryan Berry, "Henry James and the Heavenly Light," *First Things* 167 (November 2006): 35 (emphasis original).

glance James's image—whatever we think of the novel's ending or the author's larger devotion to human consciousness as an end in itself—seems like it does not connect much with Eccl. 12. But the texts' thematic interface between personal tragedy and social complexity resonates at a deeper level, if we open ourselves to multiple, complementary reading perspectives.

Of the levels of interpretation discussed above, the only one that seems unworkable is the so-called literal one taken by itself, for such a literal approach does not work as a plain sense of "the way the words go"! A metaphorical or internally allegorical approach with respect to the human body seems necessary, at minimum. In certain cases the most natural reader response is to allegorize a detail, such as the grinders becoming few, with respect to the aging process. Audiences will not agree on every detail according to that type of approach, but most readers readily agree on some, providing a baseline. Apocalyptic imagery regarding potentially cosmic catastrophes suggests itself in some cases, though not as readily in others. Jerome blended the old-age approach with allegory regarding destruction of the temple. This he did by taking Jewish interpretation quite seriously, motivated by the classical pagan tradition.[27] One can appreciate that the destruction of the temple would apocalyptically threaten communal foundations, as a funeral might do for a particular household. Other Christian readings, meanwhile, "tend to conflate the allegory of an individual old man with that of the decline of the Church (and with it individual piety) and the end of the world" (Christianson 2007: 228).

The brevity of a human life is set within a larger context—not just creation standing before its Creator (albeit that too, very prominently), but also intermediary communal networks. We live with households, economies, streets, and roads. We acquire complex moral duties, while receiving pleasurable opportunities, within these contexts. In this way Henry James's novel is not wrong to borrow its title from Ecclesiastes after all: "Maggie gives others full play until the moral implications of their deeds reveal themselves fully—as God does with us."[28]

Cosmic and communal circumstances need terrify us no more than our own death—which, notwithstanding its tragic elements, remains but a limited catastrophe. Life goes on, whether in God's future giving or the mourners we leave behind or even the natural rhythms of the created order functioning without us. Earthly life has God-given value—witness the objects of 12:6 with which it compares—but remains temporary. If that is all there is, then 12:8 provides a necessary conclusion: all is *hebel*. Yet *hebel* is only a preliminary or partial conclusion, for 12:9–14 is a fitting epilogue, matching the rest of scripture's testimony concerning resurrection from the dead.

27. See Matthew Kraus, "Christians, Jews, and Pagans in Dialogue: Jerome on Ecclesiastes 12:1–7," *Hebrew Union College Annual* 70–71 (1999–2000): 183–231, which has helpful historical charts.

28. Berry, "Henry James and the Heavenly Light," 37.

CONCLUSION

THE END OF THE MATTER

Ecclesiastes 12:8–14

> But I've developed a great reputation for wisdom by ordering more books than I ever had time to read, and reading more books, by far, than I learned anything useful from, except, of course, that some very tedious gentlemen have written books. This is not a new insight, but the truth of it is something you have to experience to fully grasp. . . .
>
> I know this is all mere apparition compared to what awaits us, but it is only lovelier for that. There is a human beauty in it. And I can't believe that, when we have all been changed and put on incorruptibility, we will forget our fantastic condition of mortality and impermanence, the great bright dream of procreating and perishing that meant the whole world to us. In eternity this world will be Troy, I believe, and all that has passed here will be the epic of the universe, the ballad they sing in the streets. Because I don't imagine any reality putting this one in the shade entirely, and I think piety forbids me to try.[1]

Quoting the book's dominant motif, "vanity of vanities," 12:8 transitions to the conclusion—whether from the Sage or an editor. The third-person reference in "says the Teacher" continues in the third-person discourse of the following verses. Combined with the expectation of a further ending after 12:7, without which the book would feel unfinished, this introduces the authorial ambiguity. Ambiguity also arises concerning how to take "Qoheleth" (→1:1). The definite article points

1. Ames, the narrator in Robinson, *Gilead*, 39, 57.

to a function rather than a proper noun. The nature of that function becomes clearer in succeeding verses, whereas the word's translation—given today's various, often professionalized notions of preaching and teaching—remains perilous. The rationale behind the rendering "Sage" concerns Qoheleth's character, which becomes an explicit focus in 12:9–12.

Transition to summary. The summary nature of 12:8 is evident due to the inclusio created vis-à-vis 1:2; like two pieces of bread, these *hebel* slogans sandwich all that lies in between. Yet this literary principle can be taken too far, as if *hebel* were the book's comprehensive and only conclusion. Summary begins as early as 11:7. Moreover, the *hebel* slogans are sufficiently terse that they announce the theme of a quest more than its conclusion—about which one must say more. It is better, therefore, to see *hebel* as the dominant contextual factor around which the Sage's material orbits. His message is broader than this particular motif—containing not only observation and reflection about *hebel*, but also advice on how (and how much) to address it. Accordingly, the exhortations to *carpe diem* and to remember one's Creator in the preceding section are vital to the book's message. Furthermore, the summary exhortation in 12:13 regarding the fear of God is not an orthodox appendix desperately trying to domesticate an unruly Sage. Instead, it recapitulates—in traditional language, to be sure—a significant component of what the Sage communicates. But this is jumping ahead.

Summary of the Sage. Ecclesiastes 12:9 clearly shifts into commentary on the book's main text. In keeping with biblical wisdom, the first assessment must concern the character of the author himself. Qoheleth was truly wise. Against the view that this is entirely a professional designation and not at all moral, we have plenty of functional description to follow. Something must distinguish this comment from mere overlap with teaching knowledge and collecting proverbs. Ethics is the obvious concern of 12:11–12, so it is hard to believe that the moral realm escapes the editor's first concern in 12:9. Affirmation of Qoheleth's wise character is all the more significant in view of the book's preoccupation with its author's life experience and interior gaze. If, as argued earlier, Ecclesiastes is ambivalent at best and unfavorable at worst regarding Solomon (even his wisdom; esp. 7:23–29), then here is another hint of distance between the author himself and the recurring Solomonic persona. The royal element of 1:12–2:26 has disappeared. Hence the Sage adopts the literary persona of a morally ambiguous figure, the flawed human paragon of wisdom, but the summary judgment on Qoheleth's own character is positive.

This sage taught knowledge, largely by means of proverbs. These he carefully studied and arranged. The latter activity, in particular, precludes Ecclesiastes containing sheer randomness. Modern expectations regarding structure go unfulfilled, but arrangement is present. Reference to "proverbs" is a general literary claim, rather than ostensive reference to the canonical book of Proverbs. The overlap with Proverbs in Eccl. 12:13–14 should not be overstated: "fear *ʾĕlōhîm*," not "fear YHWH." Nevertheless, the similarities are notable between the beginning of wisdom in Proverbs and the concluding evaluation of Ecclesiastes. The two books largely share common judgments about how to flourish in the divinely created cosmos, although they do not express this agreement via entirely overlapping themes.

Proverbs presents God's wisdom primarily through clever summaries of parental teaching, focusing on the usual blessings of righteousness while tacitly acknowledging the apparent successes and actual temptations of wickedness. Ecclesiastes explores the inner life of one who gained Wisdom but left her behind, having encountered such temptations while enjoying such successes. As Solomon retained skillful elements of wisdom, so too the book has proverbs and esthetics all its own, with its cleverness rendering complex and even problematic the standard sapiential formulas. The moral of the story is that wisdom offers no guarantee of either lasting earthly success or even fear of the Lord. Because in this life no joy is more than fleeting and no knowledge has more than contingent application, true wisdom transcends enlightened earthly self-interest. Ecclesiastes ensures that "all has been heard" in order for young people to embrace its truth realistically; Proverbs, while making few if any absolute promises, emphasizes the consequences of choosing foolish alternatives. Ecclesiastes concedes that wisdom, despite limitations, generally provides protection from self-imposed tragedy; Proverbs concedes, by the strenuousness with which it deconstructs alternatives, that tragedy can befall the wise—and the tragedy of temporary success for the wicked has befallen the cosmos.

In short, we need these two books near each other for the sake of rhetorical checks and balances. The truth, goodness, and beauty of Wisdom's appeal would not shine through if Proverbs did not make its case vigorously. The youthful skeptic would not embrace Wisdom if Ecclesiastes did not prosecute the case against her to the full before mounting the defense. One could perhaps communicate similar judgments prosaically in one book, but the message comes across more powerfully in two books that dialectically push their points to the limit. So, while its epilogue reiterates that Ecclesiastes can be friendly to its canonical neighbor, two distinctive voices can be heard at the backyard fence.

Evaluation of the Sage's book. Ecclesiastes 12:10 expands on the Sage's aim and accomplishment: *dibrê-ḥēpeṣ* ("pleasing words") and *dibrê 'ĕmet* ("words of truth") are parallel. The NRSV implies that the focus of the Sage concerns delight, whereas the focus of the editorial assessment concerns truth. However, the syntax is very difficult, and other possibilities allow that there might be no such distinction. Another tricky issue involves the phrase "sought to," because elsewhere in Ecclesiastes "seek" does not result in finding what one hopes (e.g., 7:24–29; 8:17). Does this imply that the editor is lukewarm (at best) about Qoheleth's achievement, subtly undermining it?

Against such cynicism is the passage's structure, in which 12:9 and 12:12 begin with *wĕyōtēr* ("furthermore") and then 12:13 with *sôp* ("finally"). Such particles suggest continuity with what the Sage has said. Moreover, the adverb *yōšer* ("plainly") likely has a moral component. Given the thrust of its usage, it denotes more than simply honest or plain speaking. The epilogue is acknowledging the uprightness of the Sage's writing.

Summary of wisdom's shepherding function. Within this concluding frame all of Old Testament scripture is covered—wisdom (e.g., 12:11), Torah (12:13), and prophets (12:14). After 12:9–10 deals with aspects of the Sage's approach, 12:11 shifts to the effects of his work. The structure is chiastic: "goads" and "nails" on the inside, "sayings" (*dibrê*) and "sayings" (*baʿălê ʾăsuppôt*) on the outside. The latter two need not be closely synonymous as the NRSV implies; to the contrary, there is evidence for a translation such as "masters of collections" at the end (Longman 1998: 276n67). If this is correct, then the plurality indicates consciousness of other wisdom books—even collectors and collections of them—likely including Proverbs.[2]

The goads instigate movement while the nails provide stability. The words of Kafka point to the profitable function of the pain at stake from prodding: "I think we ought to read only the kind of books *that wound and stab us*. . . . We need the books that affect us like a disaster, that grieve us deeply, like the death of someone we loved more than ourselves, like being banished into forests far from everyone, like a suicide. *A book must be the axe for the frozen sea inside us*."[3]

The multiple sayings stand in juxtaposition with the "one shepherd" by whom they are given. Commentators whose take on the book tends toward pessimism are not inclined to identify God as the shepherd, worrying that this simplistically forces all the material to be orthodox. Yet God is the most natural referent connected to giving, especially given the preponderance of this theme in Ecclesiastes. And *ʾeḥād* ("one") is not merely an indefinite form, but instead points toward a specific shepherd. The unity of wisdom sayings, as of all scripture, derives ultimately from their divine origin. That biblical identification of God as a shepherd appears in Ps. 23 but not in other wisdom texts and that Ecclesiastes nowhere else trumpets the oneness of God hardly mitigates the likelihood of the divine referent for canonically shaped audiences. A human shepherd eventually points toward the divine prototype in any case.

The reverse can also be true: the divine shepherd is a prototype for the human shepherd. Thus classic commentators long applied this text to the task of preaching. The preacher must confront sin; since biblical words are like "goads" and their collected sayings like "nails," they sting while being fundamentally beneficial. Though the words may not always appear coherent to just anyone, to those with ears to hear they are perfectly unified due to God's shepherding (e.g., Origen, *Commentary on Matthew* 2, in ANF 9.413; *Commentary on Matthew* 14.4, in ANF 9.496). This makes space—let it be noted—for not domesticating everything in a book like Ecclesiastes under a prematurely orthodox rubric. The divine coherence may reside in the spiritual depths rather than at the literary surface.

2. Gerald T. Sheppard, "The Epilogue to Qoheleth as Theological Commentary," *Catholic Biblical Quarterly* 39 (1977): 188.

3. E. G. Singgih, "An Axe for the Frozen Sea: The Emerging Task of Theological Education and the Role of the Librarians," *Asia Journal of Theology* 12 (1998): 202–3. Emphasis added.

Additionally education and agricultural activity, which have frequent metaphorical overlap, are connected. As classicist and farmer David Grene attests: "My joy in books and the way I learned were enhanced by the work of the farm and vice versa. I have found that confirmed and strengthened in the years since. It is perhaps not very good for one to spend one's time working incessantly physically, but it emphatically is most risky for someone to live off thoughts, expressing them and writing them down, with no ballast in manual work."[4] Some of the early Solomonic troubles may have stemmed from too much pleasure mixed with internal dialogue. In Eccl. 12, the Sage operates as a shepherd. Not everything taught or preached produces visible results at once; instead, some plant seed, others water it, and God must give the increase (1 Cor. 3:1–15). Closer to the present metaphors of goads and nails, the preacher provides hooks on which to hang thoughts for the longer term, yet also engages in a more immediate steering operation, providing guidance and provoking the flock to move away from danger. Preaching is long-term work, as we should expect if the goal is cultivating wisdom. The paradox is that simultaneously preaching requires focus on the here and now, on what a congregation needs—or must avoid—in the present moment. One should not design a preaching program as if people will memorize most of what one says, storing it away systematically for a rainy day. Regarding the small percentage of words people remember, the content varies considerably from person to person based on what strikes them at the moment, both focally and tacitly. The Sage preacher seeks pleasant arrangements to augment memory's capacities, but cannot predict or control what will take root. Pearls one may polish, withholding them from obvious swine (Matt. 7:1–6), but some seed still falls on rocky soil (13:1–23). Or, in other words, shepherds lead sheep.

Worrying about the present state of preaching, which so frequently involves "a Power Point outline of seven Christian principles for living," David Heim comments: "Christianity cannot be reduced to bullet point principles, but it does contain a tradition of wisdom, and people are hungering for wisdom about how to live. Megachurch preachers are often exceptionally skilled at presenting a version of the Christian wisdom tradition regarding family, friends, marriage, work and money."[5] The contemporary challenge is not to eschew wisdomlike communication in favor of solely reciting biblical narrative or doctrinal propositions or poignant illustrations, but to include wisdom texts from scripture while setting them within their implicit redemptive-historical contexts. Ecclesiastes 12 provides an example, tethering its very this-worldly orientation to the fear of the Lord and thus to reflection on ultimate ends. Contemporary wisdom, by contrast, usually deals with death by telling us how to avoid it.

4. David Grene, *Of Farming and Classics: A Memoir* (Chicago: University of Chicago Press, 2007), 11.

5. David Heim, "Hunger for Wisdom," *Theolog*, www.theolog.org/blog/2007/08.

So many books. Ecclesiastes 12:12 adds self-critical irony regarding the book itself. It is disputable whether to translate "furthermore, of these," or "of anything beyond these" (as in NRSV): the former would include Ecclesiastes itself among the sayings of which to be wary, noting potential dangers after acknowledging their wisdom. Even if the latter is correct and 12:12a speaks only of texts beyond the purview of such wisdom—hence other than Ecclesiastes—12:12b still offers a note of caution about study. Preferring the latter interpretation is the slight parallel to the end of Deuteronomy, forbidding addition or subtraction (Bartholomew 2009: 369).

Whether or not Solomon himself is at stake, subtle irony is involved. Lest we think the editorial comment jabs only at the Sage and not the text or its editor(s), the book's re-presentation rather than destruction joins the frame narrative supportively to the rest. There is indirectness between some of the Sage's words taken in isolation and divine teaching in the canon as a whole. Little third-person asides occasionally put verbal tongue in cheek. Yet it is implausible that a panicky editor expected to subvert an unorthodox book or transform it into a safe one, solely using a short epilogue. It is much more likely that the canonical editor(s) believed Ecclesiastes to be worthy of wisdom, rightly read. It is hard to see how a few concluding verses could adequately rewrite the audience's experience of the Sage's thought after the fact.

Recognizing this, we realize that Ecclesiastes presents canonical shaping, explicitly signaled. In addition to elements already highlighted, "my child" is familiar from Proverbs. Hence, though royalty is not explicit at the surface, the Sage is positioned as an instructor of the people, a shepherding figure who thereby fulfills an aspect of a true king's responsibilities. When details present interpretative conundrums, as in 12:10–12, this canonical intentionality supports discernment of the overall theological message, even if confidence on some particulars remains elusive. For instance, one might take 12:11 to be appreciative and 12:12 cautious, as here; but others take 12:11 to emphasize wisdom's sting and 12:12 to include Ecclesiastes itself in its warnings; whereas still others take 12:10–12 positively except for a minor caution at the end. Regardless, from a canonical perspective Ecclesiastes *can* be read within wisdom's basic frame promoting fear of the Lord, while always evoking at least some tension with more settled readings of the core tradition. This back-and-forth reality of pressure and counterpressure keeps any one interpretative dilemma from leading us off the rails.

Along with the spiritual dangers, most readers of the present commentary empathize with the physical weariness involved in much study—although we have it quite good compared to actual shepherds or others who do manual labor for a living! Additionally, readers can worry over the endless proliferation of books. It is a weighty feeling to face far more written on Ecclesiastes than a person can usefully assimilate without neglecting the original text. Origen's comment is droll yet apposite:

> I, for my part, am inclined to shrink from toil and to avoid that danger which threatens from God those who give themselves to writing on divinity; thus I would take shelter in scripture in refraining from making many books. For Solomon says in Ecclesiastes, "My son, beware of making many books; there is no end of it, and much study is a weariness of the flesh." For we, except that text have some hidden meaning which we do not yet perceive, have directly transgressed the injunction; we have not guarded ourselves against making many books. (*Commentary on the Gospel of John* 5.preface, in ANF 9.346)

Later on, Origen writes:

> We started from the words of the preacher, where he says: "My son, beware of making many books." With this I compare a saying from the Proverbs of the same Solomon, "In the multitude of words thou shalt not escape sin; but in sparing thy lips thou shalt be wise." Here I ask whether speaking many words of whatever kind is a multitude of words (in the sense of the preacher), even if the many words a man speaks are sacred and connected with salvation. If this be the case, and if he who makes use of many salutary words is guilty of "multitude of words," then Solomon himself did not escape this sin. (*Commentary on the Gospel of John* 5.4, in ANF 9.347)

Evidently the Alexandrian school did not have "publish or perish" as its operative principle for gaining tenure.[6]

Ellul 1990: 144 explores the author's side of the equation:

> We must remember, as we examine this indictment, that the individual being of the wise person is not forgotten, but rather everything he was able to contribute. Remembering this is essential in our world, in which great works, creations, and thoughts are numberless yet disappear into total oblivion. Do not make the objection that books survive, such as Qohelet's! His book is drowned, disappearing in a cataclysm of hundreds of thousands of books. Each is hailed as a work of genius, as the key for understanding our world, only to be forgotten within ten years. Before long, we will have a civilization based on images, so that even books will disappear, crowded out by immediately visible replacements. At that point, since the images on television or even in films are designed to be consumed rapidly and then to disappear (in spite of the video recorder), no kind of recourse or return to the sources of wisdom will be left. In any case, wisdom matures slowly—how could anyone transmit it by television?

This vision, albeit too dark, alerts us that, however quixotic words and books might be, culture is even more dangerous without them.

6. This is tremendously ironic, given how prolific Origen was as a writer, for which Jerome calls him *adamontios* ("man of brass") (Letter 33, in NPNF[2] 6.46). Further revealing the extent of Origen's reputation are Jerome's disputing the claim that he produced six thousand volumes (Letter 82, in NPNF[2] 6.173) and Melania's supposedly reading his three million lines (Palladius, *Lausiac History* 55.3, in Ancient Christian Writers 34.136). Thanks to Michael Graves for these references.

The end of the matter: human duty. Ecclesiastes 12:13 empathically delivers the summary of summaries; with "the end of the matter" we reach the end of "words" (*dibrê*). This weary activity may take a break. "All has been heard": part of the canonical purpose of Ecclesiastes, surely, is to provide a fair hearing for even the most dissonant voices. The Bible does not call for fearing God while hiding the disputable or contrary evidence. Yet, in the end, to fear God and therefore keep the commandments is "the whole duty of everyone" (parallel uses of *kol-hā'ādām* occur in 3:13; 5:19; 7:2).

Ellul 1990: 294 quotes Lacan: "This famous fear of God accomplishes a sleight-of-hand feat, transforming all fears into perfect courage, in an instant. All fears—'I have no other fear'—are exchanged for what is called the fear of God. However constraining it may be, it is the opposite of fear"! What is the worst that can happen? To fall into the hands of the living God, who definitively reveals himself in Jesus Christ to be "merciful and gracious, / slow to anger, / and abounding in steadfast love and faithfulness" (Exod. 34:6).

Many commentators assume that the Sage's deity is whimsical or despotic. Instead, our preferred deity is tame, leaving us to ourselves. But that is tempting only because much of the time we (think we) have heaven on earth. For many sectors of society or parts of the world who live on the margins, everything we fear is their present reality; God is their only recourse. All the *hebel* heard in Ecclesiastes, given its many echoes of Gen. 1–3, reverberates with the cries of Abel's blood. Everyone is subject to such *hebel* whether or not they realize where their only true hope lies.

The end of the matter: divine judgment. The final verse locates our only hope for justice in future divine judgment. Earlier texts aside, this judgment is eschatological, given the reference to what is "secret." Such language reappears in New Testament texts that presume universal judgment since all humans are God's creatures. The character of the judgment may vary for those who fear God in Christ and for those who do not, but its fact remains for everyone.

On this basis Athanasius argues that Christ the divine Word cannot be (only) a creature, for then he would be subject to judgment (*Four Discourses against the Arians* 2.14.6, in NPNF[2] 4.351). Indeed, as our human representative he has undergone judgment already. Because the Creator Logos undertook this redemptive position on our behalf, it is possible to read of judgment with fear operating as a kind of faith instead of driving us away from God in terror. Since the works addressed by judgment include everything inward—every apparent secret—I do not know how a person could face the Lord through any other way than Christ.

As we have just seen, the epilogue of Ecclesiastes acknowledges both the potential dangers of bookish wisdom and the devotional value of the Sage's teaching. Neither wholly positive nor wholly negative readings of the book will therefore suffice. On the one hand, the Sage is not simply a preacher of joy. At too many places, he reports potentially unorthodox perspectives that he once considered or still wonders about. While the ultimate tone is not despairing, considerable frustration is apparent along the way. On the other hand, the Sage's perspective is not simply secular, for at least two reasons.

First, the divine judgment acknowledged here is sought after and sometimes affirmed by the Sage himself. The epilogue plausibly claims that the Sage was wise, that his words were delightful and true, that they goad people toward divine obedience, and so forth, because they wrestle so often with our mortality in the face of God. It is good for us to learn our limitations and to develop noncalculating fear of God as a result. Divine sovereignty and future judgment should not foster the pursuit of wisdom as predictive control; to the contrary, they authorize placing ourselves in the hands of God and nothing else.

Second, the very term "secular" can be misleading, whether used by biblical critics who deny Qoheleth's orthodoxy or by popular conservatives who denigrate most of the book as a divine deconstruction of unbelief. Underneath such a dismissal of the Sage's reflections is unhealthy dualism. As Eric Gregory notes, Augustinianism contrasts "secular" with "eternal," not "sacred."[7] This is consistent with the emphasis in Ecclesiastes on transience. The *saeculum* is not free of God's sovereignty, but rather its natural and cultural orders remain the objects of divine giving even if they presently reflect the curse of human opposition to the Creator. There is no purely natural realm, and Ecclesiastes values the goods of its *carpe diem* passages—food, drink, family, and so on—for the provisional delight they bring and the gratitude they elicit toward their Giver.

Thus the Augustinian contrast between two loves is relevant too: Ecclesiastes does not reject earthly goods, but rather idolatrous human *enjoyment* of them—instead of their *use* for enjoying God. Martin Luther and Dietrich Bonhoeffer, among others, offer a linguistic update for this position, by highlighting that Ecclesiastes speaks of earthly delights. Yet, despite the freedom to speak of enjoying creaturely goods, the text's conceptual pattern remains basically Augustinian: these earthly joys are penultimate—sometimes hard to get, harder to control, and impossible to keep. That is because ultimately they point us to God. For this reason God gives us a good hard look "under the sun" in Ecclesiastes: not just to deconstruct an unbelieving perspective, but also to develop believing realism. The critical readings of the Sage as a skeptic fail to do justice to the book's frequent speaking of goodness, divine gift-giving, human delight, and the like. The conservative readings of the book in apologetic terms fail by letting both the church and the world off the hook. It is not that the world only looks dark under the sun, as if that is an evil perspective opposed to God; instead, God gives us the glimpse of secular *truth* that we need for avoiding idolatry, wherever we find ourselves on spiritual pilgrimage.

Ecclesiastes has great value for contemporary culture. Though the book does not confront modern atheism directly, it does explore questions such as the apparent

7. Eric Gregory, *Politics and the Order of Love: An Augustinian Ethic of Democratic Citizenship* (Chicago: University of Chicago Press, 2008), 11.

indifference of nature and history toward humanity, the justice of divine sovereignty and its plausibility in connection with human freedom, the possibilities of human mastery over cosmos and culture, and so forth. Ecclesiastes explores alternatives to traditional belief in God, particularly whether human efforts to control our own flourishing procure viable options. By ensuring that "all has been heard," the book joins Proverbs in providing a powerful one-two punch for "youth" of whatever age. Its exhortation to remember our Creator reflects the hard-won experience of one who did so initially but became wrongly enchanted with worldly enjoyment. There is value in phenomenological description under the sun for believer and unbeliever alike, because the appeal of idolatry cuts right through all human hearts this side of Eden. Moreover, realism about the way of the world will prevent dangerous forms of naïveté, such as unbelievers and gullible youth assuming that the Bible is glibly idealistic, or believers assuming that the joy expected in scripture requires constant smiling or supererogation.

The resulting ambiguities between dealing with our fallenness and acknowledging our finitude are likewise useful. The difficulty of discerning when the Sage faithfully explores created human limits versus falling into self-absorption speaks to the postlapsarian dilemma that all humans face. Ecclesiastes is traditionally connected to the Feast of Tabernacles, remembering Israel's time of wandering in the wilderness (Christianson 2007: 31). Reading Ecclesiastes therefore continues to address the pilgrimage in which humans find ourselves—even Christians "between the times" of Christ's first and second advents. The outlines of future resurrection may be clearer now, but details of that hope remain fuzzy, and daily life under the sun is not as different from BC as we desire. So, in the meantime, we plant, water, fear, hope, and finally celebrate; these cycles remain ingredient to all our endeavors. Failure to accept this finitude as a divine gift is ingredient in our fallenness.

Reading Ecclesiastes therefore should have the purgative effect envisioned by the church fathers, despite the need for clearer appreciation of creaturely goods. We must learn to read biblical materials on wisdom both for their depictions of human flourishing and for their incompleteness apart from Jesus Christ—both celebrating an objective order divinely preserved in creation and confronting the subjective folly through which we persistently fail to realize *shalom*. Wisdom provides an interpretative paradigm that resists easy polarities of nature and grace. Against the dominance of nature in critical biblical scholarship, we must read the texts not only for what they directly say but also for what remains open in God's promises. Against the dominance of cheap grace in churchly circles, we must make the Sage neither more nor less righteous than he actually is. Ecclesiastes 12:14 reminds us that even our acts of biblical interpretation must reflect the fear of God; all their moral and spiritual complexity will come to light.

Toward that end, Ecclesiastes leads us to remember our Creator as our Redeemer, without despising God's good earthly gifts. Like everything else, the book will remain ultimately ungraspable in this life. Yet, may the Spirit, the Sanctifier, minister this divine word in such a way that we do not simply chase the wind.

BIBLIOGRAPHY

Frequently cited works are listed here. Other works are documented in the footnotes.

Bartholomew, Craig G. 2009. *Ecclesiastes*. Baker Commentary on the Old Testament Wisdom and Psalms. Grand Rapids: Baker.

Bonaventure. 2005. *Commentary on Ecclesiastes*. Works of St. Bonaventure 7. New York: Franciscan Institute.

Christianson, Eric S. 2007. *Ecclesiastes through the Centuries*. Blackwell Bible Commentaries. Oxford: Blackwell.

Ellul, Jacques. 1990. *Reason for Being: A Meditation on Ecclesiastes*. Translated by Joyce Main Hanks. Grand Rapids: Eerdmans.

Hall, Stuart George, ed. 1993. *Gregory of Nyssa, Homilies on Ecclesiastes: An English Version with Supporting Studies: Proceedings of the Seventh International Colloquium on Gregory of Nyssa (St. Andrews, 5–10 September 1990)*. Berlin: de Gruyter.

Krüger, Thomas. 2004. *Qoheleth: A Commentary*. Translated by O. C. Dean Jr. Edited by Klaus Baltzer. Hermeneia. Minneapolis: Fortress.

Longman, Tremper, III. 1998. *The Book of Ecclesiastes*. New International Commentary on the Old Testament. Grand Rapids: Eerdmans.

———. 2006. *Proverbs*. Baker Commentary on the Old Testament Wisdom and Psalms. Grand Rapids: Baker.

Waltke, Bruce K. 2004. *The Book of Proverbs, Chapters 1–15*. New International Commentary on the Old Testament. Grand Rapids: Eerdmans.

———. 2005. *The Book of Proverbs, Chapters 15–31*. New International Commentary on the Old Testament. Grand Rapids: Eerdmans.

Wright, J. Robert, ed. 2005. *Proverbs, Ecclesiastes, Song of Solomon*. Ancient Christian Commentary on Scripture: Old Testament 9. Downers Grove, IL: InterVarsity.

SUBJECT INDEX

SCRIPTURE INDEX

Printed and bound by CPI Group (UK) Ltd, Croydon, CR0 4YY

13/04/2025

14656460-0002